The Alcoholic Empire

THE
Alcoholic Empire

VODKA & POLITICS IN LATE IMPERIAL RUSSIA

Patricia Herlihy

OXFORD
UNIVERSITY PRESS

2002

OXFORD

UNIVERSITY PRESS

Oxford   New York
Athens   Auckland   Bangkok   Bogotá   Buenos Aires   Cape Town
Chennai   Dar es Salaam   Delhi   Florence   Hong Kong   Istanbul   Karachi
Kolkata   Kuala Lumpur   Madrid   Melbourne   Mexico City   Mumbai   Nairobi
Paris   São Paulo   Shanghai   Singapore   Taipei   Tokyo   Toronto   Warsaw

and associated companies in
Berlin   Ibadan

Copyright © 2002 by Patricia Herlihy

Published by Oxford University Press, Inc.
198 Madison Avenue, New York, New York 10016

Oxford is a registered trademark of Oxford University Press

Library of Congress Cataloging-in-Publication Data

Herlihy, Patricia.
The alcoholic empire : vodka and politics in late Imperial Russia /
Patricia Herlihy.
    p.   cm.
Includes bibliographical references and index.
ISBN 0-19-513431-1
1. Temperance—Russia—History.   2. Alcoholism—Russia—History.
3. Russia—Social conditions—1801–1917.   I. Title: Vodka and politics in
late Imperial Russia.   II. Title
HV5513.H47 2002
362.292'0947—dc21   2001036216

9 8 7 6 5 4 3 2 1
Printed in the United States of America
on acid-free paper

ACKNOWLEDGMENTS

All projects have a beginning. This one was encouraged by my late husband David Herlihy when I asked him if he knew that Russia had enacted prohibition as early as August 1914. Although he was a historian, he admitted he had not known that fact, suggesting that I should investigate the reasons for Nicholas II's edict. I was working on a book about Moscow but dropped it in order to follow the vodka trail. That path brought me to Russian libraries and to the Slavic Division of the Helsinki University Library, where for an entire month David assisted me in gathering material. When his life was cut short some twenty months later, he left three incomplete book projects, mute testimony to the sacrifice of time he had made on my behalf. This book is dedicated to his memory.

The Kennan Institute for Advanced Russian Studies, of the Woodrow Wilson International Center for Scholars, provided me with a five-month fellowship in 1990 that enabled me to begin my research. I wish to thank them for a pleasant and productive stay in The Castle. Two of my colleagues at Brown University, Abbott Gleason and Ulle Holt, read all of the following chapters. I drew not only on their scholarship but also on their sustaining friendship. Other colleagues in the profession, Daniel Field, Stephen P. Frank, Gregory L. Freeze, and Richard Stites, also read the manuscript and helped me greatly in the process. Nancy Frieden read the chapter on physicians. I appreciate their valuable comments as well as those of several anonymous readers, all of whom saved me from many, but undoubtedly not all, errors.

So many librarians deserve recognition for their assistance, but special note must be made of extraordinary efforts rendered by Natasha Grishina and Susanna Tsaturnov, formerly at the State Historical Public Library in Moscow. One of the happy accidents of my research has been the formation of strong bonds with these wonderful women. My Odessa scholar friends, Oleg Gubar', Valeria Kukharenko, and Irina Nemchenko, contributed material as well. I wish to thank Clifford Wunderlich, Head of Public Services at Andover-Harvard Theological Library, Harvard Divinity School, for furnishing me with copies of broadsides from the library's collection. In Russia, John Davies found many of the photographs included in this book. Beth Weinhardt of the Westerville Public Library in Ohio and Edward Kasinec, head of the Slavic, Baltic, East European, and Eurasian Collections of the New York Public Library, also provided me with materials. To describe Helen Schmierer as a librarian who assisted me would not do her justice; she is a researcher par excellence, computer guru, gourmet cook, and avid gardener who coaxes into life ingredients in my yard to go into her cooking. Her versatility and generosity made it possible to carry on this endeavor. To Richard Gagnon, who organized my life, and to Vlad Tenenbaum, my "cyber sleuth" friend, I also raise my glass.

Teaching takes time away from research, but not when I taught for several years a senior seminar, "The Social History of Alcohol in Russia." I benefited from student papers, comments, and insights. I thank Eileen Kane, Molly Kertzer, and Tyler Langdon, Brown University undergraduates who were especially helpful; Thomas LeBien for suggesting the title of this book; and William Rorabaugh for his cheerful acquiescence to my echoing the title of his well-known book. Susan Ferber has shown the virtues of patience and perspicacity, partial explanation, no doubt, of why she is editor.

My children help me to grasp what makes life worth living. To Maurice, Christopher, David, Felix, Gregory, Irene, and their families my gratitude and love.

CONTENTS

The Alcoholic Empire

INTRODUCTION

There is nothing in the world worse than drunkenness. No evil, no misfortune, can be compared with it. Fire, famine, flood, do not produce such devastating consequences as does drunkenness. The destruction of the family, incurable diseases, terrible crimes, premature death—all of this comes from drunkenness.

—D. G. Bulgakovskii,
temperance priest, 1913

There will come a time, and it will probably come soon, that the history of the temperance movement in Russia or, to tell the truth, the history of the struggle of the people against their intoxication by alcoholic beverages will be told by an impartial historian.

—Dr. N. I. Grigor'ev,
temperance physician, 1911

Vodka and its use and abuse in Russian society generated a flood of printed material in the Russian press for three decades before its prohibition in 1914. People of various walks of life and political persuasions used the perceived problem of alcohol as an explanation for a host of other social ills, as did Father Bulgakovskii, cited in the epigraph to this chapter. Allegedly, alcohol was hurting the health of the people, debilitating their mental and physical energies, provoking accidents and absenteeism in the workplace, and contributing to suicides and crimes.[1] Purportedly, more people died of drink in Russia than were murdered. A writer for the temperance journal *Deiatel'* came to the gloomy conclusion that "madness, crime, idiocy, and death are the fateful companions of this social ailment."[2] Other observers cited crime statistics to demonstrate that there was a correlation between drink and crime. For example, M. D. Chelyshev, an ardent temperance crusader in the Third Duma, reported that in 1902, when 62 million vedros (one vedro equals twelve liters) of vodka were sold, prisons held 89,000 persons. In 1909, when 90 million vedros of vodka were sold, the number of prisoners jumped to 181,000.[3] As the historian Stephen Frank concludes, "More than any other single factor, drinking was blamed for the peasants' dreadful moral state and the rise of rural criminality."[4] A priest estimated that each year 200,000 persons in Russia died from alcohol-related illnesses, accidents, murder, and suicide.[5]

Allegedly, too, drunkenness was a significant factor in the poor performance of the Russian military and in the brawls, riots, pogroms, and hooliganism that darkened social life. Alcoholism among women was thought to threaten "the race with degeneracy" and to facilitate prostitution.[6] Drunken husbands reputedly beat their wives and deprived the household of money for food. Typical of the views of the Orthodox Church were those expressed by Father Bulgakovskii, who compiled excerpts about alcoholism from the Old Testament, peasant sayings, and statements made by contemporary psychiatrists. In his preface, written in 1898, he explained that "drunkenness is such a disaster and its horrors cannot be compared to wars or to epidemics. 'Demon,' 'blood of Satan,' 'serpent,' 'scourge of the human race,' 'deathly poison,' here are the names that are usually given to liquor and to cursed drunkenness."[7] Such sweeping condemnations of alcohol and assessments of its damage may betray more urgency than accuracy, but they also reflect a mounting concern, shared by numerous observers in the late nineteenth and early twentieth centuries, that alcohol was ruining Russia.

Discerning the effects of alcoholism was simpler than explaining the roots of Russian overindulgence, however. The problem was larger than one of individual weakness, concluded most investigators, including Dr. P. S. Alekseev, who stated that "the temperance question lies at the foundation of all social and political reform."[8] As a matter of fact, temperance workers almost invariably became advocates of reform, at the very least of the moral environment and, more ambitiously, of the Russian economy and even the political system. In order to gain credibility for their specific proposals for reform, temperance activists attempted to establish their credentials for solving the problem, an effort they hoped would elevate their visibility and respectability within Russian society. In 1897, the psychiatrist I. A. Sikorskii called alcoholism "the disease of our century."[9] By calling alcoholism a disease, the doctor implied that physicians were the people trained to address the problem. To stress the widespread nature of the disease, Dr. A. M. Korovin declared that "alcoholic beverages play a considerable role in the lives of the Russian people, and [alcohol] is, so to speak, a universal friend. Educated and uneducated, millionaires and poor alike, willingly have a relationship with alcohol."[10]

As each group of doctors, clergy, women, socialists, politicians, and psychiatrists stepped forward with recommendations for a "cure," they therefore had to make a "diagnosis" as well. They nearly all took it for granted that the manifestations of drunkenness in Russian society were evident. They differed, however, in their assessments of the factors that brought about alcoholism. Convinced that they (including the state itself) had solutions, they mobilized into groups to promote their particular therapies. In their effort to determine the causes of alcoholism, they generated new scientific and historical knowledge.

Temperance activists noted remarks made by foreigners in Russia concerning Russian drinking habits, many of whom concluded that the problem was more serious in Russia than in their homelands. In the 1840s, the German baron Haxthausen pronounced that "intemperance is one of the greatest evils, indeed the true plague of the Russian empire."[11] Around 1890, an American visited a village on a religious holiday and observed that although it was before ten in the morning, a twelve-year-old boy had joined the peasants in "drinking themselves into a beastly state of intoxication."[12]

Temperance writer and school teacher I. P. Mordvinov was sensitive to foreign criticism, stating that "from earliest times, all foreigners visiting Russia and writing about it unanimously testify to the extreme revelry of the Russian peasant holidays."[13] Aware of the image that Russian abusive drinking conveyed abroad, temperance advocates looked back to see when the country had acquired such bad habits. Some of them traced the problem back to the fourteenth century, interpreting the measure by Ivan III to curtail the sale of alcohol to the general population as a sign that there was a problem with drunkenness. Ivan IV, the Terrible, also allowed only a restricted number of friends and servitors, the famous oprichniki, to drink, and for that purpose he founded the first kabak, or tavern, in 1552.[14] Yet centuries later, Russians were still getting drunk, so much so that Patriarch Nikon in the seventeenth century created a council to regulate taverns.[15] By the end of the century, the emperor himself set a drunken example. Peter I, the Great, a prodigious drinker, imposed on his court and foreign visitors of rank the duty of joining him in downing huge amounts of alcohol at festive events. Peter's Drunken Synod of Fools and Jesters featured obscene ceremonies mocking the church—and it was indeed drunken.[16] Drinking bouts hastened Peter's death at the age of fifty-three.

Scholars have examined the sex life of Empress Catherine II, the Great, more closely than her drinking habits, but a leading authority on her life and career reports that she did not drink alcoholic beverages.[17] She maximized state revenue from the production of alcohol, however, by allowing people to bid for a limited number of licenses for the exclusive right to sell alcohol in a given area. Under this system, the state raised a quarter of its revenue.[18] Later, during the period of the Great Reforms of the 1860s, Alexander II abolished Catherine's tax-farming system because it had spawned too many liquor stores. Those who held licenses had attempted to sell as much alcohol as the market would bear in order to recoup the license fee.[19] Under Alexander's system, the state taxed both distillers and retailers according to output and consumption. The result, however, was the same: an increase in vodka consumption. The number of taverns and liquor stores quickly proliferated, reducing the price of the commodity so that more and more people consumed more cheap vodka. Hoping to curb drinking in the workplace, the state passed a law in 1886 that made it a criminal offense, subject to severe punishment, for employers to give their workers vodka as part of their salary. All pay was to be in cash thereafter.[20] Yet the reduction was only a drop in a bucket.

The idea for a state monopoly of vodka originated with Alexander III, but the monopoly was not fully implemented until the reign of Nicholas II, which began in 1896. When Minister of Finance Sergei Witte created the State Vodka Monopoly in 1894, he argued that the government could then control the quantity of alcohol sold to the public, as well as ensure its quality.[21] Witte expressly stated that the goal was not to increase revenue for the state. In order to control the distribution of alcohol, the state attempted to confine the sale of alcoholic beverages to government-run stores where no food was served. After purchases in the state-controlled stores, drinkers downed vodka on the street and smuggled vodka into *traktirs* (cheap eating establishments): "At present the drinking of strong beverages in almost all *traktirs* and tea establishments is freely allowed. A customer enters a tearoom and orders tea. After emptying the glass, he takes from his pocket a bottle of vodka and pours himself a glass which he drinks and then puts the bottle back in his pocket."[22] The intent of the monopoly was to separate drinking from eating, but the unintended result was that, without food, the drinker became drunk faster and more profoundly, according to Dr. A. V. Balov, a critic of the monopoly.[23] Despite Witte's declaration that the state was attempting to curb drunkenness, five years after the establishment of the monopoly, a report showed increased consumption of vodka.[24]

The replacement of taverns with state liquor stores, critics noted, also led to an increase in bootlegging. People bought stocks of vodka for resale when the liquor stores were closed. They wanted to drink in a social setting outside the home and at times of their own choosing, which bootlegging establishments provided. Before the monopoly, according to some temperance people, there was virtually no bootlegging. But following the imposition of the monopoly, "without exaggeration, one can say that for each ten peasant households there is one bootleg establishment."[25] By 1913, a study in Penza Province estimated that bootlegging accounted for at least half of all liquor sales in the countryside.[26] Or, as one respondent to a questionnaire put it, "Where in the township (*volost'*) there are three liquor stores, there will be 3,000 bootleggers."[27]

In anticipation of and in response to criticism that the state was soaking the land in alcohol, the state represented itself as a leader in temperance activity by creating a bureaucratic organization called the Guardianship of Public Sobriety to educate the public on the evils of drink and to distract them with public entertainment.[28] By establishing an official temperance society, the state made a public statement that temperance was a worthy goal. A wide variety of groups took up the cause by forming temperance societies themselves. Thus, they augmented the Guardianship's activities and sometimes denounced the state's philosophy of moderation. The irony of the state's being the sole purveyor of alcohol while piously proclaiming moderation in drink was not lost on contemporaries.

In 1912, an American critic succinctly sketched the fiscal implications of the vodka monopoly: "The Russian government takes in 750,000,000 rubles, hands over 17,000,000 to distillers for premiums, and devotes 2,000,000 to what Count Tolstoi characterized 'as either blasphemy or a mere toy,'—a feigned temperance propaganda [the Guardianship]." The same American found the abstinence festival celebrated in April 1913 in St. Petersburg to be utterly hypocritical:

> More than thirty different processions came from all parts of the Capital with ikons and banners to the plaza before the Kazan Cathedral. It was an imposing, an overpowering picture. Sixty thousand persons took part. Prayer was offered for salvation from alcohol. The miracle-working ikon of the mother of God was borne out of the church. The Metropolitan Vladimir with a vast number of clergy celebrated mass. A choir of five hundred voices assisted. A miracle was prayed for. In the giant assembly were apparently present the officials of the Finance Department, who have recently celebrated the fifty year jubilee of true service in the sale of alcohol. The tragic service must have seemed strange to them, for the whole state budget is based on this economic policy [of alcohol selling].[29]

Not only were foreigners struck by Russian drinking habits, but famous writers such as Leo Tolstoi and Fedor Dostoevskii also were concerned with alcoholism.[30] The former began a temperance education movement of his own, whereas Dostoevskii was content to criticize: "The consumption of alcoholic beverages brutalizes and makes a man savage, hardens him, distracts him from bright thoughts, blunts all good propaganda and above all weakens the will, and in general uproots any kind of humanity."[31] An earlier writer, N. G. Pomialovskii, bitterly recorded from experience the effects of alcoholism, a condition that contributed to his death in 1863 at the age of twenty-eight.[32] "I am now drinking," he wrote in a letter to a friend. "I have no strength, and my life, brother, is difficult. All the powers of my mind and will are strained but I cannot throw off this drunken life. Indeed, the worm sits inside. . . . Where are the means for salvation?"[33]

Like Pomialovskii, some Russian writers were victims of alcoholism; many others were witnesses who publicized its prevalence. In *Virgin Soil*, published in 1877, Ivan Turgenev complained, "Everything sleeps in Russia, in village and city—officers, soldiers, merchants, judges, fathers, children—all are asleep. Only the drink shop sleeps not, saturating Holy Russia with drink."[34] In one of his stories, Anton Chekhov describes the peasants of an imaginary village called Zhukovo: "On Elijah's Day they drank. On the feast of the Assumption they drank. On Holy Cross Day they drank. The feast of the Intercession was the parish holiday for Zhukovo and the villagers seized the chance to drink for three days."[35] Earlier, the great poet Alexander Pushkin celebrated "the amazing gift" of "golden wine" in his poems.[36]

I do not seek here to investigate the accuracy of the claims of a social crisis nor the deep roots of Russian alcoholism nor the validity of the belief that the situation was badly deteriorating as the old century turned into the new. Rather, I note that many observers believed that alcoholism was indeed rampant and increasing.[37] So much was written about alcoholism and temperance in Russia that by 1902 a second edition of titles of books and articles about alcoholism was published.[38] Seven years later, a substantial bibliography on alcoholism (but not on temperance) came out.[39] By 1914, N. P. Bludorov published a second edition of a 206-page bibliography of such literature. He also listed twenty-eight different temperance journals in print, but at one point a few years earlier there had been several more.[40]

My object is not to make a survey of temperance literature or even of temperance organizations but to examine how people's views on alcohol shaped their political thought and activities. The thousands of pamphlets, brochures, articles, journals, and books diagnosing the problem and advocating remedies were accompanied by action, principally in the form of temperance groups active in the city and countryside that preached not only to the individual to reform but also to society to seek a transformation, often in political terms. More than 100,000 members were enrolled in various temperance societies, with one society alone claiming a membership of 70,000.[41]

The belief that Russian society was in the grips of alcoholism stimulated in many corners of Russian society efforts by individuals, organizations, and the state to control it. For some, participation in temperance activities was a radicalizing experience; that is, they came to question the legitimacy of autocracy. Others denounced the modernizing, secularizing, urbanizing, and industrializing movements in Russia at the end of the nineteenth century and the beginning of the twentieth as the causes of alcoholism. They called for a return to what they believed were the more religious and simpler virtues of the past. But even these pious zealots for sobriety like Tolstoi could undermine the authority of the state.

Many of the temperance societies were formed along professional lines, as among physicians and the clergy. Even within these groups, however, there was no unanimity concerning the causes of and cures for alcoholism.[42] Women physicians appeared to be more concerned with alcoholism among women and children than among men. For some women physicians, securing the right to vote after 1906 was more important than addressing alcoholism. Psychiatrists vied with physicians concerning the efficacy of hypnosis as a treatment. Rural doctors hired by zemstvos were especially eager to wrest money and power from the Guardianship so that they, not government bureaucrats, could address the issue on the local level. Some physicians argued for enforced confinement of alcoholics for treatment. Others hesitated to grant greater police powers to the state and insisted on voluntary submission to treatment. Civil rights for both patients and professionals lay at the root of many debates. Some frustrated public-health doctors arrived at the conclusion that only with a socialist government would enough attention and funds be devoted to the medical needs of the people, especially the treatment of alcoholics.

The clergy were likewise divided over whether the individual or society itself had to be reformed. The most visible temperance societies formed within factories in the larger cities, such as the Alexander Nevskii Temperance Society in St. Petersburg. But a myriad of parish societies put forth their message in the countryside. Admitting that alcoholism was rampant among the clergy themselves, some priests attempted to reeducate the younger clergy to adopt sobriety. The creation of the State Vodka Monopoly coincided with the period when the church embraced the notion of creating a better society on earth. The church's vigorous social mission to improve life for workers seized on temperance as a pivotal issue.[43] Young priests in urban centers, such as the labor activist Father Georgii Gapon, advocated better working and living conditions for workers and used temperance as an issue to organize workers. His organization of workers was so successful that it led to the revolution of 1905.

Debate over the causes of alcoholism had a polarizing effect. Conservatives, such as the leaders of the Kazan Temperance Society, blamed the problem on modernization, loss of religious values, Jewish purveyors of vodka, and an increased climate of amorality. Some younger, more progressive clergy ultimately came to the conclusion, not dissimilar to that of socialists, that capitalism, greed, and tsarist neglect lay at the heart of increased drinking. Some of these clergy eagerly embraced the new Bolshevik regime and its Living Church promoted by Lenin as instruments to eradicate alcoholism among the oppressed people. They felt that they would at last have the support of the state to eliminate poverty, the cause of alcoholism.

Whereas some clergy become radicals against the tsarist state, others fought for power within the church. Disgruntled lower clergy accused monks of drunkenness, arguing that they, the parish priests, should acquire more privileges within the church. Parish priests wanted respect, recognition, remuneration, and the right for advancement within the hierarchy of the church, all of which, in their view, had been denied them.

Tolstoi, who was excommunicated in 1901, made temperance one of the cornerstones of his religion.[44] As a reading of his 1899 novel *Resurrection* shows, his attacks on the church, drunkenness, private property, the clergy, and the judicial and penal system were all of a piece. Disgust with the State Vodka Monopoly and it hypocritical adjunct, the Guardianship, only added to his antigovernment stance, one that led him to advocate civil disobedience. Had he not been such a famous writer, he would undoubtedly have been arrested, if not exiled. Other charismatic lay temperance leaders, such as Ivan Alekseevich Churikov, were also excommunicated, only to join the Living Church, which was supported by the Bolshevik regime after the October Revolution until 1923.[45] Churikov was so taken up with his temperance crusade that he began to usurp the prerogatives of the clergy by preaching, hearing confessions, and healing the sick. Conversely, Father John (Ioann) of Kronstadt remained a religious conservative while promoting the church's social mission with his temperance activity.

Temperance activists also urged restriction of drink among the military. Patriots proclaimed that drunkenness among troops and especially officers robbed Russia of military victories. Conservatives asserted that drinking in the military led to a lack of discipline, which, in turn, led to revolution. But more liberal temperance advocates wanted to use the military population as a pilot project for the modernization and sobering of a large segment of Russian society and were highly critical of the state for besotting the youth of Russia by allowing the distribution of vodka rations to soldiers and sailors. They wanted the state to use the military as a school for education in sobriety, the lessons of which would then be carried into civilian life. To interfere with such age-old drinking habits among the military would transfer more political power to lay reformers and diminish the power that the state had over the military.

Just as physicians and clergy differed among themselves concerning remedies for alcoholism, women were divided as to whether they wanted to secure more power in the household in order to sober up their husbands or whether they wanted suffrage in order to sober up the nation. Unlike women temperance activists in the West, Russian women did not succeed in forming temperance societies of their own, although they belonged to medical and other lay temperance societies. At first limiting their concern to alcoholism among women and children, they gradually became engaged in the wider problem of drunkenness in the population at large. More than gender, class determined the modality of how women assessed and addressed the problem. Poorer women used direct action on their spouses to the limit of their abilities if they perceived that the economic status of their households was threatened. Women of the upper classes were concerned with obtaining suffrage; they promised that they could reduce alcoholism once they were empowered with the vote. Wealthier women, less threatened economically by alcoholism, aspired to grander political status and latched onto the issue as a lever to raise their status within society.

Members of the Duma also used the issue to secure more power. By forming a subcommission to study the problem and recommend measures to curb drinking, they hoped to broaden their legislative powers. They also sought to diminish the power of the Ministry of Finance by denouncing the vodka monopoly itself and by criticizing the Guardianship as a cynical device to mask the state's ever-increasing revenue from selling vodka to the people, whom they were impoverishing and degrading. Duma members attempted to reduce funds allocated to the Guardianship, claiming that since they were the elected representatives of the people, they were better able than the bureaucracy to judge which methods were most efficacious in fighting alcoholism.[46] Nearly every political party had a plank in its platform concerning the necessity to combat drunkenness. The most noted of all members of the Third Duma was the vociferous and prolific leader Mikhail Chelyshev, whose only issue was that of temperance. He gathered support in 1907 to reduce alcohol production in the empire; even this proposal was regarded as an infringement on the power of the Ministry of Finance. In addition, members of the State Council, the upper house of the Russian legislature, also expressed concern over the state monopoly on alcohol. More and more officials began to denounce "the drunken budget" of the state.

Sobriety was not exclusively a concern of professionals and the intelligentsia, however. In fact, many temperance groups noted the absence of the intelligentsia in their midst. In addition to physicians, clergy, railroad workers, ethnic groups, university students, administrators, aristocrats, teachers, and workers, even the least-empowered segment of the population—peasants—built libraries, auditoriums, night shelters, clinics, and cafeterias to provide services to indigent alcoholics. Given the involvement of virtually all classes of Russian society in the issue, it would be insufficient to describe their various activities as an effort to exert social control. Their exhortations were aimed at all classes, not only peasants and workers but the upper classes as well. For example, priests and doctors, who were among the leading temperance organizers, were far from being considered the social elite. Furthermore, there were many grassroots movements among the workers and peasants themselves, so that the entire movement cannot be dismissed as a mere ploy of the frightened upper classes to model the masses after their own (sober) image. Tolstoi, for instance, claimed that the upper classes were more intemperate than the peasants. If the state's goal was social control by advocating moderation in drink and discouraging abstinence, it was then certainly a weak effort, so weak indeed that it was the object of general scorn by the many groups that attacked the vodka monopoly. While temperance activity involved social reform, it was even more concerned with political reform.

In post-1905 Russia, citizens demanded the power to veto the opening of vodka stores in their areas. They argued that if they acquired a voice in establishing local option, that is, to retain or abolish state liquor stores in their midst, they would have succeeded in wresting political power from the state. For most temperance activists, the right to associate voluntarily or participate in civic good works was not sufficient. They wanted economic and, above all, political change. For example, they organized antialcohol days, which the government viewed with suspicion because these events mobilized the masses, and the antimonopoly rhetoric of the crowd could easily slip into denunciations of the state. Such fears were not entirely groundless. Since the state had proclaimed temperance activity to be a worthy initiative, it had to endorse, although grudgingly, the right of groups to form temperance societies. Had the government fully realized how subversive some of these temperance societies would actually prove to be, it would have hesitated even more. Still, police spies were present during some temperance meetings, some of the leaders were under surveillance, and at times, police shut down temperance organizations. Twenty worker delegates to the First All-Russian Congress on the Struggle against Drunkenness, held in St. Petersburg in late December 1909 and early January 1910, were arrested. As socialists, they denounced the state for fostering alcoholism in order to gain revenue.[47]

Perhaps the most surprising convert to temperance was Tsar Nicholas II himself. A moderate imbiber and connoisseur of fine wine, he was perhaps moved by the massive antialcohol propaganda swirling around him in Russia by 1914; or perhaps he began to reconsider the reliance of state revenue on the consumption of alcohol by his people. He stated that fiscal prosperity should not be dependent on "the destruction of the spiritual and economic powers of many of my subjects."[48] Thus, some six months before the outbreak of World War I, the tsar dismissed his finance minister, V. N. Kokovtsev, who was accused by Sergei Witte of pushing alcohol sales during the war against Japan, and appointed Peter Bark to the post, specifically enjoining him to seek other sources of taxation besides the vodka monopoly. Yet it came as a shock to Russia when in August 1914, Nicholas issued an edict that during mobilization only first-class restaurants and clubs would sell vodka. The ban was soon extended for the duration of the war; meanwhile temperance advocates clamored for permanent prohibition. They pointed to the sobriety of the troops, the productivity of peasants, and the general well-being of the Russian people as reasons for eliminating vodka forever more. Prohibition, whether resulting from a supreme act of autocracy or echoing the vox populi, led to specific problems, such as the widespread distilling of *samogon* (moonshine), increased deaths from alcohol poisonings from the ingesting of dangerous substitutes, and, most critically, a shortage of grain for foodstuffs.

The temperance movement in all its variety allowed individuals to organize and to form many voluntary associations. In studying alcoholism and its causes and remedies, reformers became social critics. A few wanted to retreat to what they imagined to be a more religious society of the past. The majority associated the autocratic system and its vodka monopoly with alcoholism and its attendant social ills. They called for radical political change. For centuries, vodka had played a vital social role in the lives of Russians. It also, fatefully, came to play a major role in politics during the waning years of the Russian Empire and beyond.

2

SINGING ONE'S WAY TO SOBRIETY

· THE STATE'S GUARDIANSHIP

When the state set up its own temperance organization, the Guardianship of Public Sobriety, it inadvertently galvanized private temperance groups—headed by physicians, the Orthodox clergy, and lay societies—into proclaiming that their own methods, approaches, and expertise were superior to those of the lethargic, bureaucratic, mammoth state organization. The private groups sought to address the problem, whereas it appeared that the state attempted only to amuse and distract the people from drink. Some critics claimed that the Guardianship's use of popular theater as a vehicle for amusement and education reached the middle class more readily than the target audience: peasant workers. Others affirmed that the educational and artistic mission was successful; workers did indeed profit from plays, operas, and lectures, perhaps not in forswearing drinking but in acquiring culture. Workers gained a sense of autonomy and individuality from viewing plays; ironically, the same system that entertained them led to a heightened consciousness of their oppressive environment.[1]

The Guardianship served as a perfect foil to discredit the motivation of the state, which simultaneously appeared to be promoting alcohol consumption and then hypocritically urging drink in moderation. The visibility (and risibility) of a state that created a monopoly on vodka and then attempted to create a monopoly on temperance set loose much criticism against the tsarist regime, including harsh words from Russia's noted writers.

In November 1896, Leo Tolstoi angrily refused to meet with Minister of Finance Sergei Witte. Knowing what the topic of discussion would be, Tolstoi asked his brother-in-law Alexander Kuzminskii to convey to Witte his refusal to support the new state temperance society. In his letter to Kuzminskii,

Tolstoi sputtered at the very idea that Witte should think that their views on alcohol could be reconciled:

> In all that I have been writing this past year on social questions, I have been expressing as best I can the thought that the chief evil from which mankind suffers and the disorders of life come from the activities of the government. One of the striking illustrations is that the government not only permits but encourages the manufacture and distribution of the poisonous evil of liquor, from the sale of which comes one-third of the budget. In my opinion, if the government really was making every effort for the good of the people, then the first step should be the complete prohibition of the poison which destroys both the physical and the spiritual well-being of millions of people. . . . Thus, the temperance societies established by a government that is not ashamed that it itself sells the poison ruining the people through its own officials seem to me to be either hypocritical, silly, or misguided—or perhaps all three—something with which I can in no way sympathize.[2]

The government, however, viewed matters differently. As if to counter public criticism for establishing a state monopoly on vodka, the state itself launched the largest and best funded of the temperance movements.[3] On January 1, 1895, the Ministry of Finance set up the Guardianship of Public Sobriety. Its mission was to supervise liquor sales and advocate moderation in its consumption.[4] To divert people from pubs, they were to be provided with alternative amusements as well as cheap food and tea. Just as ancient Rome had used bread and circuses to keep its people loyal, the Russian state, despite widespread condemnation of this approach, retained its faith in "bread and circuses" as the best inducement to moderate drinking. Another project, to control drinking and fund clinics for the treatment of alcoholics, was always a minor expenditure. As Tolstoi noted, the liquor monopoly proved to be a spectacular fiscal success, helping the state to refill its coffers after the Russo-Japanese War of 1904–5.[5] A relatively small percentage of the profits, however, went into funding the Guardianship, an organization that was perceived to address a problem created in part by the state itself.[6]

Controversy attended the work of the Guardianship over nearly the entire course of its existence. In addition to the obvious contradiction of having one bureau encourage liquor sales and another within the same ministry attempt to instill moderate consumption, there was the basic ambiguity in its mission to promote some, but by no means total, abstinence from hard liquor. A temperance worker, B. I. Gladkov, described the goals of the Guardianship:

The Ministry [of Finance] found that the quantity of alcoholic beverages consumed by the population of Russia is in general not significant, but the problem is that Russian people drink rarely and immoderately; therefore, the Guardianship was charged with the obligation to never preach total abstinence but to fight drunkenness by training the population in daily moderation in the consumption of vodka; and thus, they proposed that from such measures drunkenness would diminish but the quantity of state vodka consumed would grow significantly. To fulfill such a goal was the task of the Guardianship of Public Sobriety.[7]

But, said Gladkov, the Guardianship was trapped in a vicious circle. It was trying to get the population to drink every day in moderate amounts. In order to do that, people would have to have the means to purchase alcohol, and yet their level of material well-being would not be raised unless they were abstinent. Gladkov believed that one had to either strive for complete sobriety or give up the struggle. Some members of the Guardianship, he claimed, recognized the futility of their philosophy and gave up the fight; others went on building theaters and buffets where liquor was sold, even on credit, so that they became secret pubs. People drank daily, all right, but not in moderation, he huffed. The result was that the Guardianship made the situation worse than before.[8]

As Gladkov noted, this ambiguity had a curious result. Limited in what it could advocate concerning the use and abuse of alcohol, the Guardianship made few attempts to rehabilitate alcoholics and instead devoted the largest part of its resources to educational and social projects having little direct connection with the issue of drink. Nonetheless, the Guardianship became the largest and best-supported governmental welfare institution in the Russian Empire.

Answering to the Ministry of Finance, which operated the liquor monopoly, the Guardianship sought to accomplish its mission through official committees set up in the *guberniias* (provinces) and territories.[9] These provincial guardianships in turn spawned subordinate committees in the cities and districts. The largest cities, such as St. Petersburg, Moscow, Kiev, and Odessa, had their own special urban guardianships. By 1900, there were 364 committees with a combined membership of 15,000 persons, an average of about 40 members on each committee.[10] A detailed budget for the year 1911, when the liquor monopoly was functioning in nearly the entire empire, gives a good view of the Guardianship in its maturity: there were 79 provincial guardianships; with their satellite committees, the total number of boards associated with the Guardianship reached the impressive number of 754.[11]

Several categories of membership in the Guardianship existed. In 1911, full members—the true "guardians"—numbered 15,580, an average of about 20 members per committee, and most of them were high dignitaries of church and state who were "obligated" to serve. The minister of finance had the right to name additional members, but in 1911, their total number was small (609 out of the 15,580). Finally, the president of the guardianship committees in the *guberniias* and territories could name additional members, but not many were so appointed in 1911 (only 337 out of the 15,580). This small number suggests that prominent local figures had little enthusiasm for supporting the official movement. The methods of appointing members—essentially dictated from on high, by statute, minister, or president—ensured that the committees would remain firmly under the control of the government and faithful to its policies.[12] The guardianships could not easily tap into whatever local zeal there may have been for the temperance cause.

The guardianship committees also appointed honorary members (151 for the entire empire in 1911, 126 men and 25 women). It appears these people did nothing but lend their names to the cause. Far more numerous were the "associate members" (*sorevnovateli*), who aided in the work of the guardianships but did not set policy or distribute resources. They numbered 15,200 in 1911 (13,660 men and 1,540 women), and were drawn in largest part from the ranks of the clergy, administrators, schoolteachers (who account for most of the women), doctors, lawyers, and other professionals. But the budget of 1911 states that only one-third of them (5,635 persons) were "taking an active role in the activity of the guardianships."[13] Those who were active appear to have endorsed the method of distracting the drinker through entertainment, an ambition that at least in part would satisfy the goals stated earlier by the Guardianship: "to create intelligent entertainment which might attract and raise the spiritual level of the population, widen its horizons, give it healthy nourishment, and care for its bodily health."[14]

Students of Russian urban history will note that each of the two capitals adapted the Guardianship to its own interests and historical style. The guardians of St. Petersburg, the more vibrant, artistic, and Western-looking city, promoted cultural experimentation because they were convinced that boredom and illiteracy were the root causes of excessive drinking. They tended to minimize the clinical approach to treating alcoholics. The guardians of Moscow, the ancient, religious, and patriarchal capital, were more solicitous for the well-being of drunkards, finding them suitable medical help, jobs, and cheap food and lodging.

The Guardianship invested huge amounts in education and entertainment, particularly popular theater. Most People's Houses, public facilities, contained theaters. In 1900, the St. Petersburg guardianship opened its Nicholas II People's House, donated by Nicholas II, which had a 1,500-seat theater, a dining hall, and a concert hall near the Peter and Paul Fortress, across the river from the Winter Palace. Five years later, a British journalist described the building as "a sort of crystal palace, [which] was the exhibition building of the Nizhny Novgorod Exhibition of 1896, which was pulled down, packed up, sent to St. Petersburg and rebuilt."[15] Over the course of ten years, the entertainment complex attracted 20 million visitors.[16] The same journalist observed that despite the cheap prices (30 kopecks), the food was not cheap enough for workers, so that it attracted "shopkeepers, *employés* of the lower ranks, soldiers and non-commissioned officers, and even a few officers, mostly with families, University students, and a crowd of miscellaneous persons of various classes. The 'horny-handed sons of toil' are few and far between." The location of the People's House was a long way from most workers' quarters and factories. The few workers who made their way there "feel themselves almost intruders in a building primarily designed for their benefit." The journalist concluded, "in time doubtless it will become more popular, and perhaps if wages go up they will be able to patronize its restaurant, while education will teach them to appreciate vodkaless joys; but for the present it must rank to some extent among the wasted good intentions."[17]

The 1911 budget shows clearly the profitability of entertainment. For example, the St. Petersburg guardianship earned little from its tearooms, kitchens, and shelters (19,529 rubles) and invested little in them (49,458 rubles). But it generated a huge income from its "theatrical presentations and other entertainments": 710,978 rubles. And the sum it invested in "theaters and scenery" was equally impressive: 538,213 rubles.[18]

The committee invested much psychological energy as well as material resources in planning theater for the people. In its report of 1908, the guardians endorsed playwright Alexander Ostrovskii's plea to the minister of internal affairs in 1882 that Russia needed popular theater. Though Ostrovskii had died in 1886, the St. Petersburg guardianship in 1908 declared its intention to put his ideas into practice. It was hoped that the theater would serve as a platform to preach sobriety to the people; it would also ennoble their souls by developing in them a passion for art and poetic idealism.[19] Later that year, the Guardianship sponsored ten popular theaters, including what was arguably the first popular theater in St. Petersburg.[20]

The development of an edifying temperance repertoire was no easy task. Temperance plays were discouragingly few. The St. Petersburg guardians therefore decided to commission plays written expressly with their goals in mind. Works commissioned included *The Fatherland War* and *Peter the Great* by Krylov-Aleksandrov (presumably, in the latter, Peter's prodigious drinking feats went unmentioned). Tunoshenskii was commissioned to write a play given the unstimulating title *A History of Russia*. The guardianship also supported a competition initiated by the Academy of Sciences to select the best play commemorating the two hundredth anniversary of the founding of the city (1703).

Despite the guardianship's significant investment, not all the productions were brilliant successes. One ambitious enterprise sought to summarize the history of Russia in thirty live tableaux, but the production closed after twelve performances. Still, the ten guardianship theaters in the capital in 1908 produced a total of 4,856 performances of 533 plays. In its report of 1913, the St. Petersburg guardianship claimed that during the course of fifteen years, it had sponsored 9,518 performances of 667 different plays.[21] It is not clear whether the workers, for whom these efforts were designed, or the more well-to-do composed the audience, as critics suggested. During the monarchy's tercentenary celebrations in 1913, the guardianship was enlisted to serve cheap meals and tea in their cafeterias and night shelters as well as to entertain the people as part of the show of alliance between the monarch and the people. The entertainments were held far from the center of the city in order to prevent the gathering of masses near the Winter Palace, where hostile demonstrations might erupt.[22] In this instance, it is clear that the productions were targeted for the workers.

The guardianship held a particular faith in the sobering effects of music, believing it was accessible even to the illiterate and that it would dissipate the boredom that led people to drink. Russians could choose from a plethora of musical offerings. In one year alone, 1,110 opera performances were presented. Over the course of fifteen years, 2,411 of them were given at the Nicholas II People's House. But perhaps the optimism of the effects of opera was misplaced, for a contemporary reported that "peasant viewers were seen to strain to get the words and to be confused about the ideas and even the subjects of the operas."[23] Opera was not only a luxury for the wealthy. Ticket prices were kept low for holiday performances, when poor workers were able to attend. Higher prices were charged for weekday performances, which were frequented chiefly by the well-to-do. The prices helped cover expenses and contributed to explain, in large part, the nearly 200,000 ruble profit the guardianship made from its productions in 1911. Nonetheless, some critics complained about subsidizing the rich, who "came not so much to be distracted from drinking as to spare their pocketbooks the expense of drinking in *cafés-chantants*."[24] The money the rich saved by attending Guardianship performances, it was suggested, would be spent later in drinking in more fashionable nightspots.

It was not enough to keep the people amused; they also had to be engaged in playing an instrument or singing, at least during that period when they were not drinking. In addition to the musical interludes during intermissions between acts of plays, there were concerts given by choirs and choruses. In St. Petersburg, anyone with an interest in music could join the "People's Orchestra," a major feature of many entertainments. Initially led by three hired instructors, the orchestra comprised people ranging in age from eight to thirty and from various ranks, including factory workers, sales clerks, and doormen. The People's Orchestra gave its first concert in December 1902. By 1903, there were seven instructors and the orchestra had grown to a hundred musicians. People's choirs were similarly organized. Clowns, acrobats, jugglers, animal acts, magicians, and popular singers provided less solemn entertainments on holidays. In a Bolshevik newspaper, a worker attacked these last types of amusement as fostering coarse instincts and driving workers "backward" to the tavern for drink.[25]

The guardianship sought to capture children with culture before they were captured by drink. It organized games for school children in the summer from 2 to 6 or 7 P.M. and in the winter from 3 P.M. for as long as there was light. The games were held outdoors on Petrovskii Island and at the Zoological Gardens in Aleksandrovskii Park. Pavilions, gigantic steps, swings, and ice hills were built for their entertainment. The children themselves put on plays, and they were instructed through nature walks and lectures. They were also instructed in arts and crafts, including woodwork. More than 400,000 children took part in the guardianship's many activities.

The guardianship also sponsored adult education by establishing reading rooms and libraries located throughout the city. Within a decade of their founding in 1899, fifteen libraries had lent out 131,594 books. The chosen books illuminated historical and literary themes, questions of drunkenness, its influence on the organism and on well-being. Nevertheless, the number of users remained well below the number of people who attended the spiritual talks, theatrical productions, and other entertainments. One educational forum was lectures on alcoholism illustrated by magic-lantern slides, which were given at Saturday and holiday evening church services.[26] By 1908, 490,292 people had attended 1,854 of these lectures.

The guardians also organized an antialcohol museum in the People's House, one of the first antialcohol museums in Russia. The museum displayed in anatomical, and presumably shocking, detail the pernicious effects of alcohol on the human organism. Experts at an information bureau also responded to questions about alcohol and its consumption, a version of present-day telephone "hot lines." In addition to its own antialcohol museum, the state Guardianship mounted displays in Moscow in 1908, in Nizhny Novgorod in 1909, at the International Hygiene Exhibit in Dresden in 1911, and at the International Industrial-Artistic Exhibit in Turin also in 1911. Its displays at the latter two exhibits won high awards.

The budget of 1911 suggests only a tepid interest on the part of the St. Petersburg guardianship in the material welfare of the people, but it did make some effort to provide tea, cheap food, and shelter, especially in predominantly working-class neighborhoods. The first dining rooms were built in 1898 at the Mikailovskii and Iunkerskii Riding School and on Petrovskii Island.[27] The two largest dining rooms together could serve up to eight hundred persons at any given time. With regular inspections by doctors, the guardianship made sure that its dining halls and kitchens were clean. It also ensured that good-quality food would be available at low prices, not only to nourish the workers but also to dissuade them from frequenting restaurants (*traktirs*), where illicit alcohol flowed freely. Closely following the words of the Russian proverb "no conversation without salt and bread," the guardians provided the salt and bread and hoped that workers would indulge in conversation to their cultural improvement. Light beer (under 2 percent alcoholic content) could be purchased with meals; it was hoped that the food, beer, and conversation would eliminate among the clientele a taste for stronger beverages. According to the official report, by 1913 some 11 million persons had taken advantage of these hot cheap meals. The report did not address the quality and consequences of the table talk.

The committee planned to build large workers' shelters but failed to realize this goal. The guardians did, however, convert a former glass factory into a medium-sized shelter that could sleep about 200 workers, at a charge of 5 kopecks per night. By 1908, the shelter had given hospitality to 253,972 guests.

Generous in sponsoring cultural activities, but restrained in meeting the material needs of the people, the St. Petersburg guardianship was most reluctant to invest in the clinical treatment of drunkards. Nonetheless, on May 19, 1903, five years after its founding, it set up an ambulatory clinic in a former glass plant to serve the Schluesselburg factory area. Dr. A. L. Mendel'son, "a specialist in nervous disorders, alcoholism, and psychotherapy," assumed its supervision.[28] At first open only three times a week, the clinic was soon receiving patients five days a week until late in the evening. In the revolutionary fall of 1905, due to tramway strikes, worker disorders, and billeting of troops in the clinic's building, it was transferred to the private apartment of Dr. Mendel'son, where, with the help of two other doctors, he accepted patients free of charge. By the middle of 1906, with the revolution dissipated, the clinic returned to its former site, and in 1907, three more clinics were established in various parts of the city. A fifth was set up in 1908 in the People's House with four staff doctors.

The success of the clinics seems evident. The guardianship report of 1908 noted proudly that other doctors came to the clinics to study their techniques (left undescribed) and that the clinics had been publicized in several St. Petersburg newspapers. A total of 14,801 patients had passed through the doors of the clinics. By 1913, two hundred doctors, mostly zemstvo (rural) physicians, had come to the clinic to hear special lectures on the treatment of alcoholics.[29] Nevertheless, the budgetary figures of 1911 show little interest in therapy; the guardianship allocated a miserly 22,717 rubles to the treatment of alcoholics, although by 1912, there were seven clinics in St. Petersburg under the direction of Dr. Mendel'son.[30]

To fend off criticism of its neglect of rehabilitation, the guardianship argued that, first, treatment would benefit only the comparatively few chronic alcoholics, not the great numbers of people oppressed by bad drinking habits; second, no law made rehabilitation of the drunkard mandatory; and third, massive detoxification campaigns would be costlier than the government could afford. The St. Petersburg guardianship, in sum, seems to have been willing to write off thousands of chronic alcoholics. By pursuing its "cultural war," it hoped to reshape Russians of the future. The report of 1908 concluded: "You must know how to approach people as with a child; you must interest him and, by so doing, conquer him. Any kind of forced influence [or] artful inoculation is an uncertain method and in the majority of cases will be unsuccessful."[31]

Setting aside the issue of clinical treatment of alcoholism, the St. Petersburg guardianship also asserted in its 1908 report that it was difficult to summarize its multitudinous activities and even more difficult to judge their success. Its measures were for the most part prophylactic; hence, few cures could be claimed. However, on an average holiday, some 28,000 people spent up to five hours at guardianship entertainments or food establishments. These activities were certainly successful in attracting large numbers of people, though their relevance to the alcohol problem is questionable. And yet, the time the people of St. Petersburg spent in these activities was time they did not spend in traktirs or at home imbibing vodka. And as Gary Thurston has shown, the guardianship "brought literary theatre to places where the market had just begun to grasp its popular potential."[32]

In its 1913 report, the guardianship claimed that the annual per capita consumption of vodka in the city in 1898, the year the local organization was founded, was 2.25 vedros (1 vedro equals 12 liters), but that it had fallen to 1.85 by 1906. The 1913 report further claimed that by 1913 consumption had fallen to 1.55 vedros—in all, a reduction of 31 percent.[33] The 1908 report reasserted that mass entertainment, especially popular theater, was the most promising approach to inducing moderation in liquor consumption, but the guardianship did not "in any way claim a role in the radical uprooting of drunkenness."[34]

In promoting public sobriety, the Moscow guardianship followed a far different course than its counterpart in St. Petersburg did. The Moscow committee generated only 126,327 rubles from theater and invested only 137,438 rubles in it. Its big income producers were its tearooms, kitchens, and shelters, which earned 372,880 rubles, and its principal expenditure, 653,560 rubles in 1911, was on "houses of the people," or hospitality facilities. (The comparable expense in St. Petersburg was 143,136 rubles.) In Moscow, the guardianship was primarily concerned with feeding and housing the poor and educating workers, quite unlike the St. Petersburg plan of spiritual improvement through mass entertainment.

Founded in 1901, the Moscow guardianship comprised guardians typically drawn from the exalted ranks of the military, civil, and ecclesiastical hierarchies, as was required by statute.[35] Members from the city duma and the mayor himself also joined. Honorary members were picked from the elite, including the metropolitan of Moscow, Vladimir; the minister of finance, Sergei Witte; a former minister of finance, V. N. Kokovtsev; a member of the state Council, S. V. Markov; and the steward of the imperial court, I. F. Tiutchev. By 1902 associate members numbered 53 persons, of whom 4 were women.[36] By 1912, the guardianship employed from 485 to 538 persons to run its various operations.[37]

At the committee's first meeting, on 26 June, 1901, the president, General A. A. Bil'derling, announced that "love for the working people and concern for them should be the basis of the activity of the guardianship."[38] He outlined three tasks: "the first, recreational—the establishment of popular fêtes (*gulianiia*); the second, educational—the opening of reading rooms, libraries, and auditoriums; the third, social—the organization of restaurants and tearooms." All of these institutions would keep workers off the streets and out of the taverns. He took the bloom off the liberalism of these remarks by adding that workers would have to pay for the benefits received.[39] However, those needing a cure would be treated at no charge at the clinic on Novinskii Boulevard.

The Moscow committee consistently received more public funds than any other guardianship. And the Ministry of Finance seems consistently to have turned a sympathetic ear toward its requests for supplementary appropriations. The ministry made up a deficit of 26,000 rubles in the guardianship's first year of operation. Two years later, the guardianship asked the ministry for a total grant of 593,878 rubles.[40] That it was much less successful than its St. Petersburg counterpart in generating its own revenues was a reflection of the nature of its activities. It tried to benefit the poor, who, despite General Bil'derling's expectations, were able to pay little for the benefits received.

Though well funded, the Moscow guardianship was no more generous than that of St. Petersburg in supporting private temperance societies, perhaps because it was forbidden to advocate absolute abstinence. In 1902, it aided the First Moscow Temperance Society with a grant of 4,280 rubles. In 1904, it distributed 14,210 rubles among the First Moscow Temperance Society, the Commission for Free Libraries, and the City Committee for the Poor. Over a ten-year period, the Moscow guardianship distributed only 108,750 rubles to other temperance and charitable societies out of the 5 million rubles it was allotted.[41] These sums are rather paltry given the guardianship's budget of nearly 1 million rubles a year. Clearly, the guardianship did not look on nongovernmental societies as worthy of support, or, more likely, the state was suspicious of rival associations not under its direct control. As will be discussed later, non-Guardianship temperance societies were under police surveillance.

The wealth of the Moscow guardianship was primarily reflected in its acquisition of impressive physical facilities. The report of 1902 proudly announced that within a year of its founding, the Moscow guardianship had already established nine people's houses, four tearooms, and an employment office, as well as ten libraries and reading rooms. On July 27, 1908, a grand, new people's house, costing 232,000 rubles, opened. The dining hall, embellished by a huge portrait of Nicholas II, had two outdoor terraces for serving tea, a summer kitchen, a covered terrace for dining, and another for dancing. The summer theater in the garden could seat 1,300 people. The kitchen was modern, with glass walls, a gas stove, a hot-water heater, and electric machines to clean potatoes, chop meat, and cut bread. The entire outdoor area was strewn with sand and illuminated with electric lights. In addition, there was a winter dining room, a reading room and library, an office, and a summer garden. This great complex was named in honor of the tsar's beloved and only son, Aleksei Nikolaevich, whose photograph was taken each year and hung on the wall of the huge dining room.[42]

An American, impressed by the size of the Aleksei People's House, which employed more than 200 people during the summer, was nonetheless somewhat critical: "At this establishment nothing is done except to provide amusement, eating facilities, theater performances and reading rooms without alcoholic attachments. No direct temperance work is attempted and no pledges of abstinence are solicited. It is purely a 'substitute' and as good a one as could be devised."[43]

In addition, the guardianship operated a winter theater of 1704 square *sazhen*s (over 5,629 square meters) on Novoslobodskaia Street. By 1911, the guardianship owned real estate worth about 756,000 rubles, controlled other assets worth 341,000 rubles, and had over 300,000 rubles in the bank.[44]

The Moscow guardianship seems to have functioned as a kind of showcase operation by which the regime could display publicly its sympathy for those caught in the throes of poverty, unemployment, and drink. High dignitaries were eager for association with its work. The tsar himself attended the opening of the people's house on Butyrskaia Street in 1902.[45] Dignitaries turned out in full force for the 1908 ceremonies opening the great new house of the people named for Tsarevich Aleksei. The governor-general of Moscow presided and the metropolitan of Moscow gave the opening invocation, a long sermon in which he enjoined all people, but especially women, to take up the cause of temperance. In a telegram read aloud, Tsar Nicholas expressed his pleasure with the new house and wished the guardianship every success. A telegram from the Grand Duchess Eliz-abeth Fedorovna, widow of the assassinated grand duke Sergei Aleksan-drovich, reminded the celebrants of her "dear husband, who actively em-braced the goals, development, and success of the guardianship."[46]

In 1912, Tsar Nicholas received in the Kremlin a special delegation of the city guardians, who presented him with a photograph album illustrating their handsome facilities and many worthy activities. Minister of Finance and President of the Council of Ministers V. N. Kokovtsev made a cere-monial visit to the Aleksei People's House in April 1913. He toured the premises, including the antialcohol museum, and was given a report on the deplorable spread of drunkenness among schoolchildren in Moscow Prov-ince by prominent temperance advocate Dr. A. M. Korovin. One wonders how Kokovtsev received this lament; as the minister of finance, he was, after all, in charge of the State Vodka Monopoly, the empire's chief purveyor of alcohol to the masses, and the individual accused by his predecessor Witte of promoting liquor sales after the war with Japan.

The Moscow committee took General Bil'derling's injunction to "love the working class" seriously. In dispensing its services, it paid particular attention to deprived neighborhoods. One of the poorest sections of the city, the Khitrov Market, gained both a night shelter and tearoom.[47] The tearoom could serve 136 persons at any given time. The average number of visitors per day was 651 but could more than double on exceptionally busy days. The morning hours were the busiest of all. Each visitor spent on average 5½ kopecks per visit; for this low price, he or, more rarely, she could obtain either a sandwich, a bowl of soup, boiled meat, or a pot of tea with three pieces of sugar. Tea was served in plain white cups bearing the guardianship's monogram, publicizing its beneficence.[48]

One notable service offered to residents of the Khitrov Market neigh-borhood was an employment bureau established in 1902 by the Moscow guardians after they had observed that Catholic, Lutheran, and Evangelical charitable societies were operating employment bureaus linked with their tearooms. The operation was so successful that it attracted the admiration (and inspection) of representatives of the guardianships at Odessa, Riga, Samara, and Tver. Even an English journalist, Edith Sellers, wrote about the Khitrov employment bureau in the *Contemporary Review*.[49]

The office was open from 10 A.M. to 2 P.M. daily, except for Sundays and holidays. In 1902, 5,309 men and 654 women were offered jobs. The busiest month was January, right after its opening, when 860 persons sought to hire help; the second busiest was July, when 714 prospective employers ap-plied at the bureau. July marked a shift in the yearly cycle of employment, when many workers left the city to undertake summer work back in their villages and other workers came to take their places. The labor market was slack from August to October. The onset of winter halted most work in the

countryside and enlivened the urban market. Spring was again a slack period, as workers remained in their rural homes for Easter and for spring
planting.

The employment bureau operating in the name of temperance provided
a valuable service for the highly mobile labor force of the Khitrov Market.
Another service provided for Moscow's workers was the sponsorship of
"popular conferences"; these were workers' meetings, which were usually
held on Saturday evenings and served informational, educational, and recreational purposes. Recognizing that Moscow, with about half a million
workers, was the industrial center of the empire, the guardianship sought
to keep the workers peaceful "and to solve the workers' problems." Not all
workers were invited to these meetings; those attending needed tickets distributed by the guardianship. At first, women were excluded altogether, but
their presence was eventually allowed and even solicited, since they presumably represented voices of moderation. The guardianship hoped that women
would assume a progressively larger role in the meetings, but in this regard,
the report of 1903 expressed disappointment.

Workers' meetings began with a hymn, and then speakers instructed
workers about current factory laws, such as those governing work-related
injuries and overtime pay, and money management, such as how to set up
mutual-aid funds and, for women, how to seek higher wages. The workers
in turn voiced complaints about certain managerial practices. For example,
some managers in weaving shops assigned the worst machines to those who
did not treat them to vodka and the best to those who did.[50] Just as many
of the temperance plays stressed patriotism, so, too, did some of the workers' meetings. For instance, on February 19, 1901, the guardianship organized
a huge demonstration of 50,000 workers around the monument to Alexander II in Red Square to celebrate the Tsar Liberator's freeing of the serfs.
The monarchy used the guardianship to reinforce its alliance with the people by putting on historical plays and commemorating great deeds of the
tsars.

A report for 1903 affirmed that the meetings held for weavers at the
German Market People's House were well attended and well received.[51] In
1907, in the aftermath of the revolution of 1905, the Moscow guardianship,
perhaps recalling the purported effects of music on savage beasts, distributed to workers cheap musical instruments.[52] However, the meetings organized for metalworkers and joiners did not go well and were poorly attended. Workers chaired these meetings and raised uncomfortable questions
that the guardianship was reluctant to answer. The questions must have
been provocative or contentious; at this particular forum given to workers,
it was hard to muzzle the radical voices completely. In the year 1905 alone,
however, the Guardianship sponsored 70,700 lectures in 6,716 towns and

villages. Some 7,400,000 persons attended these lectures, none of which, of course, advocated total abstinence.[53]

Lectures were especially appropriate for the illiterate, but the Guardianship hoped to foster literacy so that workers could receive the benefit of temperance literature. By 1902, the Moscow guardianship had stocked special libraries and reading rooms with 14,183 volumes (with a circulation of 263,516) and 18 different newspapers and journals.[54]

In addition to general education, from 1904 on the Moscow guardianship sponsored night classes in painting and drawing for workers. By 1907, 356 persons were enrolled in the adult educational courses. Since 70 percent of the students had completed rural or city elementary school, most courses could start at a middle-school level and continue over the four-year period required for graduation.[55] Instruction was open to both men and women without regard to religion or nationality. By 1912, the schools enrolled 650 regular students, not including occasional auditors. Given the size of Moscow's population, the number seems paltry, but the guardianship claimed that the total number of class meetings was 21,987.[56]

Even the luxurious atmosphere of the dining rooms, tearooms, and libraries was supposed to serve an educational purpose; the vast spaces, the portraits of the royal family, and the rich decorations were meant to uplift visitors. The guardians adopted an Arab saying, "Bright rooms give rise to bright thoughts." Respect for property, order, and neatness were virtues that the Guardianship hoped to inculcate in the people along with moderation in drink.[57]

While not investing as much in entertainment as St. Petersburg, the Moscow guardians, heeding General Bil'derling's inaugural message, did recognize the need for recreation. The Moscow guardianship was well aware that holiday periods were times of heavy liquor consumption, and so, to divert the imbibers from their cups, the guardianship rented the city riding school (the Manezh) to hold banquets for Christmas, Carnival (Shrovetide), and Easter.[58] The Christmas feast featured magic-lantern shows depicting the founding and early days of Moscow and various other historical scenes. Patriotic songs were sung and patriotic poetry was read around a huge decorated tree illuminated with electric lights. Although sobriety was the avowed goal of the guardianship, it rarely missed an opportunity to promote patriotism. In all, the Moscow guardianship produced sixty-four theatrical and musical performances to improve the minds and culture of the people.

More oriented toward the physical well-being of the poor than the St. Petersburg guardianship, that of Moscow also seems to have been somewhat more forthcoming in supporting the treatment of alcoholics. It established an ambulatory clinic for them in 1903, under the direction of Drs. N. P.

Kashkarov and A. V. Markovnikov.[59] Grand Duke Sergei Aleksandrovich and his wife, Grand Duchess Elizabeth Fedorovna, assisted in the opening ceremonies of November 2. In 1909, Dr. L. S. Minor, a prominent psychiatrist connected with the Guardianship's clinics throughout Russia, complained that the 13,000–15,000 rubles allocated to the Moscow clinic in the budget was insufficient for its work. He recommended that branch clinics be established in the temperance facilities in the Kozhevinskii and Lefortovo neighborhoods, and the Moscow guardianship agreed to look into the cost of setting up the clinics in those industrial areas.

A report on the work of the clinic for the years 1903–8 provides rich statistics on the nearly 10,000 patients that had passed through its doors.[60] By 1912, more than 15,000 patients had been treated in Moscow.[61] Nonetheless, in his annual report, Dr. I. N. Vvedenskii reiterated that more clinics were needed, since they had to turn down 605 persons who sought treatment. He saw in the growth of applications a sign of increased trust in the methods of the clinic; but by refusing patients, he argued, the popularity of the Guardianship would be diminished. For a city the size of Moscow and for the number of alcoholics it contained, one clinic was clearly insufficient.[62]

But Dr. Vvedenskii's pleas for more facilities were followed by alcohol prohibition in August 1914. The number of patients fell drastically. Only 20 new alcoholics were taken in by the clinic in 1915, compared to 1,995 in 1913. Since the patients were so few, it was possible to interview them at length to find out what had prompted them to lose their sobriety. Most of the patients who checked into the clinic in 1915 had been habitual drinkers before the war and now found easily obtainable substitutes, such as varnish, eau de cologne, and denatured spirits, to continue their habit. But the costs of such products, their nasty taste, and their destructive aftereffects prompted the 20 people who were treated in the Moscow guardianship clinic to seek help.[63]

The Moscow guardianship continued to function even after the wartime ban on the sale of alcoholic drinks by turning over some of its facilities, such as the Aleksei People's House, to the war wounded. It carried on with its educational mission. The minister of finance agreed to pay for the preparation of 306 antialcohol lessons, complete with slides, to be taken around to the various hospitals for wounded soldiers. Each lesson was imposed on more than 1,000 military personnel, who were deeply affected, according to the report.[64] Of course, it is possible that the emotion shown by the wounded was caused by their medical condition or even by wistfulness for vodka to deliver them from pain.

Even before the war, Moscow guardians were interested in the medical roots of alcoholism. In the early 1900s, they surveyed 200 alcoholics about the reasons for their dependency and voted to send the results to the First

All-Russian Congress on the Struggle against Drunkenness, held at St. Petersburg in December 1909 and January 1910 and sponsored by the Commission on the Question of Alcoholism within the Russian Society for the Preservation of Public Health.[65] They also distributed 1,000 copies of the scientific papers by Dr. Minor on the causes of alcoholism. Representatives, including Minor himself, were chosen to attend the congress.

The St. Petersburg guardianship, however, seems largely to have ignored the congress. Perhaps as a governmental agency in the capital, it was suspicious of the motives of the congress. Perhaps it had little sympathy for the emphasis the congress organizers were placing on the medical and social roots of alcoholism. The St. Petersburg guardianship certainly disagreed with the majority view that total abstinence was necessary and clung to the belief that cultural education was the only workable solution for uncontrolled drinking.[66]

In spite of its large budget, large membership, and numerous activities, soon after its foundation the entire Guardianship was subjected to scathing and mounting criticism, with one critic proclaiming the organization "a stillborn child."[67] As Gary Thurston noted, "The apparent irrationality of expanding liquor sales in order to finance popular theatres to distract workers from taverns would not pass unremarked."[68] The criticisms focused on the ambiguity of the Guardianship's mission, its promotion of partial but not total abstinence, and its efforts to bring forth a Russia full of moderate imbibers. As one writer in *Russkie vedomosti* pointed out in 1902, the Guardianship proposed to serve drinks "in moderation" in their tearooms. He asked sarcastically what they considered to be "a moderate quantity" of alcohol, since individual tolerance varied so much. "The uniting of temperance with the sale of vodka," he remarked, "would be an original combination which up until now, it would appear, has nowhere else been thought of."[69] He suggested that the Guardianship change its name from the Guardianship of Public Sobriety to the Guardianship of Moderation.

The Russian newspaper *Russkoe slovo* also attacked the idea of moderation, saying that the Guardianship had to look with one eye on moderate sales of vodka but close the other to immoderate sales—a situation that could only serve to undermine its authority.[70] Writing for *Vestnik trezvosti*, A. P. Kitaev reluctantly admitted that "a person of strong will could maintain himself within the bounds of moderation, but his brother or his son or someone else, because of a weak will, could not be able to do it."[71] Therefore, the moderate person served, not as an example of temperance, but as a lure for those who cannot stop before intoxication, so that "moderate persons inveigle others into immoderation."[72] If you show an alcoholic a moderate drinker, he will never believe that there is harm in drink, but if you show him a drunk, then he might be convinced. Alluding to Tolstoi's belief that the entire life of a person depends on his consciousness, Kitaev argued that liquor paralyzes consciousness, and consequently no amount of alcohol should be taken.

The privately funded Kazan Temperance Society continually attacked the Guardianship for its policy of moderation: "If the Guardianship preaches moderate drinking of alcohol as the obtuse intelligentsia and all of ignorant society wish, and if they fight against abuse [in this way], then they will increase drunkenness, for to distinguish moderate use from immoderate use is not possible: for one person a jigger is moderate; for another, a bottle." The author of the critique doubted the sincerity of those advocating moderate drinking, sarcastically asking if moderation consisted of drinking a glass of vodka before lunch and another before dinner. All drunkards begin with a glass and not a pail of vodka. It is easy to begin to drink moderately but impossible to end immoderate drinking without a serious cure, which even then was not always effective. He made a bad pun at the expense of the minister of finance, saying that in the opinion of Witte, temperance was utopia, whereas for the people it was *utoplenie,* or drowning [in alcohol].[73]

As if to support Tolstoi's accusation of hypocrisy, the Kazan critic went on to state that if those in charge of the Guardianship would tell the truth, they would proclaim that alcohol is poison and always harmful. Furthermore, he charged that the people heading the Guardianship were not without "sin" and were themselves given to drink. He recommended that the organization be turned over to the Kazan Temperance Society. Even in the Duma, people understood the issues better than the Guardianship, claimed the anonymous author, who went on to point out that the Guardianship answered to the Ministry of Finance, not the Ministry of Internal Affairs, and the Ministry of Finance, for all its pious protestations, wanted revenue, not reform. The Kazan Temperance Society writer asked why they did not preach total abstinence, since "all honest men of science" know that liquor is harmful. And if they truly think liquor is good for people, why was the State Vodka Monopoly so intent on closing down bootleggers?[74]

The resolutions and statements issued by the First All-Russian Congress on the Struggle against Drunkenness were bold. The official statement read that despite all the ostentation of the Guardianship, it was bureaucratic and devoid of popular initiative, its 2 billion ruble expenditure was a waste, and it should be handed over to self-governing organizations (city dumas and zemstvos).[75] According to a journalist who attended the congress, most people not only believed that the Guardians were hypocritical but used their literature to roll cigarettes![76]

An American observer noted that the members of the Guardianship

> were more or less officially connected with the government, and
> were generally too busy to do anything for temperance. If they did

become active, it was at the risk of coming into collision with other monopoly government officials, whose welfare depended on the amount of liquor that they sold. Russian officials as well as others know the advantage of preserving friendly relations with other government officers.

The same American noted that after ten years, the government had spent over 45 million rubles on entertainments: "Temperance, however, is but a small and indirect part of the work of these institutions. On the whole, they are for general social welfare."[77]

Critics complained that local guardianships opposed the petitions of peasant villages to abolish state liquor stores in their territories. The official response was that if the state closed down liquor stores, more bootlegging would occur. But the Kazan Temperance Society answered that bootleg places already existed alongside nearly every state liquor store, sometimes even located in the cellars below the monopoly stores![78] On the eve of holidays, when the licit stores were closed, the bootleggers brought the liquor downstairs to continue serving their clientele without interruption.

The Kazan Temperance Society claimed that the Guardianship did nothing about this situation and distributed no books about the harm of alcohol (except for one brochure written by "a crazy drunken professor from Kiev"). It did nothing to cure drunks; it simply entertained them.[79] The critics went on to describe how the Guardianship's tearooms in the countryside were closed for lack of interest, and how those in the large cities attracted hooligans and depraved people, who had been fired from their jobs and bought the cheap food and tea in order to save their money for drinking.[80] The people hired to work in the tearooms were unable to set a moral example, since the Guardians themselves never visited those places. The Guardians themselves were drinkers and even drunkards, according to the indignant writer for the Kazan society.

A priest writing for the Kazan Temperance Society reported in 1904 that he had attended two *uezd* (county) sessions of the Guardianship meetings and received the impression that the "Guardianship decidedly did not know what to do to sober up the people."[81] He criticized them for spending money on dance halls and tearooms and even buying an organ for one of them, asking rhetorically, "Why in one region did they spend a comparatively large amount and in another not a cent?" He recommended that the Guardianship build a small library for every school, stocked with newspapers as well as propaganda about sobriety. If the Guardianship would contribute only 25–30 rubles to every school for these papers and books, "these libraries would be much more useful than tearooms, musical instruments, and dances."[82]

Another critic also claimed that the Guardianship was out of touch with the people, since workers had only one day off a week, but theatricals were put on seven days a week. He argued that since the Guardianship had no idea what pleased the people, the entertainment was not suited to them, nor did the available literature do much good since it did not advocate complete abstinence from drink. Believing that money was better spent on furnishing school libraries with antialcohol literature than on entertainment, he recommended that the selection not be done by Guardianship bureaucrats, who chose publications in a haphazard manner, but instead by educators, namely teachers and priests.[83]

In the conservative Kazan Temperance Society's view, the Guardianship did not engage in enough general social welfare. The society believed that instead of establishing tearooms and theaters, the Guardianship should have simply built night shelters, fed the unemployed, educated them about the harm of alcohol, and helped them find jobs by teaching them a trade. They thought that the Guardianship's money should have been spent on building an asylum for alcoholics and the unemployed in each province, staffed by a priest, a doctor, and teachers of literacy and trades. Each establishment, far from cities and villages, should have vegetable gardens and fields for pasturing cattle, allowing it to be largely self-supporting and requiring an annual subsidy from the Guardianship of probably no more than 50,000 rubles. The unemployed and alcoholics should spend at least a year at the asylum unless they committed a crime while there, in which case they should be sent to a correctional institution or to Siberia. This regime, the society argued, would correct the unsystematic way the Guardianship was treating alcoholism. In conclusion: "If you look at the list of reading given out during the entire existence of the Guardianship, you will see that there is little to read about drunkenness, as if the struggle against drunkenness did not constitute its raison d'être; and even the members of the Guardianship, in the majority, are drinking people, so that they can preach only moderation, that is, drunkenness."[84]

As time went on, the Kazan Temperance Society's conservative (even reactionary and anti-Semitic) temperance journal *Deiatel'* attacked the Guardianship more sharply, claiming that the Guardianship's theater in St. Petersburg provided dirty jokes, allowed people to bring in vodka, sold beer and red wine, and even permitted child prostitution on the premises.[85] In 1909, these accusations prompted the newspaper *Novoe vremia* to dub the organization the "Guardianship of Hooliganism."[86] Even the liberal jurist A. F. Koni complained in the same year that during a theatrical intermission at the Guardianship theater, singers dressed up as hooligans sang bawdy songs, which he condemned as the "apotheosis of drunkenness" in an establishment dedicated to the eradication of drunkenness.[87] Joining the conservative and liberal condemnations was the Left. A socialist worker wrote that the Guardianship performances "not only do not ennoble audiences but vulgarize and corrupt them."[88]

The guardianships at Moscow and St. Petersburg were in large part show-case operations. Both enjoyed large budgets and carried on their activities in the glare of favorable self-advertisement through their glossy reports, from which most of the statistics cited in this chapter were mined. Indeed, if the reader has found the recitation of numbers to be rather stultifying and bureaucratic, then the chapter has served as a mimetic device to reflect how the vast majority of Guardianship critics viewed the organization, namely, as one huge impersonal state institution generating mass facilities and amusements with no sincere attempt to reach the individual drinker. Even the guardianships far from the capitals, which received little money, were largely staffed by bureaucrats who were forced to serve, put minimal energy into their mission, had little rapport with the people, and little un-derstood their problems.[89] As one doctor put it, had the government decided to create a Guardianship for the Development of Popular Drunkenness, it would have chosen the same people employed for temperance. He con-cluded that the Guardianship now "plays a completely negative role" in reducing popular drunkenness.[90]

Despite 5 million rubles given as a subsidy to the Moscow guardianship and its ten buildings by 1911, only about 3 million persons visited the fa-cilities during that year, only half as many as five years earlier, a telling sign of its lack of success. If Russian critics claimed the Guardianship spent too much money fruitlessly, French critics noted that the state gave a smaller percentage of subsidies compared to revenue in 1904 than it had in 1899 and called the Guardianship operation a "trompe-l'oeil."[91] By 1909, the Guardianship received a budget of only 2 million rubles, or less than half the 1903 allotment.[92]

Rarely were the guardianship committees able to recruit members from the local intelligentsia, who remained indifferent or even unsympathetic to their efforts.[93] In 1911, only one-third of the associate members was listed as authentically active, a figure we can safely assume was inflated. As early as 1900, when an internal investigation was made, it was reluctantly noted that many meetings were canceled because they could not raise the quorum of five members (despite the huge official enrollment) and were unable to "enlist the sympathy of uezd intelligentsia."[94]

The Guardianship sought to elevate the population materially and cul-turally. The many activities of the St. Petersburg and Moscow committees were indeed impressive.[95] But to many, such a broadcast approach seemed wasteful. There was no necessary correlation between hard drinkers and those entertained and fed cheaply. In fact, in one survey, a worker stated that the People's Houses were so elegant that, lacking suitable clothes, he could not visit them. In Odessa, Kiev, and Sevastopol, the Guardianship sponsored "popular balls" but set the time at an hour when workers were not likely to attend.[96] Providing bread and circuses no doubt made the lives of some of the urban poor a bit more tolerable, but apart from the all-too-few clinics they sponsored, the Guardianship made little effort to reach individual drinkers.

Writing in the official Guardianship paper in 1904, V. Maksimov noted that the zemstvo meetings had constantly criticized the guardianships, especially the zemstvos of Kostroma, Smolensk, Kherson, Kaluga, and Moscow. At the Moscow Province zemstvo meeting on January 19, 1904, thirty-two members voted for, and twenty-five against, petitioning the Ministry of Finance to transfer all the duties of the official Guardianship to them.[97] Unlike the highly bureaucratic official Guardianship, the local zemstvos argued that they could put the money into general education, as well as specific training in matters of hygiene, including antialcohol information. To take over such expanded educational facilities would of course enhance the powers of the zemstvos as well. Meanwhile, the monarchy was taking advantage of the Guardianship to distribute monarchist literature in the countryside.[98]

Physicians were also constant critics of the Guardianship, especially the Commission on the Question of Alcoholism of the Russian Society for the Preservation of Public Health. In 1908, the commission commented that despite all the entertainment facilities built by the Guardianship, it had not built sufficient employment offices or clinics. The Guardianship ineffectually attempted to remedy the lack of enthusiasm of the membership by frequently changing its personnel.[99] In language framed in the post-1905 revolutionary era, doctors, like the zemstvos, were clearly attempting to carve out more power and authority for themselves. They called for the Guardianship to close down and transfer its funds to the zemstvos and municipal dumas, which would enlist members from social organizations (such as physician groups) concerned with the health and welfare of the poor and individuals who were genuinely interested in the problem of drink, rather than from government agencies.[100] Further, they urged, temperance societies thus constituted with activists should be established in every city and province where liquor was sold in state stores and should receive subsidies from the Ministry of Finance of no less than 10 percent of its annual revenue from the sale of alcoholic beverages, a tenfold increase over current expenditures.[101]

Zemstvos and physicians were not alone in advocating the disbanding of the Guardianship. As early as 1904, M. Chelyshev in the state Duma and V. P. Cherebanskii in the state Council said point-blank that the Guardianship should be abolished. Only doctors and representatives of professional societies and private temperance societies should be involved in the struggle against alcohol, and the state should stop funding the Guardianship.[102] Others wanted to turn over the Guardianship People's Houses to the people as universities.[103]

By 1912, the Ministry of Internal Affairs was considering a bill to restructure the Guardianship and put it under its jurisdiction.[104] Those who committed a crime while under the influence of alcohol would serve their time in a workhouse. There would be special care for children whose parents suffered from alcoholism. The Guardianship would also attempt to uproot bootlegging and the making of moonshine (*tainoe vinokurenie*), as well as ensure that the state stores and private enterprises serving liquor would abide by the rules regulating public health and morals. As these concerns indicate, the Ministry regarded alcoholism more as a police problem than one requiring entertainment. At least if the Guardianship was taken from the Ministry of Finance, the linking of the State Vodka Monopoly and the official temperance society within a single ministry (which Tolstoi found "hypocritical, silly, and misguided") would disappear. While nearly all segments of society and even some state institutions recognized the deficiencies of the Guardianship, and many were eager to take over its functions and to receive the subsidies, the inertia of governmental operations resulted in no change. Critics continued their carping at the wastefulness and futility of the "stillborn child."

The Guardianship is an excellent example of the dirigisme of the tsarist regime; its desire to lead all reform movements, including the battle against alcoholism, was made more intense by its own monopoly's wide distribution of cheap alcohol. The state did not create the problem, of course, but it did try to veil its contribution to the problem and perhaps alleviate its bad conscience by creating the Guardianship. Paradoxically, however, in fostering popular theater, it might not have induced sobriety to any appreciable degree, but as Gary Thurston has argued, by portraying highly diverse characters and suggesting choices in life, popular theater allowed the masses to acquire a sense of their possibilities for autonomy and self-creation, a sense that manifested itself during the revolution of 1917.[105]

3 . . . .

DRUGS ARE OUR BUSINESS

- ## PHYSICIANS STAKE A CLAIM ON THERAPIES

-
-
By the 1890s, the perceived dimensions of the liquor problem
demanded the ever closer attention of the medical profession,
especially, but not exclusively, of psychiatrists. In 1897, the eminent professor of psychiatry I. A. Sikorskii called alcoholism
"the disease of our century."[1] In 1913, Dr. D. P. Nikol'skii, a
factory doctor, instructor of industrial hygiene at the Tech-
nological, Metallurgical, and Polytechnic Institutes, and a specialist in alcoholism among the youth, proclaimed that "alcoholism is the greatest social disaster, bringing with it
economic destruction, physical degeneration, and moral and
mental decline into the midst of the population."[2] He stressed
that "alcohol is a poison, destroying the organism, acting de-
structively not only on those who drink but also on the de-
scendants of drinkers."[3]

Russian physicians were interested not only in ridding the
country of alcoholism but also in promoting their status in
the community and winning a voice in the government's decisions concerning the kind of environment they felt was conducive to the public's health.[4] Russian physicians from many
social strata came to feel a certain esprit de corps through their
work for the zemstvos (rural boards) and by their participation and leadership in the Pirogov medical societies.[5] Although
by the late nineteenth century, three-quarters of Russian doctors were paid by the state, physicians began to view themselves not simply as bureaucrats executing governmental di-
rectives but as experts with an ethos derived from their
profession. As such, their confidence, commitment, and need
for autonomy were sharpened by their experiences during the
famine and cholera crises of the early 1890s. When the government denied their expertise or antagonized them in their
attempts to improve society so as to eradicate famine, physicians rapidly became alienated from their employer and con-

tributed to the radicalization of their profession, leading finally to their involvement in the revolution of 1905.[6] After 1905, the medical profession became more factionalized as some doctors continued to guard their autonomy jealously while others looked to the centralization of medicine as a means to obtain greater financial support or to achieve better standards of public health.

A physician, D. P. Nikol'skii, was one of the earliest specialists in alcoholism. He stressed that only physicians could address the problems of alcoholism successfully and proposed the dissemination of scientific readings and visual aids on the subject suitable for various readerships: those with minimal reading skills, the working class, the intelligentsia, teachers and pupils, and schools campaigning against alcoholism. In the past, he claimed, most literature treating the theme of alcoholism was either religious or fictional but seldom medical.[7]

A milestone in the medical investigation of alcoholism was the establishment of the Commission on the Question of Alcoholism, under the auspices of the fifth section of the Russian Society for the Preservation of Public Health in St. Petersburg in May 1895.[8] For unknown reasons the commission did not begin to function actively until December 1897, with its first meeting held in January 1898. Thereafter, under the presidency of Dr. M. N. Nizhegorodtsev, a psychiatrist, member of the St. Petersburg City Council, and editor and founder of *Vestnik trezvosti* (Messenger of Temperance), it performed prodigious labors.[9] By 1901, it included 170 members, predominantly physicians but also lawyers and administrators.[10] Its *Trudy*, or proceedings, up to 1912 regularly fill the pages of the society's journal and were published separately in twelve volumes. They represent, in the society's own assessment, "a veritable encyclopedia of alcoholism."[11] Reports were given not only on alcoholism but also on how to combat it. The society invited suggestions from socialists as well as the Russian Orthodox clergy concerning the roots of and therapies for alcoholism.[12]

The commission also sponsored the First All-Russian Congress on the Struggle against Drunkenness, which met in St. Petersburg in December 1909 and January 1910.[13] Even deciding upon a name for the congress involved a vigorous debate.[14] Not surprisingly, the physicians wanted to call it the struggle against alcoholism, whereas the majority of the organizing committee, who were not physicians, carried the motion to call it a congress against drunkenness, a term they insisted would be more widely understood by the public. Physicians proved to be major participants in organizing the congress and attending it. Of the 453 attendees, 163, or 36 percent, were physicians or medical people; therefore, many of the reports presented at the congress concerned medical aspects of drinking.[15]

The founder of the commission, Nizhegorodtsev, admitted that despite the many years of study, the subject of alcoholism was far from exhausted.

Nevertheless, much information on the subject had been disseminated among the intelligentsia and the masses concerning the causes of alcoholism, its harmful effects, and the means for combating it. He was also proud of the impact the ten volumes of research articles had had upon the state Duma and the state Council when they began to formulate legislation on the subject of alcohol.[16] In order to make the research more accessible to members of the government and to the intelligentsia in general, Nizhegorodtsev organized the findings of the commission into three parts: the effect of alcohol on humans, the causes for alcoholism among the population, and the means to combat alcoholism. This war on alcohol had to be conducted by both the government and society.[17] Small units of self-governing organizations, activists, and private initiative should be mobilized for the fight.

Nizhegorodtsev expressed confidence that now that the state Duma and the state Council were beginning to pass laws on limiting the availability of alcohol, matters would improve. Still, he cautioned, the experience of other countries has shown the ineffectiveness of governmental measures without the full participation of society and the recognition by the masses of the harm caused by alcohol. The effort should also be politically nonpartisan. He felt that physicians needed to keep a careful watch on the government and recommended an examination of laws that would place alcoholics against their will in special institutions.[18]

As for the causes, Nizhegorodtsev argued that they were various and interrelated, having both biological and social roots.[19] Just as the causes were manifold, so, too, should be the means for fighting alcoholism, including improving the economic position of the people and raising their cultural level. The sale and availability of alcohol should be curtailed, but he did not advocate prohibition. He also noted that there was no direct correlation between class and alcoholism. Since some well-to-do and even rich people were alcoholics, poverty could not be the explanation for all cases. Dr. A. M. Korovin agreed that alcoholism could afflict the wealthy, quoting the adage "The rich drink when they want, the poor when they can."[20]

As of 1900, zemstvo doctors, with few exceptions, had not systematically studied the problem of alcoholism, claimed Korovin. Unlike a public-health threat such as an outbreak of diphtheria, rural doctors did not rush to defend the population against alcoholism. Yet, the masses of people adversely affected by alcohol merited attention, and Korovin argued that if the rural doctors attacked this problem together, they could have a real impact. At the Twelfth Guberniia Congress of Zemstvo Doctors of the Moscow Guberniia, he commended Dr. V. I. Iakovenko (1857–1923), a psychiatrist, for his study of alcoholics living in his area.[21] Iakovenko's recommendation was to decentralize psychiatric care in order to increase the authority of local psychiatrists over state officials.[22] After the 1905 revolution, he developed a theory that political activity was good for mental health: "His primary intent was less to advance scientific understanding than to comment on political events and to exhort his colleagues to [political] action."[23] A Bolshevik physician, he died in 1923, not for his political activities, but from typhus while fighting the disease.[24]

Nearly all doctors writing on the subject attempted to establish the etiology of alcoholism. In 1900, Korovin, a noted specialist who made a study of Moscow worker alcoholics, said he could not as yet establish the causes for alcoholism because only recently had "the thinking part of Russian society" shown interest in the problem.[25] Debates over the influence of "nurture or nature" divided the medical profession in Russia as elsewhere. By 1912, Dr. I. M. Dogel', a professor of pharmacology at the University of Kazan, came out staunchly in favor of the opinion that social environment was the determining factor leading to alcoholism, arguing that "alcoholism does not depend on the individual but on the general exterior conditions of life."[26] He then elaborated on workers' long working days, poor housing, bad food, and insufficient rest, conditions that often led to dependency on alcohol, a product, in his view, that was all too cheap. He conceded that even the extremely wealthy become alcoholics, so poverty was not the sole cause. He scoffed at what was called the "bears and bees" theory developed by scientists who claimed that just as bears and bees have (supposedly) an instinctual love of alcohol, so, too, some humans have an innate thirst for it. In his opinion, alcoholism was an illness, which affected people's health and reduced their economic well-being but was not a fatal, inescapable misfortune of humanity.

Dogel' attributed his emphasis on social factors to the studies of Dr. A. A. Dril', a distinguished psychiatrist at the Psychoneurological Institute of St. Petersburg, advisor to the Ministry of Justice, and a lawyer, who believed that by changing workers' environment, drinking patterns could be altered. He convinced the Commission on the Question of Alcoholism to endorse his plan to create a building society that would furnish decent living quarters for workers, who would be required to buy at least one share at a low price in order to teach them thrift and responsibility and to spare them the stigma of being on public welfare.[27]

Environmentalists felt that there was no need to attempt to change human nature; rather, they believed that an exterior world should be provided that would deter people from seeking drink. To this extent, they would probably have supported the Guardianship philosophy of providing distractions and substitutions for alcohol rather than attempting to change individual behavior. Extreme environmentalists contended that the causes of alcoholism were rooted in the very structure of Russian society and advocated reform, even the overturn, of Russia's autocracy.

The antienvironmentalists, however, blamed the individual himself. Such was Dr. L. O. Darkshevich, founder of the first clinic for alcoholics in Russia at Kazan, who in 1910 dismissed social factors entirely:

> I cannot agree that the cause of drunkenness is in the unfavorable circumstances of life: poverty, insufficient education, . . . , etc. Those reasons that the majority point to are not the causes, and I am all the more convinced by my supervision of the hospital which I founded in Kazan and in which more than 500 persons have been patients, among whom there have been educated and unlearned, rich and poor, people of all classes, all faiths. . . . I have seen in the hospital and in night shelters alcoholic people with the highest university and academic education, students from all faculties and other higher institutions of learning, priests deprived of their office, merchants of the first guild and their children, landowners having up to 2,000 *dessiatins* of land, officers of the infantry and of the guard. . . . [28]

The causes of drunkenness, in his estimation, were the same as for smoking opium, using morphine, smoking tobacco, drinking tea, or anything else. One develops a taste for it and it becomes a habit. And the habit is formed because "the consumption of alcohol is not considered a crime, due to the ignorance of society. Because of the ignorance of society, not one meal, not one holiday, and not one gathering can be had without alcohol, so that drunkenness is a necessary accompaniment to festivities."[29] Putting an end to ceremonial drinking rather than putting up houses was his solution to excessive drinking. His views were supported by Dr. P. S. Alekseev, a physician from Riga and pioneer in the field of the study of alcoholism, who enumerated the "dangerous" circumstances leading frequently to excessive drink, which also produced crime and violence: Sundays, holidays, bazaars, fairs, court days, and *pomoch'*.[30]

Darkshevich also faulted the custom of rewarding services with vodka. He asked: "Who rewards sober Russian people with vodka for their diligent labor, who gives vodka for service to the plain people? The drunken intelligentsia themselves cannot live without vodka. For vodka they receive labor, for vodka the coachman works and all who serve get vodka; wealthy bureaucrats, propertied merchants, all the Russian people drink; for them vodka is as necessary to consume at home as bread and salt."[31] Darkshevich went on to say that he owned a factory, which employed 150 workers. They were not paid in vodka and never treated to vodka, and they did not drink because they knew that he did not drink. They also knew, he claimed, that drinking workers produced less and were consequently paid less. He remunerated his employees more since they were sober. In general, however, he made the connection between industrial conditions and alcoholism, "It is well known that often a fellow who enters the workforce in the city a sober person returns to the village a drunk."[32]

Not content to probe the causes of alcoholism, Darkshevich also had his prescriptions. The way to fight drunkenness is to give to parishes sober priests, give to students sober teachers, and give to workers sober masters. In his view, the depraved intelligentsia, who for the most part knew neither the life of the people nor their souls, could not distinguish good from evil and thus were of no help. Schools had to teach children that alcohol is a poison that harms the body and eventually kills it. And more instruction in the ways of sobriety were needed than priests had been able to provide over the past forty years. He opposed entertainments such as dances, spectacles, plays, and games, believing that they were against the nature of the Russian people, who considered such pleasures a sin and therefore needed to be drunk to participate. An ultraconservative, typical of the Kazan Temperance Society, he urged that all liquor stores and pubs be closed, citing the experience of a village in Sviiazhsk County, Kazan Province, where there had been all kinds of disorders until the liquor stores and taverns were shut down. Thereafter, the village was peaceful and free of crime. In Turkestan, drunkenness had been rare and the peasants well-off until the military allowed the opening of pubs in 1897; after that, there had been drunkenness, poverty, and crime.

Darkshevich was not alone is his gloomy forecasts of the effects of alcohol.[33] Even earlier, in 1906, Alekseev claimed that degeneracy occurred because alcohol, although quickly absorbed into the bloodstream, also "passed to some glands and genital secretions." One of the proofs he cited of the link between degeneracy and alcohol was that more illegitimate children (presumably conceived under the influence of alcohol) were "degenerate" than legitimate babies. Epilepsy is also associated with chronic alcoholism, Alekseev claimed. He insisted, however, that alcoholics are sick individuals and should not receive excessive punishments for their illness, no more than other sick people are punished. Instead, they should be treated in special clinics with a regime designed to cure their minds and bodies, just as lepers in the Middle Ages had their own asylums.[34]

He asserted that the moderate use of alcohol was the cause of drunkenness since all drunks begin with one glass; he had known many who were not drunks in their youth but in their middle years between thirty and forty had died before his eyes of alcoholic paralysis. Vodka was not aqua vitae, "the water of life," as the ancients referred to alcoholic spirits, but the water of death, water of the devil, which has shackled humanity.

One of the reasons physicians described the effects of alcohol consumption so dramatically was that the Russian people still commonly believed alcohol to have curative effects. As late as 1909, in the province of Vladimir,

47 percent of the people thought that vodka was good for one's health. They considered that it made them stronger and used it as medicine for tooth-aches, stomachaches, headaches, and sore throats; women used it after childbirth and men after hard labor. The adage "The devil doesn't drink and he lives in hell" is a sign of how addicted people were to spirits, ac-cording to Alekseev.[35]

The physicians who believed that a poor environment was conducive to excessive drinking wanted to change society and at times even the govern-ment; physicians who thought individuals were responsible for their alco-holic plight urged them to change their habits and exhorted them to dis-cipline themselves. Physicians were also divided on what specific measures were necessary to eliminate the problem. Dogel', who favored total absti-nence, argued that if alcoholism is an illness, then measures can be taken to cure it. This is the attitude, he claimed, of all the governments of Europe and America. As far as he was concerned, the best means to combat alco-holism was to enact total prohibition and to educate children from the earliest age on the dangers of alcohol.[36]

Alekseev, one of the first Russians to write a study on alcoholism, said that increased taxes on vodka did not produce increased sobriety. In his opinion, oaths to abstain for at least two years were the most effective means of overcoming the illness. Also effective was treatment in alcohol-free clinics. The biggest obstacle to public sobriety, he argued, was the huge fiscal and personal financial interests invested in the production and sale of alcoholic beverages. He could only have been indicting the government for encouraging drink among the Russian people.[37]

Dr. I. V. Sazhin also felt that clinics for alcoholics were desperately needed, noting that only three such clinics were in operation. The first, called Turva (shelter), established in Finland in 1890 by a temperance so-ciety, had helped 100,000 sailors. After eight years, there were only 148 patients, of whom about 40 percent were cured. When Turva first opened, sick persons were kept in the clinic from two to three years, producing a higher rate of success; but because of lack of money, later patients were kept there only one year. Had Turva not been subsidized, it would have gone out of business.[38]

The second clinic (and the first in Russia proper) was opened in Kazan by the Kazan Temperance Society in 1896. Although it was large enough for only twenty people, in the three years of its existence it had treated ninety-one persons.[39] The third clinic was built in the village of Vseviatskii a few miles from Moscow in 1898 at the expense (about 200,000 rubles) of Ko-rovin. Patients paid between 15 and 25 rubles a month, but there were only ten of them. Evidently, few could afford losing wages while paying for treat-ment in clinics.

In addition to residential clinics, alcoholics were treated on an outpatient basis. The St. Petersburg Temperance Society opened a clinic in 1895 that admitted only men on their own volition. Also, a Lutheran pastor, A. Masing, opened a clinic in which alcoholics paid 25 rubles per month for a room, but it soon closed because of financial reasons.[40] The state did not invest in clinics dedicated to the cure of alcoholism, and few groups could afford to maintain clinics where patients did not have the means to pay.

Since so little treatment was provided, most physicians, including Korovin, sought to prevent alcoholism through intensive sociological and medical studies. He made some interesting observations. One was that consumption of alcohol often rose if salaries rose. He also noted that if people had no higher cultural interests, then greater portions of incomes went into drinking. Further, many persons did not associate drinking with illnesses. He noted that in places like Yalta and Piatigorsk, where people went for cures of syphilis and tuberculosis, the consumption of alcohol was even higher than in nonresort areas.[41]

The medical strategies advanced by Russian physicians at the time were primarily drug therapy, notably the use of strychnine, to overcome the addiction to alcohol; the confinement of the alcoholic for an extended period in a sanitarium; and hypnotic therapy administered at ambulatory clinics.[42] These methods were much discussed, and none of them proved entirely satisfactory.

At times, applying drugs required hospitalization. In 1908, N. V. Farmakovskii, a zemstvo doctor, reported in a paper presented to the Commission on the Question of Alcoholism of the Russian Society for the Preservation of Public Health on his use of drugs (a kind of early application of the idea of methadone for heroin addicts). He said that a few years earlier, he had experimented with injecting increased doses of strychnine into alcoholics. There were some successes among the fifty patients he treated, but they were only temporarily cured, he reported dejectedly. Once they returned to their old habitats, they returned to their old habits as well.[43] Drug treatment required hospitalization. Russia was too poor to maintain an adequate number of sanitaria, and forced confinement rendered patients hostile to treatment.

Alekseev noted in 1906 that the gold cure was practiced everywhere in America. A secret and costly combination of gold, strychnine, and atropine, it was no longer injected under the skin as it had been ten to fifteen years earlier. Instead, as alcoholics were taken off alcohol, they were given stimulants in the form of infusions and decoctions of the drugs that were formerly injected under the skin, he reported.[44]

There was another weapon in the medical arsenal—hypnosis—and it was wielded by psychiatrists, many of whom diagnosed alcoholism as a form of mental illness. Psychiatry as a medical specialty was a novelty in the first quarter of the nineteenth century in Russia, but by the end of the century hundreds of students were being trained as psychiatrists in Russian universities.[45] Like other physicians, psychiatrists had to struggle to obtain recognition and the autonomy they felt their due. One psychiatrist lamented in 1895: "How little respected are honest work and knowledge in our society. . . . Officials want neither knowledge nor honest labor but only deference and obedience."[46]

Although psychiatrists and physicians shared an antagonism toward the state in their struggle for recognition and rewards, they were by no means allies. According to one historian who has assessed the situation, they were rivals: "To some degree the opposition of other physicians to psychiatrists was rooted in their perception that efforts by psychiatrists to establish an independent professional identity ran counter to the interests of the larger medical profession."[47]

Psychiatrists had had little success in "curing" the insane, in managing asylums, and even in determining who should be inmates after the government began sending political prisoners to their asylums.[48] No wonder psychiatrists seized upon the problem of alcoholism, proclaiming that they were equipped to address it. Given the rebuffs they had suffered within the context of Russian politics, they developed a special investment in establishing themselves as experts in the field of alcoholism. By the turn of the century, many psychiatrists diagnosed alcoholism as a form of mental illness and attempted to classify alcoholics. Some of these classifications were merely descriptive, while others outlined progressive stages.[49]

In 1905, Dr. S. A. Pervushin, a psychiatrist who studied how income affected patterns and quantities of alcohol consumption among urban workers and peasants, concluded that the principal means for effecting a cure was through hypnotism, either in hospitals or ambulatory clinics, although he did not recommend this therapy for those who suffered severe mental disease or who were criminals. He proposed a lengthy "cure" for alcoholics that involved sending them to residential clinics to work at trades in cities or in agriculture in the countryside to habituate them to an alcohol-free environment while they learned marketable skills for the future. Besides adopting habits of industry, they would also receive intelligent entertainment and educational readings and engage in discussions for their mutual benefit. Body, soul, and mind would be treated under this regimen for one or two years. Some alcoholics would be motivated to come on their own; others would require the intervention of a relative, friend, doctor, or priest to persuade them to commit themselves. Countries such as England and America had already considered this problem, Pervushin asserted, and attempted to cure the alcoholic in ways that benefited the alcoholic himself as well as society. This project of asylum-colonies for alcoholics would require money, although income from the inmates (called "clients") would help defray expenses. Because the state would save money from the reduction in free psychiatric care, it should be induced to allocate funds to support them.[50]

Hypnotism was cheap, and drunkards were, allegedly, easily hypnotized. In 1901, psychiatrist F. E. Rybakov reported on the methods and results of his treatment of 260 men through hypnotic suggestion at the Moscow Psychiatric Clinic.[51] He hypnotized his patients first once a day, then at longer intervals: twice a week, once a week, two times a month, once a month, and even less frequently, in accordance with their progress. However, nearly one-half (47 percent) of his patients simply disappeared without completing the treatment, and he could claim successful cures (sobriety maintained for a full year) for only 20.8 percent of the original group. Rybakov still maintained that hypnotic therapy was the cheapest and most feasible cure for alcoholism and urged its wide adoption.

Hypnosis was the most effective treatment, according to Rybakov, since about 90 percent of the population was susceptible, although it might take five to ten sessions before the patient was hypnotized.[52] He stated that public opinion held that only the nervous and hysterical were susceptible, but this incorrect notion arose from the fact that most doctors used the method only on people suffering from nervous disorders, who actually prove less susceptible to hypnosis than healthy people. It is also false, he stated, that people of weak will are more apt to respond to suggestion. On the contrary, strong-willed people respond more easily. And although all ordinary people are liable to suggestion in normal life, people in a hypnotic state are especially susceptible to suggestion.

Three years later, in 1904, instead of a 20 percent cure rate, Rybakov announced that he had improved his success rate to 40 percent in an experiment he conducted in a Moscow clinic. Relatively more people reverted to drink within the first six months than during the second six months, so the longer the duration of the treatment, the more successful it became. He therefore recommended that a year should be the minimal duration for therapy. His study also demonstrated that the least-habitual drinkers also had a higher rate of cure. As if to explain the relatively high rate of success, he went on to say that just as a person could be cured of typhus and then at some point fall ill again to the same disease, this kind of lapse was also possible for alcoholics.[53] Take the example, he continued, of a drunkard who had been drinking for twenty years but after seeking help from the doctor drank less and less often, would that not also be considered a cure? While, he admitted, it would be better for that individual not to drink at all, it was still a marked improvement for that individual. Quite clearly, this doctor believed that it was possible for an alcoholic to learn how to drink in moderation.

Although alcoholism was definitely an illness, Rybakov claimed it was one that required the assent of the patient to cooperate in the treatment, unlike other illnesses, which can be cured even if medicine is administered against the will of the patient. Unless the alcoholic wants to be cured, there can be no success, according to his Moscow experiments. Rybakov preferred treating patients in a sanitarium, but he admitted that Russia, especially after the war with Japan, was not in a financial position to construct a sufficient number of sanitaria. Hypnotism on an outpatient basis, he therefore believed, was the most useful treatment for Russian working people who could not take a year off from work to enter a special hospital.

In 1904, another psychiatrist, A. A. Pevnitskii, claimed a high rate of cure. His paper given before the Russian Society for the Preservation of Public Health at a meeting of its Commission on the Question of Alcoholism stated that he had achieved a cure rate of 80 percent using hypnotic suggestion in the clinic of Dr. V. M. Bekhterev.[54] At about the same time, Dr. A. P. Mendel'son began treating many alcoholics at two free clinics. At first, he harbored a great deal of skepticism about the use of hypnotism, but as the years went by, he became convinced that it was the most successful medical treatment available for patients susceptible to suggestion. However, he would not argue that alcoholics could be cured only through hypnosis.[55]

According to Mendel'son, cures could be effected only if the patient was treated for a minimum of two months; total abstinence was required, and suggestion seemed to be the most successful mode of treatment. Although Mendel'son's criteria were not specified, he claimed that from January 1, 1908, he treated 294 patients for no less than two months. Of those, 64 percent were completely cured, 22 percent were remarkably better, and 15 percent he considered unsuccessful cases. By 1913, the percentages had altered slightly to 64 percent, 16 percent, and 20 percent, respectively.[56]

In 1904, Korovin wrote an article for a French temperance journal explaining the way Russian medicine used hypnosis for curing alcoholics. Korovin claimed that about half of those who were not seriously ill with alcoholism were cured by working with temperance societies. But those seriously afflicted with alcoholism needed medical treatment, which up until recently had been ineffectual, whether in hospitals or in mental institutions. In the past six years, he reported, many clinics had been established especially for alcoholics, and the outpatient clinics were the most effective for they permitted the patients to live at home and keep their jobs.

Suggestion alone was also considered by some doctors to be efficacious. In 1905, Dr. B. N. Sinanu claimed to have cured sixty-two alcoholics in his ambulatory clinic without the use of drugs or hypnotism.[57] But during the first decade of the twentieth century, psychiatrists discovered psychoanalysis, which in some cases supplanted hypnosis and suggestion. By 1911, Pevnitskii had switched from hypnosis and suggestion to psychoanalysis as a method of treatment. His paper "On Psychoanalysis for the Curing of Alcoholics" was read before a meeting of the Commission on the Question of Alcoholism on February 10, 1911. Dr. Mendel'son noted that at one time Pevnitskii had been an ardent supporter of hypnotism, but now, a decade later, he had dropped it in favor of the new Freudian method of psychoanalysis. Mendel'son stressed that psychoanalysis was only an evolution from earlier psychiatric methods, which all along had supposed that without exploring the psyche of alcoholics, doctors would be unable to treat them. How ironic, Mendel'son stated, that he himself, who had once been a skeptic concerning the method of hypnotism, was now an ardent supporter, whereas Pevnitskii had gone "from extreme optimism to full negativism" with regard to the effectiveness of hypnotism. In short, he and Sazhin scarcely concealed their doubt concerning the applicability of Freudian theory to alcoholism. Both psychiatrists noted that even Pevnitskii admitted that a recovering alcoholic needed the support of a temperance society or brotherhood for long-term success, along with Freudian psychoanalysis.[58]

Other doctors also emphasized being attentive to social factors in the treatment of alcoholics. It is curious that these leading Russian scientists, adumbrating some of the techniques of Alcoholics Anonymous, noted that the support of fellow alcoholics was vital for the maintenance of sobriety, citing how sectarians were known for their sobriety and how certain other church groups with influential leaders (who in effect possessed the powers of suggestion) were also successful in sustaining the will not to drink.[59] In their view, it was necessary to combine psychiatric help (suggestion, hypnotism, and possibly Freudian psychoanalysis) with what might now be called group therapy or support groups.[60]

Earlier, St. Petersburg psychiatrist V. E. Ol'derogge advocated isolating alcoholics by putting them on islands. He identified three islands in the Gulf of Finland and other islands off the coast of Riga and in the Black Sea where alcoholics could be removed from all temptation and yet could not escape. He succeeded in persuading the governor-general of Finland to sell him an island for 2,500 rubles and to rent him another on which he established colonies of alcoholics where alcoholic beverages were strictly forbidden.[61]

As the example of being shipped off to an island suggests, it was accepted in some medical circles that alcoholics could be confined against their will. For example, a subcommission of psychiatrists of the Russian Society for the Preservation of Public Health approved involuntary commitment. They recommended a law that would permit medical authorities to judge whether a person was a danger "to himself, to those around him, and to society" because of his alcoholism. Authorities could then force the individual to undergo a cure in a clinic for a period of from six months to two years.[62] Although drafted and submitted to the Commission on the Question of Alcoholism, the bill was never adopted as law.[63]

Rural physicians denounced involuntary confinement, arguing that such a practice would only enhance the police powers of the state.[64] Russian doctors argued over the necessity for repression of alcoholics, that is, keeping alcoholics in clinics against their will. In a country traditionally devoid of civil rights, liberal physicians resisted repression, especially in the post-1905 revolutionary period.[65] The debate centered on balancing the rights of the individual against social benefits derived from therapy effected under restraint. A commentator stated that in England, public drunks could be sent to prison, and in many countries, railroad workers were required to be teetotalers.[66]

Although psychiatrists were not in agreement concerning forced incarceration for alcoholism, almost all insisted that they possessed a special expertise in treating the problem. Among Russia's prominent psychiatrists was Lazar' Solomonovich Minor, who became a noted Soviet neuropathologist.[67] Educated at and later on the faculty of the University of Moscow, Minor observed Western approaches to the problem of alcoholism while traveling abroad from 1881 to 1887. He reported his findings to the first congress of Russian psychiatrists in 1887 and published his observations on alcoholism and treatments in America, Australia, New Zealand, England, Germany, and elsewhere.[68] In 1889, he represented Russian doctors at the Third International Congress against the Abuse of Alcoholic Beverages, held in Christiania, where he was elected one of the vice-presidents. During the 1890s, he actively advocated the establishment of a clinic for alcoholics in Moscow, urging ceaselessly that treatment should not be left to amateurs but should instead be entrusted to scientists. He recommended that clinics maintain close relationships with the University of Moscow laboratories. In large part through his efforts, the Guardianship funded the first such clinic in Moscow proper in 1903. As many doctors, and psychiatrists in particular, showed a mounting interest in alcoholism, they looked to the Guardianship or to private temperance societies for the funds needed to support clinics. In 1900 and 1901, Minor headed a commission that recommended that the government discontinue the gratuitous distribution of vodka rations (the *charka*) to military personnel. He continued his lifelong battle against alcoholism even after the revolution.

Dr. S. S. Korsakov, who died in 1901 at the age of forty-seven, was, and perhaps remains, the most noted Russian psychiatrist who occupied himself with the subject of alcoholism. He published his dissertation *On Alcoholic Paralysis* in 1897, and in the same year, his work was recognized by the international medical community at a congress in Moscow.[69] By 1914, there were at least 400 works discussing his investigations on alcoholic paralysis and alcoholic paraplegia, which is still called "Korsakov's disease."[70] As one Russian biographer wrote, "the study of alcoholic paralysis by S. S. Korsakov can be considered the first step in the study of alcoholic disease in Russia and in the struggle against alcoholism."[71] Perhaps it should be expected that a country in which alcoholism posed such a large problem would also produce a world-renowned scientist in the field.

Another doctor, V. M. Bekhterev, held the first chair in psychiatry at Kazan University and was instrumental in the founding of the Kazan Temperance Society (one of Russia's most active temperance groups) and the first Russian clinic for alcoholics in the same city.[72] A participant at many congresses, including one on white slavery held in 1910, he used every rostrum he could to warn against alcoholism and, incidentally, to denounce the imperial government for creating a nation of alcoholics out of budgetary interests.

Bekhterev's great ambition was to see the St. Petersburg Psychoneurological Institute built and to secure a chair on alcoholism there, a goal that was realized in 1912. Rather belatedly, the Ministry of Finance had come to recognize that alcoholism needed medical treatment and spent 320,000 rubles on the institute and allocated an additional 400,000 rubles for its future support. Ironically, V. N. Kokovtsev, chair of the Council of Ministers and former finance minister in charge of the vodka monopoly, was present at the institute's inauguration, along with dignitaries from the vodka monopoly such as L. B. Skarzhinski, who said in their speeches that the subject must be approached from a variety of disciplines. Of course, many temperance advocates felt that the monopoly itself was largely to blame for the problem.[73]

Perhaps out of conviction, perhaps because he was supported by the State Vodka Monopoly (as his enemies noted), Bekhterev sought a formula that could determine how much alcohol a person of a certain weight could consume safely and concluded that one tea glass of vodka (which he later modified to a few teaspoons) could be consumed daily by an individual without harm.[74] Obviously, this kind of steady but moderate consumption would fill the coffers of the state treasury, as advocated by the Guardianship.[75] For some doctors, even those abroad, therefore, the institute represented a tool of the state because of its justification for the consumption of alcohol; others felt some solid scientific results would emanate from it. Although Bekhterev appeared to have reconciled medical knowledge with the tsarist state policy of advocating moderation in drink, he minced no words in 1910, calling capitalism, not alcohol, "the fundamental evil of our era."[76] Internationally recognized for his scientific work, he continued his campaign against alcoholism into the Soviet period.[77]

In 1899, another psychiatrist, I. A. Sikorskii, a professor at the University of Kiev, produced the most systematic analysis to date of alcoholism in

Russia and its social cost.[78] He carefully compared rates of consumption with child and adult mortality, murder, and crime, concluding that alcoholism was the "disease of our century," and that "the *alcoholic epidemic* penetrates everywhere, amid which perish the health, strength, and morals of the best of European peoples—the Russian people."[79]

By 1911, some doctors were no longer content to write papers and give reports on the causes, effects, and therapies for alcoholism and decided to become activists as well. Consequently, they organized in St. Petersburg the Russian Medical Society of Doctors Promoting Temperance, which noted physicians active in the temperance movement joined, including A. M. Korovin, A. L. Mendel'son, I. V. Sazhin, N. I. Grigor'ev, and A. I. Verzhbitskii.[80] Within three years, Ivan Vasil'evich Sazhin became chair of the new society. He gave courses on the medical aspects of alcoholism to doctors, *feld'sher*s (medical assistants), midwives, and students, as well as giving public lectures on the subject to middle schools, military students, and factory workers. He presented a paper based on his dissertation, "On the Influence of Alcohol on the Developing Organism," to the international congress in Finland on family education. He published several books and many articles in the periodical press and in scientific journals, promoting his belief in the necessity for complete abstinence.[81] As an example of his dedication to the cause, it should be noted that he was also vice-chair of the Commission on the Question of Alcoholism, a candidate member of the Council of the All-Russian Alexander Nevskii Brotherhood of Temperance, and founding member of the All-Russian Working Union of Christian Temperance Workers. At the All-Russian Hygiene Congress exhibit he received an honorary degree for his tireless work in the field. He is a good example of how some physicians devoted their entire scientific lives to fostering sobriety.

Nonetheless, rifts remained among physicians as to the causes of alcoholism and therapies for it. There also continued to be a tug-of-war between some physicians and psychiatrists over which group possessed the greater expertise on the issue, not only out of professional pride but also because social and political prerogatives in Russia depended on such claims. The solidarity exhibited by physicians before the 1905 revolution began to erode as they contested proprietorship over this particular issue, but by 1911, at least some physicians and some psychiatrists were able to work together in the Russian Medical Society of Doctors Promoting Temperance. As their opposition to the state monopoly grew, they were drawn closer together. Just as physicians in 1904 declared that no headway could be made on the problem of alcoholism until people had civil rights, so, too, did psychiatrists come to the conclusion by 1910 that the political structure of Russia had to change before material conditions could improve.[82]

There were tensions as well between the medical profession and the Duma. While physicians wanted to influence the Duma in their legislative choices, they did not want to surrender control of the issue to the law-makers. Nor did most of them condone the state-established Guardianship, although some scientists were willing to accept subsidies from it and other governmental agencies. Those scientists who believed in total abstinence (and they seem to have been in the majority) defied the official policy of moderation advocated by the state through the Guardianship and had nothing but contempt for the Guardianship's ineptness, if not outright hypocrisy. Only some physicians were environmentalists, but the preponderance of psychiatrists believed that "prevention of the physical and psychological degeneration of the population was dependent upon fundamental political and economic reform of Russian life."[83]

Not only did many doctors experience a profound sense of alienation from the state, which led to their participation in the revolution of 1905, but many of them, including Korovin, and especially psychiatrists, such as Minor and Bekhterev, threw in their lot with the Bolshevik regime—a group that promised "fundamental political and economic reform"—in the hope that alcoholism would not be compatible with socialism.[84]

4 . . . .

BATTLING BOOZE

- ## STRATEGIES FOR SOBRIETY IN THE MILITARY

The campaigns in Manchuria resembled a scuffle between a drunken guardsman and a sober policeman. All the evidence goes to show that vodka had the right of way as unquestionably as Milwaukee beer in the Spanish-American War. Perhaps more so. One recalls the Russian naval attack on the trawlers of the Dogger Bank, an episode which awakened the hilarity of the whole world. It has usually been attributed to the alcoholized visions of Japanese warships.

       —Ernest Gordon, *Russian Prohibition*

The army is a composite of the nation, so that the alcohol problem there is a matter of the greatest social and governmental importance.

       —Dr. I. V. Sazhin

A British war correspondent who spent two years with the Russian army in the Far East assessed Russia's defeat in the war with Japan in 1905: "A great people with a great army, who could not defeat the Japanese in a single battle, must first have been the victims not of the enemy, but of themselves." He further identified the problem by saying that "the chief enemy of an army is the nation's moral diseases," which he defined as corruption and gambling and, above all, alcoholism.[1] A German correspondent had the same idea when he observed: " 'Who defeated the Russians?' ask foreigners, and they answer, 'The Japanese did not conquer, but alcohol triumphed, alcohol, alcohol.' "[2]

Although Russian war correspondents did not play up

drunkenness in the military, individuals did note the role played by alcohol in the debacle.[3] The entry dated October 7, 1905, in the diary of a Russian engineer on board one of the ships of the Baltic Sea fleet en route to the Tsushima Straits (where he would lose his life) reads:

> The crews of the ships at Port Arthur asked leave to go to the advanced positions, and returned under the influence of liquor. No one could understand how they became drunk. In the towns liquors were not sold, and yet men went to the advanced positions and returned intoxicated. At last it was discovered, and how do you suppose? It appears that the sailors went to the front in order to kill one of the enemy and take away his brandy-flask. Just imagine such a thing. They risked their lives to get drunk! They did all this without thinking anything of it, and contrived to conceal it from the authorities.[4]

Not only did the military drink before and during the war, but financing the war increased consumption at home as well. Sergei Witte, who had created the State Vodka Monopoly when he was finance minister, recorded in his memoirs that his successor had helped finance the war through liquor revenues:

> When the war with Japan began, the then finance minister Vladimir Nikolaevich Kokovtsev began to use the liquor monopoly primarily as a means of increasing revenue, by raising liquor prices and increasing the number of liquor stores. And the work of excise officials was judged by increase in revenue rather than by decrease in alcoholism.[5]

As Witte explained, "Kokovtsev did not set the price high enough to discourage consumption but yet high enough to be ruinous for the poorer classes: the result was increased revenue from liquor sales and increased alcoholism."[6] In fact, receipts after 1904 from vodka nearly doubled, showing a net increase of 500 million rubles. As a point of comparison, in 1914 only 160 million rubles were allocated to the Ministry of Public Enlightenment.[7] Since many of the recruits for the war were members of the poorer classes, this price hike, combined with general unwillingness to fight an unpopular war, perhaps helps to explain the recruits' attacks on vodka monopoly stores.[8]

Typically, recruits began to drink, according to a Russian ethnographer, as soon as they were scheduled to appear before the draft board. All the able-bodied men (*godnye*) went around the village drinking up their money, which was supplemented by contributions from their grieving parents.[9] Playing music, smashing windows, and other "pranks" were expected of the draftees, whose habits were so universal that the expression arose "drunk as a recruit." A skilled worker from a peasant family explained this behavior:

> The village lads, together with the new recruits, moved in crowds from village to village; they played their accordions, sang outlandish songs in their strained voices, shouted, danced their village dances, drank vodka, acted rowdy, and fought over girls with the boys of other villages. This bravado and drunken revelry was their way of drowning the dread they felt in anticipation of their coming departure from their dear ones for many long years of soldiering, harsh barracks life, and perhaps even war.[10]

In 1904, these able-bodied men presumably continued their drinking by looting en route to the mobilization points. An American journalist described the scene:

> In the mobilization for the Japanese war the soldiers were carried, dead with intoxication, to the train. When they came to stations, those who could walk tore wildly out of the coaches for the saloons, and if barkeepers refused to sell, they broke bottles over their heads. In terror the drilled troops in charge of recruits telegraphed ahead to stations to have two hundred or more soldiers on hand when the train went through. Even under such surveillance the men sometimes broke open the doors of the trains and tore up the railroad stations.[11]

An American prohibition advocate citing a passage from the Moscow newspaper *Golos* reported in more detail:

> The reservists searched every man as he entered the barracks. All had vodka. The searchers always threw it into the street. In one peasant's rags eleven bottles were found. His eyes ran with tears when he saw them broken. The heap of shattered glass grew. A dirty stream of vodka flowed through the courtyard. Many threw themselves on their knees and, in spite of the dirt, tried to drink from the pools. They were kicked back. Three truckloads of broken glass were transported.[12]

Historical accounts of earlier Russian wars are replete with stories not only of the undoubted bravery of Russian troops but also, if the supply was available, of their penchant for drinking. According to the historian N. I. Kostomarov, Russian troops, when fighting the Prussians in 1758, lost a battle after they found a supply of vodka and drank it; some 20,000 of them were captured by the enemy.[13] And again:

> Napoleon, in his bulletins, informs us that the progress of the Russian army, which came to the assistance of Austria, in 1805, was marked by riot and intemperance; and that they spent the night preceding the day on which the battle of Austerlitz was fought, in drunkenness, noise and revelry. . . . This circumstance may have assisted to produce, or at least to heighten the disasters of that fatal day.[14]

Despite such anecdotes, military historian John Keep considered Russian soldiers to be more sober than the population at large. Noting that although ordinary soldiers (not officers) were allotted three vodka rations, known as *charkas,* or a total of 10 ounces a day, while on campaign, Keep pointed out: "Russian soldiers generally stuck to *kvas,* or native beer, and had a better reputation for sobriety than their officers or most civilians. From 1819 onwards they were not allowed to visit taverns and had to be content with the regulation issue of alcoholic beverages."[15] In 1910, an expert on alcoholism also declared that the incidence of alcoholism among the military was no greater than among the population at large.[16]

Dr. B. M. Shapirov even went so far as to claim that about 20 percent of those entering service did not drink at all, whereas 25 percent of those leaving service did not drink. He concluded that, for soldiers, service had been a school for sobriety. He did not consider the possibility that perhaps the drinkers had died during their lengthy service in the military.[17]

Russian soldiers were paid so little that they had to earn extra cash if they wanted to drink or perhaps even to eat well. Doing work on the outside while in the military was common practice at the end of the nineteenth century according to an American observer:

> It is curious to see soldiers in uniform working in the harvest fields or mending the roads. . . . The Russians are permitted to hire out as laborers or artisans—anything they can find to do. In the cities, the soldiers of the garrison usually have the preference over others as supers in the theaters, and among them are musicians of considerable talent. In the provinces they work at harvesting, plowing, ditch-digging, or anything the large landed proprietors can find for them to do.[18]

Many critics and reformers believed soldiers were working for drink money because they had become accustomed to hard alcohol through the allocation of vodka rations.[19] In the early eighteenth century, Peter I had allowed his sailors a ration of vodka only three times a week, whereas by 1761, it was customary to give daily *charkas* (1/100 of a *vedro,* or about 3.36 ounces) to the sailors, and in 1797, Emperor Paul I made it part of Navy regulations. During the Russian war against Napoleon in 1812, Nadezhda Durova, a woman posing as a male junior officer in the cavalry, wrote, "I honestly never thought to find a use for the two winecups of liquor that are distributed every day to us as well as the soldiers. But obviously nothing should be disdained."[20] The army also received the *charka* daily, but after 1886, a daily ration was given only to those men serving on Sakhalin Island, and the lower ranks, serving elsewhere: received vodka nine times a year, paid for out of funds collected by the soldiers themselves. In addition, vodka was given under special circumstances such as "when it was necessary for the maintenance of health and the strength of the lower ranks, as in bad weather, increased labor, and marches." Even inspections merited 1/200 of a *vedro,* or about 1.68 ounces.[21] Those who preferred could receive money in lieu of alcohol. It was forbidden, however, to give away one's portion of vodka to a companion.

The first serious debate over the *charka* was raised in the 1870s when other reforms of the military were implemented.[22] A physician, A. V. Sobolevskii, pointed out that the military reform of 1874 established the principle that military service should serve "as a school of living for the improvement of the Russian people." Serving liquor appeared to teach the wrong lesson, noted General P. E. Keppen in 1874, who believed that "the festive and toasting soldiers' *charka* will always be an obstacle to the spreading of the correct view on drunkenness among the military."[23]

General Keppen, in an 1899 speech before a subcommission of the Russian Society for the Preservation of Public Health devoted to alcohol in the armed forces, wanted to apply some lessons from America to the Russian army.[24] Quoting an unnamed American general, "Alcoholic liquids are the curse of the army," Keppen said that during the American Civil War General Grant shut down all the taverns in the District of Columbia for two months when his troops were nearby. Each colonel in the United States had the right to forbid the use of alcohol among his troops, and General Keppen said an American soldier told him that it was obvious which troops were which by looking at their level of cleanliness or orderliness. He also related that some French soldiers during the Franco-Prussian War resorted to drink, thinking that it would give them strength and bolster their morale. He did not need to add that they lost the war.[25]

When it came to practical measures to curb drunkenness in the army, Keppen gave a historical outline of the various severe punishments that had been meted out in the past, noting that Ivan I, Ivan III, Aleksei, Peter I, and Catherine II all attempted to change drinking habits, usually by regulating the manufacture and sale of vodka. But for the present, the best way to tackle alcoholism, he asserted, was through educating the young in school. He also recommended adopting the American method of considering drunkenness as a disease, which could be cured in special hospitals, claiming that in the American experience with these hospitals, two-thirds of the patients return to "a reasonable life." As for Russian soldiers, they did not turn to drink because of inadequate food. The craving for drink was not physical but a complicated psychological need. Cultured persons turn to music, to conversation, to books, or to the theater, but the soldier with little literacy is apt to turn to conversation with his companions, and he feels the need for vodka to liven up the discussion. This, according to Keppen, was a habit learned at home.

Keppen went on to say that so rooted was the association of vodka with entertainment and relaxation that it had become a universal medicine, the need for which a man brought into the service with him. The time to change this pattern was when he entered the army as a recruit. In new surroundings, it was necessary to impress upon him the need to change old habits, such as associating relaxation with liquor. Unfortunately, the *charka* perpetuated this link and the opportunity to break the associative chain was lost.[26]

In an 1883 issue of *Voennyi sbornik*, G. N. Butovskii claimed, unlike Keppen, that many army recruits had never drunk alcohol at home and that it was the military that taught them to drink by issuing the *charka*. He said that proof of the fact that the army was a school for drink lay in the fact that "the percentage of soldiers who drink grows in proportion to the number of years they serve."[27] Eventually, the sober soldier will succumb to peer pressure and accept the *charka*, according to Butovskii. Dr. N. I. Grigor'ev, founder of the noted monthly St. Petersburg temperance journal *Vestnik trezvosti*, reported that 11.7 percent of St. Petersburg workers began drinking vodka in the army. As late as 1910, reformers insisted that peasants who had never drunk alcohol before their service returned to their villages as drunks.[28]

Butovskii also noted that drinking soldiers complained more about army life, and it was useless to offer soldiers a few kopecks in lieu of their portion of vodka because they would be so mercilessly teased that they would eventually give in to drink. The only solution, according to Butovskii, was simply to abolish the *charka* completely. Since the military sought to give the rank and file a moral and mental education, teaching the illiterate to become literate, the unskilled skilled, and the lazy diligent, it should also teach the drunk to become sober. He also pointed out that it would be cheaper to give soldiers tea with sugar twice a day rather than the *charka*.[29] In response to those who advocated reducing the occasions for the *charka* to three, others countered that if that were the case, by giving out alcohol so infrequently, the ordinary soldier would come to believe that vodka was even more special and precious so that, by limiting the occasion for drink, the military would be sending the wrong message concerning the desirability of alcohol.

Not all articles in *Voennyi sbornik* were antialcohol. One writer staunchly defended selling beer and vodka in the army cafeterias on the grounds that the quality would be better and the price cheaper than at the local markets (mostly owned by Jews). He recommended that drunken soldiers should be expelled from the army stores and forbidden to use the facilities for an unspecified length of time.[30]

In 1896, Iu. Lossovskii discussed measures to limit drunkenness among the military. Unlike Butovskii, he did not favor abolition of the *charka* the Russian peasant was so accustomed to celebrating important moments of his life with drink that he could not do without an occasional *charka*. He therefore recommended that the term of service be shortened so as to reduce exposure to drink. Military chaplains should also speak individually to the ranks about the necessity for sobriety. Military doctors should explain to the soldiers the harm of alcohol to the body, especially the likelihood of contracting syphilis when drunk. Lossovskii advocated opening up tearooms and buffets for the military and encouraging them to save their money instead of spending it on alcohol. By comparison, he noted the practice in the Finnish army of having the most exemplary soldiers organize temperance societies. Instead of forbidding alcohol, the author recommended that promotions and leaves of absence be based on sobriety.[31]

In the late 1890s, temperance physicians argued that temperance societies within the military would reduce crime. Dr. Shidlov claimed that the military in British India had a temperance society with 25,000 members. Its efficacy was shown by the fact that ten times as many drinkers were sentenced for crimes than those belonging to the temperance societies.[32] One of the most frequent crimes committed by drunken Russian soldiers was absence without leave.[33]

In 1913, a Russian temperance writer claimed that alcohol was the primary cause of crime in general and that studies of crime in the military, not only in Russia, where 60 percent of those punished in the army were alcoholics, but also in Germany and Great Britain, would support that assertion.[34] He wanted to show that young civilians who were not disposed toward crime were driven to it in the army in their desire for drink. He argued that when the recruits arrived, they were carefully looked over by the doctors and many were rejected. Thus, only the healthiest with clean police records were accepted. Furthermore, they had no concerns about food, lodging, heat, or clothing—such worries purportedly drove people to drink. Since they were also closely watched, it was not easy for them to commit crime. Leading such a sheltered and well-provided-for life, soldiers had to be desperate for vodka to break the law. The commentator admitted that there were special factors in the army that might lead to crime, such as homesickness and the severe discipline. Still, he argued, compared to the advantages conferred by being in the army, the disadvantages were insignificant.[35]

Like Butovskii, Sobolevskii concluded that the *charka* must go. At one time, people mistakenly thought that the physical well-being of the soldier would be improved with alcohol, but once this was disproved scientifically, the retention of the *charka* became seen as a traditional holdover. Sobolevskii also noted that alcohol was not necessary to relieve boredom, even though the *Primary Chronicle,* the first written record of Russian history, stated 900 years earlier that "the joy of the Rus' is to drink," this does not mean, concluded Sobolevskii, that "we are not able to live without it."[36] The subcommission on drinking in the military decided to ask representatives of the military to send more data on the extent of alcoholism among the personnel.[37]

Another misconception, according to Sobolevskii, was that alcohol warms the body. In fact, it lowers the core temperature of the body, making alcoholics more susceptible to hypothermia.[38] For this reason, too, vodka was never given on winter marches. Nor, testified Sobolevskii, does vodka aid digestion, as some believe.

In 1900 and 1901, Dr. Minor headed the subcommission on alcohol in the armed forces of the Russian Society for the Preservation of Public Health. Under his leadership the subcommission presented a petition to the minister of war stating that alcoholism was less widespread in the services than among the population in general.[39] Nonetheless, they recommended ending the distribution of the *charka* and advocated measures to ensure that soldiers could not procure drink. Alcohol would be forbidden in the barracks altogether and in artels (living cooperatives). Tea rations would be provided instead. Priests and doctors should give lectures on the harm of vodka consumption, and textbooks should be amended to eliminate passages suggesting that moderate use of alcohol was healthy. Cheap food and drink, reading rooms, and amusements such as lectures and theatricals should be available to the soldiers. Outdoor sports should be encouraged. Above all, the subcommission stressed that it was the duty of officers to serve as examples and to teach the lower ranks the harm of alcoholic beverages.[40]

A minor reform was enacted on February 15, 1899, when an *ukaz* (edict) forbade trade in alcohol in soldiers' artels in the St. Petersburg region. The next year, the temperance leader Dr. Korovin said that the military was becoming concerned about drinking because of the number of recruits rejected on the basis of alcoholism. According to a fifteen-year survey made by Dr. A. Iu. Zuev, when tea was substituted for vodka, soldiers cheerfully went on the most difficult marches under the worst climatic conditions. Yet in the military artels near camps, more money was spent on vodka than on any other single product—as much as 20 percent of the expenditures of the artel.[41]

The response after the Russo-Japanese War to the drinking during the war was fairly insignificant; in 1906, a ban was placed on the sale of vodka in regimental shops. In some regiments, one could purchase beer, but not more than one bottle per soldier. In other regiments, officers refused sale of any alcoholic beverages to the troops. Instead of giving out the allowance of vodka on days honoring the tsar, some officers supplied the soldiers with chocolate, coffee, and other nonalcoholic drinks.[42] Regulations varied considerably at the discretion of the commanders. Not until 1908 were bans on the sale of alcohol such as the one promulgated in St. Petersburg extended to the entire army. By 1910, some soldiers were members of military brotherhoods of temperance.[43]

Not only physicians and military temperance advocates were involved with reforms in the military. During the Third Duma, in 1909–10, the Commission on the Means for the Struggle against Drunkenness, among its many proposals, recommended that the *charka* in all the military services be abolished outright, with money to be given to service people instead, a measure that was adopted in 1914.[44]

There appear to be no reliable statistics comparing levels of intoxication between troops and officers. Probably the old Russian adage "The poor drink when they can and the rich when they wish" applied to the military as well. And there are no statistics to show how many soldiers and sailors became alcoholics because of taking the *charka*.[45] Some experts claimed that alcohol caused a high rate of suicide, psychoses, and fatal intoxication among soldiers and officers alike. According to an anonymous writer, however, there were thirty times more officers than soldiers in military hospitals undergoing treatment for alcoholism.[46]

Despite all the debate concerning distribution of the *charka* to the lower ranks in the military, most allegations of drunkenness were leveled at officers, in both peacetime and wartime. With respect to the peacetime situation, John Bushnell commented, "There is literally no officer's memoir published or unpublished that does not report either individual cases of drunkenness to incapacitation (with no negative consequences for the officers' cases) or a uniform pattern of heavy drinking."[47] A senior officer reported at the beginning of the nineteenth century: "I saw company commanders who were so drunk that they could not keep their seat on horseback when fording streams; they fell in and had to be fished out by their men."[48] The poet Denis Davydov, who served in the Russian army as a hussar during the war against Napoleon, wrote: "We wanted to slake our thirst with milk in the cottage (it's clear how bad things were if we had to resort to milk—there was not a drop of liquor to be had)."[49] An American temperance advocate linked the debacle of the Crimean War with drinking, claiming that "there were times when the siege of Sebastopal [sic] came near being ruined by drunken officers."[50] The great writer Leo Tolstoi acknowledged that when he was fighting in the Crimean War as a young officer, he led a "dissipated military life."[51] Officers in favor of abstinence in the military were the rarest exceptions, claimed General Keppen.[52]

Drunkenness was prevalent among Russian officers in the Russo-Japanese War:

> An eye-witness of the Manchurian campaign (Ulrich) describes in various passages the drunkenness among Russian army officers. When we come to alcoholic psychoses . . . these amounted to 34.56 per cent of the total. Adding to this figure percentages for acute alcoholism, 5.63, we have a total of over 40 per cent. This goes far to explain the mismanagement, bad generalship, and final debacle on the steppes of Manchuria in 1904.[53]

According to a noted Soviet historian, Grand Duke Aleksei Aleksandrovich, younger brother of Alexander III and a grand admiral, was drunk at critical moments during the Russo-Japanese War and hence responsible for defeats.[54] General A. N. Kuropatkin recorded in his account of the war that it was difficult to obtain fresh officers for the front among those stationed in European Russia, the Caucasus, and Turkestan: "Some of them were quite useless owing to alcoholism, others to the irregular lives they had led, while several got drunk and became violent even on the way out."[55] Yet it was this same Kuropatkin who, when he was minister of war, had refused Sergei Witte's invitation to send troops to the Guardianship popular theaters so that the troops could act in the entertainments. Kuropatkin thought it beneath the dignity of soldiers to act, but he did allow military bands to play for Guardianship theaters.[56]

In his 1905 novel *The Duel*, Alexander Kuprin, who had served four years in the army, noted: "Heavy drinking, both at mess and in their own homes, was widespread amongst the officers."[57] The dialogue in the novel was restrained compared to what Kuprin wrote to his wife after she was insulted by a group of drunken officers in a St. Petersburg restaurant: "Sooner or later, I'll write about our 'valorous' army—our pitiful, downtrodden soldiers and our ignorant officers wallowing in drunkenness."[58] The impulse for the novel came from Kuprin's army experiences during the mid-1890s. When the hero joins in a drunken orgy, he is challenged to a duel, in which he loses his life; the themes of tedium, drunkenness, and savagery during peacetime propel the plot.[59] The fact that Kuprin's novel was published in the midst of Russian defeats in the Far East made it appear all the more prescient because of the association of drunken officers and lost battles. Its publication "produced a furor among both the critics and the reading public, and the ensuing controversy continued until 1917. Most commentators saw the novel as an attack not only on the army but on the autocracy itself."[60] Kuprin, like many other members of the educated public, as well as many temperance workers, traced alcoholism to the autocratic regime.

Military disorder during mobilization for the war against Japan was inconsequential compared to the many mutinies during 1905 and 1906, the years of war and revolution.[61] Drinking became a political statement during this period. While monarchist officers demanded alcohol, "revolutionary" officers made a point of shunning vodka.[62] And yet an article promoting the reactionary party, the Union of the Russian People, called the disturbances of 1905–7 "the drunken revolution."[63] Another conservative writer asserted that "a drunkard is one of the best followers and propagandists of revolution." Agreeing with Tolstoi's views, he said that since drink results in the loss of a sense of morality, and no salary is sufficient for the drunkard's thirst, he is easily enlisted into the revolutionary cause.[64]

Proof of this connection between drunkenness and revolution was offered in the same journal by an author who claimed that the first target for all mutinous crowds was the state liquor stores, which were broken into and the contents seized whether they were in Odessa or in Kronstadt or even in the countryside. According to the newspaper *Novoe vremia*, Jews contributed to the spread of revolutionary ideas in the army because most of the troops were located in the Pale of Settlement and quartered in Jewish villages where Jewish taverns and stores sold soldiers liquor either legally or through bootlegging. So Jews "systematically got young soldiers drunk" in order to spread revolutionary propaganda. Since by all observations, Jews were rarely alcoholics, this was one way for anti-Semites to tie Jews into an explanation of revolution as a product of alcoholism.[65] According to the newspaper *Birzhevyia vedomosti*, revolutionary parties might seek support from the alcoholic, but "monarchists have absolutely no use for him even as a political ally. Monarchists by nature are people of order, legality, and creative work."[66]

As for the uprisings and pogroms that resulted in the revolution of 1905, one historian claimed that tsarist officials were reluctant to call on the troops to subdue the rioters because they feared their possible involvement in drunken anarchy since "troops frequently fraternized with the rioters and participated in their looting and drunken excesses." In fact, he asserted, the Kronstadt rebellion of 1905 was a result of drunken anarchy when the sailors were denied permission to purchase alcohol.[67]

In an article in *Russkii invalid* of January 5, 1910, A. Bil'derling suggested that prohibition was the only way to cure the country of alcoholism and that the only question to be solved was how to find a substitute means of filling the treasury. He cited the case of Sweden as proof that prohibition could work: for months, Sweden had been totally dry because of widespread strikes, and the resulting sobriety was remarkable. He observed that if for some reason it was impossible to implement prohibition in the entire country, at least the Russian army of more than a million men should be dry, to serve as a seedbed of sobriety for the entire nation.[68] In fact, the army could serve as one vast temperance society so that peasants entering the service would not return to their villages as confirmed drinkers. On the contrary, arriving in the service as drinkers, they would go home confirmed teetotalers after their military service. So far only half measures had been taken with the ban on sales of vodka in military stores and tearooms, but drink establishments were allowed in the vicinity, as were state liquor stores. Bil'derling proposed that state stores be closed, and the *charka* cease being given out on the tsar's feast days and other occasions because once the soldiers tasted the vodka, they would want more and buy it at their own expense. All temptations should be removed from soldiers. He cited the wealth and health of the Molokane (a sect founded in the late seventeenth century who drank milk during fasts and did not observe Russian Orthodox rites) in the Caucasus and the German colonists in south Russia, who did not drink vodka. Russians would follow their example once they learned sobriety in the army.

The navy also addressed the issue of the *charka*. In 1897, Dr. A. Iu. Zuev spoke before a society of navy doctors and recommended the abolition of the *charka*. He believed in a gradual reduction by decreasing the number of holidays celebrated and the size of the vodka rations; he went so far as to advise that sailors should be given vodka only at sea. This was a concession to tradition, he admitted, for in the American navy no liquor was given out at all.[69] In 1908, the *charka* was still a subject of controversy. Those who opposed giving out vodka argued that in times past sailors' lives were much harsher than those of modern sailors, who only needed alcohol during illnesses or under particularly stressful conditions.[70]

Eventually steps were taken to reduce drinking in the navy:

It was in this historic year [1913] that the vodka ration in the Imperial Navy was abolished, and soon after, the sale of vodka was prohibited in the restaurants attached to all government works and institutions. The sale of vodka is also forbidden in all places of amusement, including theaters, and the legal strength of all vodka sold was reduced to 37 per cent alcohol.[71]

In 1914, the minister of the navy allowed the *charka* be given to seamen only if they were aboard ships and under certain conditions, that is, when the voyage was long or during stormy weather or as medicine. Instead of giving out daily rations, a sum of money would be set aside for the sailor so that, for example, after five years of service, he would receive from 140 to 150 rubles, a nice nest egg. Formerly, a sailor was given his *charka* in two rations: two-thirds before lunch and one-third before supper.

The 1908 ban on the sale of alcohol to military personnel was followed by much propaganda against alcohol in the leading military journal. Beginning in January 1910, *Russkii invalid* ran a five-part series entitled "The Struggle against Drunkenness," by L. V. Evdokimov, in conjunction with a special exhibit on alcoholism that opened on January 17, 1910, in the Nicholas II People's House.[72] Specially targeted to a military audience, it recommended total abstinence from alcoholic beverages, claiming that even moderate drinking led to excessive consumption.[73]

Evdokimov presented a series of statistics to demonstrate that a greater proportion of officers than of troops got drunk and died from drinking. He cited British Field Marshall Roberts, who claimed that thirteen thousand sober men were equivalent to fifteen thousand soldiers who drank (which in fact represented a modest 17 percent increase of efficiency). The Russian military temperance advocate summarized steps taken by other armies: in 1910, the British army had more than 500 temperance societies, whereas the French, German, and Italian military authorities educated their troops by way of signs and slogans against drinking. Not since 1838 was alcohol sold in barracks or on ships in America. The publication of this long series of articles in the military journal suggests that the reforms of 1908 were not entirely successful.

In 1912, however, the military authorities, much to the disgust of a temperance worker, issued an order that allowed the sale of alcohol in military barracks, with the stipulation that drunken soldiers were not to be seen on the street. One critic construed this injunction to be an admission that authorities were reconciled to the idea that soldiers would get drunk but wanted to avoid the embarrassment of the soldiers' appearing drunk in public.[74] He continued by saying that unlike some critics, he did not believe the military authorities had entered into an agreement with the people in charge of liquor sales, but rather, this was a kind of compromise by which soldiers could drink in the camps and, therefore, not have to go to cities for that purpose. The consequences, he predicted, would be that the public would no longer hear noisy drunken soldiers in cities, but that the soldiers would quietly and quickly become alcoholics in the barracks. Not much earlier, it appeared the military was on the verge of abolishing the *charka*, but now for reasons unknown they were facilitating the procurement of liquor on military bases.[75]

Prohibition came to Russia in incremental steps, beginning with a ban on all alcohol sales during mobilization in August 1914: "Simultaneously with the orders for the general mobilization of the Russian troops went the order to close, immediately, all vodka, wine and beer shops in the Empire, an exception being made in the case of first-class restaurants."[76] The ban was then extended to cover the war period, and in October 1914, Nicholas II finally declared that he would abolish vodka sales "forever" in Russia.[77] An American temperance advocate observed: "Absolute prohibition of the trade in intoxicants of every sort prevailed throughout the districts in which the Russian armies operated. The success of the prohibition during mobilization was such a vast improvement over any other mobilization ever attempted in Russian history that the lesson was too apparent to be ignored."[78]

Prohibition would come at a price, however. Dmitry Shlapentokh has asserted that it was precisely the abolition of the *charka* in the navy that provoked drunken violence after the February Revolution. Sailors from a Baltic naval base seized public buildings, drank wood alcohol, moonshine, formalin spirits, and whatever they could lay hands on, and began taking potshots and organizing looting expeditions as far as Petrograd. Once again, as in 1905, sailors at Kronstadt became drunk and unruly.[79]

A directive issued by Minister of War General V. A. Sukhomlinov in 1914 outlined the ways in which the military was combating drunkenness among both the officers and the enlisted ranks.[80] Buffets in officers' clubs could not sell liquor on credit nor could officers take liquor to their residences. The buffets could sell it only at mealtimes—including breakfast! This measure shows that officers' clubs were considered to be the equivalent of first-class restaurants—that is, an exception to the general rule of prohibition. In compensation, propaganda was stepped up. Sukhomlinov urged officers to join "societies of abstainers" under the guidance of clergy, where they would have reading rooms, lectures, sports activities, and foreign-language and music instruction. Much like the Guardianship solution to cure alcoholism, abstainers were also encouraged to attend the theater when possible.

Recruits, the directive continued, were to be denied alcohol altogether. It was no longer allowed in the clubs for enlisted men (so well described by Kuprin in *The Duel*). Soldiers should be urged to join the regimental temperance societies. Clergy should speak to them once a week on the moral evils of drink, and physicians once a month on the physical evils. Sunday readings, literacy schools, and even trade schools should be organized. The walls of the barracks should be covered with pictures and posters on the evils of alcohol and the library stocked with antidrink pamphlets. Gymnastics and sports should be cultivated, and dances held. And barracks life should be improved, with better and more varied food served and room temperatures kept at comfortable levels. Sober, happy soldiers supposedly meant more effective soldiers for Russia.

On August 27, 1914, the armed forces issued amplification of Sukhomlinov's directive, stating that all lower ranks would be given money in lieu of vodka rations; when given the choice previously, only 6–7 percent of the soldiers took their *charka* in cash. After October 1, the statement continued, beer sales would be permitted to troops with the permission of the military command.[81] The *Petersburg Gazette* remarked that the complete abolition of drink in the army would serve as a good learning experience for the masses of peasants who serve as soldiers. It would also benefit officers on maneuvers, on the march, and in the presence of the lower ranks. The paper expressed grave doubts about the success of the project, however, noting that historians claim that Charlemagne was the first to forbid drinking in the army—with little success—and that drinking continued in the British, German, and Austrian armies despite regulations forbidding it.[82]

According to the *London Daily News* in September 1914, civilians, re-servists, soldiers, Cossacks, sailors, and even hooligans were all "sober as judges," partially because a fine of 3,000 rubles was imposed on those who sold alcohol. General Sukhomlinov declared that alcoholic drinks should be banned in the country as long as the war lasted.[83] He extended the no-drinking policy for the Russian army whenever it went beyond Russian territory.

An English tourist noted:

Quietly, correctly, without fuss, the soldiers reported themselves at their various stations. Officers, lamentably aware of the weakness of the moudjiks [peasants], have told me of their amazement at the way the men appeared and behaved. The tempestuous drunken dis-orders when the Army was sent to the Russo-Japanese War were re-called, and officers, not at all given to prayer, were devoutly grateful at the change.[84]

The army orders of Grand Duke Nicholas also dictated that liquor shops be closed as soon as the Russian troops occupied a town, and that no liquor should be supplied to the soldiers under any circumstances.[85] Three months later, a military journal reported that women were petitioning authorities to send vodka to their husbands, who were suffering from cold in the trenches.[86] In March 1916, Nicholas II allowed weak grape wine to be sold at the front.[87]

Contemporaries saw the consequences of the ban on vodka as momen-tous. The *London Times* wrote on September 21, 1914: "The great victory over drunkenness in Russia has received far too little attention in this coun-try. Since China proscribed opium, the world has seen nothing like it. We have been well reminded that in sternly prohibiting the sale of spirituous liquor Russia has already vanquished a greater foe than the Germans."[88] A military journal crowed that the Social Democrats in Germany were citing Russia as a model for their own country and worried that Russia's less abstemious allies, the British and the French, might take it into their heads to supply Russian troops with sherry, brandy, and wine. Stanley Washburn, correspondent with the Russian army, noted in the *London Times* on March 5, 1915:

> One cannot write of the Russian mobilization or of the rejuvenation of the Russian Empire without touching on the prohibition of vodka; the first manifest evidence of the increased efficiency was, of course, in the manner and promptness with which the army assembled; but, from that day, the benefits have been increasingly visible, not only in the army, but in every phase of Russian life. . . . In nearly six months' association with the armies in many different theaters of operations I have not seen a single drunken or tipsy officer or soldier. This, then, was the first sign of what New Russia intended to do in this war. At one stroke she freed herself of the curse that has paralyzed her peasant life for generations. This in itself is nothing short of a revolution.[89]

Russia's humiliation at the hands of Japan was not to be forgotten, and by World War I, the sober state of the troops was often contrasted with the drunken mobilization of 1904.[90] But perhaps the contrast was not as great as it appeared. A British military attaché in Russia in 1914 reported that a group of Russian soldiers told to destroy a supply of vodka on an estate could not bring themselves to do it until they had drunk themselves into a stupor.[91] Dmitry Shlapentokh recounts that the troops, resenting prohibition, looted liquor supplies before leaving for the front and that many of them deserted.[92] Boris Segal likewise attributed desertion and growing anarchy after February 1917 to the scarcity of vodka.[93] Shlapentokh also noted that "by the first days of the February Revolution bands of excited 'drunk soldiers and hooligans' roamed the streets shooting in doors and windows." He continued, "By March–April of 1917, Petrograd was in a condition of unrestricted drunken frenzy, with contemporary cartoons depicting the Russian mob as drunken whores."[94]

After the fall of the tsar in February 1917, and especially after Order Number 1 was issued by the socialists the next month, which undermined discipline in the army, officers as well as troops began to drink and participate in drunken orgies. According to letters from Russian soldiers sent home from the front, when the enemies were not fighting, as on holy days, Russian soldiers gave German troops bread, sugar, or other foodstuffs in exchange for vodka and other alcoholic drinks.[95]

During the storming of the Winter Palace in October 1917, the wine cellar was looted; private wine collections were also at risk.[96] The desire for an efficient mobilization and a sober fighting force in 1914 (as opposed to 1904–

1905) was the prime reason for the tsar's launching of the first of a series of orders that would culminate in prohibition, to be continued even after the war. But it was difficult to go against centuries of habit; when alcohol could be procured, it was, and when it was unavailable, surrogates were consumed. The Russian military drank during the Russo-Japanese War, and they drank during World War I. The major difference was that the state received revenue to finance the first war from legalized drinking but received no revenue from the illegal drinking in the second war. Neither war, of course, was lost solely because of excessive drinking.

Breaking the law of the land repeatedly within a three-year period did result in a disregard for the rule of law, never perhaps very firm in Russia. Nonetheless, this scoffing at the law probably made the insurrections of February and October 1917 less difficult for members of the military as well as for civilians. As noted, when discipline eroded in the military because of the issuance of Order Number 1, a measure intended to introduce democracy into the military at the height of World War I, officers saw little reason not to drink with their troops—democracy could work both ways. Shlapentokh has asserted that a political culture of drunken anarchy was the natural state for the Russian populace, including the military, unless they were forcibly restrained; when those restraints broke down, the February and October Revolutions occurred.[97] This indictment is at once too simple and too complex. One can conclude, however, that a constant pattern of breaking the alcoholic ban made it easier for people to disregard the laws of the land, whether those of the tsar, of the Provisional Government, or even of the Bolsheviks.

Reformers, acutely conscious of the disparity in drinking habits between the Russian military and the Western world, spent decades attempting to arrive at a solution to the problem of drunkenness within the forces. Recognizing that recruits brought their culture into the army, they dared not alter customs drastically. And in the end, they were probably correct. Depriving the military of alcohol in 1914 had a demoralizing effect on those who had many other reasons to become disillusioned as the conflict dragged on.

ПРОСВЕЩЕНИЕ

ИЗБА-ЧИТА...

ШКОЛА КЛУБ

САМОГОНЩИКОВ ИЗ ДЕРЕВНИ ВОН!

ВОН ИЗ ХУТОРА! ВОН ИЗ СЕЛА!
КОМСОМОЛЕЦ! КРЕСТЬЯНИН! КРЕСТЬЯНКА! ЭЙ!
ЖИТЬ ЧТОБ ЖИЗНЬЮ СЫТОЙ И ВОЛЬНОЙ,
БЕЙ ЗЕЛЕНОГО ЗМИЯ КНИГОЙ! УЧЕНИЕМ БЕЙ!
ХВОСТ ЗАЖМИ ЕМУ ДВЕРЬЮ ШКОЛЬНОЙ!

ИЗГОНЯЙ, КТО ПОИТ, ВЫГОНЯЙ, КТО ПЬЕТ!

В. Маяковский.

Preceding page.
A Russian slaying
the Green Serpent
(alcohol). Courtesy of the
Hoover Institution
Library and Archives.

This page.
Night shelter for workers,
organized by Guardians
of Public Sobriety,
St. Petersburg. Courtesy of
Central State Archives
of Photo Documents,
St. Petersburg.

Dr. V. M. Bekhterev treating alcoholics by hypnosis. Courtesy of
Central State Archives of Photo Documents, St. Petersburg.

Drunken revelers on a church holiday. Courtesy of the Hoover
Institution Library and Archives.

Village Easter Procession, V. G. Perov

Temperance activist,
Ivan Churikov.
Courtesy of Central
State Archives of
Photo Documents,
St. Petersburg.

Initiates of the Alexander Nevskii Temperance Society taking oaths of sobriety. Courtesy of Central State Archives of Photo Documents, St. Petersburg.

The Monastery Refectory, V. G. Perov

"I Will Not Allow You to Enter," V. V. Mayakovskii

Effects of Vodka. Courtesy of Andover Theological Library,
Harvard University.

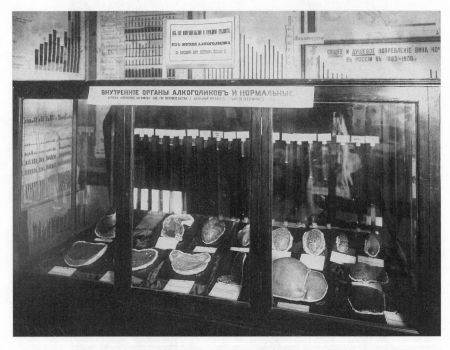

Exhibit of normal and diseased organs in the People's House of
Emperor Nicholas II, St. Petersburg. Courtesy of Central State
Archives of Photo Documents, St. Petersburg.

5 . . . .

THE CHURCH'S NEW SOCIAL MISSION

For centuries, individual members of the Russian Orthodox Church had viewed drunkenness as a vice and a sin.[1] That is not to say, however, that preachers against drunkenness favored total abstinence. A fourteenth-century Russian cleric declared: "the holy fathers did not forbid us to drink and to eat within the law and at a fitting time, but they rejected overeating and drunkenness."[2] Saints' lives and miracle tales frequently reflect tolerance for moderate use of alcohol and tolerance of those who abused it. The Mother of God is supposed to have admonished: "Know, child, that it is not evil to drink wine, but it is evil to drink too much to [the point] of drunkenness, outside of the proper time."[3] While pious literature condemned drunkenness, it also showed compassion for those who drank to excess, especially laypersons.[4]

This empathetic approach is typical of the nineteenth and twentieth centuries as well. Although from time to time, terms such as "evil" and "sin" were used with regard to drunkenness, most clerical temperance workers in the late nineteenth and early twentieth centuries, like their earlier counterparts, regarded alcoholism as a disease. In 1909, Metropolitan Vladimir made an important distinction between dissoluteness and drunkenness, claiming that the former was a result of a natural instinct, whereas the latter was a result of custom and habit, which could be changed.[5] Clerics seldom made "fire and brimstone" speeches, nor somewhat surprisingly, did they characterize drunkards as morally depraved persons. Rather, they were depicted as individuals who, with kindness rather than wrath, could be saved from the grip of alcoholism.

Father P. Mirtov, one of the most dedicated of the church's temperance leaders, remarked: "Look at the loving care with which the Russian people regard the 'little drunken ones.' Does not the Russian popular proverb, 'Whoever is drunk and clever has a double advantage' directly reflect the kindly attitude of the Russian toward alcoholism?"[6] One of the most active priests in the temperance movement in the nineteenth century was Father D. G. Bulgakovskii, whose sympathy is evident: "Never despair of reforming an alcoholic and do not pronounce accusatory verdicts in a definitive fashion upon him. It is better to warm him with your love, forget everything even to the point of forgiving his scandalous behavior as the consequences of a weakening mind and failure of the will."[7]

The church's tolerance was perhaps due to the degree that alcoholism had been a problem among the clergy.[8] One of the difficulties in enlisting priests in the battle against alcoholism was that many of the older clergy had themselves long been given over to drink.[9] The church was more censorious of drunkenness in monasteries than in village parishes, for monks and nuns "had supposedly adopted the 'angelic form' of living." To aid monks in achieving their lofty aspirations, many abbots forbade alcohol completely within the confines of the monasteries.[10] It was much more difficult, however, to monitor married parish priests living among the peasantry in the countryside. For many of them, excessive drink appears to have been an occupational hazard.

The connection between poverty and drink is the theme taken up in about 1858 by a parish priest, I. S. Belliustin, who in a remarkable position paper spelled out the havoc that poverty wreaked among the rural clergy. It forced seminarians to live in cheap boardinghouses, where they were exposed to and often came to participate in excessive drinking. Even worse, in attending class, the seminarian was likely to find that his underpaid instructor was drunk and incompetent.[11]

The rural parish to which the new priest might be assigned had no legal existence, could not own property, and hence had no "benefice," or living, attached to it. The parish priest usually had to work the land with his own hands, and this hard labor sometimes deprived him of the energy he needed to perform his priestly tasks. This lifestyle also often undermined his moral and social standing within the community. Inevitably, it also drew him into the habits of rural drinking.[12] Among the most pernicious of these customs was a practice called *pomoch'*. *Pomoch'*, or help with particularly urgent or heavy labors, might be requested at any time of the year—for plowing in spring, harvesting in late summer, mowing hay in autumn, or digging potatoes, milling grain, and cutting and carting wood in winter, or rebuilding a burned cabin at any time—but it most frequently was sought during the harvest and was all the more demanding because the season was short. Belliustin described the results: "The essence of *pomoch'* is to gather the largest possible number of parishioners for one or another kind of task. . . . When [the peasant] does come, he does so not to work, but primarily to drink: *pomoch'* is inconceivable without vodka. The work begins with vodka, it continues with vodka, it ends with vodka."[13]

Surrounded by drinking, lacking respect and status, the demoralized priest sought forgetfulness in drink. Drink was all too available, as every transaction and every activity in rural settings were awash in vodka, particularly at the events where priests' participation was required: christenings, marriages, and funerals. "He [the rural priest]," Belliustin concludes, "has to perform the priest's duties . . . But before everything comes the bottle." His grim account continues: "For him the epitome of pleasure is to fraternize with the peasants in noisy, wild drinking bouts; with joy he sets off to the tavern, drinking house, whatever—just so he is invited; if they do not invite him, he will unabashedly go and get senselessly drunk with a friend from his parish."[14]

In 1898, Bulgakovskii presented a paper before the Russian Society for the Preservation of Public Health in St. Petersburg. In it, he reviewed both the historical and the contemporary causes of clerical intemperance. The clergy of ancient Rus', he claimed, were sober, holy, and much revered by the people. But from the time of the Mongol domination onward, the village priests "lost their independence, even their self-respect." The priest, Bulgakovskii explained, "was not only subject to his superiors but also to the manorial lord, the village leaders, and the prosperous members of his community, to whom he had to submit, as his material situation was entirely dependent upon their goodwill."[15] Bulgakovskii laid primary stress on the need to provide benefices or support to the village priests. He was thus seeking to address Belliustin's concerns of half a century earlier. Economic self-sufficiency would free them from exhausting labor in the fields, render them independent of their rich and powerful parishioners, increase their moral stature, and allow them to chastise their parishioners when they saw fit. He advocated the total exclusion of alcohol from all church functions (baptisms, weddings, funerals, and the like) and the elimination of its use as the ubiquitous lubricant of nearly every social interaction in the countryside.

Allusions to drunken village priests fill the sources of nineteenth- and early twentieth-century social history. The writer Ivan Turgenev reflected popular opinion when one of his characters, a landowner, exclaimed to a young priest, who refused vodka, "What rubbish! You say you're a priest and you don't drink!" He pressed on him the glass, badgering the prelate until he felt obliged to drink the alcohol down.[16] Priests themselves admitted to sometimes being drunk continuously for as long as one or two months.[17] Typical of satirical representations of tipsy priests is Vasilii Perov's painting *Easter Procession in the Countryside* (1861).[18] It depicts priests and villagers, all inebriated, setting forth to celebrate Easter. Not until late in the century did the church attempt to impose sobriety upon its priests. And, not surprisingly, these efforts sometimes encountered resistance. In 1894, an advisory body to the church in the Kaluga diocese directed that temperance brotherhoods of the clergy be founded throughout the diocese. But the priests who composed the general assembly of the Kaluga clergy objected, claiming that a temperance brotherhood of clerics would damage their reputation.[19]

Other priests, such as Father Bulgakovskii, Father P. I. Poliakov, Archpriest P. Mirtov, and Bishop Mitrofan, vigorously sought to raise the material, educational, and moral level of the priesthood (including sobriety), especially in the countryside.[20] A lay teacher, S. A. Rachinskii, might have been the most influential person in spurring the clergy to give up their drinking habits and to preach temperance. His 1898 publication *Letters to Young Clergy on the Subject of Temperance* was widely read and cited by clergy devoted to promoting temperance.[21]

By the turn of the century, clerical temperance activist Mirtov, called "the apostle of antialcoholism in the Russian church," was the pastor of a large church in St. Petersburg serving the Orthodox Society for Religious-Moral Enlightenment. An American temperance worker described him in 1915 as "a man of sympathetic personality, of tall figure, vigorous fresh manner, flowing brown beard and leonine mane."[22] At the First All-Russian Congress on the Struggle against Drunkenness (1909–10), he presented a full program for the reform of seminary education to ensure sobriety among future priests and also convert them into effective temperance crusaders.[23] Specifically, he called for the introduction into the seminary curriculum courses that explained the chemical nature of alcohol as well as the physiological and social ills flowing from its abuse. The courses would also advise on the most recent, scientifically founded methods of treatment. Seminarians and priests themselves would be called upon to take a pledge to maintain sobriety.

These many proposals scarcely conceal an intense discontent on the part of articulate churchmen with the circumstances of rural priests, their training, and their traditional relationship with society and government. Implicitly, they were arguing that the parish priest should be freed from the need to labor like a peasant and from economic domination by the local kulaks and gentry. In effect, these reformers were reassessing the traditional mission of the Russian Orthodox Church. Since medieval times, the principal functions of the church were viewed as liturgical and didactic: the performance of the sacred liturgy and the teaching of the sacred truths. But the new plan of education and the new role envisioned for the rural clergy assigned to them a pastoral mission. Pastors, confirmed in sobriety and armed with the latest medical knowledge of alcoholism and its treatment, would lead their flocks to a life of temperance. To teach seminarians the chemistry of alcohol and the most recent medical therapies was to stress their pastoral responsibilities, their need to care for the social and moral welfare of their parishioners. The crucial issue of alcoholism lent a sense of urgency to the proposed reforms and inspired a new definition of the church's place and program in society.

In villages and provincial towns there was no single organization that established temperance societies. They were usually initiated by a priest or at the request of parish members. It does not appear as though urban reformers "went to the people" to exhort them to sobriety. At times local governments or even the official branch of the Guardianship of Public Sobriety, if there was one functioning in the vicinity, helped to finance activities of existing societies. Urban professionals, members of the intelligentsia, and the state were motivated to work diligently to eradicate alcoholism in the countryside by fears of disorder, wishes for greater productivity, and a desire to make peasants conform more closely to their own norms.[24] Those concerns were certainly expressed and legislative attempts to curb drinking made, but it is difficult to trace specific rural temperance societies to secular organizations. Since there is no systematic survey of rural temperance societies, it is difficult to gauge their numbers or assess how widespread they might have been. But some telling examples do exist.

In Tsaritsyn, a town with a population of 200,000, a priest named Alexander Petrovich Strokov founded a temperance society dedicated to St. Nikolai in November 1909. By 1914, the society's membership was 5,105, and it had won silver and bronze medals at the International Congress against the Abuse of Alcoholic Beverages for its antialcohol exhibit. Members of the society built their own House of Sobriety by donating money and labor and taking out loans. They opened up a bakery, a press, a dining hall, a cinema, a credit cooperative, a choir, a kindergarten, a job placement bureau, which also gave out free legal advice, and a free outpatient clinic for alcoholics. To promote family outings, each summer the society organized steamship excursions on the Volga. As many as 800 people would sing as a choir during the day, have picnics, and enjoy nighttime fireworks displays. On Easter and Christmas Eves, the society organized special free parties for members and their families, which as many as 3,000 children attended.[25] It was, in short, a miniature social-service agency, run under the auspices of the local church.[26]

In 1903, a parish temperance society was formed in the village of Il'inskii in Iaroslav Province. At its opening, Father Alexander Khrustalev gave a moving sermon, placed the society under the protection of the Theoforovskii ikon of the Mother of God, and urged the members to take an oath of abstinence for at least six months.[27]

Father M. G. Sretenskii founded a temperance society in the village of Spas-Zaulkovskii in 1910, with only eight members.[28] Both laymen and clerics were officers and members. The chair of the society was a peasant, Ivan Stepanovich Fuleev. Honorary members included the metropolitan, the governor-general of Moscow, and merchants. In memory of the fiftieth anniversary of the liberation of the serfs, the society's library was named for Tsar Alexander II, and the annual general meeting was timed for February 19 to commemorate the emancipation. Unlike many religious temperance societies, this one did not attempt to abolish the use of drink altogether. For that reason, the Guardianship donated 100 rubles to the society. To justify moderate use of alcohol, the report of the meeting cited the biblical observation "Wine is useful for human life," and no oaths were taken to abstain from liquor, but instead simple honest brotherly declarations were given to live a sober life. Those who were alcoholics, however, did promise not to touch alcohol for at least a year. After one year, membership grew to seventy-nine persons, who paid 2 rubles each for dues.

From the 1880s on, it had been the village priests who, with the help of peasants, founded temperance groups in the village.[29] In 1901, one village priest described his experience in forming a parish temperance society. At first, membership consisted of only a handful of peasants, but soon nearly seventy peasants had joined, the membership growing "almost without any effort on my part."[30] He noted that sometimes peasants would come to him, often the worse for drink, with tears in their eyes and beg to be enrolled in the society. The priest told them to return when they were sober enough to make the decision to take the pledge.[31] Dues were voluntary, since many could not afford fees of any sort. He also noted that "from the local intelligentsia a few felt sympathy for my activity, but the majority were scornful."[32]

At times, individual priests acquired a particular reputation for being able to cure alcoholics. One such clergyman was Father S. Permskii, who founded the St. Sergius Temperance Society at Nachabino-Bankov, a village near Moscow, which attracted as many as 6,000 persons a month.[33] Another notable society was located at St. Sergius Trinity Monastery near Moscow, where Father Paul founded a free school for the children of alcoholics.[34] At first the school, along with a library and dining room, was supported by private contributions, but then the Ministry of Finance gave the school 2,500 rubles for the construction of a separate building, and a yearly subsidy thereafter. Local peasants donated the land for the school, and the Holy Synod equipped the school at the cost of 3,500 rubles.[35] The pupils, both boys and girls, took classes in the usual variety of subjects: language, arithmetic, singing, religion, handicrafts, and, of course, lessons on the harm done by liquor. In handwriting lessons, they invented sayings against "the green dragon [alcoholism]," and they also wrote essays on the theme of sobriety. An American, Miss E. Ia. Smith, taught needlework to the girls three times a week. Father Paul justified devoting special attention to children by saying, "What is sown in the child and in youth gives good results in the soul of the adult."[36]

Father Paul extended his ministry to adults as well. Near the school, more than 300 recovering adult alcoholics labored in a workhouse in exchange for food and clothing. Father Paul estimated that about 10 percent of them became good workers and remained sober. Further, the peasants successfully petitioned the government to close the local liquor store in the village near the monastery. Enrollment in the society in 1908 included 1,070 adult members, 80 students, and 151 donors.

Before the founding of Father Paul's society at the most famous monastery in Russia, Dr. A. M. Korovin, speaking at the Seventh International Congress against the Abuse of Alcoholic Beverages in 1899, called the efforts of parish priests to form such societies, to date, "mediocre."[37] Reportedly, only 3,000 of the 45,000 parishes in the Russian Empire in 1914 had temperance societies.[38] But while provincial and rural societies were relatively sparse and distributed randomly over the countryside, urban temperance societies grew rapidly, especially in the capital, St. Petersburg.

The best-known example of the new pastoral activism was the Alexander Nevskii Temperance Society, founded in 1898 by a young priest, Father Alexander Vasilievich Rozhdestvenskii. A professor at the St. Petersburg Ecclesiastical Academy, Rozhdestvenskii had been placed in charge of the Orthodox Society for Religious-Moral Enlightenment, which spearheaded the new social mission of the church.[39] He viewed drunkenness as a vice that separated the individual from God and opened the door for other sins and believed it was imperative that the Orthodox clergy address it.[40] He became well known among factory workers, to whom he spoke about sobriety "not with stern but with tender and kind words."[41] His success was phenomenal. Within a year and a half, the Alexander Nevskii Temperance Society claimed nearly 10,000 members, a number that had jumped to 70,644 by 1906.[42]

The society eventually established nine branches in factories in St. Petersburg and operated four schools, two technical schools (*masterskaia*), and one printing press.[43] In 1911, the lay Russian Society for the Preservation of Public Health awarded a gold medal to the Alexander Nevskii Temperance Society, praising it for its "fruitful activity and for its publications," which soon numbered from 300,000 to 700,000 copies of pamphlets and books a year.[44] Among its activities were organized boat trips to the monastery in Valaam, which were part excursions, part retreats, and part pilgrimages.[45] When Rozhdestvenskii died prematurely at the age of thirty-three in July 1905, hundreds of workers and their families attended his funeral.[46]

In their mission, Rozhdestvenskii and his fellow workers in the factories of St. Petersburg labored to create the kingdom of God on earth, where there would be justice and no poverty. It is not surprising, therefore, that one of the society's more famous members was Father Georgii Gapon, whose Assembly of Russian Factory and Mill Workers took part in the industrial strike of January 1905 and the march to the Winter Palace, events that precipitated Bloody Sunday and led to the outbreak of the 1905 revolution.[47]

The heart of the strategy espoused by the Alexander Nevskii Temperance Society was to secure a moral commitment from the drinker and to offer him or her constant support in maintaining it. Crucial to this strategy was the practice of taking the pledge. The drinker was urged to take a public pledge, usually in church and before sacred ikons, to abstain from drink for some prescribed period of time.[48] The society advocated total abstinence and not mere moderation, but they compromised this rigor by inviting the drinker to enter the sober life in temporary stages. The advantage of this policy was that the periods of abstinence and drinking could be tailored to fit the calendar of traditional beverage consumption in Russian life. Pledges of sobriety would be taken up to the next great holy day, which was usually also the next great occasion for binge drinking.[49] If the pledges seem less than sincere, at least they probably did reinforce cultural restrictions on drink and limited its social damage. It was an attempt to limit drinking to traditional village practices instead of the more frequent and regular rhythm of urban drinking occasions.

In the typical church society, support for the newly sober was provided by its regular meetings and activities. The logic behind forming permanent associations of reformed drinkers was to create a support system. Those who wavered in the sober life were urged never to depend on their own resources but to seek out help from fellow members at once. A temperance pamphlet published by the Valaam monastery in 1904 instructed:

> Feeling your weakness, don't despair. Turn to relatives, friends, ac-
> quaintances; ask them for counsel and help. If they can't help, be a
> man, resist evil temptations, turn to the pastors of the church and
> in general to spiritual people, known or unknown. Believe that you
> will find good people who, from their Christian duty, out of love
> for their neighbors, will help you, set you on the road to salvation,
> and support your uncertain steps.[50]

The Alexander Nevskii Temperance Society included a special team of fifty chosen lay assistants (*vybornye*), who regularly visited the membership on Sundays and holy days, brought the waverers to meetings and to church, and confirmed them in their sobriety. Each assistant was given a specific territory in St. Petersburg to cover. They attended special training sessions and were instructed to act toward their weaker brothers not as spies or policemen but as brothers and sisters of mercy.[51] Members of the clergy also visited members of the society. One city priest made it a point to announce by mail that he was coming to visit a member of the temperance society and his family without charge in order to pray with him in order to give him strength to keep his pledge. Many societies recommended saying the Jesus prayer in order to obtain that strength.[52]

The Alexander Nevskii Temperance Society model was adapted by the Pokrovsko-Kolomenskii Church in St. Petersburg. Taking the pledge against drinking was far from casual. An elaborate certificate was signed by the person seeking sobriety. He also filled out a questionnaire that asked his occupation, marital status, the duration of the pledge, how many times he had taken pledges previously and if they had been fulfilled, and, finally, the amount of his donation. This was followed by a brief catechism session entitled "Verdict of Reason against Drunkenness," in which a series of questions were asked, such as "Who is poor?" and "Whose wife and children are unfortunate?" with the refrain to each being "a drunkard."[53] Twenty of the lay assistants, one from each part of the parish, were present as witnesses and to offer support to those taking the pledge. After taking the pledge, each person would contribute from 5 to 30 kopecks for the certificate of sobriety, the reading material, and the magic lantern shows and other entertainments put on each Sunday and sometimes on Thursdays in the parish.

After two and a half years, Father V. A. Akimov summarized the results of his urban parish society at the Pokrovsko-Kolomenskii Church by noting that nearly 93 percent of the 1,949 members were peasants, most of whom were in the construction business, followed by those who did artisan work, day labor, and street peddling.[54] Since much of the construction work was seasonal, a large number of those pledging were only temporary members of the parish who came to the city and took pledges between April and the beginning of June, depending on the timing of Easter. Another big surge of vows was right after Christmas when workers vowed to remain sober until Easter; more vows were taken up until Christmas or Trinity Sunday. Not only did this system allow workers to celebrate the holidays in the usual manner with drink, but it also acted to restrain them from spending their pay in the interim and to encourage them to remit some of it back to their families. Some explicitly took pledges "until my return to the village."

The workers who took the pledges were generally young: over 76 percent of them were between the ages of twenty and forty. Nearly 79 percent of those taking the oath were married, and 50 percent of them had children. According to the priest, the statistics showed that the work of the church was especially useful because it affected the most productive members of society, those who would set an example for their families. More than half of those taking the oaths had done so for a second or third time, even up to eighteen times! Given the short duration of the pledges, this is not surprising; 39 percent of them took the pledge for three months, 27 percent for six months, and only about 12 percent for an entire year. Only four persons took the pledge for life, including one inhabitant of a flophouse. Women constituted only 1.3 percent of all the pledgers; most of them were either single or widows, and they ranged in age from thirty-six to forty.

The most remarkable sign of success, according to Akimov, was the fact that 92 percent of the people taking oaths were faithful to them. The people themselves recognized this method to be effective, and the number taking pledges grew 189 percent from 1910 to 1911. Women marched their husbands into the church to take the vow. Employers often demanded from their workers certificates of sobriety given out by the church and renewals when they expired. Workers themselves recognized the cash value of such testimony and were eager to sign up. Of the 8 percent who broke their pledges, the reason given was usually "from weakness." Some were more specific: "I was unhappy," "I was sick," or "My comrades tempted me." Most commonly, they encountered some ordinary ritual, a birthday or a deal concluded, that always required a drink, and then the pull of habit was too strong.[55] On the whole, Akimov found the results of his survey gratifying. Workers recognized that with the aid of parish pledges, they could remain sober for specified stretches of time, during which they retained their wages and helped their families.[56]

One of the priests zealous in stamping out alcoholism and in helping individuals find gainful employment was Father Ioann (John) of Kronstadt (later canonized a saint), a charismatic preacher and confessor who was a member of the Alexander Nevskii Temperance Society and other temperance groups.[57] Rather than blaming alcoholics for their drunkenness, Father Ioann criticized those who gave them drink.[58] Struck by the high rate of unemployment in Kronstadt, Father Ioann built shelters and workshops called Houses of Industry (Doma Trudoliubiia), where temperance was preached and the unemployed were taught skills.

Founded in 1899, Father Ioann's church temperance society was among the earliest of the 261 clerical organizations that opened before 1900. By 1914, it was one of 1,818 church temperance societies in Russia and had the sixth highest membership.[59] Most of the members of the society were peasants or *meshchane* (townspeople). There were a few bureaucrats (even of the highest ranks) and a handful of physicians. A few priests, deacons, and psalmists also joined, though the priest noted that they were only a small portion of the clerics and church functionaries who needed help and most of those who did belong could not fulfill their pledges. The majority of the 530 members were Russian Orthodox, but there were some Old Believers, Lutherans, Catholics, and even a few Jews.[60] People came from other parishes to join the society; some came on the recommendations of their pastors, and others joined despite public denunciations of temperance by their own priests.[61]

Father Ioann's movement began to spread from one *uezd* (county) to another; soon the entire province was covered with temperance societies. People arrived to join at all hours of the day, and even on Easter Saturday and Christmas Eve. "I met them at 4 A.M., at 11 in the evening, and sometimes I went to church five times a day with them, if necessary. I feared," Father Ioann said, "to push aside those thirsting for salvation with even the slightest hint of a rejection."[62] Some of them added to sobriety pledges a vow not to swear, gamble, or use tobacco.

Father Ioann boastfully noted that when members took pledges in front of him, they tended to observe them more faithfully than when they went to the other priests, although "the others were all wonderful pastors, sober, attentive, instructive."[63] Members were given a copy of the rules of the organization, a membership card, an ikon, and antialcohol booklets and brochures. In his society, only about 10–15 percent could not carry out their pledges to the end of the period, and these people reenlisted for a period of no less than three months. Some, he claimed, observed the pledge beyond its termination, and indeed for the rest of their lives.

The priest's major concern, apart from the health of individuals, was the poverty that drunkenness brought into the household.[64] From close acquaintance with his parishioners, he saw household misery and violence, at least part of which he attributed to alcoholism. So he carried his mission for sobriety into the schools in an attempt to dissuade children from following the path of their elders. He organized School Unions for children and their parents, in which children promised not to drink, smoke, swear, gamble, mistreat animals, or steal. "Women from those families where formerly their husbands got drunk," he reported, "were especially satisfied. They could not find words to express their gratitude."[65]

As in Ireland, where Father Matheu, a charismatic priest, managed to get 5 million Irishmen (out of a total population of 8 million) to pledge complete abstinence in the 1840s, temperance societies were most successful when led by a person revered for a saintly life and who could touch the emotions of the afflicted. This was true of Rozhdestvenskii, Ioann of Kronstadt, and of a group known as *trezvenniki*, who like the Ioannites, were deemed to be too pietistic by the official church.

Charisma counted far more to seekers of sobriety than whether the political bent of the leader was conservative (like Father Ioann) or radical in some respects (like Tolstoi).[66] Although the church was eager to promote sobriety, it feared its position was threatened by schismatics of all sorts after a 1905 law granted tolerance to all religions. One such charismatic leader, Ivan Alekseevich Churikov, and his followers were eventually judged by the church to be sectarian. A peasant trader from Samara Province, Churikov settled in a poor working-class neighborhood of the capital in the mid-1890s. Influenced by Father Ioann of Kronstadt, he began to warn workers against alcohol and, although he was a layman, to preach the gospel, heal the sick through prayers, and hear public confessions. After a short stint in an insane asylum (presumably for claiming powers of healing) and then imprisonment in the Suzdal' Spaso-Evfimev monastery for a few days, he returned to St. Petersburg, where, like Rozhdestvenskii, he became immensely popular among urban workers.[67] His friend Ivan M. Tregubov, a follower of Tolstoi, recorded some of his weekly revival-like prayer meetings in St. Petersburg, where workers made public confessions, and unlike the decorum observed in Orthodox services, congregations shouted back after Scripture readings. The hierarchy frowned not only on the charisma of this layman who also claimed curative powers but also on the group's "leftist" association with writer Leo Tolstoi, temperance advocate and founder of his own religion.[68] Conservatives feared that Churikov and his followers might be radical, and after Tolstoi was excommunicated, it seemed more likely that Churikov might be sectarian, too.[69] His preaching and his wearing of a pectoral cross like a priest's no doubt also antagonized some of the clergy.

Churikov had both detractors and supporters. Among his detractors were some of the relatively new professional missionaries, who prided themselves on their effort to rationalize Orthodoxy.[70] These missionaries believed that logical debate was the way to win converts and so condemned those they perceived to be "mystical sectarians," who, by 1913, had 100,000 "converts" in St. Petersburg and Moscow alone, as well as followers in Omsk, Kostroma, Iaroslavl', Novgorod, and Ukraine.[71] Churikov had some liberal clerical protectors, such as Metropolitan Antonii of St. Petersburg, who defended him precisely because of his success in rehabilitating alcoholics; Churikov was not excommunicated until after Antonii's death in 1912.[72]

Churikov's success among alcoholic workers was akin to the success of Baptists in drawing support in the Soviet period. The spiritual movement appealed to peasants who had recently moved to urban settings and who were frightened by the anonymity, anomie, poverty, and lack of community in their new environment. Sermons, singing, and shouting likely provided emotional experiences that allowed uprooted persons to become part of a brotherhood, a tight community of people who cared for each other. Churikov preached the comforting and optimistic message that people could take charge of their own lives and live in sobriety and decency with discipline and loving help from the brotherhood; in sobriety they could find a kind of heaven on earth. The revival meetings, an innovative urban phenomenon, bore little or no resemblance to their religious experiences in the countryside.[73]

Opposition to Churikov and other *trezvenniki* came mainly from the Orthodox hierarchy, who had already alienated parish clergy and many of the lay intelligentsia by excommunicating popular liberal priests.[74] Not only was the hierarchy afraid of sectarians, but it was also suspicious of lay leadership in religious matters. While the Alexander Nevskii Temperance Society had encouraged lay activism, the official church felt that Churikov had gotten out of hand. It was not because he advocated absolute abstinence from alcohol, also promoted by many priests, but because the church did not want laypersons to take over religious services and the temperance movement. Dispute over the role of the laity in the church was one of the stumbling blocks that prevented parish reform before the 1917 revolution.[75]

While the official church mistrusted *trezvenniki,* the centrist Octobrist Party supported them precisely because they did not act under the direction of the hierarchy or the Holy Synod, with whom they were struggling in the state Duma over who should be in charge of reforming the church. Octobrists preferred the *trezvenniki,* who might be considered radical but, unlike the socialist temperance advocates, still believed in private property.[76]

The church's opposition to the *trezvenniki* was soon extended to another group, but this time not laymen but clerics who entered politics without the approval of the hierarchy. The Group of Thirty-two (later called Renovationists), convinced that social work demanded political activism, engaged in what they called Christian politics in order to stamp out alcoholism, the reason for poverty and other social ills. They saw a connection between real life and religious faith and intended to change society. The duty of the church was to support the principle of justice, which meant that the church should speak for the poor and powerless and defend them against exploitation. The religious, they concluded, must participate in politics, often in opposition to the state.[77] The rise of this group illustrates how the fight against alcoholism served as an opening wedge into the political arena. The tardiness of the official church in addressing the issue give rise to the independent creation of urban Alexander Nevskii Temperance Societies, to the charismatic *trezvenniki,* and finally to radical members of the clergy who believed social and political structures had to be altered in order to eliminate alcoholism.[78] An ardent advocate of abstinence, M. D. Chelyshev, a member of the Third Duma, summarized the church's temperance activity: "After [Patriarch Nikon], for two hundred years the church has slept."[79] But even Chelyshev recognized that by 1912, "much has changed." The church, by the time he was speaking, supported the largest and most widespread temperance movement in Russian society outside the government's Guardianship of Public Sobriety and, we shall see, took the leadership of the temperance movement away from parish priests.[80]

One of the reasons for the long delay in the church's involvement was that fiscal interests of the imperial government had long discouraged the clergy from speaking in favor of total abstinence. Some members of the clergy argued much later that the church temperance societies of the late 1850s, created with the approval of the Holy Synod, had been so successful that the *otkupshchiki* (tax farmers with licenses to sell vodka) made complaints, denouncing antialcohol sermons to the Ministry of Finance as "illegal" and "inconsistent with the Christian religion."[81] Some members of the clergy claimed that the minister of finance, fearful of losing revenue, forced the clerical societies to close.[82] Another anonymous author also claimed great success for the midcentury temperance societies and blamed the minister of finance for quashing them for fiscal reasons.[83]

Though the church attempted to reform and broaden its social mission to improve the morals of the urban and rural masses in the 1860s, it was not until June 1889 that the Holy Synod invited priests to preach temperance. It sent a circular to parish priests advising them "on their spiritual authority to take certain measures for the eradication of drunkenness," perhaps inspired by the mounting dimensions of the problem and desiring a more direct engagement with society. Among its recommendations was the formation of parish temperance societies.[84] All alcohol was to be renounced, not just vodka, as had been the case in 1858–59.[85] Less than a year later, in March 1890, a temperance society was founded at the St. Petersburg Seminary to prepare future priests and deacons as clerical temperance workers for the provinces, but according to Korovin, it found little sympathy among the seminarians and did not last long.[86]

The establishment of a parochial temperance society required the approval of only the local *eparkh,* or bishop, which made setting up clerical temperance groups a far easier process than setting up lay ones, which involved a tortuous bureaucratic process through the Ministry of Internal Affairs. The number of church societies grew rapidly; 205 were founded in 1889–91, the largest of which included 600 members.[87] According to N. I. Grigor'ev, the clergy founded 890 temperance societies before 1900.[88] By 1909, according to the over-procurator of the Holy Synod, there were 950 church temperance societies, with a membership of 508,716 persons.[89] An Estonian temperance leader noted that church temperance societies had existed in Podolia since 1892 and that there were 150 such societies in Tambov. He also reported that many churches had over a thousand members who had pledged total abstinence for a lifetime or from one to ten years. Some societies had succeeded in closing down liquor stores.[90]

St. Petersburg set the tone, but other cities also witnessed the establishment of church societies. For example, in Moscow the Danilovskii Branch of the First Moscow Temperance Society, led by a priest, Luke Liubimov, gathered every Sunday and holiday in a tearoom to sing hymns and pray. Even if the membership numbers were somewhat exaggerated, they were impressive. "The army of Danilov temperance people grows and grows.

Having begun with 25 persons, it has now reached the number of 50,000 members, with the society commanding a hundred thousand rubles, a school for children, a Sunday school for adults, a reading room, a library, and so on."[91]

After 1905, the Holy Synod was determined to gain greater control over the large and growing temperance organizations. At the First All-Russian Congress on the Struggle against Drunkenness (St. Petersburg 1901–10), there had been only a couple dozen priests among the more than four hundred delegates. The clergymen urged the congress to adopt a resolution to introduce moral and religious education into all schools as a weapon against alcoholism, a resolution that failed to pass. Rebuffed and disappointed with the meeting, some of the clergy called for a second all-Russian conference against alcoholism to be held, which would be dominated by clerics rather than a broad spectrum of laypersons.[92] In August 1912, Father Mirtov summoned the first All-Russian Congress of Church Temperance Workers—called "the Practical Activists."[93] The congress, whose mission was to combat alcoholism with Christian love, mutual help, and unconditional abstinence from alcohol, ran for six days at the Moscow Seminary;[94] 706 delegates attended, 236 from Moscow and the remaining 470 from all over the empire.[95] In his opening speech, Archbishop Arsenii of Novgorod suggested that the Guardianship was ineffectual and lamented the absence of the intelligentsia from the ranks of temperance societies. He claimed that clerical temperance groups, whose duty was to save drinkers, furnished a more solid basis of support for drinkers, especially by means of pledges. In reviewing the history of church temperance societies in the 1850s, he concluded that then (as well as in his own time) "the people themselves were seeking and found with joy a refuge in them from their drunken lives."

Since priests heard confessions and were thus intimately acquainted with "the secret nooks of the human conscience," they were best suited to help their parishioners who wanted to be cured of their illness. He cited the American physician Benjamin Rush as saying, "I am forced to believe that only religion is effective against drunkenness. I am convinced by my many years of experience that purely human means have no effect on it."[96] The archbishop criticized the 1909–10 congress for placing too much emphasis on social and economic conditions leading to alcoholism. While admitting that these factors played a role, he claimed that mankind had never been a slave to material conditions and that man's spiritual nature, mind, and will all must come into play against drunkenness. "Drunkenness is not only an illness, but also an evil, the moral breaking down of the people, which is the result of many causes, but primarily the decline of faith."[97]

Bishop Mitrofan, who was also a member of the state Duma, asserted that drunkenness was a decline not only of faith but also of morals. He linked the increase of hooliganism in the land to alcoholism. A sign of the decline of morality, he claimed, was that it used to be considered shameful to be drunk, but this was no longer the case. The clergy therefore should inculcate morals among the youth in schools.[98]

Noting the growth of temperance work in the church, Arsenii hoped that the conference of clerical temperance workers would lead to renewed efforts and greater success as one united and purposeful organization.[99] Another speaker, Father Vetlin, also emphasized the need to form a spiritual brotherhood of parishioners, who would extend to each other loving mutual help.[100] In contrast to the self-congratulatory tone of most of the speeches, the conservative metropolitan of Moscow and a total abstainer, Vladimir, was more restrained in his words of greeting to the 1912 congress: "To be sure we cannot say much about our successes or compliment ourselves in this field. Our work is a new, very modest, and little noticed activity. Our church-parish temperance societies are not numerous and not well known, with the exception of two or three societies in the capitals. We do not have many cultural or material resources."[101]

The clergy minced no words about how the Ministry of Finance indirectly contributed to the spread of drunkenness with its monopoly on liquor.[102] This outspoken condemnation of the vodka monopoly appears to contradict the statement of an American temperance worker, William E. Johnson, who claimed that the Holy Synod received about 14 million rubles a year from the monopoly, so that it dared not criticize the state institution. Although it remains unknown whether the Holy Synod received funds from the monopoly, priests at the antialcohol congress of 1912 asked for state subsidies to support clerical temperance groups—a request that demonstrated their low opinion of the work of the Guardianship, already supported by state funds.[103] One priest, who described himself as a "humble toiler in the provinces," denounced alcoholism among the clergy and demanded that the State Vodka Monopoly be abolished.[104] Another priest said no alcoholic had the right to be in the priesthood, because each parish had to have a sober priest to lead a temperance society.[105] These statements from parish priests also show that in their view, educated society, the intelligentsia, was not doing anything about the roots of alcoholism.

No congress concerning alcoholism would have been complete without Duma member Chelyshev, who, at the penultimate session, spoke on legislation pending in the state Duma and lost no opportunity to excoriate the Ministry of Finance for intoxicating the Russian people. He cited statistics on the increased number of state liquor stores and the increased per capita consumption of alcohol since the introduction of the monopoly. And he postulated that only if women were allowed to vote in the village assemblies would liquor stores be closed.[106] At the conclusion of his speech, the clerical congress passed a resolution supporting the legislation pending in the Duma, which, as described by Chelyshev, included giving women the right to vote in peasant assemblies on the issue of alcohol, but on no other issue. Arsenii agreed that women, especially wives of priests, should be called upon to take an active role in temperance because of their influence on the family.[107]

The second and much more radical resolution proposed by Chelyshev, that the emperor himself ban the sale of all alcohol everywhere in the empire, was neither discussed nor voted on at the congress, despite his repeated requests. The congress did adopt about fifty resolutions, which stemmed from the more than 100 reports given.

After the congress of church temperance workers, the Holy Synod began taking increased control over temperance groups. The Alexander Nevskii Temperance Society, renamed the All-Russian Nevskii Brotherhood of Temperance, expanded its ministry throughout the empire, but under the supervision of the Holy Synod.[108] The Holy Synod also kept an eye on lay temperance groups, having condemned as "sectarian," the *trezvenniki* popular movement. That the church was taking over temperance societies was further suggested by the emergence of the All-Russian Working Union of Christian Temperance Workers. On September 29, 1911, they sponsored an "antialcohol day," to be observed all over Russia by special liturgies, processions, lectures, and entertainments. Even the Duma participated in observing the antialcohol day by holding a prayer service in Aleksandrovskii Hall.[109] People were to refrain from alcohol that day, something like the "smoke-out days" recently observed in the United States. Streetcars covered with placards advertised the campaign. Women, escorted by members of the cavalry, went to the busiest city streets to sell brochures, pamphlets, and postcards for 15–20 kopecks; business was brisk in government buildings, banks, and factories and in the Gostinii Dvor, the Passage, and other shopping centers. A rich American merchant who contributed to the event told Bishop Mitrofan that he had originally refused to donate to a temperance society, believing it had nothing to do with him, but he changed his mind when his wife and children were nearly killed in a train derailment caused by a drunken engineer.[110] Over 7,000 rubles were raised that day.

By the eve of World War I, the All-Russian Working Union of Christian Temperance Workers declared the first three days of the Easter holiday days of sobriety, a time traditionally given over to much drink.[111] To designate the Easter holiday as a time for abstinence went against tradition. Many people looked forward to drinking after the forty dry days and nights of fasting. In fact, as one temperance writer noted, since no one could abstain for so long a period, it was customary to prolong the Carnival drinking time right into the first week of Lent and then to refrain from abstinence during the last week of Lent in anticipation of the great holiday. But the All-Russian Working Union of Christian Temperance Workers was vigorous in lobbying the government to close liquor and even beer stores during the first, fourth, and seventh weeks of Lent, and it chided officials for canceling the Guardianship's religious readings and shows on the grounds that Lent was not a time for "spectacles."[112]

Going against tradition, therefore, on April 6–8, 1914, all the state liquor stores were closed in St. Petersburg, as well as taverns, pubs, and second- and third-class restaurants—all of which were normally closed only on Easter Day itself. On Easter Monday, a religious procession of thousands of people from all the churches of the capital arrived at Alexander Nevskii Monastery. Metropolitan Vladimir, along with many other clergy, celebrated the liturgy, and Mirtov preached to a crowd, which included many youths. That night, at the Kalashnikov Grain Exchange, Dr. A. I. Verzhbitskii was the first of many speakers on the dangers of alcohol consumption. Simultaneously, in lecture halls around the city, other doctors, including N. I. Grigor'ev, I. V. Sazhin, and N. P. Strudentsov, also gave lectures. The speeches were followed by orchestral performances and children's choruses. Beginning at dawn the next day, about 1,500 persons took to the streets to distribute 75,000 temperance medals in the capital. A million or more medals were given out in the provinces. The celebration was capped by a temperance banquet on April 23, tickets for which cost 1 1/2 rubles. Among the attendants was Minister of Finance P. L. Bark, the man then in charge of the State Vodka Monopoly. As usual, the banquet (doubtless vodka-free) ended with a concert.

While such special events garnered much publicity and some funds, the clerical societies quietly engaged in social services. For example, the Malo-kolomenskaia Church Temperance Society in St. Petersburg, founded in 1870, had established a home for the elderly, a shelter for boys, and a day care center for girls by 1900. Likewise the Blagoveshchenskaia Church provided a school, library, bookstore, shelter for girls, and housing for the elderly.[113] The Temperance Fraternity of the Predtechenskoe Church fielded a mobile medical clinic and a pharmacy to treat alcoholics.[114]

In 1913, Metropolitan Vladimir of St. Petersburg urged every parish to organize a brotherhood based on the successful All-Russian Nevskii Brotherhood of Temperance; since these brotherhoods would be built on religious principles, they should be directed by the parish priest himself. In this way, the priest could unite all those in the parish desirous of attaining sobriety, and he himself could serve as a model of the sober life. Vladimir recognized how difficult it was for an individual to drink moderately when in the company of tipplers, but in a group, each could support the other in his resolve, giving each other strength and calling upon the help of God.[115]

The emergence of Vladimir as a leader in the temperance movement in his official capacity of metropolitan of the capital city is indicative of how the official church after 1905 began to take charge of many of the formerly spontaneous social-religious activities, including those of temperance.[116]

Ivan Aivazov, a zealous antisectarian missionary associated with the excommunication of Churikov and a lay professor at the St. Petersburg Ecclesiastical Academy, praised Vladimir for "taking on his shoulders the broadest organization in the struggle with national drunkenness, not only in taking under his protection the First All-Russian Congress of Practical Activists in the struggle with alcoholism but also in fighting for a sober Rus. In this, he has accomplished a veritable *podvig* (a heroic feat)."[117]

Although many officials were honorary members of church temperance societies, and even the minister of finance attended some of the more public functions of church temperance groups, there was still a fundamental divergence in their goals. The church's insistence on total abstinence worked against the state's objective of promoting moderate alcohol consumption among the masses.[118] Clerical societies clearly attracted a broad following, while the Guardianship appeared only to amuse, but not necessarily to sober up, the population. Bureaucrats, not alcoholics, formed the membership of the Guardianship. The small subsidies given to church temperance activities by the Guardianship revealed the ambivalence the state felt about the growing crowds attracted to such societies as the Alexander Nevskii organization.

To be sure, the Holy Synod, a bureau within the state, had invited pastors to join the state in promoting sobriety. It could not, however, and did not muzzle the sharp criticisms emanating from the clergy concerning the Guardianship, the State Vodka Monopoly, and even, at times, the tsarist regime, which permitted such a noxious institution.[119] When the Holy Synod saw the extraordinary success of the Alexander Nevskii Temperance Society throughout the empire, it insisted that it come under its protection. The fact that the Holy Synod called on monasteries to help in the struggle against alcoholism perhaps showed that they were easier to control than parish organizations.[120] The 1905 revolution certainly warned the Holy Synod that societies helping workers to gain sobriety and better wages, even if led by a priest, could be dangerous. Father Gapon's society touched off Bloody Sunday, when peaceful workers marched to the Winter Palace and were met with lethal shots by tsarist troops. Clearly, in the Holy Synod's view, such autonomous clerical temperance societies should be closely monitored.[121] For example, the activities of Father Mirtov, formerly of the independent Alexander Nevskii Temperance Society, now came under the auspices of the Holy Synod, including sponsorship of his 1911 lecture tour to Perm, Ufa, Ekaterinburg, and other eastern cities.[122]

Clerical societies sometimes ran afoul of the authorities.[123] For example, one commune led by a priest voted to close down the state liquor store in the area, but when the petition reached the government, the local bishop was told to tell the priest that he would be punished if he persisted in this effort. Mirtov complained that a church temperance society could not get official permission to open a library and also that officials shut down reading rooms. He condemned "the intrusion of officialdom and its dark influence on the matter of temperance."[124]

There was no doubt that clerical temperance societies on the eve of world war were growing. Tens of thousands of people participated in the Alexander Nevskii Temperance Society's pilgrimages and meetings, and more than a million people a year visited the church where the society was located.[125] Determined to eradicate drunkenness, which was "a shameful stigma that has long marked the Russian," and asking, "If Muslim kingdoms can live without vodka, why should our Orthodox Christian state be worse?" clerics all over Russia formed parish societies.[126] The church did not win them all over to the cause of sobriety, of course. One respondent to a questionnaire in Vladimir Province wrote of the clergy, "They give sermons, but they almost never move anyone." Another said, "The clergy gives sermons from time to time, but their influence seems to be little, and in general, respect for the clergy by the people is remarkably undermined, because they themselves drink even more than the people, so they seem to me only to implant drunkenness."[127]

Nonetheless, the church, in its new mission to minister to society with pastoral concern, found in the issue of alcoholism a powerful lever to wrench itself out from under state tutelage. The problem was, as far as the Holy Synod was concerned, that they would have to be careful not to allow any more loose cannons (or canons) within the church itself, such as the pietistic *trezvenniki* or the militant Father Gapon. The encroachment by the Holy Synod on the activities of independent church organizations was a sign that the state recognized that the Orthodox Church itself was more sympathetic to the victims of drunkenness than to the regime that provided a social environment that drove workers to drink. Not only were powerful ecclesiastics critical of the state monopoly and, more indirectly, of the regime that permitted it, but several individual priests active in the temperance movement, convinced that a radical change in society was necessary to solve the problem, were in later years all too eager to join the radical Bolshevik alternative Orthodox Church, the Living Church.[128] One such person who turned against not only the state but the church as well was the charismatic *trezvennik* Churikov, who, excommunicated in August 1914, joined the Living Church in December 1922. As Richard Stites has noted of sectarians, they "seemed to want some kind of merger between Bolshevik economic forms and a vibrant sectarian Christianity infused with brotherhood, equality, and harmony."[129] Another cleric began his career as a temperance worker and ended as an atheist. Mikhail Galkin (later Gorev), an ordained priest and a temperance activist who coedited the journal *Trezvye vskhody* (Seedlings of Sobriety), underwent a tortuous spiritual odyssey, which led him to renounce his clerical status and to become an editor of the leading antireligious communist newspaper, *Bezbozhnik* (The Godless).[130] Some religious temperance workers apparently became so caught up in attempting to establish heaven on earth that they eliminated belief in an afterlife.

As those careers illustrate, liberal parish priests who worked with the urban poor and who had hoped to create a better life on this earth were frustrated, first by the conservative hierarchy and then by an orthodoxy that would not combine it tenets with socialism. Finally, some, disillusioned by all religions, turned to socialism, which had promised to eliminate not only religion as the opiate of the people but also the preferred opiate of the people—vodka.

6 . . . .

WOMEN'S PHYSICAL AND POLITICAL USE OF ALCOHOL

[The drunkard] drinks the tears, blood, and life of his wife and children.

—H. F. Lamennais

Unfortunately, for the present, Russian women are indifferent to the problem of alcoholism.

—I. M. Dogel

We must not give women [voting] rights or they will close all the taverns.

—Peasant from
Tver Province, c. 1908

In 1899, a correspondent from Orenburg Province related an incident in a village he identified only as "P." A widow ran an illegal tavern, which was also a house of prostitution. The wives of the village, angered that their husbands were her regular customers, secretly denounced her to the fiscal authorities but would not make their accusations publicly and officially. When the local fiscal agent finally accumulated enough evidence to arrest the widow, the other women thanked him— but still privately. "Thus are the habits and customs," the correspondent observed, "in our backward corner of the world."[1] Presumably, women were afraid of retribution from the woman or from their husbands who patronized the business.

The alcohol trade activities of peasant women made a contribution to the family budget. A questionnaire circulated by the Alexander Nevskii Temperance Society of St. Petersburg among Russia's rural clergy reveals the role peasant women played in the alcohol trade. A priest of Dankovskii in Riazan Province reported: "Women usually do the bootlegging, and this is especially sad, as up to now they have been models of sobriety and also martyrs to the drunkenness of their savage husbands and sons, but now they themselves spread drunkenness for profit, from which greater and greater sufferings will be their lot."[2] In a church periodical, however, some peasant women justified their bootlegging as moral since out of their profits they lit candles and gave donations to the church.[3]

A priest surveyed from the Pskov Province described how a peasant, after a spree in the tavern, "very often continued to drink in his own home, buying the vodka from his wife, daughter-in-law, or daughter."[4] The women, he says, even prepared hors d'oeuvres (zakuski) for the customers. His words imply that the women bootleggers operated quite independently of their husbands. He claimed, too, that the bootlegging, largely done by women, was changing drinking habits in the countryside from occasional sprees to continuous inebriation. For women, bootlegging was an opportunistic crime if they had a house, store, or tavern in which to sell vodka illegally.[5] Women also went to fairs and bazaars, where, for a price, they produced vodka and glasses to save the thirsty traders the trouble of finding taverns. What is more, bootlegging was particularly attractive because the money that married women earned was their own (like the produce from their gardens) and did not have to go into the household economy. If the women were single, the profits might go toward a dowry, or if widowed, they might support their children. The attractiveness of the business to women is reflected in the statistics. Women constituted a little less than 10 percent of all persons convicted for felonies; yet between 1874 and 1913, women made up 20–30 percent of those convicted for bootlegging.[6] Over time, they got away with these crimes less often because state authorities, loath to lose revenue, arrested and convicted more and more women.[7]

Some temperance advocates even blamed peasant women for the drunkenness of their men, and not only those who were bootleggers. For example, in 1909, a temperance advocate accused a peasant woman of not keeping an attractive home for her husband and sons and, as a result, driving the men to seek a more satisfying social life in the tavern.[8] Making the home welcoming by providing a clean and quiet environment was a common theme among temperance advocates. Women were urged to keep their houses clean but not to offer guests vodka. Rather, wives were advised to indulge in "jokes, laughter, smiles, sweet and charming words," in order to make men forget about alcohol.[9] Danish and German temperance advocates likewise rebuked women for being inadequate housewives and guardian angels of the home, driving nagged and bored husbands to the tavern; as one summed up the relationship between married life and drink, "Almost all men who are unhappily married are drinkers."[10]

With the establishment of the State Vodka Monopoly in 1894, which closed taverns where only drink was served, men were said to have begun to drink more at home, with the result that "women and children became acquainted with vodka."[11] Ironically, one of the reasons for closing taverns was purportedly to place men under the disapproving eyes of their wives at home, should they imbibe too much. Vodka, however, was nearly always proffered to guests, so it is unlikely that the creation of the vodka monopoly was responsible for the introduction of alcohol into the household.[12] One writer pointed out that since women controlled what was consumed in the household, they limited the serving of alcohol to occasions involving guests. After the introduction of the monopoly, he claimed, the unbridled drinking that had occurred in the taverns no longer took place, so that total consumption of vodka was reduced.[13]

In 1906, Dr. A. Bulovskii, a tsarist official, boasted that the government's policy, in effect since 1894, of prohibiting the consumption of alcohol where it was sold had succeeded in restoring domestic peace. In former times, peasants who brought their various products to town markets had returned completely inebriated, having drunk the money received for their grain and other commodities. In consequence, they arrived home in a foul humor, treated their families in a very nasty fashion, and easily got into arguments, which often degenerated into brawls and fights. But now, according to his optimistic report, the peasant "returns happily to the bosom of his family, counts out the remaining money, and is happy to be able to show to his wife the money that he has earned, which he gives her for safekeeping."[14] Bukovskii's report, however, sounds more like propaganda for the State Vodka Monopoly for the benefit of foreigners than a realistic picture of life in Russia.

Most of the temperance literature asserted that women drank far less, and less often, than men.[15] The survey of the Alexander Nevskii Temperance Society supports this observation while looking more closely at and illuminating patterns of drinking among rural women. According to a priest in Kostroma Province, men moved to the capitals during the summer for more lucrative seasonal work. The women, left behind to carry out heavy rural labor by themselves, drank as a release and perhaps to ease their pain. Many priests observed that women, like men, were given to binge drinking; they drank especially heavily after completing major seasonal tasks such as sheep shearing and on holidays and holy days. Unmarried peasant women had their own celebrations, such as on Whitsunday (the seventh Sunday after Easter, or Pentecost), when they would go into the woods, "drink beer, sing, decorate birch trees, and learn their fortunes by tossing wreaths into a stream."[16] The laments of wives and fiancées in popular songs relate frequent mistreatment by drunken men, but there are also songs in which women recall with satisfaction how they returned home drunk or tipsy from parties.[17] Although women shared the same culture of holiday drinking as men, they were censured more severely. The psychiatrist I. A. Sikorskii called it a "perversion" of the nature of females for them to drink excessively.[18] This tension between the traditional inclusion of women in festive drinking and a newly emerging sense of the impropriety of heavy drinking by women is expressed by a historian:

> There can be no doubt that women in pre-industrial society drank more than home-brewed weak beer; they also drank spirits, although perhaps not in the same quantities as men. It seems as if this practice underwent a change with the development and spread to all social classes of the bourgeois ideal of woman during the second half of the 19th century.[19]

Factory women were, however, more apt to become alcoholics than were peasant women.[20] Like men, women transferred rural habits to the city, but with the increased flow of cash, they drank more frequently than they had done at home.[21] The working woman Z. I. Zapechina described in her memoirs that in the predominately female spinning mill where she worked in 1914, women would report to work tipsy on the Thursday before Whitsunday. On the Monday after a wedding, a bride would bring vodka, beer, candy, cookies, and nuts to work to treat her companions. On one such occasion, Zapechina reported, "Merriment, songs, and dances began, until it looked like the machines would collapse. [The bride] was put in a cart ... and we began to wheel [her around]."[22] A temperance worker who said that he had observed factory life for a quarter of a century reported that "alcoholism is increasing greatly among women. Already in England, France, and Belgium, it is now, unfortunately, beginning to spread in Russia, especially in the large cities and factory regions. Now it is not unusual to meet women together with their husbands and children on Sundays and holidays going to a *traktir* [cheap restaurant], where they drink this poison."[23] Just as women in Russia were joining the workforce and showing signs of adopting a male urban drinking culture, a new construct of femininity developed: "Around 1900 alcohol was perceived as a symbol of masculinity and sobriety as a symbol of femininity." Society expected women to conform to its ideal of accepted behavior, with women's drinking becoming unfeminine and men's sobriety becoming unmasculine.[24]

In cities, alcoholism among women was closely tied to another major social problem—prostitution. Just before World War I, an American temperance writer claimed that the 18,000 prostitutes in Riga made taverns the center of their trade. He also declared that drunkenness was much more prevalent in Riga than anywhere in America.[25] Russian women themselves linked alcoholism with prostitution. Some professional women believed prostitution, rather than drunkenness, to be the more pressing "women's issue" in the early 1900s.[26] Prostitution, however, was directly related to the liquor problem. In a report delivered in 1901 to the Russian Society for the Preservation of Public Health, Dr. Maria I. Pokrovskaia, a physician who had earned a high reputation in the field of public health, told how madams distributed vodka to their "girls" in order to sustain them in their work, especially on holidays, when the number of customers was great. Another purpose was to addict them so as to prevent them from leaving the bordellos.[27] Women would join the customers in drinking, not only because the sales were profitable to the house but also because the imbibing customer might tip more. It was expected that the women would encourage the men to drink by drinking along with them. A survey among hospitalized prostitutes revealed that all of them demanded vodka, and more than half of them in considerable quantity. A majority of the women reported that "without alcohol, they were unable to ply their trade."[28] They were also unable to face the official humiliating health inspections without drinking copiously beforehand. Pokrovskaia concluded one article by stating: "In contemporary society, prostitution and alcoholism are tightly connected. One often serves as the cause for the other. Therefore, for the successful struggle against alcoholism, it is necessary to battle prostitution, and vice versa."[29]

Long an active feminist, Pokrovskaia founded the journal *Zhenskii vestnik* (Women's Messenger) in 1904.[30] As its articles show, she was chiefly interested in equal rights for women, job opportunities, education, and the suppression of the "houses of tolerance" (brothels). Author of a widely read book on women workers in St. Petersburg, she was also the founder of the Women's Progressive Party, which agitated for equal legal rights for women, the vote, and the suppression of prostitution.[31] There was much less discussion of temperance in her journal. After the proclamation of prohibition in 1914, however, the Women's Progressive Party held a meeting in St. Petersburg on the topic, "Alcoholism and the Public Mood during the War," showing a belated interest in the subject.[32]

Countess Sofia Panina, a liberal active in the Kadet Party, also was interested in saving women from prostitution through temperance. In 1902, along the lines of the Guardianship activities, she had a People's House built in a red-light district south of the Moscow railroad station to offer theater and courses to the working class.[33]

By century's turn, there was widespread fear that alcoholism among women was increasing, which was blamed for the rise of drinking among children. An inquiry into the drinking habits of rural schoolchildren in Moscow Province established that 67.5 percent of the boys and 46.2 percent of the girls were drinkers.[34] The writer N. G. Pomialovskii, who died of alcoholism at the age of twenty-five, admitted, "I was drunk for the first time when I was seven. From then on until I finished my education, my passion for vodka developed crescendo and diminuendo."[35] One reason children began to drink, apart from the example set by their parents, was that distilleries often employed children, where sometimes their pay was partly in alcohol.[36] Strong believers in the inheritance of acquired characteristics, the reformers dreaded that drunken fathers were passing on their propensity for drinking to their offspring, daughters as well as sons.[37] And, allegedly, drunken mothers and wet nurses were also imparting that deadly thirst through the milk that their babies suckled.[38] One writer claimed that the effect of alcohol on women's organisms was greater than on men's since women were weaker. In addition to the destructive influence on the body of women, alcohol also destroyed their morality. "The maternal feelings suffer and alcoholism often leads to sterility or premature births."[39] Drunken women not only ruined themselves but also threatened the race.[40]

Women were, however, more commonly the victims, not of drunkenness, but of drunkards. Metropolitan Vladimir of St. Petersburg quoted a German work called *Macrobiotics,* which alleged that women lived on average three years longer than men principally because men drank more spirits.[41] A survey of women in Vladimir Province taken in 1910 claimed that 51 percent of women drank from time to time, but the rest never drank.[42] Women figure much more prominently as the innocent victims of inebriated husbands and fathers. In 1900, Evgeniia Chebysheva-Dmitrieva, a teacher and writer and one of the few women prominent in the temperance movement, claimed that 75 percent of all family disorders were attributable to the drunkenness of the male.[43] A. Ol'ginskii described the lot of wives of drunkards, saying they suffer from "fights, filth, arguments, poverty, hunger, cold, and illnesses."[44] One doctor, noting the abuse suffered by women at the hands of their drunken husbands, stated that they had no one to turn to, for their parents were probably also drunkards, the police were too brutal and unwilling to interfere in domestic affairs, and women could not seek redress in courts because there were no nurseries in which to place their babies while litigating. Divorce was difficult to obtain on the basis of abuse, he continued, because few witnessed the harm done to wives.[45]

A temperance advocate wrote that drunken husbands destroyed family happiness and peace and thus demoralized the children, who then began to drink themselves. "Observing factory life for more than twenty-five years," he said, "I can barely describe the terrible scenes and the facts of their lives: unhappy families, the tears of wives, the groans of women beaten by their husbands."[46] The flamboyant and persistently antialcohol delegate to the Duma from Samara, M. D. Chelyshev, became a temperance crusader after one of his tenants returned home drunk and murdered his wife: "This incident," he said, "had such an impact on me that I decided to fight vodka with all my strength."[47]

Women interested in temperance looked for allies among other temperance advocates. Women were fairly numerous as physicians—perhaps more numerous than in any other liberal profession, apart from teaching—and as physicians, they appear as benefactors of secular temperance societies. Women even founded some of these societies, but no women's temperance society lasted for long.[48] For example, the *First Women's Calendar* for 1903 in St. Petersburg listed charitable organizations, mutual-aid societies, educational and housing support, and various clubs for women but not a single organization devoted specifically to temperance.[49]

Although women participated in various temperance organizations, they seldom predominated in them. Only in one were they in the majority. In 1902, two women, M. M. Volkova, a physician, and E. A. Chebysheva-Dmitrieva, attempted to rally women to the cause of promoting sobriety among women and children. In a letter sent to medical journals and also privately circulated, they announced the formation of a special section of the Society for the Preservation of Women's Health, which itself had been founded in 1898 as part of the Society for the Preservation of Public Health.[50] Apart from studying the drinking habits of schoolgirls, there appears by 1902 to have been little investigation into the drinking habits of women, so it is not clear to what extent the founders of the society felt there was a need to "protect" women from alcoholism. Alcohol, the two women stated, was destroying both morality and health in Russia—the two chief concerns of women. In Europe and America, hundreds of thousands of women had taken up the battle for temperance, but up to the present, they wrongly claimed, not one Russian woman had joined the fray.

The new section first met on November 2, 1904, after a liturgy, and invited both women and men to participate. Of the twelve persons in attendance at the first meeting, E. A. Chebysheva-Dmitrieva was elected chair; Count L. B. Skarzhinski, vice-chair; N. D. Gattsuk, treasurer; and Z. A. Rodionova, secretary.[51] The honorary patron of the organization was Princess Evgeniia M. Ol'denburg, whose husband was a well-known temperance advocate. She sent a telegram conveying her best wishes to the new group, whose name, the Section for the Struggle against Alcoholism among Women and Children, clearly stated its mission.[52] Volkova, a physician and president of the Society for the Preservation of Women's Health, gave a keynote speech describing the negative influence drunken mothers had on their families and promising that the parent society would work closely with this new section. Dr. M. N. Nizhegorodtsev, the first president of the Commission on the Question of Alcoholism, presided temporarily until the election of officers could be held. In his opening remarks, he told the women that their organization was important since "a woman is the best guardian of the idea of temperance and morality."[53]

Chebysheva-Dmitrieva, chair of the organizing committee, explained that the section had been conceived as early as 1900, but it could not be formed sooner because of certain "formalities," which suggests that it was difficult to obtain official permission to establish such an organization. Financing such an organization may also have proved challenging. Even at its founding, the section's treasury contained only 445 rubles and 16 kopecks. Telegrams of congratulation came from Countess M. A. Sol'skaia, Princess Shcherbatova, Professor of Hygiene V. Shidlovskii, the Kazan Temperance Society, and others.[54]

At the first meeting, the section set out its goals and activities. In order to promote sobriety among women and children, they planned to establish tearooms (for women and children only) and give lectures on the harm of alcohol, as well as distribute books, brochures, and leaflets. They also decided to build a clinic for alcoholic women and children and appointed three physicians to be in charge: Vol'te, Mendel'son, and Grigor'ev.

Membership would not be restricted to women, nor just to those who were members of the parent group, the Society for the Preservation of Women's Health. The yearly dues would only be 1 ruble. In order to raise money for the organization, they would hold benefit musical evenings and sell Chebysheva-Dmitrieva's brochure *The Role of Women in the Struggle against Alcoholism*, of which Vostok Press donated 2,000 copies. They also hoped to charge for general educational lessons in order to distribute free literature and finance their free lectures with magic-lantern slides. Thanks to the solicitation of the vice-chair, Count Skarzhinski, the St. Petersburg Guardianship of Public Sobriety gave the new society a 3,000-ruble subsidy to establish its tearooms and shelters.

The section for the Struggle against Alcoholism among Women and Children soon set to work. Their first tearoom and modest library for women and children were set up in a tobacco factory. Most of the group's activities consisted of sending speakers to various halls and temperance societies to give lectures on such topics as "Alcohol and Health," "How the Alcoholism of Parents Affects the Children," and "Drunken Children." Nearly all such lectures were accompanied by magic-lantern slides, and when well-known experts such as Dr. N. I. Grigor'ev spoke for them, the attendance was usually as high as 700 persons. The section also engaged in clinical work, thanks to the free services of Dr. S. S. Vol'te. She volunteered to cure women and children alcoholics through hypnosis, three times a week for several hours. No reports were found on her rate of success.[55] Despite the energy devoted to the section and the variety of its activities, the section quickly disappeared from the historical record. According to one observer writing in 1907, "A few years ago, a woman's temperance society was formed in St. Petersburg, where they opened two dining rooms, but what they are doing now or how many members they have is unknown."[56]

The paucity of women and children alcoholics, certainly by comparison to the numbers of male alcoholics, probably accounts for the tepid response of educated women to that cause. Of all the social problems besetting urban

Russia—lack of housing, low wages, poor working conditions, prostitution, crime, and male alcoholism—the plight of those relatively few women and children did not attract much fervent attention. Those women doctors who took up the cause of women and children alcoholics may have done so because they had not been allowed to treat males before 1902. Perhaps, too, since in Russian culture men were expected to drink and women were expected to drink less frequently, if at all, women and children might have been considered the "deviants" from cultural norms and thus more amenable to treatment. At any rate, it appears that the efforts of women fighting for women's sobriety could not sustain much interest.

While we can hypothesize about the choice of women to combat alcoholism among their own gender, and the reasons for the lack of response to this issue, we can look more concretely at the failure of another temperance society, one that fought alcoholism in both men and women and had male and female members. R. Baudouin de Courtenay, one of the few prominent women intellectuals involved in temperance matters, gave a paper at the All-Russian Congress on the Struggle against Drunkenness in 1909 in which she recounted her role in organizing the first temperance society in St. Petersburg to insist on complete abstinence.[57] She had been in close contact with its members, who included students, workers, tailors, and laundresses. She observed that it took no effort to attract them; they came of their own volition to participate in the lectures, literary and musical evenings, and tours of the Hermitage and of the city. She had hoped to increase membership beyond 170 people, but potential members were frightened off by the soldiers posted in the temperance tearooms, who stared in an intimidating manner at the temperance workers. Finally, after a year and a half, the government disbanded the society under some flimsy pretext.[58]

Baudouin de Courtenay remained friends with some of the former temperance workers, and they continued to further their cause as educators rather than in formal organizations. She suggested that they took up advocating abstinence in a clandestine manner. But, she added hopefully, at present they were awaiting the confirmation by the *gradonachal'nik* (city chief) of regulations for a new society for absolute abstinence. Furthermore, she stated, they were all following with great interest debates in the Duma on legislation to permit localities to close down liquor stores altogether.

Baudouin de Courtenay was typical of women involved in temperance issues in that she was more interested in women's rights than in alcoholism; both matters she subsumed under worthwhile "ethical-social" movements. She cited Finland as being in the forefront of the battle against drunkenness, which she characterized as a new humanitarian struggle. She admired how the Finns studied the issue through biological, physiological, and psychiatric experiments and were able to prove scientifically that degeneration of offspring resulted from alcoholism among pregnant women and nursing mothers. She cited experts' calculations that 60 percent of the children of drinking parents became epileptics and that alcoholism produced more than half of all insane patients. In the St. Petersburg hospitals, 47 percent of the insane patients were alcoholics. She further claimed: "Mankind paid the price of billions of rubles for this seedbed of physical and moral poison each year."[59]

Baudouin de Courtenay urged that the war against alcoholism be waged on new grounds: not with words but by personal examples of abstinence, by establishing rapport with uneducated alcoholics, and by participating in temperance societies. Russian temperance societies, like the American, English, and Finnish ones, should, she urged, build better houses for the working population. She advocated more legislation limiting the sale and use of alcohol. The battle, she repeated, was not simply against drunkenness but against ordinary drinking, since many scientific studies showed, she claimed, that even moderate consumption of alcoholic beverages was harmful. And, indicating that there was recognition of fetal alcohol syndrome, Baudouin de Courtenay pointed out that alcohol spoils and poisons the elementary cells of the fetus, putting future generations at risk.[60]

In 1911, nearly ten years after the first society to combat alcoholism among women and children was established, a second one was organized. This time Chebysheva-Dmitrieva became chair.[61] Various well-known temperance doctors, such as A. L. Mendel'son and I. V. Sazhin, were among the more prominent members, as was Chelyshev.[62] The mission of the society was to provide useful occupations and wholesome entertainment for children and to spawn similar societies in the provinces. Again, membership dues were low, only 1 ruble. No accounts exist of any accomplishments this group might have achieved over the years, so it seems that, once again, temperance elicited little sustainable enthusiasm.

As a kind of preventive measure, some women organized leisure time activities for other women, to serve both as a deterrent to drinking and as a means to escape their drinking husbands. For example, in Voronezh in 1903, women opened a tearoom for women and girls thirteen years of age or older. In 1905, as many as 823 women attended these Sunday gatherings, where they engaged in uplifting conversations, knitting and sewing, reading, singing in a choir, dancing, and playing games. Attendees may simply have wanted to enjoy their leisure time in the company of other women. Strictly speaking, it was not a temperance society of women. For the men of Voronezh, there was a regular temperance society.[63]

The seeming indifference among educated women to the problem of alcoholism disturbed many male temperance leaders, including doctors, the writer Tolstoi, and Duma representative Chelyshev. In 1914, Chelyshev wrote an open letter to Russian women in which he compared Nicholas II's rescript of January 30, 1914, to the emancipation proclamation of Alexander

II in 1861, to argue that now all the Russian people would begin to be liberated from drunkenness.[64] He solicited the support of Russian women for this new démarche for sobriety by telling them that they should test their powers and use their influence to reduce alcoholism. The Duma representative noted that if German women were moved to take charge of the temperance movement in their country, where alcoholic psychoses were five times fewer than in Russia, then how could Russian women be less involved? The statistics Chelyshev cited were alarming. Each year in St. Petersburg, he stressed, 9,000 women died from drinking. Even in villages, there was much prostitution, he claimed, and statistics showed that 75 percent of all prostitutes began plying their trade when drunk. He challenged Russian women to fight for their suffering sisters.

He praised American women for their temperance activities since 1852, and the power and influence energetically expended by the women of England, Sweden, Norway, Germany, and other European countries on the movement. "Can Russian women, who suffered much from the war against Japan," he asked rhetorically, "be indifferent to the fact that even in Port Arthur on December 6, 1888, thirty-eight Japanese women founded a women's temperance society? By 1904, six hundred women of the best Japanese families had taken charge of antialcohol propaganda."[65]

Even Polish, Finnish, and Lithuanian women were organized in temperance movements, Chelyshev claimed. Some 12,000 Finnish women had signed a petition to the Third Duma requesting that the state liquor stores be closed. And as soon as the Finnish parliament was open to them, they spoke in favor of prohibition. Baltic women were especially active in the First All-Russian Congress on the Struggle against Drunkenness, he reminded Russian women.

He concluded that despite all the sufferings of their sister peasants and workers, female members of the Russian intelligentsia were in last place when it came to helping others. Seemingly determined to shame the women into action, he barraged them with facts and figures. Some 4.5 million children saw their mothers buried before their fourth birthday; more than a million working and nursing mothers went from the tavern to their graves; hundreds of thousands of women alcoholics filled the hospitals, which had too few beds to contain the 275,000 women made mad by alcohol; millions of women traded their bodies; and 800,000 female criminals were in prison. He appealed to all women—whether lawyers, doctors, teachers, patronesses, wives, sisters, daughters, and especially mothers—to be united in the war against alcoholism and become real sisters of mercy.[66] It is interesting, however, that he did not attempt to appeal to women by talking about alcoholism among men.

In 1905, the Kazan Temperance Society also chided Russian women, noting that in America women formed societies in which they took an oath never to marry a man who drank ("Lips that touch liquor will never touch mine") and to divorce him if he succumbed to drinking after marriage. The anonymous author of an article in the society's journal remarked on the great influence these women exerted, whereas

> our women up until now, not only have not entered into an active war against drunkenness, the scourge of mankind, but on the contrary, very often in the capacity of hostess, they distribute this evil. Just look how warmly in the midst of our families the mistress treats her guests with vodka, begging them to drink again and still more and how happy she is if the guests actually do drink a substantial amount. All hostesses, even those who themselves do not drink at all or who in other circumstances would not encourage people to drink, do this.[67]

The critic went on to state that such was the force of habit that it was presupposed that people needed to drink in order to loosen their tongues and to have a good time. For those who viewed the visit of guests as a pretext for drinking, there was no hope of sobriety, he stated, but for those who enjoy guests and want to remain sober, they could entertain without vodka and have pleasant conversations while quite sober. This would allow women to save money, tens of rubles per year, to have sober husbands, to keep their children free from the temptation to drink, and to learn to enjoy company without proffering the bottle. The author concluded by saying that he knew many families that enjoyed lively company and conversations during gatherings where no liquor was served.

One of the leading experts on alcoholism, Dr. N. I. Grigor'ev, made a special plea to women in 1911 to enter the battle. He conceded that to be truly effective in this battle, women had to achieve civil equality and independence, because, he claimed, "wherever women receive rights and freedom, they energetically and productively lead the battle against the use of alcoholic beverages, establishing temperance societies, and presenting the government with laws limiting the consumption of alcohol."[68] He stressed that women from all classes needed to be involved, as women of the intelligentsia had little rapport with victims of alcohol.[69] The doctor then went on to describe how American women in the 1870s agitated for temperance. He presented a short history of the Women's Whiskey War in Ohio, carried out by upper class women, concluding this account with the founding of the Women's Christian Temperance Union (WCTU) by Frances E. Willard.[70] He then summarized the history of temperance in Great Britain, including a general outline of a children's temperance society that had been established there, before moving on to women's involvement in temperance movements in France, Switzerland, and Belgium.

On the eve of World War I, some Russian women began to imitate those famous American women who attempted to destroy saloons in the nineteenth century. On Saturday, July 5, 1914, about fifty workers, after receiving their pay, entered *traktirs* and pubs near their factory, New Aivaz. A group of women followed them and poured out the men's beers and broke their vodka bottles. The workers acceded to the demands of the women and left the establishments without resistance.[71]

While wives of workers took direct action, many temperance workers questioned why women members of the Russian intelligentsia found it difficult to subscribe to the idea of total abstinence. In 1903, A. I. Tomlina, a Russian woman, was making a European tour and by chance was in Geneva during the World Christian Temperance Women's Congress, so she attended the meeting. Although she was immensely impressed by so many women from all over the world combating alcoholism through prayers, speeches, songs, and demonstrations, she felt unable to give a written promise of total abstinence as they required. Though a nondrinker herself, she could not promise to refrain from having alcohol in the house to serve guests, for the "total abstinence demanded by members of that organization [WCTU] violated Russian codes of hospitality."[72]

Women of the upper classes found it impossible to counter the culture of hospitality, and working women did not want to contest the prevailing drinking culture either. Laura Phillips has argued that working women did not form temperance societies because "their opposition to male drunkenness was founded in intermittent circumstances rather than in a categorical antipathy toward drunkenness. In fact, the perception of drinking as normal masculine behavior was an outlook working-class women shared with their male counterparts."[73] She explained that each woman negotiated with her husband in her own way to reduce his drinking, at least to the point of being able to support his family. In short, drinking was acceptable until the household economy was threatened, and only then were measures taken, such as wives appearing at factory gates on paydays to secure the pay packets from would-be celebrants. These women waiting to tow their husbands home on paydays were known as *buksiry* (tugboats).[74]

Another, more subtle approach by women was to drop a packet of a product such as "Alkola" (a concoction of bromide, soda, licorice juice, and dandelion root) in the unsuspecting husband's tea. These concoctions were advertised in the penny press to guarantee loss of interest in vodka. One woman claimed to have adopted the more direct (and perhaps more desperate) technique of pouring ammonia into her husband's bottle of vodka.[75] Thus, women negotiated individually with husbands they judged to have drinking problems, and some of the strategies appear to have been unilateral ones, even sneak attacks.

If women members of the intelligentsia and working women were con-
spicuously absent from official temperance organizations in Russia, peasant
women were more visible and audible, but in their own way. In 1907, in
the village of Oksiukovo, Ustiug District, Novgorod Province, peasant
women started a "peasant women's strike," a *babii bunt*. When they could
no longer stand the drunkenness of their husbands, they petitioned local
officials to close down the state liquor store. While awaiting the official
response, they took matters into their own hands. They pooled their resources, bought a lock and key, and locked the door to the liquor store at
night, which the clerk attempted unsuccessfully to break into the next
morning. For their act, sixteen women were arrested, as well as four of the
men who stood up for their wives.[76]

In the village of Gorninskii, Iaroslavl' Province, women also closed down
the liquor store, alleging that their husbands, brothers, and even their children were complete drunkards. In July 1909, about sixty women went to
the cashier of the Central Asian Railroad to ask that their husbands be paid
only once a month, instead of twice, to help reduce their drinking.[77]

Women took action within their households and on a local level and in
some cases took their grievances to the government. In 1908, forty-three
women who called themselves "wives and mothers" of Polei Village, near
St. Petersburg, sent a petition to the state Duma. Their salutation was "To
the Representatives of the People!" Stating that they turned to the Duma
as protectors of their interests, they recounted how, when there was a bootlegging tavern in their village before the creation of the state monopoly,
their husbands and fathers spent all their money there, making life very
hard for the families. When the state liquor store opened, they had experienced a ray of hope that the men's drinking could be controlled. But then
a *traktir* began to serve bootlegged vodka when the store was closed, such
as on holidays. For the past eight years, they claimed, their condition has
been worse than before. They concluded their petition by imploring: "Close
this cursed *traktir*, which is responsible for all of our misery! Stop all sales
of alcoholic beverages in our village. We hope that our request will be
fulfilled."[78]

The petition of the wives and mothers of Polei Village was dated June 3,
1908. The Duma registered it as document number 1593 and sent it to the
Commission on Petitions on June 23, which decided to return it to the
women. But the women did not give up and sent it to the Revenue Department in St. Petersburg. When the local police heard of the request, they
argued that the *traktir* was legal. Again, the women stood their ground.
Revenue officials then came and spoke of the illicit vodka sales that would
result if there was no *traktir* and, in the end, declared it a matter for the
local officials to decide. As this case illustrates, official determination to

gather revenue often frustrated women's attempts to close state liquor stores.

At times, women turned to provincial governors. In 1899, a provincial paper reproduced a petition addressed to "His Excellency" sent by an unspecified number of peasant women of the village of Monastyrka to the governor of Nizhnii Novgorod Province. The women asked that the two taverns in the village be closed because, not only were their husbands drinking up all the money, but they were hocking household items to pay for vodka, dragging out all their clothes, furnishings, and even hard-boiled eggs from their huts to satisfy the "bloodsucking tavern keepers." The paper concluded tersely with the notation that the petition, which had been sent "with tears," was passed on to the zemskii nachal'nik (a representative of the central government).[79] Presumably, no action was taken.

In dealing with the drinking problems of husbands, wives of workers and peasants worked in collusion with the church, encouraging husbands to take the pledge.[80] Some wives even urged their husbands to become sectarians so that sobriety would become a way of life. While there is some evidence that daughters and wives of priests gave counsel on domestic abuse and alcoholism, it is difficult to assess their unorganized efforts.[81] A village priest, however, attributed his success in opening a temperance society at his church to the help of the women in his parish.[82]

Dr. Korovin, a militant temperance advocate, related how women could run into difficulties when they attempted to engage in temperance activity. One unnamed woman, the wife of a doctor, in a small town in the Volga region, founded a temperance society but was strongly opposed by the intelligentsia. The clergy, seeing this opposition, refrained from supporting the organization until the "powers," that is, the governors of the city, showed sympathy for the undertaking. Only then did the enemies become well-wishers.[83] The monk Pavel, founder of the Sergievskaia School of Temperance in 1904 outside St. Petersburg, welcomed the help of an American woman, E. Ia. Smith, who taught temperance at the school.[84]

As an example of the priority given by educated women to suffrage, it should be noted that at the end of February 1905, about thirteen women activists in Moscow formed the All-Russian Union of Equal Rights for Women.[85] Their first congress was held May 7–10, 1905. The union advocated the emancipation of women in conjunction with the emancipation of the entire people. The congress made a special appeal to peasant women. Equality and the right to vote would enable them to take action against the two "major enemies of the peasantry": alcoholism and war. The franchise would allow peasant women to close the shinki, the illicit taverns in their villages, which, they claimed, sustained the high levels of rural drunkenness. First should come the right to vote, and then action against alcoholism.[86]

The 1909–10 St. Petersburg congress against alcohol abuse also provided a stage on which women could express their views on alcoholism and its linkages with women's rights. Three hundred ninety-three men and sixty women participated in the congress. Chebysheva-Dmitrieva, who attended the congress, complained that there were too few teachers, school doctors, mothers, and educators at the congress.[87] She also asserted that Russian women were far behind in the temperance movement, claiming that about 3,800 Finnish women were active in the affairs of 200 societies, and several were even in leadership positions.[88]

Among the women delegates to the congress was Dr. Pokrovskaia. She presided over a section meeting of the congress held on January 5, 1910, to which she read the proposed resolution of the Petersburg Women's Club of the Progressive Party on the necessity of granting full voting rights to women. Suffrage was to precede temperance work. Once prohibition was proclaimed in Russia, however, women appeared to stand behind it, as in 1915, when a women's magazine noted that only in those countries where women led the antialcohol battle was there some measure of success.[89] Russian educated women were not visible in large numbers proposing prohibition, but once it became law, they supported it.

Women's demands for greater control over property, passports, and the right to vote were also exhibited in the resolutions made by the women at the 1909–10 congress. They argued that they needed power in the household if they were to extirpate drunkenness and that a wife should at the very least be able to vote in the village assembly in order to close down liquor stores especially if her husband was a drunkard. They also asserted that alcoholism should be grounds for divorce.[90]

In their presentations to the congress, women agreed that unemployment, homelessness, and poverty were the chief roots of alcoholism in the cities. They urged the establishment of shelters, settlement houses, and employment bureaus. They laid even greater stress on family life and culture, underscoring the critical connection between the roots of drunkenness and the oppression of women. How could it be, a delegate to the congress, E. M. Dobrotina, demanded to know, that children reared by women who hated vodka still grew up to be drunkards? It must be simply because mothers had not sufficient legal and moral authority within the home to offer their children a powerful example.

Ironically, while women were making demands for greater power in national and family life at the congress, they received shabby treatment there. In the sessions held on January 4, the women were not allowed sufficient time to present their reports. On the following day, several protested "against such an unjust treatment of the voices of women, mothers and wives" and proposed that women walk out of the congress to show their indignation. But other women recommended that they remain, given the importance of the cause, and they prevailed.

The importance of legal rights for women as a prelude to freeing them to engage in temperance work was made evident by one of the resolutions adopted by the congress:

> Whereas the reduction of drunkenness is intimately connected with raising the economic and spiritual level of the people, and whereas the improvement of the living conditions of the masses depends directly on an improvement in the material and legal situation of women, the congress acknowledges that the struggle with the use of strong drink will fully succeed only if women can enter it as citizens of equal rights.[91]

These sweeping proposals to give women political power may seem out of place in the resolutions of an antialcohol congress. But they are a good example of how many groups and parties used the alcohol issue as a platform from which to advocate profound reforms in Russian society and to advance their own standing. Even some men made the association between the civil status of women and their entry into the battle against alcohol. In 1907, D. Nikol'skii claimed that success in fostering temperance "depended on the legal position of women, on their social and political life, and their civil independence." He noted that in Norway, because women had the right to vote in local elections, eleven out of thirteen cities voted for full prohibition of alcohol. He concluded by saying: "In Russia, a backward nation, where women are oppressed and dependent, they cannot voice their opposition to this evil [alcoholism]."[92]

In Chebysheva-Dmitrieva's view, one of the positive results of the congress was that M. D. Chelyshev introduced a bill into the Duma in November 1911 for antialcohol instruction to be made obligatory in elementary schools. The second positive result was that the church began training priests to give antialcohol sermons, not only on moral grounds but also buttressed with scientific data. She urged priests, somewhat gratuitously, to take part in the temperance movement by giving talks on the dangers of alcohol.

Chebysheva-Dmietrieva was concerned principally with education, but most women favoring temperance wanted the vote. The latter supported the 1909 proposal by the Duma's Commission on the Means for the Struggle against Drunkenness that women (mothers and daughters of household heads) be given the right to vote in village *skhody* (assemblies) on whether to close down liquor stores in their village or to ban proposed new liquor stores. The Ministry of Finance opposed this by claiming that it was against rural tradition to have women vote. The commission pointed out, however, that the change was not so radical, since female heads of households already voted on other matters in the village *skhody*. Clearly, the commission hoped that women would add to the majority vote needed to ban liquor stores, whereas the finance officers feared the ban and subsequent loss of revenue.[93]

As the proposal explained, "In designing this article [to allow women to vote], the commission had in mind that women in some countries of Western Europe, and especially in the North American United States, had a huge significance in the matter of fighting drunkenness."[94] The commission stipulated, however, that village women could vote only on the issue of banning liquor. All women could vote on an alcohol ban, whereas before only the very few women who were heads of households could vote in village assemblies. Women had used the alcohol issue as leverage to argue for complete suffrage, but they were thwarted by this measure, which gave them only partial voting rights. The bill became law. Thus, by February 1913, women did have the right to vote on banning liquor in their localities, but little more than a year later, prohibition went into effect, giving them little opportunity to exercise their limited franchise. Women in Russia received the right to vote in national elections in 1917, three years after prohibition.[95]

Some critics attributed the weak participation of Russian women in temperance activities to their indifference to alcoholism, but contemporary accounts point to the need for other explanations. In looking at the experience of women in temperance movements in the United States and Europe, it is rather noticeable that in those countries where Protestantism predominated, women took a more active role in combating drink than in Catholic countries.[96] Since Russian Orthodoxy more nearly resembles Catholicism than Protestantism, the weaker presence of women in such movements in Russia might be expected.

In the Russian Empire, Baltic women, especially in the Protestant areas of Livonia and Courland, were more active than Russian women.[97] Even the women in Kovno, a Catholic and Jewish city, organized a congress of Lithuanian and Latvian women in 1908. They petitioned for prohibition of the sale of alcoholic drinks except as medicine prescribed and available in pharmacies. In August 1909, a congress of Estonian women in Narva protested against the consumption of alcohol by their youth and denounced the State Vodka Monopoly. And Latvian women introduced a resolution at the 1909–10 St. Petersburg congress that all schoolchildren should be taught the harm of alcohol consumption.[98] Both Chelyshev and Chebysheva-Dmitrieva stressed the importance of Baltic women in leading the way in temperance matters within the Russian Empire.

Why should Protestant women have been more visible in temperance movements than their Catholic or Orthodox counterparts? To begin with, Protestants, in general, organized temperance societies earlier and more efficiently, so that one could expect women to follow suit.[99] Women, both

ministers' wives and members of the congregations, were traditionally involved in the pastoral work of Protestant churches and were often socially
active and experienced organizers. Perhaps, too, within Protestantism there
was a strain of Puritanism that had a lower threshold of tolerance for alcoholism among its faithful than Catholics and Orthodox.

It is also possible that there was greater latitude for public expression
and freedom of the press to oppose the dominant culture in Protestant
countries than in some Catholic areas and, certainly, more than in Russia.
As one study of French suffragists noted, "British and American women
received political education, for example, through the Anti–Corn Law
League or the abolitionist movement." They translated these experiences
into political action in seeking the vote, especially in Protestant nations.
The explanation could hold for women in the temperance movements also;
as de Tocqueville wrote, "Amongst almost all Protestant nations, young
women are far more the mistress of their own actions than they are in
Catholic countries."[100]

There is also some evidence that Tsar Nicholas I encouraged temperance
societies in Finland (which was under Russian rule) but not in Russia itself.
After meeting with Robert Baird, a temperance worker, Nicholas ordered
Baird's book to be translated into Swedish in 1843 and to be distributed
among the Finns, but he did not sanction a Russian translation.[101]

In Protestant countries, ministers' wives were often in the forefront of
temperance societies, whereas priests in Catholic countries were unmarried
and Catholic women played a smaller role in church affairs. In Russia,
where parish priests were married, poverty and low levels of education probably prevented clerical women from organizing temperance societies, although there is some indication that females from the clerical estate un-
dertook individual counseling against alcoholism.[102]

The Orthodox Church in Russia recognized that part of the appeal of
the Stundists, fundamentalist Evangelical Christian sectarians who won over
large groups of peasants in southern Russia, lay in their insistence on total
abstinence. Although in 1894 the Stundists were labeled "especially dangerous," and their prayer meetings outlawed, the state decided to combat the
sectarian group by encouraging Orthodox Church temperance societies near
Kiev. Tsar Alexander III himself noted that "the chief reason that the majority of Stundists in one village joined the predominant church [Orthodox]
was the fact that the parish there established a temperance society with
worthy local priests at the head."[103] Not until 1912, however, did the Holy
Synod endorse the formation of a society of clerical temperance workers,
called Practical Activists. At the same time, the Holy Synod summoned the
wives and widows of priests to become engaged in temperance work as
well.[104]

Just as Protestant women were more active than Orthodox women, so, too, were sectarian women. The Dukhobors were a large and prosperous sect who settled in the Caucasus Mountains. They had originally been a sober people, but during the mid–nineteenth century, drunkenness had spread among them. Then a woman named Luker′ia Vasil′evna Kalmykova succeeded her husband as the sect's leader. She initially imposed on her many followers a regime, not of total abstinence, but of temperance in the use of alcoholic beverages. She forbade her followers to frequent the taverns (apparently run by Armenians), curtailed the consumption of alcohol at weddings, and ordered that drunkards be publicly whipped. By the end of her life in 1886, she seems to have insisted on total prohibition. She is one of the few examples of a woman leading a small segment of Russian society into temperance—or even abstinence—and well before the establishment of the State Vodka Monopoly.[105]

After Nicholas II proclaimed prohibition in August 1914, a women's journal, although it had not been much concerned with the issue earlier, featured on its first page an editorial on temperance. Its author, I. Popov, congratulated the tsar (and not the women's movement) for having issued a ban on the sale of liquor and for closing down liquor stores. "Women, who are the victims of suffering if there is alcoholism in the family, must rejoice and insist that even after the war, the ban on vodka continue," proclaimed the editorial. It was a vague exhortation to virtue after the fact considering that Russian women had done little to organize themselves as a group against alcoholism.[106]

Yet it would be unfair to criticize Russian women as being indifferent to the problem of alcohol. Many felt strongly that since they lacked legal and social standing within Russian society, they were bound to be less effective than men in the struggle. Only when they were accorded civil rights, including the vote, might they mount a campaign for temperance. Power was a prerequisite for advocacy. For twentieth-century Russian women, power lay in civil rights. Earlier, according to religious tradition, women went out to preach publicly against drunkenness only after they were emboldened by apparitions from the Mother of God, who gave them heavenly instructions to combat drunkenness.[107] Twentieth-century Russian women wanted to be like men in their civil rights, but some men feared that if they were too active in the public sphere, demanding to vote like men, they might also begin to drink like men. Could emancipation of women also mean freedom to drink like men?[108]

To a certain extent, Russian female activists enjoyed what the economic historian Alexander Gerschenkron called the "advantages of backwardness." Since neither Russian culture nor tradition nor even government authorities favored private temperance activity, women sought to achieve more meaningful and comprehensive rights first and only then to tackle the issue of alcoholism. As for illiterate village women, they had little experience of collective and organized action; some profited from illegal sales of alcohol while others resorted to spontaneous demonstrations, like Carrie Nation, although without her large following. Simple nagging and threatening could be efficacious as well. As Tolstoi noted, "Last year a footman who used to have fits of drunkenness, and when in the village kept himself from it for five years, when living in Moscow without his wife, who used to keep him in order, began again to drink and ruined himself."[109]

It appears that working-class Russian women accepted drinking as part of their culture, but each woman was left to determine when the bounds of custom within her household had been exceeded. At that point, she took steps, whether to seek his pay packet, slip aversion concoctions into his drink, drag him to church to take a pledge, or ask him to convert to a sober sect. A few exacted retribution. An American traveler described the actions of one Russian woman around 1890: "Her opportunity occurs whenever her lord and master comes home helplessly intoxicated. While he is thus powerless to defend himself, she seizes a stick and repays with interest every blow she has received from him since his last drinking bout."[110]

Russian women remained somewhat ambivalent about alcohol. During the first months of World War I, when alcohol was forbidden in the land, some women petitioned the governor of Petrograd to send vodka to their husbands, who were suffering from cold in the trenches.[111] The alleged warming effects of alcohol as well as the cultural construction that it was manly to drink died hard among Russian women and men. While many men urged women to be guardians of sobriety in their homes, only the more radical temperance leaders wanted to share public space with women temperance advocates, who almost all appeared to have a broader agenda. Professional and socialist women, for the most part, were interested in grander causes, notably, in obtaining suffrage, which would give them the power to address, among many social issues, the problem of alcoholism.

7 . . . . . .

TEA AND SYMPHONY

• THE LAITY MOBILIZES AGAINST ALCOHOL

The history of the struggle against alcoholism is altogether modest; its deeds are unaccompanied by any stir, its heroes remained unknown, and their names are not recognized in the pantheon of glory.

—A. Rubio

As if to balance the large number of virtually unknown lay temperance leaders, perhaps the most famous writer in Russia, Count Leo Tolstoi, organized his own temperance society, the Union against Drunkenness (Soglasie protiv P'ianstva), in 1887. It preceded the establishment of the State Vodka Monopoly by eight years and the first large lay temperance society in St. Petersburg by three years.[1] Significantly, the regime that would later subsidize the Guardianship of Public Sobriety refused to recognize his organization. The state's interest in temperance came only with the introduction of the vodka monopoly in 1894.[2] In 1896, nearly ten years after creating his own temperance society, Tolstoi was made an honorary member of the First Moscow Temperance Society, which was organized by laymen, but he was expelled after his excommunication by the Orthodox Church in 1901.

It is understandable that Tolstoi would take action to combat alcoholism: drunkenness for the philosopher was not simply one of a host of sins but *the* cardinal sin, the root of all evil, for without drunkenness violence and sins of the flesh would not occur. Hence, it played an imposing role in his personal philosophy and religion.[3] For him, the founding of the temperance union was not a casual affair, but the beginning of a lifelong campaign: "Intoxication, no matter of what kind, is the sin, abandonment to which makes struggle with any other sin impossible; the intoxicated person will not struggle with idleness, nor with lust, nor with fornication, nor with the love of power. And so in order to struggle with the other sins, a man must first of all free himself from the sin of intoxication."[4]

When Tolstoi began his temperance society, about 150 individuals pledged not to drink alcohol or to buy or serve it to others. They also promised to publicize its harmful effects. The number of members grew to 559 men and 165 women by February 1888. Many of these 724 members of the Union were Tolstoi's personal friends, including Nikolai Nikolaevich Miklukhi-Makla, the gymnast Verevkin, the artist Nikolai Nikolaevich Ge (the younger), and Ignat Sevas'tianovich Makarov, all of whom were residents of Tolstoi's country estate, Iasnaia Poliana. One of the most famous members, apart from Tolstoi himself, was Thomas G. Masaryk, thirty-eight years old at the time and the future founder of Czechoslovakia.[5] Not all of its members joined voluntarily, since 16 of the females and 101 of the males were under fifteen years of age, and 2 were under the age of five. Most of the members were in their twenties. Only 6 women and 12 men enrolled who were older than sixty. Presumably, by that age one was either committed to drink or was not enticed by it; the former would not take the pledge and the latter had no need of it. Unfortunately, most of the members did not identify themselves by estate or profession, but there were at least fifteen writers, including Tolstoi himself.[6] As he wrote to the artist Ilya Repin, "our Union against Drunkenness, in spite of its indeterminate shape, is expanding and embracing more people, i.e. it's having an effect."[7] At its peak in 1891, the membership embraced 1,100 persons, although little is known of its activities.[8]

Tolstoi enrolled some of his children—Tat'iana (age twenty-three), Lev (eighteen), Maria (sixteen), Andrei (ten), and Misha (seven)—but their names were later erased from the list (by their mother?). Like their father in his youth, the sons sometimes drank to excess, a problem that colored Tolstoi's demeanor toward them. His wife, Sofiia, complained constantly of her husband's lack of interest and disappointment in some of their numerous children, particularly with their son Ilya. It can be conjectured that part of Tolstoi's disillusionment stemmed from Ilya's excessive drinking. Even Sofiia, whose life largely revolved around her children and helping her husband, noted in her *Diaries* in 1893: "When I got back I had a serious talk with Ilya, Andrusha, and Vanka, warning them of the evils of alcohol and strongly urging them not to touch it. All my sons' failings and mistakes have been due to excesses of wine."[9]

In 1887, at the time of the founding of his Union, Tolstoi asked the elder of the village near his estate to summon all the peasants. Tolstoi gave a lecture on temperance and then called for the peasants to step up to sign a pledge not to use alcohol or tobacco. Although the women urged their husbands to sign up, one man protested that they could not get along at weddings, births, and baptisms without vodka—tobacco perhaps but alcohol certainly not. "Our fathers always drank it; we must do the same." Tolstoi replied, "You can substitute sugared rose-water. In the south rose-water is always served with sherbets thick as honey." According to a biographer of Tolstoi, "The muzhiks crowded up to the table; the women were radiant; even the children seemed to realize that something great was happening; the idea of sugared rose-water enchanted them." Yet some peasants wanted clarification after they had signed, "So then no more vodka, no more tobacco?" The sage replied: "No, there's an end of smoking and drinking. You have promised."[10]

In 1911, less than a year after Tolstoi's death, the newsletter of the Tolstoi Museum noted that many of those who belonged to the temperance society might still be alive and possess some precious remembrances of and correspondence with the great writer concerning his temperance activities. The museum solicited whatever material readers could contribute for publication in the newsletter and for preservation in the museum. But in the last two issues of this periodical ever to be published, which covered the years 1912 and 1913, there was no more mention of Tolstoi's temperance union or of any memorabilia retrieved.

Giving up drink was part of Tolstoi's new way of life after his religious conversion in the late 1880s. He became a vegetarian, teetotaler, and non-smoker, living in the countryside on his estate, teaching peasant children, and doing agricultural chores. He admitted to a dissolute life in the past:

> I cannot recall those years without horror, loathing, and heartache. I killed people in war; summoned others to duels in order to kill them, gambled at cards; I devoured the fruits of the peasants' labour and punished them; I fornicated and practised deceit. Lying, thieving, promiscuity of all kinds, drunkenness, violence, murder ... there was not one crime I did not commit.[11]

As the capstone of sins, alcoholism was a central issue in Tolstoi's idiosyncratic interpretation of Christianity. In his essay "Why do People Drug Themselves" (1890), Tolstoi said that when one asked people why they used drugs, they responded, if they had thought at all about the matter, that it was because it was pleasant, it made one feel joyous, or it passed the time. Tolstoi, however, believed that those were not the true reasons and posited that all men have two natures: the physical, which is blind, and the spiritual, which can see. This sight, or ability to judge one's actions, is called "conscience." He continued, "It is not because of taste, pleasure, or amusement that a person consumes hashish, opium, liquor, tobacco, but because of a desire to suffocate the demands of conscience."[12] He came to this conclusion after overhearing a cab driver saying in connection with committing a crime, "It would be a shame to do that if one were not drunk." That comment provided a sudden flash of insight: the purpose for getting drunk was to put oneself in a condition to rob, rape, murder, and commit other shameful acts not permitted by conscience. This theory was confirmed for him when he learned that a servant had tried to murder an old woman related to Tolstoi because she had dismissed the servant's lover, but he could not bring himself to do the dreadful deed until he took two glasses of vodka.

Not only were 90 percent of all crimes committed in a state of inebriation, claimed Tolstoi, but half of all women who lost their virtue were drunk at the time. The connection between crime and drunkenness is no accident, he said. A soldier must be drunk to kill, so the army gives him vodka. In short, Tolstoi did not see drunkenness as an existential problem, a desirable state sought for its own sake, but rather, drunkenness was teleological: a person deliberately sought the deadening of conscience because he had some sort of nefarious goal that he would be incapable of accomplishing were he sober. "They drink and they smoke, not from boredom, not to become merry, not because it is pleasant, but in order to stifle their conscience."[13]

In addition to his temperance society, Tolstoi wrote numerous essays, short stories, and several plays to combat the use of alcohol. *The First Moonshiner; or, How the Demon Earned His Bread,* which was his first morally instructive play, was staged for factory workers in St. Petersburg in 1886.[14] Like the official Guardianship of Public Sobriety, Tolstoi felt that he could make his point through popular theater. The plot of this lively comedy is simple: the demon in charge of peasants was not hauling as many souls as Satan wished into hell, but the demons in charge of noblemen, merchants, priests, women, judges, and even monks were meeting their quotas with no difficulty. As for the demon in charge of lawyers—his success was phenomenal. Impressed by the record of other demons and driven by diabolic emulation, the peasants' demon hatched a scheme. For a long time the demon had not been able to make a certain peasant curse even when the demon had stolen his only crust of bread. The honest peasant even wished the unknown thief (the demon) a hearty appetite! So the little devil returned to the home of this good peasant and transformed his meager grain into a bumper crop, which overflowed the granary. Posing as a farm laborer, the demon told the peasant that *he* knew what to do with the surplus grain:

> *Farm hand.* What to do with it? From this grain here I'll make
>   such good stuff for yuh that yuh'll be happy the rest of yur life.
> *Peasant.* What'll yuh make?
> *Farm hand.* A drink, that's what. Such a drink that if yuh's tired,
>   it'll pick yuh up; if yuh're hungry, it'll fill yuh; if yuh're restless,
>   it'll put yuh to sleep; if yuh're sad, it'll make yuh happy. If

yuh're afraid, it'll give yuh courage. that's the kind of drink I'll
make.[15]

Needless to say, the honest peasant and his wife, indeed all the men in
the village, began to drink, then to dance, then to curse, then to fight, then
to fall down from inebriation. The final orgiastic scene drove home the
message:

> Farm hand. Did'ya see? Now their pig's blood is talkin'. They've
> turned from wolves into pigs. [Points to peasant.] There he is,
> like a boar in muck, gruntin'.
> Chief [Satan]. You've done it! First like foxes, then like wolves, and
> now they're like pigs.

The last line of the play has Satan speaking to the demon in charge of
peasants: "Good boy! You've earned your bread. Now if only they'd keep
on drinking booze, we'll always have them in our hands."[16]

This play is only a sample of the kind of didactic and popular pieces
Tolstoi turned his hand to in the mid-1880s. In 1884, with his friend and
disciple V. G. Chertkov, he founded a nonprofit publishing house, Posrednik
(Intermediary), in Moscow expressly to disseminate such literature to a
popular audience.[17] Because of the moralistic tone of these publications,
many of them were stocked by the Guardianship libraries, despite Tolstoi's
personal disdain for the state organization.

Between 1878 and 1910, most of Tolstoi's writings were nonfiction pieces
such as Stories for the People, which included such famous stories as "What
Men Live By" and "How Much Land Does a Man Need?" Even Tolstoi's
last long novel, Resurrection (1899), criticized contemporary society from
a religious viewpoint and included a condemnation of drunkenness. The
great artist's preoccupation with his crusade against drink is reflected in his
letters. At the end of January 1888, Tolstoi wrote to his artist friend I. I.
Repin that he was writing three essays on drunkenness. Impressed by the
cover Repin had drawn to illustrate the physical harm done by syphilis, he
asked him to produce three illustrations: "Choose the subjects of all three
yourself, but make them as terrible, powerful, and directly relevant to the
subject as your picture on syphilis." Tolstoi went on to state, "I have not
been well recently and because of that it is taking me a long time to finish
my article on drunkenness ["Time to Come to Our Senses"], and I want
to get it up by the roots. It is a subject of enormous importance. Give me
encouragement." Repin replied that he would be happy to send illustrations,
asking if he wanted them for a cover or for the interior of a book. Two
years later, Repin sent an illustration for The First Moonshiner, but for
unknown reasons, only a few copies were printed.[18] Tolstoi soon asked

another artist, N. N. Ge, one of the members of his sobriety union, "Could you draw a picture about drunkenness? I need two—one big one, and also a vignette for all publications on this subject."[19] Tolstoi was churning out antialcohol pieces, and he wanted good-quality illustrations to enhance their appeal.

Oddly enough, in 1909, it was Tolstoi's turn to make an antialcohol drawing. Duma representative M. D. Chelyshev, who was elected on an antivodka platform, asked him to design a label to be put on all bottles of state vodka.[20] His design, a skull and crossbones, was accompanied by a simple warning: "Poison!"[21] The Duma voted that all bottles of vodka would be so labeled, but the Council tabled the bill.[22] Had it passed, Russia would have been eighty years ahead of the United States in warning that alcohol is a health danger. By the time the Council dismissed the idea, Tolstoi was dead.

Although Tolstoi wrote his morality plays and tracts for peasants and workers, he did not consider them to be alone in their overindulgence. He reserved some of his more vitriolic words for the intelligentsia, as in 1889, when he lambasted in an article the drunken behavior of the Moscow intelligentsia in their celebration of Tat'iana Day, January 12, the foundation day of Moscow University.[23] He exhorted the intelligentsia not to demean themselves and set a bad example before "lackeys, cab drivers, porters, and village people." Although it was true, he said, that peasants spend from 20 kopecks to a ruble during their parish holiday celebrations, educated people spend from 6 to 20 rubles on alcohol on Tat'iana Day. The article was republished and hotly debated in many journals. Students at Novorossiskii University wrote in the local paper, *Odesskii listok,* that they had read his diatribe against Tat'iana's celebration and in defiance gathered together to drink to Tolstoi's health. They said as long as they were young, they would drink during their parties, but perhaps in old age, no doubt alluding to Tolstoi himself, they might shut themselves up in a shell.[24]

It might be expected that Tolstoi the populist would attack the intelligentsia, but other social critics also singled them out for upbraiding. A writer for the newspaper *Utro rossii* condemned clergymen, officers, students, doctors, surveyors, teachers, merchants, traders, writers, artists, journalists—professionals who drank themselves into a stupor. "Alcoholism is the dreadful ailment of our nation; this is the scourge of our time. If we are to fight it, the struggle must begin with the healing of the intelligentsia."[25] In his view, virtually all the intelligentsia were in the grip of drink, "Alcoholism surrounds the entire life of the intelligentsia. The member of the intelligentsia who is not in such a state is actually considered a lunatic, an abnormal person."[26]

Tolstoi and the author of the article agreed that although it was lamentable that workers and peasants were also afflicted with alcoholism, the artistic, cultural, and spiritual life of the country and its future were in the hands of the intelligentsia. Tolstoi rejected moderate drinking for the intelligentsia, as for anyone else. He insisted that humans must always be fully conscious. Drinking moderately in some ways was worse than total inebriation, for it was an escape from solving problems. When people said to him, "Look at all those people who have achieved so much in the arts, science, and politics and who drink in moderation," Tolstoi would answer, "But think of what they might have done had they been completely sober."[27] The fact that some temperance workers accused members of their own professions and class of alcoholism weakens the argument that temperance workers were attempting to turn the lower classes into upstanding, virtuous, hardworking people, created in their own (bourgeois) image.[28]

Tolstoi was concerned not only with the individual but with society as a whole. He thought that a drunk could not love his neighbor, and since society must be built on Christian love, the good of the nation required renunciation of drink.[29] In his brochure *Christian Teaching*, Tolstoi exhorted people to flee the desire for the stimulation of drink. The solution lay in intense introspection.[30] By the wide cultivation of interior enlightenment, society would get rid of its present drunken leaders and experience rebirth. Since Tolstoi did not believe in an afterlife, it was extremely important to him that individuals perfect themselves and society here on earth, a goal attainable only through sobriety.

Although Tolstoi created his own temperance movement, he was respected by leaders of other organizations, including the physicians involved with the Commission on the Question of Alcoholism of the Russian Society for the Preservation of Public Health. On the occasion of his eightieth birthday, they sent him a telegram of congratulations and noted that they were in the process of planning the All-Russian Congress on the Struggle against Drunkenness. But Tolstoi, already very ill, could not attend; indeed he died during the congress.[31] Afterward, the Commission on the Question of Alcoholism held a meeting commemorating the life of Tolstoi.[32] All the members of the meeting rose in respect for the memory of two outstanding temperance leaders who had just died: Tolstoi and Dr. D. A. Dril', whom they called an indefatigable warrior for public sobriety. They noted that while Tolstoi waged his war on religious principles, Dril' waged his on economic and biological principles.[33] Speeches and papers were dedicated to Tolstoi's struggle against alcohol. Chelyshev said that Tolstoi was listened to only by the lower classes and urged that sobriety be preached to all classes.[34] And yet, no one was more militant about reaching all classes than Tolstoi, who proclaimed that "the ugliness and, above all, the meaninglessness of our life stems primarily from the constant state of drunkenness in which the majority of our people of all classes, callings, and positions are now to be found."[35]

Tolstoi's passionate views on alcoholism may seem not to have gained a following beyond the small group of his committed disciples, but an American temperance writer credited him for having helped the tsar arrive at the idea of prohibition, claiming that "the temperance teachings of Tolstoi have filtered into the remotest corners of Russia."[36] It is impossible to estimate how many people Tolstoi persuaded to accept his views, but it cannot be assumed that his message touched only the politically conservative such as the tsar. Vladimir Bonch-Bruevich, a socialist and defender of sectarians, was solicitous in 1911 to save all the memorabilia of Tolstoi's temperance union for the Tolstoi Museum. He later became a Bolshevik physician put in charge of a committee to quell riots fueled by alcohol after the 1917 revolutions.[37] In 1933, he and Stalin's director of culture, Anatoly V. Lunarcharsky, edited some of Tolstoi's works.[38]

Although Tolstoi's organization was a precocious experiment, there is not much recorded about its activities. We do have, however, records of many other temperance organizations established in cities by laypersons, although doctors and priests were frequently among the chief activists. The Finnish and Baltic areas of the empire led the way. Some Finns of the Russian Empire were organized as early as 1816. Various temperance societies were formed in the 1840s, 1850s, and continuously thereafter in Russian Finland. The first temperance journal emerged in 1883, as did tracts against alcohol published in Finnish.[39] In 1887, a Finnish merchant tailor founded the temperance society Alku, which had not only a large membership in Finland but also a branch in St. Petersburg numbering about 200 members in 1898.[40] Even Finnish and Estonian convicts in Siberia formed temperance societies.[41]

The Finnish movement was influenced by American, British, and German temperance societies.[42] There was even a branch of the American organization the Women's Christian Temperance Union in Finland.[43] But the Finnish movement was not limited to the middle class, women, or the educated. Some 70,000 workers, male and female, staged a "strike" against alcohol on May 1, 1898, when they vowed not to drink for an entire year and made a series of demands, including the closure of liquor stores. These demonstrations took place in various Finnish cities at the same time. The workers were sending a political message that they wanted the Russian vodka monopoly out of their territory. In 1907, the Finnish parliament went so far as to vote in favor of prohibition, but neither the Finnish Senate nor Russian imperial authorities approved the law, so that it did not take effect until prohibition was declared throughout the Russian Empire in 1914.[44]

The numerous Finnish organizations emanated primarily from the working class, as in all the Baltic area. Part of the antialcohol protest was a class protest, but it certainly also involved ethnic and religious rebellion against Russian hegemony as well.[45] An American temperance worker claimed that

the temperance movement there was considered "as being generally promoted by the revolutionary element [so] that the Russian government has
always been suspicious of the Baltic anti-alcohol reformers. . . . It represents
a revolt against the baronial brewer and the Russian government vodka
monopoly."[46]

The official tsarist view was that not only were temperance organizations
subversive but because so many had originated in Protestant sects, they
might also lead to sectarianism among the Orthodox. For example, an
American temperance crusader, Reverend Robert Baird, author of the
widely translated and distributed *History of the Temperance Societies in
America,* visited St. Petersburg in 1835 and was received by Nicholas I. We
do not know what transpired during that visit, but we do know that in
1836, a Latvian pastor published information from Baird's book, and in 1842,
when he attempted to form temperance societies, Nicholas I would not
permit them, "lest they should be mistaken for separate religious sects."[47]
The vigor with which the Russian authorities suppressed temperance organizations among the Letts, even forbidding the clergy to speak against
alcoholism, indicates that they feared ethnic protest as much as lost liquor
revenues.[48] By 1909, even the Catholic Church had established a temperance
union in Latvia, which made clear that their purposes were not political.
Hence, it was tolerated.

Given St. Petersburg's proximity to the Baltic and Finnish areas, it is not
surprising that it was the home of the first Russian lay temperance society
after Tolstoi's Union against Drunkenness.[49] Founded in 1890 during a cholera epidemic, the St. Petersburg Temperance Society counted among its
members physicians, politicians, priests, professors, and princes.[50] They
seem to have pioneered the idea of substituting amusements for alcohol, a
strategy adopted later by the Guardianship and other temperance societies.
They offered balalaika concerts and other popular entertainments, for which
active members paid dues of 3 rubles per year, whereas honorary members
paid 5 rubles. They put on plays: nearly ten thousand performances between
1900 and 1913, with a repertoire of 667 different plays. One Russian critic
claimed that although the society had built tearooms for workers, these
tearooms did not match the number or amenities of those of similar organizations in Western Europe.[51] What they lacked in tearooms, they com-
pensated for with their meals-on-wheels, fielding "twenty-two moveable
lunch rooms using nine horse wagons, three automobiles, six platforms and
four hand carts," from which they served hot meals just before World War
I.[52]

The society in St. Petersburg enjoyed the support and encouragement of
some of their more important members, such as Count Tol', chief of the
port and, later, governor of St. Petersburg. Admiral Verkhovskii had an
auditorium built that could hold 2,000 persons and obtained from the Min-

istry of the Navy a subsidy of 1,000 rubles to build a tearoom and cafeteria near the port.[53] In 1894, General Studzinskii got 1,500 rubles from the Ministry of War to build a tearoom for the workers in a gunpowder factory. Countess Panina contributed a public reading room with a rich collection of books in 1896. By 1898, the society estimated that it would spend 23,000 rubles on building cheap housing outside the city.[54]

As is evident, the lay society in the capital adopted many of the strategies later used by the Guardianship; they opened tearooms, asylums, clinics, and libraries; provided clothes and cheap living quarters; and distributed antialcohol literature. They also organized orchestras, choruses, shows, parties, and lectures. How many alcoholics were lured away from drink as a result of all this activity is impossible to know, but some material and cultural improvements were brought into the lives of workers. And as they attended these mass entertainments, they became used to being part of large assemblies.

Medical assistance was somewhat less in evidence, since it took six years for the St. Petersburg Temperance Society to build a clinic. It opened in 1896, supported not with state funds but with large donations from merchants. Patients who volunteered to come for treatment maintained their anonymity, except with the doctors, and they paid only if they could afford it. The average length of stay, which included both medical treatment and physical labor, typically lasted from four to six months. The St. Petersburg Temperance Society envisioned eventually opening about twenty-five clinics in the environs of the capital, including some for women and children who were not receiving clinical care.[55]

Whereas the St. Petersburg Temperance Society was a citywide organization, some advocates of temperance dedicated their time and resources to a single factory; for example, E. L. Nobel' had a People's House built at the Liudvig Nobel' factory in St. Petersburg in 1901. The elaborate building contained an auditorium where workers were treated to lectures on science, history, geography, and literature, as well as the usual concerts, including worker choirs that provided cheap entertainment in the evenings, on Sundays, and on holidays. The purpose of instructing and amusing workers was undoubtedly not only to keep them out of taverns but also to shape a more reliable workforce.[56]

The capital was also the site of a nonclerical religious organization, the All-Russian Working Union of Christian Temperance Workers, which began its work in 1911, under the protection of Grand Duke Konstantin Konstantinovich; its primary target was young people.[57] One member, Dr. Verzhbitskii, claimed that in St. Petersburg there was universal drinking among children. For example, in a school with fifty girls aged eight to sixteen, only two never drank. Of those who drank, thirty-eight drank beer and ten drank vodka. In a working-district school for children aged eight to eleven, of the forty-three students, nine drank a glass of vodka each night before dinner, fourteen drank on holidays, and sixteen had gotten drunk at least once in their lives. The physician concluded that parents gave children access to alcohol and that the All-Russian Working Union should attempt to address this issue.

The society sponsored an "antialcohol day" on September 29, 1911.[58] It began with a public prayer service held in the Aleksander Hall of the city duma. Members, many of them students, then fanned out throughout St. Petersburg with boxes for donations and with temperance brochures, which were purchased chiefly by working women and had sold out by three in the afternoon. They collected over 7,000 rubles in sales and donations that day. An indication of how the state equated social activism with subversion is the fact that when Father Tikhomirov, a chaplain in the army, was selling brochures for this event in the Nikolaevskii railroad station, a person in full military dress uniform asked him to leave. Authorities also barred temperance activists from the waiting room of the Tsarskoe Selo station. Despite some incidents of harassment by the police, the day of campaigning ended with a choir concert.

Five years after the founding of the St. Petersburg Temperance Society, a counterpart was established in Moscow. The First Moscow Temperance Society was organized "by simple workers from the factories who wished 'to conduct themselves well.' "[59] Members were primarily factory workers, artisans, and petty traders, mostly with little education. Tolstoi accepted honorary membership in this society since its goals matched his own.[60] Three years after its founding, it had sufficient funds to build five tearooms and libraries and put together choruses and Sunday schools to teach literacy. According to an account of the first ten years of its activities, the Til' factory was the headquarters of a new branch with 90 members, which soon grew to 276. In 1900, in addition to the tearoom, a library opened for reading, lectures, and magic-lantern shows, and the following year, a new cafeteria was opened to entice workers away from taverns. By 1908, the society offered evening courses to adults. Workers and factory managers played a leading role in the life of the Moscow society, whereas the St. Petersburg Society appeared to comprise professional groups and notables.[61] The Moscow society's official report gave the names of the workers most active over the decade, noting that there had been 1,500 members in all as of 1908. Over the decade, the library grew to 1,500 volumes, the tearoom served 90,000 people, and 100,000 rubles had been invested in the temperance society.

The first Exhibit on Alcoholism, which opened in Moscow on December 8, 1908, was sponsored, not by a temperance society, but by the Moscow Society for the Building of Popular Libraries and Reading Rooms. The initiative for such an exhibit came from one of the members of the society,

Actual State Counselor V. D. Levinskii, but the support came from the Ministry of Finance.[62] The infusion of temperance ideas into other societies is difficult to measure, but this is one clear manifestation of how temperance percolated throughout another organization.

It is impossible to gauge how much sobriety was induced by all these efforts, but the growing temperance societies composed of workers encouraged literacy, the forming of credit unions, and the notion that workers could take control of their lives. A skilled worker noted around the turn of the century: "We thought of our contributions [to credit unions] as going not to ordinary mutual-aid funds, but to the goal of revolutionary struggle."[63] The societies created a milieu conducive to a serious examination of their urban, work, and home environments, as well as contemplation of how to remedy deficiencies. It is not surprising, therefore, that in large urban areas with temperance societies involving workers, such as Moscow and Odessa, the police unions organized by Sergei Zubatov took hold. Zubatov himself told workers: "Your task is to study and teach the workers a general educational knowledge, to fight against drunkenness, and defend your economic rights; political struggle is a 'pastime for the high and mighty.' "[64] Zubatov intended to keep workers' agitation limited to economic issues, but political demands entered their agendas, resulting in unexpected strikes. These unintended consequences led to Zubatov's dismissal from government service.

Even the workers' association headed by Father Gapon included among its prominent activities a temperance society. He was the leader of a peaceful protest in January 1905, when Nicholas II's police fired on the crowd, resulting in the infamous Bloody Sunday. When workers actively took part in temperance associations, they learned that they had to renew their own lives, but they also learned that society could be renewed as well; many of them resolved to do both.

Temperance societies flourished not only in the two capital cities and the Baltic regions but also on the eastern periphery of European Russia. Tatars, who in general did not drink alcohol, were not in the majority in the city of Kazan. In 1917, they made up only 22 percent of the city's population. Seventy percent of approximately 207,000 urban inhabitants were Russians, with Jews forming only 4 percent. The rest were of a dozen different ethnic groups. There was a sizable population of factory workers, about 20,000.[65] Unlike many important temperance societies, the one in Kazan was founded in 1892 principally by professors from the local university, although it was supported by the local metropolitan and governor, who were honorary members. By the end of 1904, the Kazan Temperance Society had 2,882 members. By 1898, the society had put up 56,882 paying and 1,292 nonpaying guests in their night shelters. It had also founded a home for orphans, where they were taught to read and do various crafts. Seminarians visited the orphanage and night shelters to conduct religious conversations. The Red Cross helped the society open a dining hall.[66] The opening of the first clinic in the entire Russian Empire for the cure of alcoholics in 1896 was a welcome addition to the many services already performed by the Kazan Temperance Society.[67]

The ceremony opening the clinic included prayers led by Archbishop Vladimir of Kazan and speeches given by the governor, the city chief, the rector of the university, the president of the temperance group, A. T. Solov'ev, and other dignitaries. The hospital had nine beds (for men only) and would treat chronic alcoholics who wanted to be cured of their addiction and those suffering nervous illnesses as a consequence of alcoholism. All patients would enter voluntarily. If the patient wanted to take on an assumed name while in the hospital to protect his identity, that would be possible. The hospital would keep patients busy in a homelike atmosphere.[68]

Earlier that year, an anonymous writer offered the opinion, in an article published by the Kazan Temperance Society's journal *Deiatel'*, that "there is no doubt from the scientific point of view that chronic alcoholism is an illness with the predominance of a spiritual disorder more or less clearly manifested."[69] Tolstoi, who once studied at the University of Kazan, would have been in full agreement with that statement. The author claimed optimistically that there was a 30–50 percent cure rate, although he admitted that some of the internal and external medicines were of dubious effectiveness unless the drinker himself changed. Only if a chronic alcoholic changed his habits and activities that accompanied his drinking patterns could he be cured. He noted that the wealthy could change the environment that led to their drinking, but the poor found it more difficult to change their work, their companions, and the occasions for drink. Since Russia was relatively poor compared with Western Europe, it could not match the hundreds of societies abroad in Europe and America with their hundreds of thousands of members and dozens of hospitals devoted exclusively to the cure of alcoholics. As an indication of conditions in Russia, he claimed that in St. Petersburg alone each week, some 900 persons were found dead from drink on the streets.[70] Most drunks sober up, return to their everyday existence, get drunk again, and either perish on the streets or in ordinary hospitals as a consequence of their drunkenness. Many of these individuals, he argued, could be saved if only there were clinics expressly for the care of alcoholics.

A professor from the University of Kazan and the chief doctor of the society's clinic, Dr. L. O. Darkshevich, submitted a report in 1896 in which he stressed that all patients must come to the clinic voluntarily, as their cooperation was necessary for their cure, even if at times their stay was lengthy. To force the unwilling would be tantamount to providing free shelter indefinitely, an expense too great for the society.[71] Once patients made progress, they were released to return to work. They could return to the clinic, however, as outpatients and, if necessary, receive free meals and shelter. Patients were urged to report immediately to the clinic should they feel they were about to take a drink. But the decision to return had to be made by the alcoholic himself. The doctor recounted "a case in our hospital in which a sick person came in on the insistence of his wife, stayed six weeks in the clinic without drinking, but left without our permission only to pursue his intemperate life."[72]

Darkshevich condemned the Guardianship's policy of entertaining the masses and criticized the content of the plays for not being sufficiently moral. He called for measures that, if enforced, would have been tantamount to prohibition. No less sweeping were the demands made by the society's president, A. Solov'ev, who in 1910 asked that no new liquor stores be allowed without the express permission of the local inhabitants. That would put power in the hands of the people, who could petition only for the closing of existing stores, and since relatively few such petitions received favorable responses, it was important that people have the power to veto the establishment of liquor stores in the first instance. Other stated that communities should have the right to close down bootlegging places and that vodka should be sold in reduced strengths and in large bottles only, so as to discourage consumption of the contents on the spot. Solov'ev presented these recommendations to members of the state Duma, who were discussing legislation for reducing alcoholism.[73]

When the vodka monopoly was introduced in Kazan, the society had approved the introduction of state liquor stores, believing that drunkenness would be reduced because of the purity of the product.[74] As time went on, however, the Kazan society became more and more unhappy with the Guardianship and with the vodka monopoly. As noted earlier, they went so far as to call members of the state Guardianship drunkards and subversives.

The journal of the Kazan society, *Deiatel'*, contained many articles that reveal the extremely conservative nature of the organization, its nationalistic fervor, and its increasing anti-Semitism. The ultranationalism of the society is reflected in their comparisons between French drunkards and Russian ones. French workers, reported one article, drank coffee with rum or cognac at six in the morning, a half liter of wine at eight, a glass of absinthe at half past ten, another coffee with rum at noon, and a half liter of wine at four o'clock, topping the evening off at six with another glass of absinthe. The French worker purportedly spent one-half of his pay on this tippling. Death from drinking was not unknown to French youths of fifteen to twenty years. Furthermore, the article continued, patients in French hospitals consumed 3 million liters of red wine and 3,000 liters of rum in 1898. The author claimed that the idea of a special hospital for alcoholics was not raised in France until 1899 (three years after the opening of the clinic in

Kazan), but even when one was opened, hospitalized French alcoholics had access to wine. *Deiatel'* concluded that even less has been done in France than in Russia to combat alcoholism.[75] The situation in Germany, according to *Deiatel'*, was not much better. The consumption of alcohol grew annually, and not until 1880 were temperance societies formed that demanded full abstinence from drink. This staunch patriotic author also claimed that workers in Germany were worse off than in Russia, since more than half of them had no permanent lodgings, only night shelters.

Although the Kazan Temperance Society claimed that Russian workers were not as bad off as European workers, they denied that granting Russian workers civil rights would contribute to their sobriety. Singling out an individual with an obvious Jewish surname, L. M. Gol'dmershtein, they derided him as "a liberal dignitary." He had told the Commission on the Question of Alcoholism set up by the Duma that people would not be inclined to sobriety until they had civil rights. Father Mikhail Galkin, later the editor of *Bezbozhnik,* said the reason the lower classes had so few personal rights in Russia is precisely because they *were* drunks.[76] "Look at the United States," he exclaimed; "there where there is a rule of law, people drink twice as much as in Russia. Or look at England, Germany, or Austria, where they also drink twice as much, or look at the 'free Belgians,' who drink five time more than Russians, and as for the French Republicans, terrible to say, even seven times more. No," the priest concluded, "Russians are not to look to 'drunken Europe,' . . . but we are to look to our own Muslims and Old Believers who don't drink at all."[77]

Not only did Father Galkin reject Europeans as models for sobriety, but he also denied that alcoholism was a result of poor living conditions, low wages, and long hours of heavy work. He claimed that women, especially Tatar women, worked extremely hard for as many as sixteen hours a day, yet they did not turn to drink. He concluded that "in the large cities, there are more places of entertainment, and the more that people amuse themselves, the more they drink. In the city, they eat better, are better housed, and earn more than in the countryside, but they also drink more. In the city, there is more so-called enlightenment and more drunkenness."[78] This conservative writer did not want the blame for drinking to rest with the tsarist regime, which was being denounced by radicals for creating poor living and working conditions and denying workers civil rights. The Kazan Temperance Society appeared to be even more patriotic than the First Moscow Temperance Society and more conservative than the clerical temperance societies in general.[79]

While the distant Kazan society appears to have been extremely conservative, the Odessa Temperance Society, founded in 1891, was more radical. According to the newspaper *Odesskie novosti,* G. Iaryshkin, a member of the lower class, dominated everything in the society. "He himself composed the books, wrote the reports, and wanted no one to function outside his authority." The more educated members of the group sneered at him.[80] We have already seen that Odessa students mocked Tolstoi's injunction to university students not to drink. Resistance to temperance in Odessa was manifested also in the fate of Sergei Balashov, who suggested that a tavern be closed, a proposal that so irked some drinkers that they murdered him. The Odessa Temperance Society debated whether to name a school for him or erect a monument to his memory.[81] When temperance days were proclaimed in the city in the spring of 1914, there was massive noncompliance. Even though some vodka-dispensing places closed, drinkers quickly found alcohol at buffets in railroad stations and in theaters so that they got even drunker on those dry holidays, unlike the more upstanding citizens of the capital, who supposedly observed the dry days.[82]

Virtually every region had its own temperance societies. To provide the names of a few, the Archangel Society was founded in 1892 on the shores of the White Sea. It enjoyed the support of the intelligentsia and the governor of Archangel. The Kiev Southwestern Temperance Society had branches in Podolia and Volynia; its members were required only "to lead upright working lives and to use alcoholic drinks moderately." In 1898, lay temperance societies were founded in Tula and in Astrakhan. Nearly all of them were established after the state took over the vodka industry.

In the early twentieth century, lay societies such as the Society for Fighting against Alcohol in the Public Schools began to target certain drinkers, including children. In the Russian branch, Professor A. A. Kornilov of the University of Moscow was president, and the president of the Moscow Temperance Society was an honorary member. A good many physicians also were members of the society. It is apparent that like Tolstoi many temperance activists belonged to more than one society.

All lay societies had to support themselves from membership dues and donations, although occasionally the Guardianship disbursed small subsidies. In 1904 and 1905, for example, the Guardianship distributed 180,487 rubles per year, or about 5.8 percent of its funds furnished by the Ministry of Finance. The small sum was distributed unevenly among various provinces, with some receiving none at all, since it could not fund projects or groups advocating total abstinence. The paltry amount given to lay societies went principally to support amusements, an activity it endorsed. The Guardianship gave out only 6,000 rubles to subsidize antialcohol periodicals.[83]

As this brief survey illustrates, lay temperance societies were as diverse as Russian society itself. Some were organized along ethnic lines, such as Alku, a society for Estonians in Estonia and Estonians living in St. Petersburg. Others were organized by occupations, such as physicians or railroad workers, who formed their own society with sixty-nine branches throughout the empire by World War I.[84] Even university students had their own organizations.[85] Other societies were formed to minister to particular groups, such as workers and children. In his summary of temperance activity in Russia at the turn of the century, the activist Dr. A. M. Korovin said that the most gratifying aspect of the lay societies was the support they gave to workers in factories, such as the Narva cloth mill and the Poliakov factory in Moscow Province, the Tver factory and the Votkinsk works in Viatka Province, and the Nizhne-Tagil' factory and the Nev'ianskii works in Perm. What was so remarkable, he claimed, was that in a ten-year period, there had been such intense and widespread activity, reaching as far as Siberia. The societies had been a force for education, moral uplift, and creation of a more hygienic and democratic life: "The temperance societies have made it possible to destroy those social barriers which remained as a consequence of emancipation, so that the simple people are trained to see in the *intelligent*, not the *barin* (master), but simply a mortal to whom he can relate with trust and respect for scientific truth. Conversely, the educated have had an opportunity to get closer to the people and to learn their daily customs." He also noted that it was the simple people, not the educated, who took the initiative to form temperance societies in the countryside. This phenomenon showed clearly how much the people wanted to improve their existence; these self-help temperance societies would "certainly leave deep traces in the history of culture in Russia."[86]

It is impossible to judge if Korovin's sanguine conclusions were accurate. It is safe to say, however, that thousands of laypeople organized societies to promote sobriety in ways they saw fit. It is evident that they were formed not only by the educated class but by all classes of people. All of them were in agreement that the Guardianship was not the answer to the problem of alcoholism. The Kazan Temperance Society frowned on their entertainments for being too worldly, whereas other groups claimed the Guardianship was simply ineffectual because of its bureaucratic structure and refusal to preach total abstinence from alcohol.

Lay temperance organizations fostered solidarity among various professions and ethnic and religious groups, but they also appeared to have adapted very much to the culture of their location.[87] The laity emphasized entertainment in St. Petersburg, the welfare of workers in Moscow, and the peculiar combination of medical care, ultranationalism, and anti-Semitism in Kazan. To the extent that workers themselves learned to read, think, and organize within temperance groups, they became more powerful agents in determining their future and that of the empire. It was not only that professional people were engaging in civic activities, the much discussed volunteerism of late imperial Russia, but their frustrations and the workers' frustrations led at times to the conclusion that the regime had to be changed or, since the altered state of drinkers was so difficult to eradicate, the state itself would have to be altered by radical measures.[88]

The nature of debates over alcoholism and sobriety led to diverse political opinions. Even the views of Tolstoi are difficult to place on a political spectrum. His belief that a weak will and a desire to stifle one's conscience, rather than poverty, caused drunkenness would place him on the Right. Like the conservative priest Father Galkin of Kazan, he did not subscribe to the environmental theory that the tsarist regime's indifference to poverty and suffering caused excessive drinking.[89] For Tolstoi, it was a question of an individual's morals. Yet his rejection of both the official church and the state—his refusal to obey their laws, pay taxes, or serve in the military, as a protest against war and the vodka monopoly—puts him on the Left. His close associate Vladimir D. Bonch-Bruevich, who in 1899 worked in V. G. Chertkov's publishing house in England, which printed Tolstoi's books, was active in trying to preserve Tolstoi's temperance memorabilia. After the Bolshevik revolution, he became a communist coeditor with Lunacharsky, Stalin's director of culture. As the careers of Bonch-Bruevich and numerous others confirm and as the state correctly surmised, when laypersons formed temperance societies, they might easily escape the state's control.

8 . . . .

THE POLITICS OF ALCOHOL

That politics was at the heart of the temperance movement is shown by the fact that physicians and liberals hailed the October Manifesto of 1905, which created the Duma and guaranteed civil rights, as the instrument that freed them from silence on the causes of alcoholism. As Dr. A. M. Korovin exulted in October 1905: "Words were straining to be free but were held back in vices. We spoke earlier of drunkenness but not in connection with the circumstances that generated it." Up until now, he said, one could thunder against alcoholism as an evil, as a sickness, but one could not identify the causes, such as insufficient education, inadequate food, low wages, or the long working day and unhygienic working conditions. Korovin had been blocked by the authorities from delivering a paper entitled "The Alcohol Problem and the Working Class," but he boldly asserted that it was the fault of Tsar Nicholas II himself that he had been muzzled. He railed against the arbitrariness of the censorship that would not allow him to connect alcoholism with indigence or, more pointedly, with the regime:

> It is not permitted to say that alcohol becomes one of
> the tools of oppression, namely, that it helps keep the
> working class in the state of being deceived and in
> penury, and weakens the mind and will that they pa-
> tiently bear their yoke with little material security. It
> was forbidden to say that alcohol suppresses their an-
> ger over their fate, that alcohol is one of the factors
> that hinders the workers' consciousness of their unat-
> tractive existence, that fills their hearts with thousands
> of stupid hopes "that it will be better."[1]

Even more subversively, Korovin suggested that only if they formed unions could workers improve their conditions. To create unions was a function of the brain, he claimed, and because alcohol harms the brain, all those who want to take control of their future must be sober. He compared the manifesto of October 17 to the emancipation, saying that now not only serfs but all Russians had been freed. "Thank God, today we are citizens! We can, we dare, speak publicly that which is in our minds and hearts. . . . We can meet and form unions for the betterment of the people."[2]

Whereas Korovin considered political freedom to be a necessary condition for getting to the root cause of alcoholism, another socialist physician, G. I. Dembo, believed that the lack of political rights itself caused alcoholism.[3] For Social Democrats, alcoholism was an offense against socialist discipline and ethics. Employers took advantage of alcoholic workers by paying them low wages, supplying them with vodka to keep them on the job. Drunkards could not sustain successful strikes, but they often became strikebreakers. Certainly, drinking prevented workers from reflecting on their miserable status, a process necessary for raising their political consciousness. In short, workers had to be physically conscious before they could become class conscious.[4] Workers could not be blamed for drunkenness because it was rooted in their misery.

That the issue of vodka was politically charged was made manifest at the First All-Russian Congress for the Struggle against Drunkenness. At times, the proceedings almost degenerated into farce as various groups threatened to or actually did walk out. At the end of 1909, P. A. Stolypin, president of the Council of Ministers, convinced that the bourgeois intelligentsia had renounced its revolutionary mood of 1905 and having been assured that politics would not enter the discussions, not only endorsed the conference but also gave the organizing committee 10,000 rubles for expenses.[5]

The Society for the Preservation of Public Health under the auspices of its Commission on the Question of Alcoholism organized the 1909–10 antialcohol congress. They sent out 1,600 invitations to various institutions, organizations, and private persons to participate.[6] Those in attendance included a large contingent of physicians and others from the medical community, women (mostly from the teaching and medical professions), clerical delegates, members of the state Duma, and representatives from city dumas, zemstvos (provincial assemblies), universities, learned societies, and the Guardianship of Public Sobriety. A sizable delegation of socialist workers also appeared, alongside representatives from the Ministry of Finance and the usual contingent of police. With such a volatile mix, it was predictable that the congress would bristle with controversy, arguments, walkouts, denunciations of the regime, and arrests. The published reports are filled with frank, angry, and radical words by many of the participants.[7] Academics lashed out at restrictions on university autonomy, women demanded more legal rights, the church insisted on religious and moral education in all schools, representatives from organs of local government wanted to enlarge their powers, ethnic minorities sought more autonomy, and the socialist workers called for the right to organize, ostensibly in cooperatives but in reality in unions.[8] All of these political demands, it was claimed, had to be satisfied before the various groups could satisfactorily deal with the issue of drunkenness.[9]

When the congress failed to adopt a resolution that would include moral and religious education in the campaign against drunkenness in schools, the clergy felt rebuffed and stalked out; they thereupon organized their own All-Russian Congress of Church Temperance Workers, which met in Moscow in 1912.[10]

The Bolsheviks, encouraged by Lenin and sanctioned by the illegal newspaper *Sotsial-demokrat*, sent a delegation, which was considered suspect by the police. In preparation for the conference papers, workers in various regions, including St. Petersburg, Baku, Riga, and Narva, were polled concerning their views on the causes of alcoholism.[11] For months before the conference, workers from trade unions, workers' clubs, educational and cultural societies, as well as workers' temperance organizations, had researched the issue of alcoholism by sending out questionnaires. They had done all of this openly, meeting once a week on Sundays in order to discuss the problem, and yet a dozen workers were arrested and were put in prison for two months.[12]

During the conference the police from time to time took the names and addresses of workers and once ordered the chair to interrupt and forbid the presentation of one report, "The Development of the Relationship between Poverty and Alcoholism." Even Professor M. N. Nizhegorodtsev, the chair of the congress, asked the minister of the interior for an explanation for the arrests.[13]

Others were deemed too politically pernicious and were stopped by the government officials from delivering their papers on aloholism. One such was V. G. Chirkin, who linked the capitalist system with oppression and alcoholism and was forbidden to read his report by order of the city governor.

If the delegates had difficulties presenting papers because of their political content, they had even greater problems with their fellow delegates in attempting to pass acceptable resolutions. There were strong differences in ideologies and opinions on the touchy subject of alcoholism, as was manifested in the drawing up of resolutions at the conclusion of the congress. The worker delegates sought to delete the clauses on the importance of religious-moral education in the schools from a resolution and also defeated the doctors' clause insisting on total abstinence. The worker A. I. Iapynevich, a delegate of the Sampsonievskii Educational Society from the Petersburg Vyborg District, explained that total abstinence from alcohol would not be possible until workers had greater political rights. Calling total abstinence an unrealistic goal in contemporary circumstances, he argued, "the practical realization of this propaganda is impossible in the face of the existing political arbitrariness, with the lack of the right to gather, or of unions, or free speech in general for workers."[14] The Social Democratic deputy to the Third Duma, A. I. Predkal'n, defended the resolution of the working group with the same argument.

Instead of blaming workers for their drinking problem, socialists put the blame squarely on the regime itself by condemning its fiscal arm, the State Vodka Monopoly, putting forth a resolution at the plenary session of the third section of the congress on January 5, 1910, stating:

> The state monopoly in Russia, with close relations with landlords, with bureaucrats, and with the uncontrolled authority of the state economy, allows a wide scope for the enrichment of distillers at the expense of the entire population. Any kind of palliative measures such as decreasing the strength of liquor or raising its price would not change the pernicious system but on the contrary might lead to increasing the poverty of the masses.[15]

The workers did not spare the Guardianship either, another creation of the state, saying that it had "a pretentious, ostentatious character" and that the 2 million ruble annual subsidy was a waste of public money. Only if the Guardianship was transferred into the hands of local government and workers could it lead to practical results. Again, the chair muted the angry tone of the resolution at the last meeting, but not without protest from the workers' delegation. In the end, the resolutions of the delegate working groups were neither accepted nor rejected, since they were not put to a vote. The presidium no doubt feared the closing down of the congress with such incendiary resolutions.

Russkoe znamia, the Black Hundred reactionary paper, attacked the workers, claiming that "at this congress was a horde of agitators whose task it was to wreck the congress and deprive it of the possibility to take up the question of drunkenness with any kind of practical results."[16] The government showed its agreement. During the night after the closing of the congress (from January 6 to 7) and in the course of the following day, the police arrested about twenty worker delegates to the congress.

Not having carried the day at the congress, the socialists took their case to the Duma, where indeed the topic of drunkenness had been an issue since the convening of the Third Duma in 1907. As John Hutchinson has noted, "for the loyalist parties of the centre and the right, the government's complicity in the drink problem was a source of embarrassment, while for the opposition parties it was one of the most useful weapons in their arsenal of political slogans."[17] In 1907, the Duma created a Commission on the Means for the Struggle against Drunkenness, one of whose first resolutions passed was a request to the government that it not sell alcohol in districts suffering from famine.[18]

Within the Duma, the most outspoken opponent of the State Vodka Monopoly, or indeed to the dispensing of any alcohol, was M. D. Chelyshev, the formidable delegate from Samara. Like Tolstoi, he dressed as a peasant and promoted total abstinence, although he was a wealthy merchant and a self-educated man.[19] When he was mayor of Samara, he had urged his city duma to adopt a measure to forbid the sale of alcoholic beverages every-where—stores, inns, and hotels despite the fact that the city itself earned more than 30,000 rubles annually just from the liquor licenses of *traktirs* (cheap eating establishments). Since those suffering from abuse of liquor filled prisons, jails, and night shelters, which were costly to the city, the income was not worth the expense, he claimed. To balance out the accounts of the state treasury, he proposed that the city make a donation of 300,000 rubles per year to the state, raised from taxes on real estate, rather than have that amount derived from vodka sales to its 100,000 inhabitants.[20] If the provincial powers would not allow this measure, then Chelyshev pro-posed to lay it before His Imperial Majesty himself. The bill passed the city duma, but the government would not accept the appropriation in lieu of vodka sales. Chelyshev, who allied himself with the Octobrist Party, had the temerity to stand up on the floor of the Duma and state, sounding like a socialist, "It then dawned upon me that the Russian bureaucracy did not want the people to become sober, for the reason that it was easier to rule autocratically a drunken mob than a sober people."[21]

Once in the Duma, Chelyshev attempted to enlist to his cause the Com-mission on the Question of Alcoholism set up by the public health physi-cians ten years earlier. The committee of physicians and members of the intelligentsia did not agree with him that the monopoly should be abolished. Some of the physicians wanted sweeping social and economic reforms, not administrative changes.[22] Chelyshev then used the Duma as his forum to propose antialcohol legislation, calling for a voice vote in the Duma when-ever there was voting on matters pertaining to alcohol so that opponents to his proposals would be clearly identified.

In December 1907, he and thirty-two other deputies in the Duma proposed a one-eighth reduction in the production of alcohol and a simultaneous increase in its price over a period of four years beginning in 1909. To compensate for the reduction of vodka consumption in Russia, distilleries could increase production of industrial alcohol for export abroad. In May 1909, at the time of the debate on the bill in the Duma, members of the Left entered into the fray, stating that it was useless to tinker with controlling amounts and prices of vodka when the fundamental issue was a political one. People had to be given civil rights before they would choose to become sober, and the state should not profit from alcohol consumption. The Socialist Democratic delegate Predkal′n declared that civil rights were essential and if the government wanted to destroy drunkenness, it had to get rid of its revenue from vodka. Dziubinskii, another socialist, recommended making tea drinking cheaper by lowering taxes on sugar, and then perhaps the poor would reduce their consumption of cheap vodka. From the fall of 1908 to 1910, the commission did not move beyond debating the issue.

Although critics pointed out that there were many defects in the current bills pending in the Duma on the alcohol question, Cheylshev rose to the defense of the Duma, reminding critics that the Duma was fighting interested parties, including members of the Ministry of Finance, whose revenues depended on vodka sales.[23] By 1911, Chelyshev and his colleagues had proposed a new bill, which included legislation to impose fines of from 15 to 50 rubles and imprisonment for up to fourteen days for engaging in bootlegging. The bill proposed that sales of vodka be limited to only one bottle of vodka per person per day. Village assemblies, in which married women could vote, would have the power to forbid the introduction of state and private liquor stores.[24]

The bill also stated that liquor would not be sold in state buildings or places of amusement. Train engineers, ship captains, and others in the business of transportation and responsible for the safety of others would be checked for sobriety. The bill required better packaging of vodka so that it could not be consumed on the street.[25] It recommended the rapid development of temperance societies in every parish and the spreading of information in schools and the press on the harm of strong drink. The Duma's commission's bill also urged the government to think of other means to raise revenue rather than taxing vodka, to close brothels and bootlegging establishments, and to open government clinics for alcoholics. The state Guardianship was criticized for its failure to police irregularities in the sale of vodka.

As Hutchinson has pointed out, nearly all parties had criticisms of the state and its vodka monopoly. Centrists, such as the Octobrists, felt that the revolution of 1905 had revealed that the decline of social order had been brought about partially by the availability of alcohol. They were eager to enlarge their power over the state budget, which would happen if they could propose alternative taxing measures. They wanted to make Russia a great power, a status it would never achieve in its current degraded condition. They favored the help of the public in attacking drunkenness, that is, the public's participation in temperance activities, rather than extending the state's police powers to curtail hours of sale and step up arrests, measures that were only going to arouse opposition and another potential revolution.

Some on the Right used the issue of drunkenness to castigate the state for its modernization program, which encouraged industrialization and urbanization; they claimed that drinking had been controlled in the countryside. A right-wing populist group, the Russian Association, strong in southern Russia as well as Kazan, seized on temperance as a strategy to mobilize the masses.[26] *Deiatel'*, the journal of the Kazan Temperance Society, more and more stridently anti-Semitic, revealed the strength of reactionary forces that blamed Jews, especially as purveyors of drink, for all the social ills of Russian society.

Kadets and other parties to the Left used the issue to insist on extending local self-government and university and professional autonomy. They proposed that the administration of the Guardianship, medical research on alcoholism, and the medical treatment of alcoholics be handed over to the zemstvos.[27] Kadets, as well as zemstvo leaders themselves, were eager to use the issue of drunkenness as a means to enhance their own powers to collect revenue and enact legislation.

Had the Duma been able to effect all the measures proposed by Chelyshev and the commission, the Duma would certainly have enlarged its legislative powers. The bill was given to the state Council, where it was vigorously debated for two years until 1911.[28]

In the same year, Chelyshev wrote a book, *Have Mercy on Russia*, in which he gathered the letters and telegrams he had received from all over Russia that supported his efforts to shut down the state liquor stores.[29] People from all walks of life testified before the commission, such as two twenty-two year-old peasants from Poltava Province, who "humbly" requested that the government stop producing vodka. The first All-Russian Congress of Gold and Silver Industrialists also said on the record that alcohol sales increased absenteeism in the mines and reduced miners' paychecks, which in turn depressed local businesses. The congress of miners asked the Duma to request that state liquor stores not be located near mine sites.

When at last the bill emerged from the state Council, it did allow peasant assemblies to vote to close state liquor stores in the villages. Baron A. F. Meyendorf, a member of the Duma, pointed out that all reports of the Duma were a result of compromises among individual opinions. He continued, "I myself do not agree with the report of our commission." He felt it was impractical to give peasants the right to vote to close down liquor stores, because even if they decided on that measure, other peasants would soon demand their reopening. Unless there was additional legislation to punish peasants for changing their resolution to close the liquor stores, he felt it was futile.[30]

In 1912, a writer in *Vestnik trezvosti* asserted that the state had reneged on its promise to allow local *skhody* (village assemblies) to decide on the opening and closing of liquor stores. "The practice of the last several years has shown that the resolutions of the *skhody* to close liquor stores have been met with reprimands from the state."[31]

The commission on alcohol in the Duma did pass two resolutions: first was to reduce the alcoholic strength of vodka from 40 to 37 percent, and the second was to call the attention of the clergy to the evils of alcoholism (as if priests had not been actively engaged in temperance work for decades!). The commission itself was so divided, it could not agree on how to address drunkenness with stiff regulations on the vodka trade without stepping on the toes of the Ministry of Finance.

By 1911, much doubt had been raised about the efficacy of putting laws on the books reducing hours and days of sale. Although state vodka stores had long been closed on Sundays and holidays, it was common to see people drunk already before church, according to Father G. Kucherovskii. Liquor stores had been closed on court days, yet witnesses appeared in court drunk, clearly having been bribed with vodka. On bazaar days, the stores were closed, yet drunkenness and fights reigned from dawn till dark. Kucherovskii said more laws would not help, since even the existing ones were not enforced, especially with regard to bootlegging. Even temperance societies were only palliatives in his view. Since all poisons are sold only with a doctor's prescription and alcohol is a poison, he asked why it was not subjected to the same laws.[32]

In anticipation of objections that such a severe measure would only encourage bootlegging and moonshine, he answered that those objections were made by distillers, whose interests lay with alcoholism. Everyone knows how inert the peasant is, he claimed, so that making moonshine would never enter into his head. The only solution lay in the government's shutting down completely all distilleries.[33]

In 1913, another member of the Duma, I. N. Tuliakov, entered the debate concerning the vodka monopoly by scoffing at the explanation of a member of the Ministry of the Interior, who had claimed that alcoholism was a result of the severe climate in Russia. Tuliakov asserted:

> The fundamental reason which brings the Russian people to the vodka evil is not the climate, but poverty, oppression, lack of justice, dreadfully long hours of labor, low pay, terrible housing conditions, the arbitrary rule of the police, the trampling under foot of the human personality, and regularly recurring famines. The condition of laborers in the enterprises controlled by the Ministry of Finance is not better and sometimes even worse than in private enterprises.[34]

Those were inflammatory words, but much could be said under cover of battling drunkenness. The government could never endorse drunkenness, so that it was forced to tolerate a great deal of criticism of its role in fostering the sale of vodka through the monopoly. Knowing of this chink in the armor of the state, temperance workers could use the issue of alcoholism as a shield under which they could emerge to do battle with drunkenness, all the time claiming more prestige, privileges, and power for themselves: the laity, clergy, women, physicians, socialists, and zemstvo and Duma members.

Duma members were not the only political voices raised against alcohol. Even the former minister of finance and architect of the monopoly twenty years earlier, Sergei Witte, expressed his dissatisfaction with the weak Duma bills, and in January 1914, he attacked his own creation in a speech before the state Council.[35] He stressed that he had proposed the monopoly in order to curb drunkenness, and not to increase revenue. The scheme might have worked, he claimed, had it not been for the war against Japan. At that time, "The picture began to change rapidly. The real object of the reform [i.e., monopoly], the suppression of alcoholism, was pushed to the rear, and the object of the monopoly became the pumping of the people's money into the government treasury."[36] The 1905 revolution, which prompted the government to lessen its support of the Guardianship (with decreased funding) as well as to monitor bootlegging, resulted in increased revenues and drunkenness. He even obliquely criticized the Ministry of the Interior by saying that the state became suspicious of its own reading rooms and tearooms and closed some of them "for political reasons."

He then asked, "what have we done for the suppression of alcoholism, the great evil that corrupts and destroys the Russian people? Absolutely nothing. As a result of our utter lack of activity in the direction of combating the evil of alcoholism, we are confronted by a new evil, the so-called 'Hooliganism.' Hooliganism is a legitimate child of alcoholism."[37]

He suggested that there be a ceiling on the amount of revenues the state could garner from alcohol (700 million rubles yearly). Any surplus would be plowed into temperance societies. Bootlegging and public drunkenness should be severely punished. Minister of Finance Kokovtsev defended the institution on fiscal grounds without addressing the issue of alcoholism, but in the end, the vodka monopoly never recovered from Witte's attack, according to an American temperance activist.[38] It was rapidly becoming indefensible.

In a way, Kokovtsev, who had been finance minister during the Russo-Japanese War, never recovered either; the tsar dismissed him from his post in January 1914. The relentless attacks by Chelyshev from the Duma and by N. Kramer from the state Council, as well as denunciations from members of the imperial family in the press, especially from Grand Duke Konstantine Konstantinovich and Prince Ol'denburg, discredited Kokovtsev and the vodka monopoly.

Perhaps to discredit the idea of abolishing the State Vodka Monopoly, Kokovtsev suggested in his memoirs that it was the drunken reprobate Rasputin who said that it was unseemly for the tsar to be the chief dealer in vodka and that it was "time to lock up the Tsar's saloons."[39] But even earlier, in 1913, Nicholas had found an ally in A. V. Krivoshein, the minister of agriculture, who introduced a bill in the Duma to restrict sales of vodka.[40] The celebrations in 1913 of the three hundred-year rule of the Romanovs resulted in local closures, an indication that the royal family favored restrictions on vodka sales and that it perceived that the people did also. On February 21, 1913, temperance societies participated in the grand pomp of the religious processions to the Kazan Cathedral that marked the election of Mikhail Romanov three hundred years earlier.[41]

Clearly, the tsar himself was moved by Witte's attack on the monopoly, for he went to Moscow and some provinces to observe the extent of public drunkenness. As a result of this personal survey, by the beginning of 1914, he was convinced something should be done about alcoholism. Thus, he appointed Peter Bark as minister of finance and at the same time issued a rescript to Bark:

> The journey through several provinces of Great Russia, which I undertook last year with God's aid, afforded me an opportunity to study directly the vital needs of my people. . . . With profoundest grief, I saw sorrowful pictures of the people's helplessness, of family poverty, of broken-up households and all those inevitable consequences of insobriety. We cannot make our fiscal prosperity dependent upon the destruction of the spiritual and economic powers of many of my subjects, and therefore it is necessary to direct our financial policy towards seeking government revenues from the unexhausted sources of the country's wealth and from the creative toil of the people.[42]

It is clear that early in 1914, the tsar had come to the conclusion that the "drunken budget" had to go. The tenor of Nicholas's rescript was not lost on the minister of the interior, N. A. Maklakov, who instructed the governors of the provinces, "In order to carry out the will expressed in His Majesty's rescript, the police must take measures to limit the abuse of alcoholic drinks and to aid all persons and institutions fighting against drunkenness by all means permitted by the law."[43]

Not to be outdone, the Duma passed a bill that allowed villages to close liquor stores for three years, a ban that could be renewed. It took only a two-thirds majority vote in the villages, in which women with property could participate. It was alleged that the reason the state Council had been so slow and so cautious in approving the bill was that many of the members had distilleries on their property or that they otherwise profited from the vodka monopoly.

The state Council might have been slow to act, but after fourteen sessions devoted to discussions of legislation to curb alcoholism, it approved a bill on February 14, which was codified by the state Chancellery. On the eve of prohibition, therefore, the Duma and the state Council were prepared to curb the consumption of alcohol principally through the means of local options to ban liquor.[44]

The tsar's expression of concern, as well as local closings, resulted in a decrease of 2.5 million rubles in revenue from vodka sales in the first half of 1914 compared to the same period a year earlier. The lowered income was attributed to the fact that from February to July more than 800 petitions for local dry areas were granted. Since the tsar had spoken up, officials could scarcely refuse the closures.[45]

In fact, there appears to have been frantic activity to take advantage of the tsar's endorsement. In October, the Council of Ministers gave provincial and local authorities the power to declare their territories dry. Many communes and cities, including Moscow, did that.[46] The city duma of Rostov-on-the-Don voted to become a dry city, as did the dumas of Vilnius, Vladimir, Ivanovo-Voznesensk, and Kiev. The fire brigade in Warsaw helped destroy supplies of vodka.[47]

The widespread local adoption of dry areas made the tsar's task easier when, in August 1914, he issued an edict that all but first-class restaurants and clubs would have to cease the sale of vodka during mobilization of the troops. Those genuinely interested in prohibition were overjoyed. Those who were using the issue as a means for criticizing the regime and obtaining power had the rug pulled out from under them by none other than the tsar himself.

The ban for the mobilization period was soon extended to the duration of the war. An American temperance worker crowed that the "financial receipts of the Monopoly collapsed like a pricked bladder."[48] He exulted in the sobriety of St. Petersburg: "A Prohibition city of approximately two million people seems, apparently to the inhabitants themselves, the most natural thing in the world." And Moscow was no less transformed, with flophouse occupancy going from over a thousand to no more than three hundred guests.[49]

A French temperance activist reported that crime was down not only in Russia, where military service was compulsory, but also in Finland, where it was not. Insane asylums contained fewer men and women than before prohibition. There were also fewer fires and accidents on feast days. Lost workdays ascribed to hangovers were reduced; workers were more productive, increased their savings, and made fewer pledges at pawnshops. Wife beatings diminished, according to a priest, who said he saw fewer women with blackened eyes and fewer brawls. Peasants went to church more often and made repairs to barns, fences, porches, and stables. Households acquired clocks, sewing machines, and pictures. Peasant women became veritable coquettes, decking themselves in new clothes and jewelry. Peasant hostesses served kvass, syrups, and lemonade instead of vodka. Although at first pallbearers refused money as a substitute for vodka, they did come to accept a meal.[50]

Robert Hercod's book *La Prohibition de l'alcool en Russia* (1919) was based on a survey taken by the Poltava Statistical Bureau, which polled people in the countryside. They obtained 1,780 answers from teachers, clergy, zemstvo doctors, peasants, and others. The majority of the replies stated that they welcomed the ban on alcoholic beverages and commented on the beneficial consequences. There were some differences of opinion, however. In those villages where there had been excessive consumption, respondents expressed the wish that the ban be continued since they were acquainted with the harmful effects of alcoholism. In those villages where consumption was more moderate, they preferred to reinstate sales of liquor after the war, although with some limitations. The strongest supporters of the ban were the former drunks, who now felt reborn. It is true that for them the first days were difficult; they even thought of suicide, but then they adopted a new life. Women were satisfied with the new way of life, although some were worried about what to substitute for vodka when giving hospitality.[51]

About 74 percent of the respondents admitted that surrogates were not unknown to them; 23 percent had used surrogates, and 3 percent avoided answering the question. Some said that in the early days of prohibition, they had on hand denatured alcohol, but experiments with it made them quickly renounce drinking it. Sometimes they missed vodka on family and church holidays, with which it was tightly connected.

They reported that at first it seemed that all kinds of social life would collapse and that any kind of gathering of people without vodka would be unthinkable. But little by little, people got used to the new situation, and holidays were celebrated without quarrels and fights. "We are clearly living in the first century of Christianity," wrote one respondent. People were convinced that christenings and weddings without vodka were cheaper. The absence of vodka was also reflected in *pomoch'* (the practice of mutual aid); it was feared that there would no longer be a desire to work, but peasants now accepted meals in payment for help.

The ban on spirits also improved village life. *Volost'* (county) elections went peacefully; no more did candidates treat the commune to a *vedro* of vodka. People were interested in public life and read the newspapers avidly for reports on the war, for which they gladly sacrificed, in contrast to the situation during the Russo-Japanese War. Family life was better. Their food was of better quality, they drank more tea, and in some homes, they even drank cocoa. They paid debts and even put money into savings. The majority said that the prohibition had a good effect on youth except for the development of gambling. There was need for good books, public libraries, popular courses and lectures, and People's Houses that sold nonalcoholic beverages. The Poltava Statistical Bureau ended its survey by noting: "The people await from the government further active help in their sobering up."[52]

Nevertheless, there were ominous signs that sobriety could not be maintained. A year after prohibition, temperance activities had not slackened. People still drank wine, beer, *braga*, and kumiss, and when these were not available, they drank denatured spirits, varnish, wood alcohol, eau de cologne, and *kinderbalsaam*.[53] In June 1916, the Duma voted into law a continuation of the ban on alcohol after the war, which made it illegal to sell spirits, vodka, beer, and other alcoholic beverages. The first offense would be punished by a jail term of from four months to a year; the second, jail from one to three years, and the third offense would bring exile. Wine could be consumed unless there was a local ban.[54] The law did not get to the state Council, but the Provisional Government approved it as one of its first acts when it came to power.[55]

Temperance journals continued to write as if fighting for temperance was still of the highest importance. In *Rodnaia zhizn'*, as late as October 1914, an article on winning Petrograd youth for temperance insisted that there be a single unifying temperance organization, specifically the All-Russian Alexander Nevskii Brotherhood of Temperance Workers, for the entire empire, with youth cells, since up until then, temperance drives had been uncoordinated and people had repeated their mistakes.[56]

In Moscow, four temperance societies—the Society of Physician Temperance Workers, the Eparchy Temperance Society, the Circle of Activists in the Struggle against School Alcoholism, and the Society for the Struggle with Alcoholism—joined to bring sobriety to war-torn Russia. First, special lessons on the harm of alcohol were taught in the various hospitals and clinics for the war wounded. The idea was that these veterans would go out in turn to preach temperance in the army and in various cities. The temperance organizations wrote an open letter to the municipal dumas and zemstvos to urge a continuation of the ban on vodka and other strong drink and to extend the ban to beer and wine as well. They also distributed warnings concerning the harm done by substitutes for vodka, especially wood alcohol. In lobbying for the continuation of prohibition, they sent telegrams to Grand Duke Konstantine Konstantinovich and to Duke Nikolai Nikolaevich. The former wired back that he had delivered their telegram personally to the tsar. They also petitioned the Ministry of Public Enlightenment to make antialcohol lessons mandatory in all Russian schools.[57]

In 1916, amid the disastrous Great War, rural parish priests were engaged in a debate with the zemstvos over who should be responsible for building temperance halls.[58] The political struggle over the "ownership" of temperance activity was quite evident in the newspapers. Apart from the fact that the clergy were better equipped to give moral-religious instruction necessary to maintain sobriety, Father Mirtov argued that parish temperance societies, like lay societies, would include choirs, orchestras, credit unions, cooperatives, tearooms, and libraries. He feared that the zemstvos would exclude priests from their deliberations and activities and would only stock their libraries with secular books. He cited how difficult it was to extract subsidies from zemstvos for church-run schools. At the very least, he implored, let priests give religious talks in the zemstvo People's Houses as they did in Tver Province.

That both the clergy and zemstvo leaders were so eager to claim leadership in temperance activities after prohibition indicates that there was still a perceived need for lessons in sobriety. Despite the hours of discussion about legislation regulating vodka before the war in both the Duma and the Council, the decision to render Russia sober came from the very top, Nicholas II. Only after his moves in that direction was the Duma effective in passing antialcohol legislation. Despite all the struggles among groups to claim the expertise to cope with alcoholism, hoping to increase their prestige and power, in the end, Nicholas exercised his power, won the admiration of temperance workers all over the world, and ultimately contributed to his own downfall.

As Orlando Figes described the matter: "It all began with bread. For several weeks the bakeries in Petrograd had been running out, especially in the workers' districts, and long bread queues were beginning to appear."[59] The bread crisis reached such a point that authorities announced on February 19, 1917, that rationing of bread would begin on March 1. Panic buying set in, and on International Women's Day, February 23, women demonstrating for equal rights were joined by women textile workers from the Vyborg District protesting against the bread shortage. Soon riots and strikes broke out all over the city; this was the beginning of the end for the Romanov dynasty. Police reported that the slogan "Give us bread!" was the most commonly heard cry on February 23, followed two days later by "Down with government!" and "Down with war!"[60] Nicholas II abdicated a month later.

The choice of such an eccentric location for the capital by Peter the Great, who defied nature and the Swedes, proved ill-advised. In a sense, the bones of the thousands of convicts, serfs, and military personnel who built Peter's window to the West obtained their revenge when the people in the capital rioted. The logistics of supplying St. Petersburg with food had always presented a problem.[61] By 1917, when St. Petersburg had a population of over 2 million, the impact of its location had become fully clear, since its adjacent countryside could satisfy only a small fraction of its food needs.[62] According to a report made shortly after the war, "In Petrograd the rise in prices had become alarming within six months after the outbreak of the war; the chief reason lay in the capital's unfavorable geographical position for it was separated by enormous distances from the centers of production."[63] Another report confirmed the problem:

> In this respect, Petrograd, owing to its geographical position, was most unfortunately situated. The shortage of food became apparent in December 1916. In the beginning of 1917, it became alarming. The dearth of supplies provoked popular disturbances, which rapidly developed and ended in Revolution, which in two days overthrew the Monarchy.[64]

The capital relied on a smoothly functioning transportation system, good harvests, and the willingness of peasants to sell their grain.

Even in peaceful times, the Russian railway system, with its hub in Moscow in the central region, was "inadequately developed, inadequately supplied with rolling stock, and could deal with only a limited number of trains a day."[65] With the disorganization of the commercial service of the railroads during the war (virtually all rolling stock was needed to transport troops and supplies to the front and to return the wounded), food and fuel became scarce and expensive commodities in the capital. As another investigator noted, "The disorganization of transport was mainly due to two causes— the scarcity of fuel and the scarcity of metal," so that rolling stock could not be replaced. "The food crisis was intimately connected with the disorganization of transport on the one hand, and the exhaustion of industrial production on the other."[66]

The scarcity of industrially produced consumer goods resulted in forced savings for the peasants, for they were getting high prices for their scarce grain, and with consumer goods scarcer still, they were acquiring large sums of money (mostly in paper currency, which the government was printing to make up for the revenue lost from abolishing the vodka monopoly). "The peasants thereupon became disinclined to take their agricultural produce to market, which could give them nothing they needed in return, except at extravagantly high prices. Thus the supply of agricultural produce gradually decreased and the deficiency in food supply became more acute."[67]

Temperance advocates attributed the sudden relative prosperity of peasants during the war to their forced abstemious life and furnished evidence quoted earlier of their savings, repairing of farms, paying off debts, and buying luxuries. This impression is supported by one group of economists, who estimated that during the war Russian peasants saved 600 million rubles a year by not drinking. The same group noted that urban populations saved 400 million rubles, so that their demand for foodstuffs and other articles rose, thus bidding up the price for industrial commodities and no doubt heightening their frustration when foodstuffs were scarce at a time when they had the cash to purchase them.[68] With extra rubles in the pockets of the population at large, no wonder consumer goods were in short supply.

Not only were peasants fetching high prices for their products, but they also received money for leasing their horses and vehicles to the government for the war effort, not to speak of wage earnings and allowances paid to families with mobilized men.[69] With *samogon* (moonshine), peasants could purchase goods and services that abundant paper currency could not buy. The advantage of vodka was its scarcity, its portability, its durability, and its desirability.

As early as March 30, 1917, the Provisional Government had published a decree by which all grain on hand as well as that of the forthcoming harvest of 1917 was declared preempted by the government.[70] When the Bolsheviks came to power, the Petrograd Military Revolutionary Committee ordered stocks of alcohol to be destroyed and appointed a special commissar for the fight against drunkenness, odd measures for a country that had been under prohibition for three years.

The new government further found it necessary to pass a law making it illegal to use grain for distilling.[71] It clearly believed it had a problem concerning the availability of vodka—that is, the prevalence of *samogon*. As early as September, 1917, the Bolshevik minister of food supply noted, "Liquor distilling is *growing* and is a serious reason for the destruction of all plans for supplying the population with grain."[72]

Thanks to the abundant, cheap, and good-quality vodka made available by the vodka monopoly, there was little need for moonshine before prohibition. It is not clear how fast the progress was from compliance to surrogates to *samogon,* but illicit distilling certainly appeared to be a problem for the Bolsheviks by the fall of 1917. The Ministry of Agriculture found 1,825 illegal distilleries in the second half of 1914, and the Excise Department recorded 5,707 cases of illicit distilling as early 1915, which authorities estimated to be only 10 percent of illicit distillers. By May 1916, a conference of governors reported that illicit distilling was occurring in several provinces.[73] Peasants began to make vodka for their own use and then recognized a resource that could be used to barter for scarce goods. Among the many testimonials to the consumption of vodka during prohibition we have the report of March 1916 from Tsaritsyn, in Saratov Province, that there was widespread intoxication among people engaged in trade and unrestrained drunkenness among workers, especially dockworkers.[74]

In sum, even before the bread riots in St. Petersburg, grain was being withheld in the countryside and turned into *samogon*. Transportation, limited as it was, was not the only problem. The reality was that peasants had no incentive to surrender their grain, and many reasons to withhold it, a lesson the new Bolshevik regime would soon learn. The eccentric position of St. Petersburg made it more vulnerable than other cities to the consequence of prohibition: grain turned into *samogon*.

In his long-standing zeal for sobriety, Nicholas contributed to his own fate, a destiny linked to the successful completion of the war both on the battlefront and on the home front. Prohibition deprived the government of roughly 900 million rubles, or about 28 percent of its income, just at a time when it needed war materiel. Sober soldiers went to the front in 1914 in some instances unarmed, and citizens in the cities, most ominously in the capital in February 1917, went unfed.

As Leopold Haimson notes, metalworkers and other demonstrators who broke into center city on February 23 used the slogan "Give us bread!" partly to rally working-class support for a revolution and partly to persuade "the law enforcement officials mobilized to oppose the demonstrations, of the legitimacy of their [workers] protest and resolute actions."[75] Haimson views this use of the slogan as a clever ploy appealing to the humanitarian instincts of Cossacks and garrison soldiers so that they would not take up arms against the revolutionaries. He emphasizes the use of the slogan as a novel tactic, asking why striking workers in the summer of 1915 did not think to take up that slogan. They did not do so because acute shortages did not begin until 1916.[76] No one would doubt that revolutionary ardor had mounted during the war and that militants cleverly realized that the cry "Give us bread!" would elicit sympathy. But the effectiveness of that particular slogan derived from its resonance, its credibility. Workers could persuade fellow workers to revolt and soldiers not to fire because they all knew in 1917 that there was no bread.

9 . . . .

CONCLUSION

The year 1913 was a most notable one in the history of the temperance cause in Russia. The elements of reform had acquired such strength among the people as well as among the powers in Petrograd that they could, without fear of reprisals from the monopoly authorities, investigate the drink troubles and speak and write freely.

—William E. Johnson,
American temperance activist, 1915

It is clear that in one foreign observer's eyes the 1914 ban on alcohol could be directly attributed to the power of the Russian people. Whether the people persuaded Nicholas to announce prohibition or whether he had made the decision independently remains moot until historians find evidence to support one view or the other decisively.[1] Also moot is the issue of whether or not the massive efforts of temperance activists reduced alcoholism in the Russian Empire. But it is significant that Russia was the first country to adopt prohibition.

There are other significant observations to be made about the mass temperance movement, however. Contemporaries themselves recognized that the temperance movement, in all its variety, was nearly unique in the Russian experience. It originated and grew without the tutelage of the state and even, in large part, in opposition to its policies. Most private societies, whether religious or lay in character, were highly critical of the state's liquor monopoly and implicitly critical of the regime that sponsored it.[2] The state in turn remained suspicious and ambivalent toward private societies, but the magnitude of the alcoholism issue won for them a grudging toleration.

Dr. A. M. Korovin of Moscow called the temperance societies "a unique phenomenon of social energy." He regarded them as "evidently destined to assume a visible place in the history of Russian culture."[3] Some, but not all, of the societies represent prime examples of what has come to be called "civil society" or volunteerism and *obshchestvennost'*.[4] Unlike many Russian voluntary associations, however, they were not all urban or confined to what might be described as the emerging middle class in Russia. They were not even all progressive: some advocated moral regeneration and a return to a preindustrial Russia. This very lack of cohesion—the capaciousness, the fractiousness of the many organizations—takes us beyond a discussion of civil society, If there was one common denominator to all their rhetoric, actions, and views, it would be an intense distaste for the status quo. The impulses for temperance in Russia emanated from many quarters of society, from many *sosloviia* (estates), from rural and urban priests, from some of the peasants, especially from women, from workers, from socialists, from military people, and even from some civil servants, by no stretch considered to be middle class. Professional people such as doctors, teachers, and jurists were numerous in the voluntary temperance associations. While many lamented the absence of the intelligentsia, such pioneers in the Russian temperance movement as Count Leo Tolstoi betray the motley nature of persons enlisted in the cause. Even the bureaucracy, in the form of the Guardianship of Public Sobriety, got into the act, as it were, by establishing Russian popular theater, if not sobriety. All of these groups and individuals had their own diagnoses for the problem and advocated their own therapies; the variety of their activities and the intensity of their efforts suggest their energies. So also do the approximately thirty-two temperance periodicals published between 1880 and 1914.[5] What one historian has noted of temperance movements in England can be said of Russian societies as well: "Like other causes, the temperance movement offered its adherents a new fraternity, based on common needs and experiences. . . . The temperance movement at this period gave prestige and responsibility to many talented working-class men and women who otherwise would have had little chance to exercise their organizational and leadership skills."[6] Although individual temperance societies differed concerning how to solve the problem of alcoholism, each society formed a certain cohesion and camaraderie.

In Russia, these observations could be extended to peasants who voted in their village assemblies to close state liquor stores. Korovin believed that although the voices of temperance workers were few and weak in the state Duma, behind them "stand tens of thousands of rural resolutions to close the state stores and conscious sober elements of the rural and city populations, who are organized into temperance societies in the name of pure love for their dear land and are true friends of progress."[7] He urged everyone in favor of sobriety to write to the Duma and petition them to abolish the

Guardianship in favor of local control over temperance measures. He supplied the address of the state Duma and asked everyone to write to the Samara representative, M. D. Chelyshev, who noted in 1914 that "from the moment of the introduction of the state sales of alcoholic drink, there were 40,000 villages that voted to have no state liquor stores."[8] Grassroots protest against the presence of liquor stores is noted by Stephen Frank: "[village] petitions from across the empire flooded government offices asking to close local drinking establishments and state liquor shops."[9]

And yet, had the peasants not feared a rift with the authorities of the state Treasury Department, more would have asked that the liquor stores be closed. Even some church officials feared antagonizing the state. For example, a parish priest and church elder succeeded in getting the peasant commune to petition the government to remove the vodka stores from their district. Soon a member of the Monopoly Department came to investigate, declaring there had been a "conspiracy" between the clergyman and the elder. The bishop thereupon warned the priest not to interfere in the affairs of the village and "on the question of temperance to limit himself exclusively to moral persuasion, taking good care to keep the same in agreement with Christian doctrines; and should the complaint be repeated, a stricter punishment would be accorded him."[10] This incident was no doubt not a solitary one.

As an anonymous author wrote in the conservative journal *Deiatel'* in 1911, the Ministry of Finance finally allowed the closing of a state vodka store in a certain village many years after the peasant commune had petitioned for the closing. The author of the article recalled that peasant communes called repeatedly for the closing of state liquor stores, but this was the first time that he had ever read that permission had been granted. The official refusal always included the question: "What is the use of the state's closing its liquor establishments when at the same time several secret bootlegging places would open and drunkenness would continue as before?" The author responded that it was not true that bootlegging would increase significantly, because as it was, state stores primarily existed as suppliers for bootleggers. Closing state stores would increase bootlegging only an insignificant degree, if at all.[11]

In effect, the author accused the Ministry of Finance of hypocrisy. If the state was so concerned about reducing alcoholism, why then did it always put so many obstacles in the way of peasant communes' decisions, arrived at after much debate, to close the liquor stores? Surely, the ministry was more concerned with the health of the treasury than with the health of the individual. The bottom line was that all liquor consumption, legal or illegal, bore the government seal. Secret distilling and bottling of vodka were relatively rare before 1914. "A huge apparatus is necessary for distilling so that secret production of spirits is extremely difficult. . . . In short, all Russia drinks grain liquor prepared by the state, whether it is sold in state liquor stores or by secret bootleggers." The anonymous author then asked why, when peasants finally decide to stop having liquor available, the state stood in the way? Isn't it reasonable to assume that if they were willing to close down state stores, they would also put a stop to bootlegging? He continued, "is it impossible to believe that the people's movement toward sobriety is sincere and unfeigned? Could not the state tolerate temperance by shutting down vodka stores?"[12]

Before 1914, the brief answer was apparently no, since the record shows that for many years, despite peasant petitions, the state resisted shutting down liquor stores. But the very effort to close state stores mobilized thousands of peasants, mostly women, who felt they had been given the power to determine whether they lived in a wet or dry area. While far from being the majority of millions of peasants, those whose attempts to exercise their power were thwarted and became further alienated from the state.

Not only peasants wanted their votes to count; women also demanded political rights. Women simply wanted the vote, claiming that they could address alcoholism only if they were full citizens. Even before the 1905 revolution, physicians demanded civil rights. The doctors who met in 1904 in St. Petersburg to discuss medical problems passed a resolution declaring that "an active and successful struggle against alcoholism, which in Russia is a social evil of the first magnitude, is possible only if we have full guarantees of liberty for our persons and words, and freedom of the press and public meetings."[13] According to Johnson, some of the physicians at the conference were punished by being transported to Siberia for having "the temerity to criticize a government institution."[14] But physicians persisted in linking civil rights to the issue of alcoholism: "Without the improvement of the economic and legal position of our people, it is impossible to think seriously about the reduction of popular drunkenness."[15]

Young urban priests in particular were eager to create a better working and living world for laborers and did not spare criticism of the government for creating a miserable milieu. To a certain extent they were advocating a form of "liberation theology" *avant le lettre*. Critics of the state also came from ultraconservative religious circles, so polarizing an effect did the issue of alcoholism have on people. They sniped at the state and society both from the Left and from the Right. Workers themselves were aware of alcoholism in their midst and attempted to unwind its coils. Worker writers regarded drunkenness "as both a sign and a cause of a weak self, a critique of workers' moral personalities. . . . Satirical and serious writings alike shamed workers for drunkenness, swearing, gambling, and other degrading 'unseemly' behavior, for lying to their wives about wages squandered on drink, and for treating women as sexual objects."[16] Some socialist workers used much the same language as some of the clergy and Tolstoi, as when a worker wrote, "Drunkenness is a disease of the will, and the will depends on reason."[17]

Perhaps under no other guise than that of a temperance worker could a person so freely criticize the government. A temperance advocate made a strong case that Guardianship funds should be transferred to the state Duma and to city dumas, stating that "the government as the first guard of the interests of its people should not extract revenue from their sick misery." He further demanded that the state Duma should be in direct charge of all revenue derived from the vodka monopoly and that it should be spent exclusively for clinics for alcoholics and to educate people about alcoholism. Temperance societies should be supported by such income, and they "should receive special privileges relating to temperance propaganda, whether oral or in the press."[18] The Duma itself was engaged in a tug-of-war with the state over extending its powers to control the manufacture, distribution, and taxation of vodka.

The issue of temperance, while of genuine concern to millions, can also be visualized as a huge Trojan horse within which stood peasants, workers, clerics, doctors, teachers, women, soldiers, and Duma members—-all prepared to attack the state for purveying vodka and minimizing the consequences and, at the same time, to advance their own political agendas.[19] When the Trojan horse was opened, and they rushed forth in 1914, the attackers were amazed to find the tsar himself leading the battle against "the green dragon." As a result, the monarchists boasted that Nicholas II did more for the Russian people by freeing them from vodka than did his grandfather Alexander II in freeing people from serfdom. Socialists, however, who had been attacking the regime for years for having created the monopoly, found themselves suddenly "robbed of one of their best propagandist weapons, [and they] raised the cry that prohibition was a tyrannical law, interfering with the people's freedom."[20] Clearly, the regime and not drunkenness was their primary enemy, as it was also for some other temperance crusaders.

EPILOGUE

*Russia is never going to be drunken again. Alcoholic beverages
have been prohibited and the Russians are getting used to
teetotal beverages.*

—John Foster Fraser, 1915

*Nobody in the world knows what [vodka] is made out of, and
the reason I tell you that is that the story of vodka is the
story of Russia. Nobody knows what Russia is made of, or
what it is liable to cause its inhabitants to do.*

—Will Rogers, 1924

An eyewitness to the 1917 revolution reported that people were
saying, "we drink cold water, and Nicholas [drinks] wine."[1] It
is true that Nicholas II liked wine, but all evidence shows that
he was a moderate drinker, unlike his father, Alexander III,
who instituted the vodka monopoly.[2] Even if the British tourist
cited in the epigraph to this chapter was correct about Russia's
sobriety, and there is much evidence that he was not, people
resented the class differentiation made explicit in the initial
ban against alcohol in 1914 when first-class restaurants were
exempt. The purported drinking by aristocrats continued to
rankle even after the royal family was imprisoned. For example, in May 1917, an article in the *Odesskie novosti* said that
"Nicholas Romanov's guards drink wine.[3] Again, in September
1917, when the imperial family was imprisoned in Siberia, a
shipment of wine was sent to Nicholas from his summer palace at Tsarskoe Selo; but, along the way, soldiers, suspecting
that the wine was destined for officers, poured it into the Ir-
tysh River.[4] After the royal family was murdered, graffiti were

found on the walls of the guards' rooms; some involved the tsar's wife and Rasputin, a disreputable, self-styled holy man, and one drawing showed Nicholas drinking wine with a scribble underneath saying that his greed was responsible for poisoning the people with alcohol, a rather belated reference to the vodka monopoly abolished three years earlier.[5] Evidence that resentment ran deep is furnished by an Englishman who fought on the side of the anti-Bolsheviks during the Russian Civil War and who said that "the chief contributory cause to the revolution was the prohibition in 1914 of the sale of spirituous liquor."[6]

Abstemious Lenin, who inherited prohibition, embraced the official so-cialist doctrine that capitalism produced alcoholism. He passed legislation prolonging the tsar's ban and nationalized both the production of alcohol and the existing stock of alcoholic beverages. By November 1917, he forbade the production of all alcoholic beverages, including wine. Anyone who pro-duced or sold alcoholic beverages was subject to military-revolutionary tri-bunals.[7] In 1918, to ferret out moonshine, he set up the Commission to Combat Drunkenness and Pogroms, which imposed harsh punishments on those caught making it.[8] Lenin did this, not only for ideological and fiscal considerations, but because he had learned his lesson from the revolution. He knew of the peasants' preference for converting grain reserves into home-brew rather than selling them on the market. Should this practice continue, the Bolshevik regime's victory might be overturned if cities with their workers went starving. He was the beneficiary of the bread riots in 1917, which forced the tsar to abdicate.[9] For fiscal reasons, however, even Lenin reluctantly ended prohibition and created a new state vodka monop-oly that went into effect in 1925, the year after his death.

Russians went back to their old drinking habits. As Dr. V. M. Bekhterev noted: "A wave of alcoholism engulfed the whole country." Everybody drank: "the well and the sick, men and women, adults and children." They drank as before the revolution at "celebrations, at weddings, at parties, on name-days, for appetite, for warmth and to refresh themselves.[10] Soon So-viet drinking eclipsed tsarist drinking levels. A family of eight in a tiny hut entertained twenty to thirty guests so lavishly on a religious holiday that they consumed 36 liters of vodka, 180 liters of home-brewed beer, a sheep, and a thirty-six-pound pig. As a result of this extravagance, the family had to eat black bread, cucumbers, and potatoes the rest of the year. One Easter celebration in Omsk District resulted in violence with four deaths and forty-four serious injuries. By the 1920s, a doctor estimated that 56–80 percent of all children drank vodka in earnest on holidays and 90 percent had tasted it.[11] As an indication of this high consumption, by 1927 excise taxes on vodka amounted to 18.9 percent of all revenues.[12] As Richard Stites has noted, the literature against drunkenness was enormous and "was hardly different in tone from that of the prerevolutionary temperance movement, and just about as effective."[13]

Physicians who attributed drinking to social environmental factors welcomed the new Bolshevik regime because they felt the socialist state would finally support both their research and their remedies. And for about a decade their views were accepted. After the revolution, they became Soviet social hygienists, who defined disease not primarily as a biological phenomenon but as a social one. "The aim of social hygiene as a science was both to describe and to prescribe: its practitioners were to examine the social conditions within which disease occurred and spread and to propose social measures which would contribute to the all-important goal of preventing disease.[14]

The disease of alcoholism appeared to be preeminently suited to this kind of approach. To be sure it was a long-term pursuit, that is, to create a social and economic environment conducive to weaning the Soviet people from drink. But in the brave new utopian socialist world, all things seemed possible. In the short term, however, chronic alcoholics could not benefit from such a leisurely cultural project. They needed immediate help, which social hygienists could not supply. Here psychiatrists stepped in, as before the revolution, claiming that they were the experts:

> In contrast to social hygienists, the psychiatrists pictured the *bytovoi* (habitual) alcoholic as a species of mental patient whose drinking was a function of his inability to adapt to the challenges of life rather than a response to his unfavorable social circumstances. Touting the results of their empirical studies of the patients in psychiatric institutions, the psychiatrists maintained that they alone had the knowledge to treat this type of alcoholic effectively.[15]

These Soviet psychiatrists believed in restricting access to alcohol and, unlike many tsarist physicians, favored forcible treatment of patients. They took over the field of alcohol studies since the public-health doctors and social hygienists had no immediate solutions to offer.

By the time of rapid industrialization under Stalin's First Five-Year Plan and its accompanying cultural revolution, social conditions were such that Stalin determined they could not bear the scrutiny of the social hygienists, who fell into official disfavor. During the turmoil of the Five-Year Plan, social hygienists uncovered disturbing social ills affecting disease, conditions that were supposed to disappear under a socialist regime. Just as public-health doctors had criticized the tsarist regime, Soviet social hygienists were poised to find fault with contemporary socialist economic and social conditions. To survive, they quietly moved into other areas of public-health work.

Temperance activists did not flourish for long under Stalin's regime either. In 1928, the state fostered the creation of the Society for the Struggle against Alcoholism with a familiar array of members: military leaders, writers, doctors, public-health workers. The society soon grew to a membership of a quarter million persons and published its own journal, *Sobriety and Culture*.[16] After a year or more of vigorous campaigning, including a demonstration of 15,000 children in Irkutsk against alcohol, the society was abolished in 1930. All temperance activity was merged with antireligious campaigns. Social energies were to be invested in fulfilling the First Five-Year Plan, so that alcoholism under Stalin became a non-issue.

With the question of alcoholism thus "solved," in 1930 Stalin ordered the production of vodka to be increased and placed directly under central government control. "New factories were built, and by 1940 there were more shops selling drink than meat, fruit and vegetables put together; the output of alcohol rose sharply as a result, although it fell again during the war and levels of consumption of the immediate post-war period were, in fact, no higher than they had been in the late tsarist years."[17]

No higher than tsarist consumption still meant that alcoholism remained a vexing problem in the Soviet Union for fifty years, but with only scant official attention given to it. According to an expert on the subject, per capita consumption of alcohol increased significantly between 1960 and 1979.[18] Russian sources indicate that between 1940 and 1985 the sale of alcohol increased 7.4 times.[19] In 1985, two months after Mikhail Gorbachev became general secretary of the Communist Party of the USSR, he signed into law a resolution entitled "On Measures to Overcome Drunkenness and Alcoholism."[20] This assault on alcohol was his first policy innovation. Within a few months, Gorbachev the general secretary, or *general' nyi sekretar'*, was jokingly dubbed the *"mineral' nyi sekretar'"* (mineral water secretary). One of Gorbachev's measures was his creation of the All-Union Voluntary Temperance Promotion Society. Just like the Guardianship of Public Sobriety under Nicholas II, this organization was composed of bureaucrats and functionaries, calling into doubt the "voluntary" aspect included in its title. To give Gorbachev credit, he hoped that this organization would result in grassroots "civic associations," which he promoted throughout his perestroika campaign. In fact, since the Ministry of Finance, the Ministry of Trade, the State Planning Commission (GOSPLAN), and some of the party elite were all against what they considered the suicidal lopping off of revenues, Gorbachev had a genuine *need* to appeal to the masses if his goal for total sobriety was to be achieved.

In retrospect, it can be seen that Gorbachev's call to citizens to implement his alcohol policy was an indication of his relatively weak position within the party and state administrative elite. Castigating the torpid ministerial bureaucrats and inert party apparatchiki, Gorbachev frequently called upon citizens to give short shrift to all the ensconced conservatives who did not support his drive for perestroika and, in particular, his antialcohol campaign. As one political scientist wrote, "In most countries advocates of sobriety tend to be sectarians appealing to a limited segment of the community; not politicians seeking national leadership."[21]

Nikolai Chernykh, the man in charge of propaganda for the Politburo, was appointed chair of the All-Union Voluntary Temperance Promotion Society. A typical example of the membership was a government official in Kiev who was handed a voluntary temperance society badge and was told to preside over a temperance group two or three nights a week. A friend of mine, a historian at the Moscow Academy of Sciences with whom I admit to sharing a glass or two of vodka in Moscow in 1989, related to me that in 1985 he had been told that he was to be president of the Academy of Sciences Voluntary Temperance Promotion Society. I asked him what he had to do. He said he had to promise not to drink for one year (his term of office, and he did renounce alcohol for that year), collect the 1 ruble dues from each of the members (which were sent to the Kremlin headquarters of the temperance society), and lead a few discussion groups. Every factory, school, and institution was told to form such voluntary societies.

In a very short time, the government organization numbered 14 million members. Like the guardianships of the 1890s, they established recreational facilities and sponsored outings and other distractions. Like the guardianships, they were criticized for being apathetic and displaying no genuine enthusiasm for temperance. Unlike the tsarist guardianships, however, Gorbachev's state organization preached total abstinence. The ultimate proclaimed goal was to produce a drug-free society.

Gorbachev certainly made it more difficult to obtain alcohol. He cut alcohol production to one-half its normal level.[22] The drinking age was raised from eighteen to twenty-one years, and state vodka stores did not open until after 2 P.M. The long lines of imbibers at the shops at that hour provided material for many jokes. Some wineries were converted to fruit juice factories, while many vineyards were pulled out by the roots. Alcohol was banned from resort areas. Alcohol-free cafes and restaurants sprang up in the big cities. In 1989, I ate in one of them in St. Petersburg, then still Leningrad. A string quartet played music most of the evening, and at one point, a woman read poetry to the diners. The same tactics of providing entertainment in lieu of alcohol prevailed there as in the nineteenth century. The stated therapy for alcoholics in Leningrad at that time was to place emphasis on "learning to utilize leisure time effectively, such as by spending holiday times together in the country, visiting theaters and movies and discussing the event afterward, and helping each other to develop new interests."[23]

The number of liquor licenses issued to restaurants was drastically cut. One disgruntled manager in Rostov complained that on the first day that his restaurant was turned nonalcoholic, his receipts fell from the normal level of 1,700 rubles to only 230 rubles.[24] In Russia, as in the United States, much of the profit in the restaurant business was in selling liquor.

As testimony to the lack of success of the voluntary temperance societies and to compensate for the cut in vodka production, moonshine was produced in vast quantities, so much in fact that sugar disappeared from the shelves and had to be rationed for the first time since World War II.[25] Buckets, also necessary for making home brew, could not be found in the stores. As under the 1914 ban, sales of products with alcoholic content— eau de cologne, window-cleaning fluids, and other solvents—skyrocketed.

The scarcity of vodka caused much disgruntlement, to say the least. On New Year's Day 1991 in Chita, Siberia, a riot broke out, with people blocking traffic, lighting bonfires, and pulling down lamp posts, all because they were unable to exchange ration coupons for wine and vodka. Blackmarket prices for vodka were five times the official prices of the scarce commodity. Part of Gorbachev's unpopularity derived from his vigorous antialcohol policies. In 1991, he had to admit that these policies contributed to a deficit of 49 billion rubles in revenue, which he compared with similar losses incurred by the Chernobyl catastrophe and the earthquake in Armenia.[26] The fact that by 1988 moonshine production became the USSR's top growth industry reduced Gorbachev's chances of convincing powerful Party people that sobriety was a battle worth fighting.[27]

Gorbachev's detractors claimed that he was using the alcohol problem as a device by which to focus attention away from more substantial shortcomings within the Soviet state. Gorbachev, allegedly, wanted to suggest that Communist Party members were not responsible for the state of the Soviet economy and society, but drunkards were. According to some Russian and American scientists:

> Persons with alcohol problems were treated as social outcasts, degraded people, or criminals. The disease concept of alcoholism was practically transformed into the concept of "moral sickness," and the term "alcoholism" became some type of swear word. It led to some unfortunate results. For example, people with alcohol problems who previously took medical advice and who received treatment in outpatient clinics or in hospitals, now went underground or without treatment. Their relatives also ceased contact with medical doctors and narcologists because they feared punitive sanctions.[28]

Under Gorbachev, confidentiality was lacking concerning medical records, so that those in need of therapy seldom requested it. "To be in treatment for alcoholism, to have the stigma of being an alcoholic, even for those who completely abstained from alcohol, was seen as a disgrace in the public's eyes."[29] It was virtually impossible for leaders, if known to be alcoholics, to remain in the Communist Party. Other officials, the military, the police, KGB officers, pilots, drivers, and railway workers were generally heavy drinkers. Since it was the accepted cultural norm in these groups to drink, "not to go along with [drinking] risked ostracism by the group, so the culture virtually enforced heavy drinking but proscribed treatment."[30]

Gorbachev's attitude was that alcoholism represented a moral failing. At the same time, people regarded restriction of alcohol consumption as a major interference with their private lives. Even Gorbachev's own temperance society admitted that 85 percent of the Soviet people were against his antialcohol program. By the late 1980s, Gorbachev faced mounting protests, riots, increases in the number of deaths from alcohol poisoning, revenue losses, illegal moonshine production, and the introduction of large-scale drug use, all of which severely diluted his policies.[31]

The medical profession's strategies for sobriety similarly echoed those of the past. An American group visiting the Soviet Union in 1987 reported that out of 1.2 million physicians, there were 7,000 narcologists, that is, specialists in alcoholism. The *Journal of the American Medical Association* published an article describing the therapies of these narcologists: "The majority of the methods used is based, it seems, on some kind of aversion conditioning."[32] Their therapy included giving alcoholics apomorphine and alcohol mixtures to smell and drink until vomiting resulted. They also used Antabuse and nicotinic acid in aversion therapy. Suggestion and hypnosis therapists forced alcoholics to stare at the bridge of the nose of the doctor, while the doctor changed the pitch of his voice and waved his arms in something "like a mystical ceremony," according to an American doctor witness. During these hypnotic treatments, each drinker was programmed for a specific length of time, never less than a year. As a final reminder of how loathsome alcohol is, the doctor sprayed a weak solution of ethyl chloride into the mouth of the patient to produce a painful shock. Since the solution resembled the flavor of alcohol, the drinker would associate drinking with pain.[33] Many of these therapies echo the old church oaths, the old peasant aversion methods, and the old psychiatric hypnosis.

These might well be traditions that in some way seeped into Soviet life from the past, but much was also forgotten by the Soviets. After 1917, temperance was a taboo subject, since the official view was that alcoholism was a capitalist aberration that would disappear under socialism. Not until Gorbachev's glasnost was the subject publicly aired again, and only slowly did sociologists begin to explore Russia's past experiences with temperance. Under Gorbachev's rule, Soviet doctors came to America to study the methods of Alcoholics Anonymous, in order to establish AA–type support groups in the Soviet Union. They had forgotten how similar the group discussions and mutual-support procedures were to those of the old Russian church temperance societies.

Despite the unpopularity of Gorbachev's measures, he did achieve some remarkable results. For one thing, the steady decline in male longevity was broken in the mid-1980s, with life expectancy for men rising two years, to 65.1 years. Since it far surpassed the simultaneous increase in female life expectancy, the increase cannot be explained by changes in nutrition, health, or environmental standards, but it can probably be attributed to decreased consumption of alcohol. Calculations combining both licit and illicit per capita consumption of alcohol show that it fell from about fifteen liters in 1984, which was the consumption rate the year before Gorbachev took office, to about ten liters in 1988, when he was forced to give up his campaign.[34] In short, Gorbachev is credited with having saved from 600,000 to 1,000,000 lives.[35] Such a record could not be prolonged, however, as a journalist pointed out that "to mobilize the old command system against such a deeply rooted habit as the taste for vodka in Russia stood little chance of succeeding."[36] At a time when people were beginning to criticize and to organize, for Gorbachev to impose unpopular measures from above, and at the same time to enlist criticism from below only contributed to his ultimate resignation.

For a while after the fall of Gorbachev and the dissolution of the Soviet Union, vodka production was privatized. In May 1992, the state monopoly was abolished, and a flood of untaxed vodka flowed into Russia, with the result of reduced prices and increased consumption. For fiscal reasons, a June 11, 1993, decree from Boris Yeltsin reinstated a state monopoly on the production, storage, and sale of alcohol. With a statement curiously reminiscent of that of the minister of finance in the 1890s, the state monopoly claimed that it had to take over all aspects of vodka distribution because of concerns over public health.[37] A desperate need for revenue drove taxes on vodka up to 90 percent of its value. By early 1994, the high domestic prices caused an 80 percent drop in vodka output; more than 140 of the Russian federations' 240 alcohol distilleries stopped their operations. As prices for domestic vodka soared, cheap vodka flowed in from abroad; its sale on the black market accounted for nearly 50 percent of lost excise taxes. Yeltsin himself had granted concession to importers to bring in foreign vodka duty-free.[38]

During World War I, many Russians believed Rasputin to be a German spy, and now ironically the consumption of the German vodka "Rasputin" forced a reduction in the production of Russia's famous brand "Kristall." Overall, German vodka exports to Russia totaled $200 million, despite the government's imposition of duties from 100 to 300 percent ad valorem. An American firm began to export vodka to Russia in 1991 under the label "St.

Petersburg." It found favor with some housewives because it came in plastic bottles with screw tops that could be used for storing olive oil and other liquids; Russian vodka bottles have no corks or reusable caps and are traditionally drained shortly after opening.[39] Israel began to export vodka called Askalon Vodka B-G to Russia in 1992.[40] In fact, in 1995 half the imported vodka came from western Europe, including the famous Swedish vodka Absolut.[41] Despite the high duties, imported vodka was preferred for its superior quality. Yeltsin attempted to restrict vodka imports by imposing quotas on them, reducing the allowable quantity from 250 million liters in 1995 to only 50 million liters. Such a measure not only irked the European Union but also favored the manufacture of more domestic moonshine.[42]

Fifteen years after Gorbachev's drive, the voluntary unions have renamed themselves the League of Sobriety and Health. Membership has dwindled from 14 million to fewer than 3 million. In the tsarist period, private temperance groups were examples of voluntary societies and manifestations of growing "civic consciousness." As we have seen, they mobilized the spontaneous energies of thousands of Russians and presented a political problem for the tsar in their harsh criticisms of social and political conditions. In the Soviet period, not only were grassroots groups not allowed, but there is no indication that there was any sizable sentiment among the people against alcoholism. And even in the post-Gorbachev period, temperance so far has not swept the country. It is still considered normal for men to drink. During the 1996 elections, Yeltsin hired the public relations firm Alter-Ego, which promoted Yeltsin as someone with whom people would want to drink vodka in the kitchen. No wonder then that Boris Yeltsin won the 1996 election. During the same campaign, Vladimir Zhirinovsky, an ultranationalist presidential hopeful, raised campaign funds by selling his own brand of vodka, which pictured himself on the label.[43] Conversely, militant communists in Cuba fought to dissociate the image of Che Guevara from a brand of spicy vodka.[44]

Boris Yeltsin, generally perceived to be a binge drinker, mounted no antialcohol drive and opened the Russian market to cheap vodka imports. Even the Russian Orthodox Church was accused of importing alcohol and tobacco as tax-free humanitarian aid and then reselling the products on the free market.[45] As a result, in the 1990s, Russia faced mounting alcoholism, drug use, and fetal alcohol syndrome and an alarming reduction in life expectancy, to 57.6 years for men and 71 years for women in 2000.[46] Russians were not only drowning in vodka but also drowning from vodka. About half the drowned individuals in Russia in 1999 were intoxicated males, a considerable number since drowning deaths in Russia are 500 percent higher than in Western nations.[47] According to a survey of the Moscow area, divorced and single persons have elevated risks of drinking relative to married persons, so the high rate of divorce contributes to alcoholism.[48]

A sad and ironic footnote is that with all the efforts of the state to generate profits from the sale of vodka, it has been estimated that during the seventy-year rule of the Soviets, they lost four times as much wealth in wasted man-hours from alcohol than they took in as revenue. Vodka quickly fills state coffers but, apparently, also quickly fills workers' coffins. Ironically, too, while revenue to the government is at an all-time low, consumption of alcohol appears to be at an all-time high. Characteristically, as taxes on vodka went up, production of legal vodka declined, as in the year 2000, but total alcohol production went up, indicating the growth in moonshine.[49] While the Russian people were drinking more than ever, the government lost an estimated 300 billion rubles ($67 million) annually, since only about 40 percent of the alcohol consumed was legal. Yelstin's attempt to reestablish the monopoly has not been successful. To reverse this revenue drain, Gennady Zyuganov, the leader of the Communist Party, who ran against Vladimir Putin in 2000 for the presidency, advocated putting both the production and sale of vodka and tobacco under a state monopoly, thus ending importation of cheap vodka. He lost the election.[50] The issue of vodka affects not only domestic politics but also strains relations between Russia and former members of the Soviet Union, such as Georgia, which in 1997 was sending 800 trucks a month of raw ethanol into Russia to be converted into more Russian moonshine.[51]

As of the year 2000, moonshine was still killing imbibers. In 1997, in the town of Krasnoyarsk, twenty-two people died after drinking illegal liquor made with methyl alcohol by three women pensioners. Poverty drove these women to make the poisonous brew, and poverty drove some people to drink it rather than the real thing to avoid paying the high excise taxes.[52] One woman in the small town of Pitkiaranta, seventy-five miles east of Finland, a mother of two small boys, makes *samogon* in her kitchen, selling each bottle for 80 to 90 cents, grossing $225 a month. She said that "people come and make orders for weddings, birthday parties, funerals—we had a lot of orders for the New Year's celebrations." Another woman across the courtyard also makes moonshine.[53] Tamara Chernyshkova, a sixty-three-year-old former schoolteacher who is practically blind, sold up to 100 bottles a day of moonshine at a Moscow subway station in 1997, after paying bribes to the police.[54] Women were active in making moonshine during the tsarist regime, and they still appear to be a factor in the trade.

By the turn of the twenty-first century, teenage Russians have less of a chance of living to the age of sixty than they had a hundred years ago. Five times as many people were treated for alcoholism in 1995 as in 1990. It was estimated that there were 80 million alcoholics in Russia in the year 2000.[55] Alcohol-related death rates in Russia are approaching 500 per 100,000, in contrast to a U.S. rate in 1995 of just 77. Pop-top, nonresealable bottles of vodka encourage the drinker to consume the entire contents in a single sitting. Vodka also comes in small plastic containers of four or five ounces like the ones in which airlines serve water and orange juice. The latest gimmick to encourage drinking is the sale of talking vodka bottles: "When you open the bottle, the caps start talking. It starts with practical instructions like 'Pour' and then, as the evening progresses, it produces an increasingly drunken mixture of shrieks, giggles, and sound effects."[56] On average, Russian adults consume about eighteen liters of pure alcohol a year, which is roughly the equivalent of 38 liters of 100 proof vodka, or a bottle of vodka of normal alcoholic content every other day.[57]

Not only is alcohol consumption causing problems, but so is its production. In the summer of 2000, three persons active in the lucrative vodka market were gunned down, gangland style, including the so-called Alcohol King, Sergei Kolesnikov, a politician and businessman.[58] Even the state attacked its own Kristall vodka plant, attempting to replace the director with one of its own choosing (ironically, a man by the name of Alexander I. Romanov), along with a dozen private security guards, although the state was not able to prove it holds any stock in the enterprise.[59] Loss of control over production and consumption of vodka is emblematic of the chaos of the post-Soviet state. One of Putin's early acts of legislation was to create an alcohol conglomerate, Rosspiritprom, controlling over fifty distilleries in which the government claims to own a majority of stocks and twenty others in which it is a minority shareholder. The state earns over $470 million in taxes from the production of alcohol, but it could double its earnings with tighter control over the manufacture of moonshine.[60]

Once Yeltsin abolished the state monopoly on vodka production, however, control has been impossible to regain. Smuggling of grain spirits from the United States by criminal elements in America and in Russia, perhaps as much as tens of millions of gallons of alcohol, deprives Russia of significant amounts of revenue. Only Russians, with their long experience in surrogates for vodka, as after 1914 and after 1985, could devise such clever ways of disguising the alcohol. The 192-proof alcohol arrives in Russia tinted with dye to pass as windshield-wiper fluid, cologne, mouthwash, and cleaning solvent. Smugglers often furnish illicit distributors with the chemicals necessary to transform the products into diluted and flavored vodka.[61] As a sign of a reverse alcohol flow, the head of the Federal Tax Police announced in February 2000 that "illegal alcohol confiscated by the tax police will be reprocessed into anti-freeze for motor vehicles and aircraft."[62] Demand for dangerous black-market and moonshine vodka parallels government tax increases on liquor. It is a vicious circle involving a tight link between taxes and death. In the first five months of 2000, tax on vodka increased 40 percent; during the same period, 15,823 persons died from alcohol poisoning, an increase of 45 percent over the same period in 1999.[63] The government is attempting to identify Russian-produced vodka for tax purposes and to assure the quality of the product by issuing stamps to be affixed on legal vodka bottles. This measure has resulted in the importation of forged stamps, so illicit identification stamps can now be put on illegal bottles of moonshine.[64]

Drinking vodka is tightly interwoven into the fabric of Russian life and has been for hundreds of years. It has perhaps made life tolerable for millions of people and certainly has added to the conviviality of even more millions of celebrants. The problems associated with excessive drinking have been explored here, but vodka itself can be celebrated, as it is for example, in Uglich, where there is a vodka library and people are being taught how to savor good vodka.[65] In June 2001, a Museum of Russian Vodka, advertising itself as "the first museum of Russian vodka in the world," opened in St. Petersburg. A combination of a historical exhibit and vodka tasting enterprise sponsored by a new Russian brand of vodka, the museum displays interesting reproductions of the tsars' laws concerning the manufacture and taxing of vodka over the centuries. The director told me that they will expand the museum to include a restaurant, making it possible to attract larger crowds to view the exhibits. At the same time that an exhibit of antialcohol posters was shown in Moscow, near Red Square could be found another exhibit, "The Five-Hundred-Year-History of Russian Vodka," which was described as "a hymn of praise to the pleasures of the silvery spirit."[66] A bronze monument was erected on the sixtieth anniversary of his birth to Venedikt Yerofeyev (Erofeev), a vodka drinker of heroic proportions "who eulogized the spirituality of booze in his classic underground novel *Moskva-Petushki* (Moscow to the End of the Line)." Six hours of programming were aired to his memory, "while 1,500 of his biggest fans crowded into a suburban train to retrace the alcohol-fogged odyssey in his famous novel."[67]

In August 1914, Tsar Nicholas II issued an edict prohibiting the manufacture, sale, and consumption of hard spirits and wine. Less than three years later, he was forced to abdicate. In 1985, General Secretary of the Communist Party Mikhail Gorbachev launched his antialcohol campaign, and within six years, he was forced to resign.[68] These sequences might well represent the fallacy *post hoc, ergo propter hoc*, but Vladimir Putin seems to have gotten the point. In February 2000, when he was acting president of Russia, he denied that the government had decided to raise the price of vodka (although it had). He said that "the government does not regulate vodka prices, they're regulated by the market."[69] In Russia, when the issue comes to restricting the production and consumption of vodka through manipulating prices or supply, by means of fiat, *ukaz*, or law, history whispers *caveat imperator*.

NOTES

Chapter 1

1. See, for example, the article "K voprosu ob alkogolizme," *Deiatel'*, nos. 8–9 (Aug.–Sept. 1897): 476, in which the anonymous author claimed that the death rate among those between the ages of twenty and thirty was five times greater for those who got drunk than for sober persons. All translations from Russian are my own unless otherwise indicated.

2. Ibid., p. 479.

3. M. D. Chelyshev, "Miting trezvosti," *Vestnik trezvosti* (henceforth *VT*), no. 231 (Mar. 1914): 17. For more on crime and alcoholism, see S. Shol'ts, "P'ianstvo i prestuplenie," *Izvestiia Moskovskoi gubernskoi zemskoi upravy*, no. 3 (Mar. 1914): 1–6; and P. S. Alekseev, "Kriminogennoe svoistvo alkogolia," *Vrachebnaia gazeta*, nos. 36 and 37 (1906).

4. Stephen P. Frank, *Crime, Cultural Conflict, and Justice in Rural Russia, 1856–1914* (Berkeley: University of California Press, 1999), pp. 21–22.

5. M. Popov, "Pouchenie o vrede p'ianstva," *Deiatel'*, no. 11 (1911), 270. The population of Russia in 1911 was roughly 150 million. Earlier estimates of deaths from alcohol are given in *Deiatel'*, nos. 8–9 (Aug.–Sept. 1897): 479.

6. Although some scholars say that the term "alcoholism" is "no longer a meaningful term in scientific usage," it will be used here as it was understood in the period discussed. See Dwight B. Heath, "Don't Oversimplify Drinking-Abuse Issue," *Providence Journal*, Aug. 26, 2000, p. B5.

7. D. G. Bulgakovskii, *P'ianstvo: Izrecheniia o p'ianstve, zaimstvovannyia iz Sviashchennago Pisaniia, i mneniia o nem drevniago i novago vremeni* (St. Petersburg, 1898), pp. 3–4. An earlier anthology of sermons of the clergy against drunkenness was gathered by I. M. Dobrotvorskii. See the reprint of his "Drevniaia russkaia propoved' protiv p'ianstva," in *Deiatel'*, no. 1 (Jan. 1897): 8–33.

8. P. S. Alekseev, *O p'ianstve s predisloviem Gr. L. N. Tolstago* (Moscow, 1891), p. 93.

9. I. A. Sikorskii, "Alkogolizm i piteinoe delo," *Voprosy nervno-psikhicheskoi meditsiny* 2 (1897): 335.

10. A. M. Korovin, "Dvizhenie trezvosti v Rossii," ZhROONZ, no. 4 (Apr. 1900): 368.

11. August von Haxthausen, *Studies on the Interior of Russia*, ed. S. Frederick Starr (Chicago: University of Chicago Press, 1972), p. 211. On p. 212, he states that the White Russians (Belarus) were "inveterate drinkers," whereas the "Little Russians [Ukrainians] drink regularly, though usually in moderation. . . . The Great Russian [Russian] does not drink constantly or daily. There are many who do not touch a glass for months and who refuse a dram when it is offered them. But then there are times and temptations when, if he tastes one drop, he is seized by a fit of drunkenness; he drinks without cease for days or even weeks." Nearly all observers, native and foreign, described a pattern of binge drinking.

12. Thomas Stevens, *Through Russia on a Mustang* (London: Cassell, 1891), p. 136.

13. I. P. Mordvinov, "Derevenskie prazdniki kak novoe kul'turnoe delo," *VT*, nos. 258–59 (June–July 1915): 23.

14. Ivan III allowed some of his courtiers to drink at any time and as much as they chose, but they were segregated and lived in a special suburb south of Moscow lest they corrupt the population at large. Ivan IV used access to vodka as one means to ensure loyalty from the *oprichniki*. See Ivan G. Pryzhov, *Istoriia kabakov v Rossii v sviazi s istoriei russkago naroda* (Moscow, 1991), p. 44. See also William E. Johnson, *The Liquor Problem in Russia* (Westerville, OH, 1915), pp. 133–34.

15. *Deiatel'*, nos. 8–9 (Aug.–Sept. 1897): 477. According to John P. LeDonne, "Drunkenness had reached such proportions by the middle of the seventeenth [century] that attempts were made to curtail the sale of liquor following the uprising in Moscow in 1648." See his article, "Indirect Taxes in Catherine's Russia: II. The Liquor Monopoly," *Jahrbücher für Geschichte Osteuropas* 24, no. 2 (1976): 173.

16. Lindsey Hughes, *Russia in the Age of Peter the Great* (New Haven, CT: Yale University Press, 1998), pp. 250–57.

17. "Catherine was also abstemious, and only at the end of her life did she take an occasional glass of Madeira on medical advice." Isabel de Madariaga, *Russia in the Age of Catherine the Great* (New Haven, CT: Yale University Press, 1981), p. 573.

18. For this farming, or *otkup*, system, see LeDonne, "Indirect Taxes," pp. 173–204.

19. Johnson, *Liquor Problem*, p. 116.

20. Ibid., p. 156.

21. Sergei Witte, "K voprosu ob alkogolizme," *Deiatel'*, nos. 8–9 (Aug.–Sept. 1897): 477. The idea was also that millions of moderately drinking Russians would supply the revenue to fund the contemporary state industrialization program. See Volodimir Pechenuk, "Temperance and Revenue Raising: The Goals of the Russian State Liquor Monopoly, 1894–1914," *New Zealand Slavonic Journal* 1 (1980): 35–48, for annual increases in vodka monopoly profits from 1904 to 1912. Even though the staffing of the monopoly required 40,000 employees, profits rose by 25 percent with the introduction of the monopoly. See Theodore H. Von Laue, *Sergei Witte and the Industrialization of Russia* (New York, 1974), pp. 102–4.

22. Ernest Gordon, *The Anti-alcohol Movement in Europe* (New York, 1913), p. 60.

23. A. V. Balov, "Vinnaia monopoliia i narodnaia trezvost', *Otdel obshchestvenno gigieny, vrachebnoi gazety*, no. 24 (1906): 59.

24. "Potreblenie vina," *Trudy kommissii po voprosu ob alkogolizme i merakh bor'by s nim*, 1899, St. Petersburg, pp. 138–39. An American expert claimed that the monopoly's gross income nearly equaled the combined revenues of Spain and Portugal. See Gordon, *Anti-alcohol Movement*, p. 75.

25. A. E. Elishev, "Shinkarstvo," *Deiatel'*, no. 10 (Oct. 1911): 243.

26. Frank, *Crime*, p. 123.

27. Dr. A. Korovin, "P'ianstvo vo Vladimirskoi gubernii," *VT*, no. 204 (Dec. 1911): 15.

28. Marc Lee Schulkin, "The Politics of Temperance: Nicholas II's Campaign against Alcohol Abuse" (Ph.D. diss., Harvard University, 1985); Andrew Kier Wise, "The Russian Government and Temperance, 1894–1914" (M.A. thesis, University of Virginia, 1990).

29. Gordon, *Anti-alcohol Movement*, p. 197 n.d.

30. Temperance advocates wrote articles on the theme of alcoholism in the works of various writers; see Aleksandr Lavin, "Tip alkogolika v proizveneniiakh Maksima Gor'kago," *Deiatel'*, no. 1 (Jan. 1905): 19–26; and P. Nechaev, "P'ianstvo i p'ianye po izobrazheniiu Chekhova," *V bor'be za trezvost'* 5 (July–Aug. 1915): 26–28.

31. D. G. Bulgakovskii, *Gore goremychnoe* (Moscow, 1911), p. 14.

32. N. G. Pomyalovsky [Pomialovskii], *Seminary Sketches*, trans. Alfred Kuhn (Ithaca, N.Y.: Cornell University Press, 1973), pp. xi–xxxvii. "When Dostoevsky invited him to a supper party, Pomyalovsky downed glass after glass of vodka, only to pass out on the floor just as supper was served" (p. xxii).

33. Bulgakovskii, *P'ianstvo*, pp. 15–16.

34. As quoted by Johnson, *Liquor Problem*, p. 142.

35. "Peasants," in *The Oxford Chekhov*, vol. 8, *Stories, 1895–1897*, trans. and ed. Ronald Hingley (London: Oxford University Press, 1965), pp. 217–18. For other comments by Chekhov on drunkenness in Russia, see Nechaev, "P'ianstvo i p'ianye po izobrazheniiu Chekhova," pp. 27–28.

36. A. V. Sobolevskii, "Pushkin o spirtnykh napitkakh," *Deiatel'*, nos. 6–7 (June–July 1901): 252–61.

37. Daniel R. Brower, *The Russian City: Between Tradition and Modernity, 1850–1900* (Berkeley: University of California Press, 1990), p. 183: "The reasons for the prominence of sobriety as a goal are not clear. Nothing in the records suggests that demon liquor had suddenly become a devastating plague." Russian contemporaries clearly thought otherwise. Dr. A. Korovin calculated that the percentage of deaths from alcoholism rose from 19 percent of all deaths in 1905 to 24 percent in 1909. "Dvizhenie trezvosti v Rossii," *ZhROONZ*, no. 4 (Apr. 1900): 376.

38. D. G. Bulgakovskii, *Alfabetnyi ukazatel' knig i statei protiv p'ianstva v noveiushei russkoi literature i pamiatnikakh drevne-russkoi pis'mennosti*, 2d ed. (Moscow, 1902).

39. M. K. Viazemskii, *Bibliografiia po voprosu ob alkogolizme* (Moscow, 1909).

40. N. P. Bludorov, *Sistematicheskii ukazatel' knig i nagliadnykh posobii po alkogolizmu*, 2d ed. (St. Petersburg, 1914).

41. The Alexander Nevskii Temperance Society of St. Petersburg. See *Ves' Sankt Peterburg na 1906 god: Adresnaia i spravochnaia kniga S. Peterburga* (St. Petersburg, 1907), col. 1049.

42. These differences in views about alcoholism were part of general differences of opinion among physicians concerning whether to seek freedom from

state tutelage or to associate more closely with the state in order to secure funding. See John F. Hutchinson, "Politics and Medical Professionalization after 1905," in *Russia's Missing Middle Class: The Professions in Russian History,* ed. Harley D. Balzer (Armonk, NY, 1996), pp. 89–90.

43. Jennifer Elaine Hedda, "Good Shepherds: The St. Petersburg Pastorate in the Emergence of Social Activism in the Russian Orthodox Church, 1855–1917" (Ph.D. diss., Harvard University, 1998); Simon Dixon, "The Church's Social Role in St. Petersburg, 1880–1914," *Church, Nation, and State in Russia and Ukraine,* ed. Geoffrey Hosking (New York, 1991).

44. Tolstoi was excommunicated for doctrinal reasons, not for his teetotalism.

45. William B. Husband, *"Godless Communists": Atheism and Society in Soviet Russia, 1917–1932* (DeKalb: Northern Illinois University Press, 2000), p. 58.

46. The Duma decided to cut down the subsidy to the Guardianship by 500,000 rubles. Johnson, *Liquor Problem,* pp. 169–70.

47. G. R. Swain, "Freedom of Association and the Trade Unions, 1906–14," in *Civil Rights in Imperial Russia,* ed. Olga Crisp and Linda Edmondson (Oxford: Clarendon Press, 1989), p. 186.

48. "31 ianvaria 1914 g," *VT,* no. 230 (Feb. 1914): 1. Also reprinted in *Golos tserkvi,* no. 3 (Mar. 1914): 179–81. Nicholas then asked the Duma and the Council to look at the laws concerning state sales of liquor, keeping in mind the needs of the people. He was clearly asking the Ministry of Finance, with the support of other governmental authorities, for some limitations on the sale of vodka despite the fact that nearly one-third of the state's revenues derived from vodka sales.

Chapter 2

1. For the blurring of proletarian theater and temperance theater with regard to repertoire and reception by workers, see E. Anthony Swift, "Workers' Theater and 'Proletarian Culture' in Prerevolutionary Russia, 1905–17," in *Workers and Intelligentsia in Late Imperial Russia: Realities, Representations, Reflections,"* ed. Reginald E. Zelnik (Berkeley: University of California Press, 1999), pp. 260–91.

2. L. N. Tolstoi, letter to A. M. Kuzminskii, Nov. 13–15, 1896, in *Polnoe sobranie sochenenii* (Moscow, 1954), vol. 69, pp. 205–6.

3. See Schulkin, "Politics of Temperance, Nicholas II's Campaign against Alcohol Abuse"; Wise, "Russian Government"; "Popechitel'stva o narodnoi trezvosti," *Entsiklopedicheskii slovar'* (St. Petersburg, 1890–1904), vol. 48, pp. 547–48.

4. The founding of the Guardianship immediately followed the establishment of government liquor stores. For a summary of the goals and obligations of the guardianships, see "Vnutrennia letopis'," *Nedelia,* no. 1 (Jan. 1895): 7. In 1896, both the liquor monopoly and the Guardianship came under the direction of the Chief Administration of Indirect Taxation and Government Liquor Sales, a branch of the Ministry of Finance. See *The Memoirs of Count Witte,* trans. and ed. Sidney Harcave (Armonk, NY, 1990), p. 243.

5. *Memoirs of Count Witte,* p. 244. See Wise, "Russian Government," p. 13: "From 1890 to 1894, the last five years of the excise system, the annual revenue from alcohol sales averaged 260.4 million rubles. In 1902, the first year in which the monopoly was fully in effect, net liquor revenues totaled 341 million rubles. By 1911, the figure had soared to nearly 594 rubles, which includes an increase of

more than 190 million rubles in profits resulting from the substitution of the liquor monopoly for the old excise system."

6. It is almost as if the U.S. tobacco industry today were to take 1 percent of
its profits to educate the public to smoke moderately. In fact, court decisions and
state programs are requiring some tobacco companies to earmark some of their
profits for education about the harm of smoking.

7. "Rech' skazannoi B. I. Gladkovym 13 fevralia 1911 goda pri otkrytii Vserossiiskago Trudovogo Soiuza Khristian-Trezvennikov," *Deiatel'*, no. 4 (Apr. 1911): 72.

8. Ibid., p. 73.

9. Both the central administration and the provincial and local committees
were called "guardianships," and their members guardians. In this chapter, I capi-
talize references to the Guardianship as a whole but use lowercase for the many
guardianship committees and individuals.

10. See *Nedelia*, no. 1 (Jan. 1895): 7, a report on the beginnings of the Guardianship. For the size of the Guardianship, see *Vestnik popechitel'stv o narodnoi trezvosti* (henceforth *VPONT*), no. 7 (Sept. 1903). For moneys distributed, see *VT*,
nos. 150–51 (June–July 1907), which lists the monetary help to various temperance
societies by the Guardianship for the period 1904–5; subsidies to other establishments averaged 180,487 rubles per year, or 5.8 percent of its own budget.

11. *Kratkii ocherk deiatel'nosti S.-Peterburskago gorodskogo popechitel'stva o narodnoi trezvosti, 1898–1912* (St. Petersburg, 1913).

12. Mikhail Gorbachev used the same method of creating a state-sponsored
temperance society by ordering "volunteers" to join. See Stephen White, *Russia
Goes Dry: Alcohol, State, and Society* (Cambridge: Cambridge University Press,
1996), pp. 75–81, 128–33, 183–85.

13. Detailed breakdowns of the membership in these and smaller categories are
given in *Kratkii ocherk*, 1913, pp. 4–5.

14. *Kratkii ocherk deiatel'nosti S. Peterburgskago gorodskogo popechitel'stva o narodnoi trezvosti, 1898–1908* (St. Petersburg, 1908), p. 3.

15. Luigi Villari, *Russia under the Great Shadow* (London, 1905), p. 31.

16. E. Anthony Swift, "Fighting the Germs of Disorder: The Censorship of
Russian Popular Theater, 1888–1917," *Russian History/Histoire russe* 18, no. 1 (spring
1991): 3. By 1900, the Guardianship had also built People's Houses with theaters in
Kiev and Cheliabinsk. Unlike the Nicholas II People's House, most of the temper-
ance theaters were located in working-class districts and functioned year-round on
a regular schedule, not just at feasts and festivals. See Gary Thurston, *The Popular
Theatre Movement in Russia, 1862–1919* (Evanston, IL: Northwestern University
Press, 1998), p. 12.

17. Villari, *Russia under the Great Shadow*, p. 31.

18. The strategy persisted even after the revolution of 1917, for in 1929, Dr.
A. M. Korovin, who had been active in tsarist times in the physicians' temperance
movement, supported the building of motion picture theaters or of using
churches for that purpose in order to entertain workers to divert them from
drink.

19. *Kratkii ocherk*, 1908, p. 67.

20. *Kratkii ocherk*, 1913, p. 5. On the other hand, the Alexander Nevskii Temperance Society, which founded a permanent, enclosed theater seating 258 people,
might have been the first to introduce popular theater into St. Petersburg. See

Gary Thurston, "The Impact of Russian Popular Theatre, 1886–1915," *Journal of Modern History* 55, no. 2 (1983): 237–67.

21. *Kratkii ocherk*, 1913, pp. 7–10.

22. Richard S. Wortman, *Scenarios of Power: Myth and Ceremony in Russian Monarchy, vol. 2, From Alexander II to the Abdication of Nicholas II* (Princeton: Princeton University Press, 2000), p. 466. In Kostroma, the ancestral home of the Romanovs, the guardianship also entertained the people to commemorate the 300 years of Romanov rule (p. 475).

23. Thurston, *Popular Theatre Movement*, p. 149. "Classics like *Rusalka, Sadko, Prince Igor* and *A Life for the Tsar* shared the stage with difficult new works" (p. 149).

24. Ibid.

25. Swift, "Workers' Theater," p. 279.

26. The magic-lantern slides, which were in black and white, were forerunners of 35-millimeter color slides and were images developed on an emulsified glass plate within the camera. To see the image, the plate was put into a lighted glass box (the lantern) and people peered through a lens at the illuminated image. Zemstvos used these slides as a way to teach peasants new methods of farming, and the technique was easily adapted for antialcohol lessons. See "Zemskaia organizatsiia narodnykh chtenii so svetovymi kartinami," *Deiatel'*, no. 12 (Dec. 1911): 315–16.

27. At first, the private St. Petersburg Temperance Society was refused permission to use the dining room at the Mikhailovskii and Iunkerskii Riding School for its operations.

28. *Kratkii ocherk*, 1913, p. 25.

29. Ibid., p. 27.

30. *VT*, nos. 210–11 (June–July 1912): 43.

31. *Kratkii ocherk*, 1908, p. 23.

32. Thurston, *Popular Theatre Movement*, p. 151. Many of the plays put on by the St. Petersburg guardianship, such as those by Gorky, Tolstoi, and Turgenev, had not been approved by the censorship, signaling that even the guardianship had its radical aspect.

33. *Kratkii ocherk*, 1913, p. 46. Other accounts cite an increase in per capita consumption of vodka under the monopoly. For example, "By 1906, per capita consumption of alcohol had increased to .63 *vedro*, up from .53 *vedro* at the time of the implementation of the monopoly in 1895" (Wise, "Russian Government," p. 14). See also John Foster Fraser, *Russia of To-day* (London, 1915), p. 39: "In 1913, the last of the drunken years, there were 80,000 fiscal drink shops and the consumption from 1904–1910 had nearly doubled."

34. *Kratkii ocherk*, 1908, p. 22.

35. *Kratkii obzor deiatel'nosti Moskovskago Stolichnogo Popechitel'stva o narodnoi trezvosti za 10 let* (Moscow, 1911), p. 3.

36. Membership grew from 53 persons in 1902 to 218 in 1915. The percentage of women members grew from 9 percent in 1902 to 21 percent in 1915. It is not clear what the precise duties of the members were.

37. *Kratkii obzor*, 1912, p. 45.

38. *Otchet o deiatel'nosti Moskovskago stolichnago popechitel'stva o narodnoi trezvosti za 1901* (Moscow, 1902), pp. 4–5.

39. *Otchet o deiatel'nosti Moskovskago stolichnago popechitel'stva o narodnoi trezvosti za 1902* (Moscow, 1903), p. 3.

40. *Otchet o deiatel'nosti Moskovskago stolichnago popechitel'stva o narodnoi trezvosti za 1904* (Moscow, 1905), p. xiv. Its usual funding was 500,000 rubles a year.

41. *Kratkii obzor*, 1911, pp. 5–6.

42. Johnson, *Liquor Problem*, p. 161.

43. Ibid.

44. *Kratkii obzor*, 1913, p. 7.

45. *Kratkii obzor*, 1902, p. vii.

46. *Kratkii obzor*, 1909.

47. Daniel R. Brower, *The Russian City between Tradition and Modernity, 1850–1900* (Berkeley: University of California Press, 1990), p. 76, states that "the slum had no place in the dreams of civic leaders, public-spirited intellectuals and progressive entrepreneurs." For a description of the Khitrov slum area, see Joseph Bradley, *Muzhik and Muscovite: Urbanization in Late Imperial Russia* (Berkeley: University of California Press, 1985), pp. 273–81.

48. The report gives a complete list of all the prices for each dish and drink (*Kratkii obzor*, 1902, pp. 54–56). In 1902, the tearoom employed twenty-four staff members. They were enjoined always to be polite to the sometimes scruffy customers and never address them with the familiar (and condescending) *ty* instead of the respectful *vy*. Staff members enjoyed one full day off each week but were required to work on Sundays, the tearoom's busiest days. Although the working day lasted between sixteen and seventeen hours, employees were granted an intermediate rest period lasting up to two and one-half hours. And if customers were few, the employees could sit and read in the tearoom, but they could not eat the food or drink the tea. The employees were given living quarters or a cash equivalent, a bed, clean bed linen weekly, and uniforms; they were allowed one bath a week. The staff received two free opera or theater tickets weekly, which were distributed in turn among the employees. It is clear that next to charity given to the poor and providing cheap entertainment, the most valuable service rendered by the Guardianship was giving employment to service personnel.

49. Ibid., p. 26. Edith Sellers's article appeared in *Contemporary Review*, no. 444 (Dec. 1901). Part of the article is translated in *Kratkii obzor*, 1903. "People go there for the simple reason it is the only place where they can receive a very cheap and complete good meal." Sellers concludes by saying, "Russia should be complimented that in it can be found so many thousands of men and women who extend a helping hand to the poor, clear away the heavy stones on their path through life and make their lives easier" (pp. xiv–xvi).

50. The Moscow guardianship's tactics of allying the government with workers against owners of industry appear to be the same as those of Sergei Zubatov, the police union organizer. The idea was to undercut the appeal of radical labor organizers. See Jeremiah Schneiderman, *Sergei Zubatov and Revolutionary Marxism: The Struggle for the Working Class in Tsarist Russia* (Ithaca, 1976). One socialist worker, Semën Kanatchikov, denounced the guardianship, calling it a reactionary organization determined to "crush workers' consciousness." See K. I. Idel'chik, M. I. Aruin, and A. I. Nesterenko, "1 Vserossiiskii s"ezd po bor'be s p'ianstvom," *Sovetskoe zdravookhranenie*, no. 2 (1972). For Kanatchikov, see *A Radical Worker in*

Tsarist Russia: The Autobiography of Semën Ivanovich Kanatchikov, ed. and trans. Reginald E. Zelnik (Stanford: Stanford University Press, 1986).

51. *Otchet Moskovskago Stolichnago Popechitel'stva o narodnoi trezvosti za 1903 god* (Moscow, 1904).

52. *Kratkii obzor*, 1907, p. xii.

53. Johnson, *Liquor Problem*, p. 168.

54. The attention given to education is notable. In 1911, Moscow spent more than twice as much on "evening and Sunday schools" than did the guardianship of St. Petersburg, though the expenditure was not lavish (8,751 rubles in the former, 4,222 in the latter city).

55. *Otchet Moskovskago stolichnago popechitel'stva*, 1908, p. 39.

56. *Otchet Moskovskago stolichnago popechitel'stva*, 1912, p. 40.

57. *Kratkii obzor*, 1902, p. 186.

58. The cost of renting the facility came to 32,500 rubles.

59. On the methods used to treat alcoholics, see chapter 3.

60. The figures are contained in a report by Dr. L. S. Minor and another doctor of the clinic, I. N. Vvedenskii, "Chisla i nabliudeniia iz oblasti alkogolizma," presented at the First All-Russian Congress on the Struggle against Drunkenness and published separately (Moscow, 1910).

61. *Otchet Moskovskago stolichnago popechitel'stva*, 1914.

62. *VT*, nos. 210–11 (June–July 1912). The Guardianship boasted that since its founding of clinics, it had treated 60,921 patients in all the empire by 1912.

63. *Otchet Moskovskago stolichnago popechitel'stva*, 1916, pp. 90–93.

64. Ibid., p. 128.

65. Ibid.

66. See "Novyi zakon o proizvodstve rabot v prazdnichnye dni," *VPONT*, no. 24 (July 19, 1904): 561. The official journal of the St. Petersburg guardianship gave credit to the zemstvos for initiating the concept of providing workers with wholesome diversions to replace hard drinking during leisure time.

67. See, for example, D. N. Borodin, "Vinnaia monopoliia," *ZhROONZ*, no. 9 (1899): 67–113; and *ZhROONZ*, nos. 10–11 (1912): 60, for the label "stillborn child."

68. Thurston, *Popular Theatre Movement*, p. 147. Thurston noted that less than 1 percent of the liquor revenue went to the Guardianship, and not all of that went to the theater.

69. Quoted in A. V. Pogozhev, ed., *Promyshlennost' i zdorov'e* (St. Petersburg, 1902), p. 9. At a meeting of the Russian Society for the Preservation of Public Health in 1908, one member said it was no secret that in some of the tea houses, the Guardianship sold vodka. See *ZhROONZ*, nos. 10–11 (1912): 60.

70. Quoted in *Promyshlennost' i zdorov'e*, p. 9.

71. Kitaev, "V zashchitu trezvosti," *VT*, no. 125 (May 1905): 40.

72. Ibid., p. 43

73. "O zhelatel'noi postanovke popechitel'stva o narodnoi trezvosti," *Deiatel'*, no. 2 (Feb. 1910): 28–30.

74. Ibid., p. 30.

75. V. A. Chernevskii, *K voprosu o p'ianstve vo Vladimirskoi qubernii* (Vladimir, 1911), p. 60. He cited as an example of waste the fact that in Odessa the guardianship gave 24 lavish balls, ostensibly for the poor, but the poor could not afford the 30-kopeck tickets nor did they know how to ballroom dance.

76. Boris Kader, *Life, I Salute You* (Cambridge, MA, 1945), p. 49.

77. Johnson, *Liquor Problem,* pp. 130–31.

78. "O zhelatel'noi postanovke popechitel'stva o narodnoi trezvosti," *Deiatel',* no. 2 (Feb. 1910): 29.

79. Ibid., p. 30. The author might have been referring to L. B. Skarzhinski, author of *Antialkogolizm v shkolakh* (1899) and *L'alcool et son histoire en Russie* (1902), who was in the employ of the vodka monopoly and argued that total abstinence was not the way to handle the problem of alcoholism.

80. "This charitable institution [Guardianship] gave the workers the possibility of saving up money for vodka" ("Popechitel'stvo o narodnoi trezvosti," *Deiatel',* no. 3 [Mar. 1910]: 45).

81. "K voprosu o narodnoi trezvosti," *Deiatel',* no. 2 (Jan. 1904): 54.

82. Ibid., p. 56.

83. *Deiatel',* no. 2 (Feb. 1910): 32. *Deiatel'* published many reprints of articles criticizing the Guardianship. Most of them spoke of the bureaucratic nature of the organization and the waste in staging spectacles. Some went so far as to suggest that the Guardianship was subversive since it included "the so-called liberation movement not only in the provincial capitals but also in the county seats." Some of the literature, it claimed, had the objective of "arousing the people against the authorities, against the existing regime, destroying the spirit of patriotism, and ridiculing the religious feelings of the people." See anonymous article, "O zhelatel'noi postanovke popechitel'stva o narodnoi trezvost" (ibid., pp. 32–35).

84. Ibid., p. 45. The government should raise excise taxes on liquor and use the money to cure alcoholism, the author advocated.

85. The Guardianship was, in the view of the Kazan Temperance Society, also destroying authentic folk dances and entertainments in favor of "vulgar" entertainments. Ibid., p. 33.

86. I. Preobrazhenskii, "K bor'be s p'ianstvom v narode," *Deiatel',* no. 8 (Aug. 1912): 188.

87. Thurston, *Popular Theatre Movement,* p. 214.

88. Quoted by Swift, "Workers' Theater," p. 279.

89. A. M. Korovin, "Dvizhenie trezvosti v Rossii," *ZhROONZ,* no. 4 (Apr. 1900): 382.

90. A. V. Balov, "Vinnaia monopoliia i narodnaia trezvost'," *Otdel obshchestvennoi gigieny vrachebnoi gazety,* no. 24 (1906): 64.

91. *Les annales antialcooliques,* Apr. 1904, pp. 65–66. A sign of the scanty support given the guardianships is the fact that although nearly all of the activity of the organization centered on tearooms, many of them, especially in the eastern provinces, had to close because they were unprofitable. See A. M. Korovin, "Dvizhenie trezvosti v Rossii," *ZhROONZ,* no. 4 (Apr. 1900): 384. The minister of finance gave a subsidy of a little over 4 million rubles to the Guardianship in 1904 and only 2.5 million from 1908 to 1912. See Wise, "Russian Government," p. 13.

92. Thurston, *Popular Theatre Movement,* p. 214.

93. *VPONT,* no. 7 (Sept. 1903), gives a critical report on the relationships of the Guardianship to the local intelligentsia in nine provinces. Dr. A. M. Korovin provided a table profiling the 4,103 members of the Guardianship as of 1896. Most of the members were civil servants, with a few hundred members of the clergy and a handful of doctors, teachers, and peasants, but there was no classification for the intelligentsia. See A. M. Korovin, "Dvizhenie trezvosti v Rossii," *ZhROONZ,* no. 4 (Apr. 1900): 383.

94. *Deiatel'*, no. 10 (1904): 369.

95. Temperance tearooms and theaters were built in the provinces, including in a northern Chernigov Province town of only 9,000 inhabitants that included a large Jewish population. The state-sponsored agencies no doubt felt that acculturation was an additional benefit as well as temperance. See Thurston, *Popular Theatre Movement*, p. 131.

96. Ibid., p. 155.

97. V. Maksimov, "Audiatur et altera pars," *VPONT*, no. 6 (1904): 149. Before the establishment of the State Vodka Monopoly, zemstvos and municipal dumas, as well as peasant communes, received revenue from the sale of liquor licenses. If they, rather than the Guardianship, received subsidies for temperance activities, then they would have regained some of that lost revenue. See Raymond Heiders, "Imperial Vodka Monopoly," in *Modern Encyclopedia of Russia and Soviet History*, ed. Joseph L. Wieczynski (Gulf Breeze, FL, 1979), vol. 14, p. 161. At the 1909–10 temperance congress, D. N. Borodin called for transferring of Guardianship libraries and reading rooms either to the zemstvos or to the Ministry of Public Enlightenment. See Thurston, *Popular Theatre Movement*, pp. 150–51.

98. Wortman, *Scenarios*, vol. 2, p. 488.

99. *ZhROONZ*, nos. 10–11 (1912): 58–59.

100. *ZhROONZ*, nos. 10–11 (1912): 59. Ten years earlier, the minister of finance had urged the Guardianship to work more closely with municipal dumas and rural zemstvos, but there is little evidence that it did so. "Obozrenie gosudarstv. econom. i obshchestv. zhizni," *Vremennik zhivopisnoi Rossii* 2, no. 82 (July 28, 1902): 234.

101. *ZhROONZ*, nos. 10–11 (1912): 59.

102. Dr. A. M. Korovin, "Neotlozhnoe delo," *VT*, no. 159 (Mar. 1905): 1.

103. Thurston, *Popular Theatre Movement*, p. 237.

104. "Popechenie o narodnoi trezvosti," *Deiatel'*, no. 8 (Aug. 1911): 193–95.

105. Thurston, *Popular Theatre Movement*, pp. 284–90.

Chapter 3

1. I. A. Sikorskii, "Postanovka dlia lecheniia i prizreniia alkogolikov," *VT*, no. 123 (March 1905).

2. D. P. Nikol'skii, "Ukazatel' obshchedostupnoi literatury po alkogolismu," *ZhROONZ*, no. 1 (Jan. 1913): 36–44.

3. Ibid., p. 36. Typical of the many articles for popular consumption on how alcohol affects the organs of the body is "Narodnoe bedstvie," *Deiatel'*, no. 2 (Feb. 1902): 81–85, reprinted from *Sel'skii vestnik*.

4. This idea is expressed by John F. Hutchinson, *Politics and Public Health in Revolutionary Russia, 1890–1918.* (Baltimore: Johns Hopkins University Press, 1990), p. xv: "The struggle to make Russia healthy was, inescapably, a political struggle, not in the narrow sense of party politics but in the larger and ultimately more important sense of a struggle to control the place that the promotion of better health would play in the political economy of Russia."

5. Nancy Mandelker Frieden, *Russian Physicians in an Era of Reform and Revolution, 1856–1905* (Princeton: Princeton University Press, 1981).

6. Frieden, *Russian Physicians*, pp. 17–18.

7. D. P. Nikol'skii, *K voprosu o p'ianstve i ego lechenii v spetsial'nykh zavedeniiakh dlia p'ianits* Moscow, 1898, p. 38.

8. The Russian Society for the Preservation of Public Health itself had been founded on Oct. 12, 1875, and given official recognition on July 23, 1877. See Vladimir Guberg in *ZhROONZ*, no. 14 (1904): 6–11, for its history and organization. For the Commission on the Question of Alcoholism, see A. V. Polozhev, "Bor'ba za trezvost'," *ZhROONZ*, no. 9 (1899): 205–12.

9. Johnson, *Liquor Problem*, p. 159, called *Vestnik trezvosti* "the first permanent temperance publication launched in the Russian Empire."

10. Dr. Legrain, "Le mouvement de tempérance en Russie," *La presse médicale* 49 (June 1901): 245.

11. Dr. M. Nizhegorodtsev, "Alkogolism i bor'ba s nim," *ZhROONZ*, no. 8 (Aug. 1909): 42.

12. See, for example, the report of the Subcommission Seeking Means to Combat Popular Drunkenness by Means of the Clergy given in 1908 and discussed in chapter 5.

13. *Trudy pervago vserossiiskago s"ezda po bor'be s p'ianstvom. S.-Peterburg 28 dekabria 1909 g.–6 ianvaria 1910 g.*, 3 vols (St. Petersburg, 1910). In 1911, an article in *VT* complained that as soon as the congress was over, the special commission ceased its activities. See *VT*, no. 193 (Jan. 1911): 1.

14. *ZhROONZ*, nos. 10–11 (Oct.–Nov. 1909): 90.

15. Of the fifty-one members of the organizing committee, twenty-two were physicians. Of the 16,000 invitations circulated, about 3,500 were sent to city, zemstvo, and factory hospitals. For the figures, see Idel'chik, Aruin, and Nesterenko, "1 Vserossiiskii s"ezd po bor'be s p'ianstvom," *Sovetskoe zdravookhranenie*, no. 2 (1972).

16. See chapter 8.

17. Dr. M. Nizhegorodtsev, "Alkogolism i bor'ba s nim," *ZhROONZ*, no. 8 (Aug. 1909): 44.

18. One of the resolutions passed at the Ninth Pirogov Congress in 1904 was against the state's administrative methods of coercive treatment of alcoholics. Frieden, *Russian Physicians*, p. 249. The issue of forced treatment was one of the many that divided physicians from some psychiatrists.

19. Nizhegorodtsev identified the general factors leading to alcoholism as material (economic and hygienic), cultural (tradition, educational level), and moral (the individual's attitudes), as well as the availability of alcoholic beverages, climate, race, gender, and age. Some of the "direct" causes he listed were biological (heredity, "degeneracy"), psychological, and physiological (the effect of ethanol). See Boris Segal, *Russian Drinking: Use and Abuse of Alcohol in Pre-revolutionary Russia* (New Brunswick, NJ, 1987), p. 318.

20. A. M. Korovin, "P'ianstvo vo Vladimirskoi gubernii," *VT*, no. 204 (Dec. 1911): 11.

21. A. M. Korovin, "Dvizhenie trezvosti v Rossii," *ZhROONZ*, no. 4 (Apr. 1900): 388–89.

22. Julie V. Brown, "Social Influences on Psychiatric Theory and Practice in Late Imperial Russia," in *Health and Society in Revolutionary Russia*, ed. Susan Gross Solomon and John F. Hutchinson (Bloomington: Indiana University Press, 1990), p. 35.

23. Julie V. Brown, "Revolution and Psychosis: The Mixing of Science and Politics in Russian Psychiatric Medicine, 1905–13," *Russian Review* 46 (1987): 292–93.

24. *Bol'shaia Meditsinskaia Entsiklopediia,* 2d ed. (Moscow, 1981), vol. 28.

25. A. M. Korovin, "Dvizhenie trezvosti v Rossii," *ZhROONZ,* no. 4 (Apr. 1900): 368. He further observed: "We Russians are only beginning to recognize our national poverty and to undertake a struggle against it. Our experiment so far has been altogether modest." As late as 1924, Korovin was writing against alcohol, stating that since the Soviet government was interested in the well-being of workers, prohibition should be stressed. See Press Bulletin, no. 30, of the International Bureau against Alcoholism, written May 19, 1924, by Dr. Robert Hercod, microfilm held in the Westerville Public Library in Ohio. In 1929, Korovin was still sending information about ways to combat alcoholism in the Soviet Union to foreign temperance groups.

26. I. M. Dogel', *Spirtnye napitki, zdorov'e i nravestvennost'* (Kazan, 1912), pp. 228–30.

27. This project, called "Workers' Harbor City" (Gavan'skii Rabochii Gorodok), comprised five apartment blocks, which were completed in 1906. They were located on Vasilievskii Island, St. Petersburg. See *ZhROONZ,* nos. 10–11 (Oct.–Nov. 1912): 121. See also John F. Hutchinson, "Medicine, Morality, and Social Policy in Imperial Russia: The Early Years of the Alcohol Commission," *Histoire sociale/Social History* 7 (Nov. 1974): 207–11. Dril' died in 1911 after a lifetime of temperance activity.

28. L. O. Darkshevich, "K voprosu o bor'be s p'ianstvom," *Deiatel',* no. 1 (Jan. 1910): 2.

29. Ibid. For popular customs surrounding drink, see Patricia Herlihy, " 'Joy of the Rus'': Rites and Rituals of Russian Drinking," *Russian Review* 50 (Apr. 1991): 131–47.

30. P. S. Alekseev, "Kriminogennoe svoistvo alkogolia," *Vrachebnaia gazeta,* no. 38 (1906). *Pomoch'* was a kind of "agricultural bee" or communal aid on a holiday to accomplish an agricultural task such as haymaking, in compensation for which the person who benefited from the service "hosted" the helpers with food and copious drink. See Herlihy, "Joy of the Rus'."

31. L. O. Darkshevich, "K voprosu o bor'be s p'ianstvom," *Deiatel',* no. 1 (Jan. 1910): 4.

32. Ibid. See David Christian, "Traditional and Modern Drinking Cultures in Russia on the Eve of Emancipation," *Australian Slavonic and East European Studies* 1, no. 1 (1987): 61–84, who argues that taverns and capitalism increased alcohol consumption.

33. For a detailed description of the medical effects of alcohol consumption, see "Alkogolism i bor'ba s nim," *ZhROONZ,* no. 8 (Aug. 1909): 49–65, including the assertion that the inebriate's "tongue is loosened, he makes feeble puns that he feels are witty," and as the folk saying went, "What a sober person has in the mind, the drunk has on his lips."

34. "Kriminogennoe svoistvo alkogolia," *Vrachebnaia gazeta,* no. 38 (1906).

35. Ibid.

36. By 1913, Russia had a special temperance society for the purpose of educating children called the Society for Fighting against Alcohol in the Public Schools. Professor A. A. Kornilov of the University of Moscow was president; well-known

temperance activists such as Dr. A. M. Korovin and Father N. P. Rosanov were members. Johnson, *Liquor Problem*, p. 165.

37. P. S. Alekseev, "Kriminogennoe svoistvo alkogolia," *Vrachebnaia gazeta*, no. 36 (1906).

38. A. M. Korovin, "Dvizhenie trezvosti v Rossii," *ZhROONZ*, no. 4 (Apr. 1900): 387.

39. Ibid. There were three classes of accommodations: first-class patients paid 75 rubles per month, second-class paid 30 rubles, and third-class paid 20 rubles.

40. Ibid., p. 388.

41. A. M. Korovin, "Vodochnye sosudy i nechastnye bol'nye," *VT*, no. 130 (Oct. 1905): 22–23. For example, while the average sum for drink spent per person in the Crimea was 10 rubles, in Yalta, where more people went for cures, the sum was 25 rubles. He concluded, "wherever there are gathered many ill persons, there the demand for strong alcoholic beverages is strengthened!"

42. V. F. Veliamovich, "Sistema ambulatornago primeniia gipnoterapii kak mera bor'by s alkogolizmom," *Vrachebnaia gazeta*, no. 8 (1901): 517–27.

43. N. V. Farmakovskii, "Materialy k bor'be alkologizmom v derevne," *ZhROONZ*, no. 1 (Jan 1909): 40–56.

44. P. S. Alekseev, "Kriminogennoe svoistvo alkogolia," *Vrachebnaia gazeta*, no. 38 (1906).

45. Brown, "Social Influences," pp. 27–29.

46. Ibid., p. 30.

47. Ibid., p. 31.

48. Ibid., pp. 31–33.

49. For a summary of these various classifications, see Segal, *Russian Drinking*, pp. 318–20. He concluded, "Most of these classifications were prototypes for modern schemas that divide alcoholics into several categories. Some writers made the crucial distinctions between physiological and psychological dependence, addictive and non-addictive alcoholism, and described alcoholism as a multidimensional process—an idea considered by contemporary handbooks as the most recent scientific achievement" (p. 320).

50. Dr. S. A. Pervushin, "Postanovka dlia lecheniia i prizreniia alkogolikov," *VT*, no. 124 (1905): 54–55.

51. F. E. Rybakov, "Lechenie p'ianstva gipnoticheskim vnusheniem," *Vrachebnaia gazeta*, no. 8 (1901): 913–14, 937–40. In the following year, Dr. E. V. Rig dismissed hypnosis as an effective cure. In his 12 years of experience treating a variety of alcoholics from all social classes, he determined that inheritance played a key role in alcoholism and that educating the youth on the harm of alcohol was more effective than hypnosis. "Bor'ba s p'ianstvom," reprinted from *Sibirskaia zhizn'* in *Deiatel'*, no. 5 (May 1902): 228–31.

52. F. E. Rybakov, "O lechenii alkogolikov voobshche i v chastnosti gipnozom," *VT*, no. 130 (1905): 40. He gives a lengthy description of what it is like to be under hypnosis.

53. Ibid., p. 37.

54. A. A. Pevnitskii, *ZhROONZ*, nos. 10–11 (1912): 116–17. For Bekhterev, see later discussion.

55. A. P. Mendel'son, *ZhROONZ*, nos. 10–11 (1912): 117.

56. Ibid., p. 28. However, an inquiry made among those treated after two to four and a quarter years revealed that only 48 percent had not drunk from the

time of their treatment. But, as the report noted, it was not surprising that the workers fell off the wagon since drinking was so widespread that "reasons and temptations to drunkenness are met at each step." According to a survey made of patients visiting the clinics, on average they drank 1.40 bottles of eighty proof vodka every twenty-four hours, or 25.4 vedros per year, spending on drink 48 percent of their wages. About 70 percent of the alcoholics inherited the problem from their parents, 67 percent showed signs of degeneration; 52 percent showed two or more such signs at the same time; 24 percent suffered from delirium tremens; 7 percent suffered epileptic fits, in most cases because they had "poisoned the brain with alcohol."

57. B. N. Sinanu, *Vrach*, no. 20 (1898).

58. Mendel'son, *ZhROONZ*, nos. 10–11 (1912): 118. Mendel'son suggested that Pevnitskii came into contact with Freud's ideas of psychoanalysis when the former was in Odessa.

59. A few examples of charismatic individuals or groups cited by the psychiatrists as influencing large numbers of alcoholics were the Alexander Nevskii Temperance Society, Brother Ivanushko, and the missionary Bogoliubov. See ibid.

60. Dr. Forel' had stressed this two-pronged attack on alcoholism at the 1909–10 congress. See ibid.

61. *Deiatel'*, no. 12 (Dec. 1896): 654.

62. "Proekt zakona o prinuditel'nom pomeshchenii privychnykh p'ianits v lechebnyia uchrezhdeniia i ob ogranichenii ikh provspon'ianits v lechebnyia uchrezhdeniia i ob ogranichenii ikh pravosposobnosti, vyrabotannyi Iuridiko-psikhiatricheskoi Subkomissiei," *ZhROONZ*, no. 10 (1900): 677.

63. The idea of legitimate intervention is an old one in Russian culture: "First, by defining alcohol abuse as a disease rather than as a sin or a vice, especially for laypeople, the ecclesiastical authors of miracle tales depicted them as deserving of healing. It became a virtue for family members, friends, and even strangers to bring them to pilgrimage sites for treatment, even by force if necessary." Eve Levin, "Miracles of Drunkenness: The Culture of Alcohol in Muscovite Hagiography and Miracle Tales," paper presented at the American Association for the Advancement of Slavic Studies Annual Conference, Seattle, WA, 1997.

64. W. Arthur McKee, "P'ianitsa von!" paper presented at the annual conference of the American Association for the Advancement of Slavic Studies, Boston, 1996.

65. The eminent jurist and member of the state Council A. F. Koni argued that alcoholics had forfeited their right to freedom from incarceration. See "K istorii nashei bor'by s p'ianstvom," *Sobranie sochinenii* (Moscow, 1967), vol. 4, pp. 376–77.

66. Ibid., p. 119. According to McKee, "P'ianitsa von!" the first state-run asylum for alcoholics opened in Binghamton, New York, in 1864. A decade later, Connecticut legalized compulsory commitment of chronic alcoholics. In 1898 in Great Britain, people who were convicted of public drunkenness four times in one year were sent to "retreat."

67. *Bol'shaia Sovetskaia entsiklopediia*, 3d ed. (Moscow, 1979), vol. 16; Kh. I. Idel'chik, "Problema bor'by s alkogolizmom v nauchnoi i obshchestvennoi deiatel'nosti professora L. S. Minora (k 125-letiiu so dniia rozhdeniia)," *Sovetskoe zdravookhranenie*, no. 3 (Moscow, 1980): 63–66. For a list of tsarist psychiatrists who

worked for the Bolshevik regime, see P. E. Zabludovskii, *Istoriia otechestvennoi meditsiny* (Moscow, 1960).

68. L. S. Minor, *K voprosu o p'ianstve i ego lechenii v spetsial'nykh zavedeniiakh dlia p'ianits* (Moscow, 1887).

69. See I. Ermakov, "S. S. Korsakov i ego rabota ob alkogol'nom paraliche," *V bor'be za trezvost'* 5, no. 1 (Jan.–Feb. 1914): 34–43, for a brief biography of Korsakov's life and work.

70. Michael L. Ravitch, *The Romance of Russian Medicine* (New York, 1937), pp. 211–12.

71. Ermakov, "S. S. Korsakov," p. 39.

72. Vladimir Mikhailovich Bekhterev was born on Jan. 20, 1857; he studied at St. Petersburg Medical-Surgery Academy, where he finished in 1878. Later, he was a Soviet neuropathologist, psychiatrist, psychologist, physiologist, and morphologist. His major contribution to science was work in the 1890s on brain morphology. See *Entsiklopedicheskii slovar'* Brockhaus and Efron, vol. 3A (43 vols.; St. Petersburg, 1890–1904), p. 647, and the *Great Soviet Encyclopedia*, vol. 3, p. 105. He, too, was an early advocate of hypnotic therapy. Michael L. Ravitch, *Romance of Russian Medicine* (New York, 1937) p. 212. Bekhterev was a prolific writer. Widener Library of Harvard University holds thirty-one of his books. Soviet scholars wrote several biographies: I. Guberman, *Bekhterev: Stranitsy zhizni* (Moscow, 1977), and V. P. Osipov, *Bekhterev* (Moscow, 1947).

73. L. B. Skarzhinski, author of *Antialkogolizm v shkolakh* (1899) and *L'alcool et son histoire en Russie* (Paris, 1902), was employed by the State Vodka Monopoly. He had always argued that abstinence was not necessary. In 1909, Skarzhinski went to the United States to gather data on the purported failure of local prohibition. In 1913, he was one of the leaders at the conference in Paris that organized the International Committee for the Scientific Study of the Liquor Question. As Johnson noted, "This is a concern of men largely identified with the manufacture of liquor and who seek to find a way to solve the drink problem without interfering with the sale of drink" (*Liquor Problem*, pp. 178–79).

74. V. M. Bekhterev, "Obratnaia storona medali," *VT*, no. 208 (Apr. 1912): 12.

75. Ibid., p. 13.

76. Brown, "Revolution and Psychosis," p. 297.

77. V. M. Bekhterev, *Alkogolizm i bor'ba s nim* (Leningrad, 1927). Brown gives evidence that clandestine political activity took place in several psychiatric institutions, including Bekhterev's institute in St. Petersburg ("Revolution and Psychosis," p. 299 n. 41).

78. I. A. Sikorskii, *Alkogolizm v Rossii v XIX stoletii i bor'ba s nim* (Kiev, 1899). For his career, see *Ukrainskaia Sovetskaia entsiklopediia* (Kiev, 1984), vol. 10, p. 54.

79. Cited in Bulgakovskii, *P'ianstvo*, p. 29.

80. *VT*, no. 203 (Nov. 1911): 27; also *VT*, no. 205 (Jan. 1912): 2. For the regulations governing the Russian Medical Society of Doctors Promoting Temperance, see *VT*, no. 201 (Sept. 1911): 25. For the career of N. I. Grigor'ev, a histologist, see *Bol'shaia meditsinkaia entsiklopediia*, 2d ed. (Moscow, 1981), vol. 26.

81. Sergei Sovetov, "Sovremennye deiateli trezvosti," *Rodnaia zhizn'*, no. 38 (Sept. 26, 1915): 13–15.

82. "The profession [psychiatry] also laid culpability for high rates of alcoholism and alcohol-related psychoses on the shoulders of the government.... Only

radical measures had any hope of success. Any efforts to teach the population about the problem would continue to prove futile, they argued: these efforts could not alter fundamental living conditions, and the government denied the opportunity to organize and propagandize freely" (Brown, "Revolution and Psychosis," p. 296).

83. M. Ia. Drozes, *Zadachi meditsiny v bor'be s sovremennnoi nervoznost'iu* (Odessa, 1907), as quoted by Brown, "Social Influences," p. 42.

84. As the Soviet historian Edel'shtein noted, the Russian Union of Psychiatrists and Neuropathologists was the first professional organization of physicians to support the Bolsheviks. See Julie V. Brown, "The Professionalization of Russian Psychiatry, 1857–1911" (Ph.D. diss., University of Pennsylvania, 1981), p. 400 n. 25.

Chapter 4

1. Frederick McCormick, *The Tragedy of Russia in Pacific Asia*, 2 vols. (London, 1909), vol. 2, p. 281. Foreign war correspondents were impressed by the level of drunkenness among the Russian military forces during the Russo-Japanese War. See also *VT*, nos. 234–35 (June–July, 1914): 13.

2. The article in the *Neue freie Presse* was quoted in a reprint of an article from *Ufimskie vedomosti* in "Golos Zagorskago obshchestva trezvosti," *Deiatel'*, no. 3 (Mar. 1912): 22. On the Russian military, see William C. Fuller, Jr., *Civil-Military Conflict in Imperial Russia, 1881–1914* (Princeton: Princeton University Press, 1985); Bruce W. Menning, *Bayonets before Bullets: The Imperial Russian Army, 1861–1914* (Bloomington: Indiana University Press, 1992); David Allan Rich, *The Tsar's Colonels: Professionalism, Strategy, and Subversion in Late Imperial Russia* (Cambridge: Harvard University Press, 1998). For temperance and the military, see George E. Snow, "Alcoholism in the Russian Military: The Public Sphere and the Temperance Discourse, 1883–1917," *Jahrbücher für Geschichte Osteuropas* 45, no. 3 (1997): 417–31.

3. Louise McReynolds, *The News under Russia's Old Regime: The Development of a Mass-Circulation Press* (Princeton: Princeton University Press, 1991), pp. 185–97.

4. Eugene S. Politovsky, *From Libau to Tsushima: A Narrative of the Voyage of Admiral Rojdestvensky's Fleet to Eastern Seas, Including a Detailed Account of the Dogger Bank Incident* (New York, 1908), p. 11.

5. *Memoirs of Count Witte*, p. 244. Not only Witte, but also Western temperance advocates, pointed to the nexus between the monopoly and the Russian military: "From 1897 to 1910 the Russian government took from the Russian people six milliards of rubles ($3,000,000,000) by the way of its spirits monopoly. Its yearly payments for the army are entirely covered from this source, and 100 million rubles in addition remain for warships" (Gordon, *Anti-alcohol Movement*, p. 160).

6. *Memoirs of Count Witte*, p. 244.

7. Johnson, *Liquor Problem*, p. 182.

8. For attacks on liquor supplies, see W. Arthur McKee, "Taming the Green Serpent: Alcoholism, Autocracy, and Russian Society, 1881–1914" (Ph.D. diss., University of California, Berkeley, 1997), pp. 348–51. John Bushnell, *Mutiny amid Repression: Russian Soldiers in the Revolution of 1905–1906* (Bloomington: Indiana University Press, 1987), pp. 42–43, attributed the disorders to the staggered mobili-

zations. The nine call-ups resulted in 123 serious disorders. He did not link these disorders to alcohol, but rather to a succession of military defeats, a confusing system of exemptions, insufficient food and equipment at the mobilization depots, and the general chaos attending these partial mobilizations. But given the riots and boycotts by peasants in 1858 and 1859 when the price of vodka was raised, it is possible that the higher cost of vodka in 1904 and 1905 as well as the demoralized situation of the recruits contributed to the disorders. Dmitry Shlapentokh, "Drunkenness and Anarchy in Russia: A Case of Political Culture," *Russian History/Histoire russe* 18, no. 4 (1991): 473, claimed, "At the start of the Russo-Japanese War, which directly preceded the revolution of 1905, mobilized soldiers, having plied themselves with liberal doses of alcohol, started pogroms."

9. Olga Semyonova Tian-Shanskaia, *Village Life in Late Tsarist Russia*, ed. David L. Ransel (Bloomington: Indiana University Press, 1993), p. 110.

10. *A Radical Worker in Tsarist Russia: The Autobiography of Semën Ivanovich Kanatchikov*, p. 159.

11. Gordon, *Russian Prohibition*, p. 11, quoting an article in the *Saturday Evening Post* written by Miss Brush.

12. Ibid., pp. 11–12. If one were to rely solely on the official publication of the Guardianship of Public Sobriety, however, soldiers in Ufa were lining up peacefully to receive extra tea, sugar, and bread from the Guardianship. See S. M., "Mobilizatsiia voisk i popechitel'stva," *Vestnik popechitel'stv o narodnoi trezvosti*, no. 3 (Jan. 22, 1905): 50–51.

13. As quoted by Segal, *Russian Drinking*, p. 75.

14. P. S. White and H. R. Pleasants, *The War of Four Thousand Years* (Philadelphia, 1846), p. 183.

15. John L. H. Keep, *Soldiers of the Tsar: Army and Society in Russia, 1462–1874* (Oxford: Clarendon Press, 1985), p. 186.

16. *Deiatel'*, no. 5 (May 1910), p. 781.

17. *Trudy vserossiiskago s"ezda prakticheskikh deiatelei po bor'be s alkogolizmom sostoiavshegosia v Moskva 6–12 avgusta 1912*, 3 vols. (Petrograd, 1916), vol. 2, p. 76.

18. Stevens, *Through Russia on a Mustang*, p. 164. He reported that a soldier received 70 kopecks a month, but Bushnell, *Mutiny amid Repression*, p. 14, found that the sum was as little as 22.5 kopecks a month before 1906. See Bushnell, *Mutiny amid Repression*, p. 112, for the ban issued in January 1906 against soldiers working as civilians. During the Soviet period and since the collapse of the Soviet Union, Russian soldiers have been working in agriculture to supplement their diets.

19. The anonymous author of "K voprosu o bor'be s p'ianstvom," *Deiatel'*, no. 5 (May 1910): 73–74, noted that "after the first *charka*, there comes a desire to drink more at one's own expense."

20. Nadezhda Durova, *The Cavalry Maiden: Journals of a Russian Officer in the Napoleonic Wars*, trans. Mary Fleming Zirin (Bloomington: Indiana University Press, 1989), p. 126.

21. A. V. Sobolevskii, "Zhurnal zasedaniia subkomissii po voprosu ob alkogolizme v voiskakh i vo flote," *ZhROONZ*, no. 8 (1900): 775. The amounts seem insignificant when compared to the American army. American temperance advocates claimed that chaplains of the Continental Army received two gallons of rum per month during the American Revolution, and officers received four gallons of rum a month as their ration. Both the Northern and the Southern armies during

the American Civil War lost battles under the influence of the bottle, whereas during the Spanish-American War, "The notorious drunkenness of our troops in the Philippines, of which the whole world knows by unimpeachable testimony, is sufficient proof of the fact that the canteen there has not been an agency of temperance" (William P. F. Ferguson, *The Canteen in the U.S. Army: A Study of Uncle Sam as a Grog-Shop Keeper* [Chicago, 1900], p. 159).

22. For military reforms after the emancipation of the serfs, see W. Bruce Lincoln, *The Great Reforms: Autocracy, Bureaucracy, and the Politics of Change in Imperial Russia* (DeKalb: Northern Illinois University Press, 1990), pp. 143–58. Although the *charka* generally referred to vodka rations in the military, the term was also used for vodka offered to employees as part of their salary or as a bonus. See V. Fanin, "Charka," *Deiatel'*, no. 14 (Dec. 1911): 6–7.

23. A. V. Sobolevskii, "Zhurnal," *ZhROONZ*, no. 8 (1900): 775–76.

24. See G. Dembo, *L'esquisse sur l'actualité de la Commission pour l'étude de l'alcoolisme (1898–1900)* (St. Petersburg, 1900), p. 37, for the names of the members of the subcommission on alcoholism in the military.

25. A. V. Sobolevskii, "Zhurnal zasedaniia subkomissii po voprosu ob alkogolizme v voiskakh i vo flote," *ZhROONZ*, no. 10 (1900): 686.

26. Ibid., pp. 688–89.

27. Nikolai Butovskii, "Neskol'ko soobrazhenii po povodu vinnoi soldatskoi portsii," *Voennyi sbornik* 12 (Dec. 1883): 295–302.

28. *Deiatel'*, no. 5 (May 1910): 74. The Soviet army also served as a school for drinking: "One soldier described the extent of drinking in the Soviet Army when he noted that, 'even if you are not an alcoholic when you go into the Army, you are when you come out'" (Richard Gabriel, *The New Red Legion: An Attitudinal Portrait of the Soviet Soldier* [Westport, CT, 1980], p. 153).

29. Butovskii, "Neskol'ko soobrazhenii po povodu vinnoi soldatskoi portsii," *Voennyi sbornik* 12 (Dec. 1883), p. 296. Both tea and sugar were relatively expensive so not only would distributing them be a treat, but tea would also act as a stimulant (most alcoholics when renouncing alcohol appear to crave sugar).

30. T. D., "O soldatskikh bufetakh v polkakh 3–i gvardeiskoi pekhotnoi divizii," *Voennyi sbornik* 12 (Oct. 1883): 284.

31. Sobolevskii, "Zhurnal," *ZhROONZ*, no. 8 (1900): 779.

32. In Russia between the years 1836 and 1855, "Disorderly conduct and drunkenness, which represent obvious violations of military discipline, also appear negligible in the crime statistics. The figures are deceiving, however, since most offenses of this type would have been punished summarily at the company or regimental level" (Elise Kimerling Wirtschafter, *From Serf to Russian Soldier* [Princeton: Princeton University Press, 1988], p. 117). As for the British military in India, an American temperance advocate declared that there was total abstinence among the soldiers in India by 1898. See Ferguson, *Canteen*, p. 202.

33. Wirtschafter, *From Serf to Russian Soldier*, pp. 140–41. In the Soviet army, 85 percent of the soldiers at all ranks gave as their reason for going AWOL "to get vodka." See Gabriel, *New Red Legion*, p. 161.

34. Aleksei Shilov, "Prestupnost' v armii i alkogol'," *V bor'be za trezvost'*, nos. 5–6 (May–June 1913): 48–49.

35. Shilov, "Prestupnost'," pp. 45–49. A more realistic appraisal of what army life was like in 1913 is given by Ellen Jones, *Red Army and Society: A Sociology of the Soviet Military* (Boston, 1985), p. 21: "The tsarist soldier, like the modern So-

viet counterpart, was very fond of escaping the harsh living conditions and physically grueling drill through drinking bouts."

36. A. V. Sobolevskii, "Zhurnal," *ZhROONZ*, no. 8 (1900): 784, "Rusi est veseli piti" did not mean "Ne mozhem bez togo byti."

37. A. V. Sobolevskii, "Zhurnal," *ZhROONZ*, no. 10 (1900): 679.

38. A. V. Sobolevskii, *Russkoe bogatstvo*, no. 7 (July 1885), quoting A. Reinbot, who said that in Russia in winter the more one proceeds to the northeast, as a general rule, the less vodka is consumed. He quoted Dr. Hooker, doctor of the James Ross polar expedition, who said that a cup of grog was very pleasant in great cold because it warms a person inside and out, but within half an hour, one is colder than before.

39. A. V. Sobolevskii, "Zhurnal," *ZhROONZ*, no. 10 (1900): 677–78.

40. James M. Reardon, *The Temperance Movement in Russia* (Minneapolis, 1905), p. 13. Segal, *Russian Drinking*, p. 332, claims that the Ministry of Military Affairs accepted these proposals in 1908.

41. A. M. Korovin, "Dvizhenie trezvosti v Rossii," *ZhROONZ*, no. 4 (Apr. 1900): 389.

42. "Mery k iskoreneniiu alkogolizma v armii," *Deiatel'*, no. 19 (May 1914): 124–26.

43. L. V. Evdokimov, "Bor'ba s p'ianstvom," *Russkii invalid*, no. 16 (1910).

44. *Prilozheniia k stenograficheskim otchetam gosudarstvennoi dumy: Tretii sozyv, sessiia tret'ia 1909–1910 gg.*, vol. 3, nos. 439–562 (St. Petersburg, 1911), p. 24.

45. In his story "Night Duty" (1899), A. Kuprin described a private who "drank no vodka except what was issued to him on grand holidays [the *charka*]" (*The Garnet Bracelet and Other Stories* [Moscow, 1938], p. 176).

46. Segal, *Russian Drinking*, p. 332.

47. John Bushnell, "The Tsarist Officer Corps, 1881–1914: Customs, Duties, Inefficiency," *American Historical Review* 86, no. 4 (Oct. 1981): 755. For two novels that describe heavy drinking in the military, see, for the tsarist army, General P. N. Krassnoff [Krasnov], *From Double Eagle to Red Flag*, 2 vols. (New York, 1927), and, for the Soviet army, Viktor Kondyrev, *Sapogi—Litso Ofitsera* (London, 1985).

48. A. I. Gagarin, "Zapiski o Kavkaze," *Voennyi sbornik* 288 (1906): 23–25, as quoted in Keep, *Soldiers of the Tsar*, p. 343.

49. Durova, *Cavalry Maiden*, p. 230.

50. Johnson, *Liquor Problem*, pp. 152–53.

51. Leo Tolstoy, *A Confession and Other Religious Writings* (New York, 1987), p. 23.

52. A. V. Sobolevskii, "Zhurnal," *ZhROONZ*, no. 10 (1900): 685.

53. Gordon, *Russian Prohibition*, p. 9.

54. P. A. Zaionchkovskii, *The Russian Autocracy under Alexander III*, ed. and trans. David R. Jones (Gulf Breeze, FL, 1976), p. 22.

55. General A. N. Kuropatkin, *The Russian Army, and the Japanese War, Being Historical and Critical Comments on the Military Policy and Power of Russia and on the Campaign in the Far East*, 2 vols. (London, 1909), vol. 1, pp. 292–93.

56. Thurston, *Popular Theatre Movement*, p. 148.

57. A. Kuprin, *The Duel* (New York, 1916), p. 87. For a discussion of this novel in the context of alcoholism in the army, see Bushnell, "Tsarist Officer Corps," pp. 753–55. For Tolstoi's opinion of the novel, see his daughter's account: *The Tol-*

stoy Home: Diaries of Tatiana Sukhotin-Tolstoy (New York: Columbia University Press, 1951), p. 326: "In the evenings we read Kuprin's *Duel,* with Papa doing most of the reading. He likes it and finds Kuprin more talented than Gorky."

58. Nicholas Luker, *Alexander Kuprin* (Boston, 1978), p. 73.

59. Duels in the military became legal on May 20, 1894. See P. A. Zaionchkovskii, *Samoderzhavie i russkaia armiia na rubezhe XIX–XX stoletii, 1881–1903* (Moscow, 1973), p. 270.

60. Luker, *Alexander Kuprin,* p. 107.

61. Bushnell, *Mutiny amid Repression,* pp. 141, 173.

62. Bushnell, "Tsarist Officer Corps," p. 756.

63. A. Volynets, "P'ianaia revoliutsiia," *Deiatel',* no. 11 (Aug. 1907): 164–67. For a discussion of how the upper classes feared sober workers, whom they considered to be conscious revolutionaries, and yet simultaneously maintained the myth of the alcoholic revolutionary, see Laura Lynne Phillips, "Everyday Life in Revolutionary Russia: Working Class Drinking and Taverns in St. Petersburg, 1900–1929" (Ph.D. diss., University of Illinois at Urbana-Champaign, 1993), pp. 85–88.

64. "Politicheskaia platforma alkogolika," *Deiatel',* no. 13 (Dec. 1911): 8–9.

65. Quoted in "Aktivnoe uchastie alkogolikov v revoliutionykh smutakh," *Deiatel',* no. 13 (Dec. 1911): 9–11.

66. Quoted in ibid., p. 10.

67. Shlapentokh, "Drunkenness and Anarchy," pp. 470, 473. The sailors of Kronstadt who revolted in October 1905 voiced, among other demands, the right to consume alcoholic beverages, "since sailors are not children under the care of their parents."

68. A. Bil'derling, "Armiia, kak rassadnik trezvosti v narode," *Russkii invalid,* no. 3 (1910).

69. A. Iv. Zuev, *Deiatel',* no. 5 (May 1910): 780.

70. Nikolai Vakulovskii, "Charka v russkom flote," *VT,* no. 165 (Sept. 1908): 3–4.

71. Johnson, *Liquor Problem,* p. 176. Sailors were to receive money instead of vodka.

72. A full description of the exhibit is given by L. V. Evdokimov, "Bor'ba s p'ianstvom," *Russkii invalid,* nos. 17 and 27 (Jan. 1910). For instance, there was a display of Russian temperance journals such as *Vestnik trezvosti* and also foreign material, including a brochure from Tasmania, materials from the Good Templars, Belgian cartoons, etc. The exhibit included *lubok*s from the seventeenth century, that is, pictures with captions that denounced alcohol, prompting Evdokimov to remark that ordinary people began temperance crusades two centuries before the intelligentsia did.

73. L. V. Evdokimov, "Bor'ba s p'ianstvom," *Russkii invalid,* no. 15 (Jan. 1910).

74. "Alkogolizatsiia soldat," reprinted from *Kolokol* in *Deiatel',* no. 9 (1912): 31.

75. "Alkogolizatsiia soldat," *Deiatel',* no. 9 (1912): 32.

76. Johnson, *Liquor Problem,* p. 194. David Christian, "Prohibition in Russia, 1914–1925," *Australian Slavonic and East European Studies* 9, no. 2 (1995): 91, cites the text of the circular from the Ministry of Finance of May 5, 1914, which stated clearly that all dispensers of liquor except first-class restaurants would be closed "immediately on the declaration of mobilization, until the dispatch of all reservists . . . from the assembly points to the army, that is, until the closure of the assembly points."

77. Johnson, *Liquor Problem,* pp. 190–200.

78. Ibid., p. 198.

79. Shlapentokh, "Drunkenness and Anarchy," p. 485.

80. The entire directive (*prikaz* no. 309) is printed in *VT,* nos. 234–235 (June–July 1914): 14–18.

81. "Rasporiazhenie pravitel'stva," *VT,* no. 240 (Dec. 1917): 16–18.

82. "Trezvost' v voiskakh," *VT,* nos. 234–35 (June–July 1914): 13.

83. Johnson, *Liquor Problem,* p. 199.

84. Fraser, *Russia of To-day,* p. 37.

85. Johnson, *Liquor Problem,* pp. 215–16.

86. L. V. Evdokimov, "Vino v okopakh," *Russkii invalid,* no. 289 (Dec. 1914): 13.

87. Christian, "Prohibition in Russia," pp. 100–101.

88. Johnson, *Liquor Problem,* p. 216.

89. Ibid., pp. 216–17.

90. Gordon, *Russian Prohibition,* pp. 11–12.

91. Sir Alfred Knox, *With the Russian Army, 1914–1917* (New York, 1921), vol. 1, p. 307; see also William Steveni, *The Russian Army from Within* (New York, 1914), pp. 31, 42.

92. Shlapentokh, "Drunkenness and Anarchy," p. 477.

93. Segal, *Russian Drinking,* p. 120.

94. Shlapentokh, "Drunkenness and Anarchy," pp. 478–79.

95. Christian, "Prohibition in Russia," p. 101. Christian disagrees with Shlapentokh's assertion that the Germans and Austrians deliberately plied the Russians with liquor so that they would lose battles. See Shlapentokh, "Drunkenness and Anarchy," pp. 481–83.

96. Segal, *Russian Drinking,* p. 120; Shlapentokh, "Drunkenness and Anarchy," p. 479.

97. Shlapentokh, "Drunkenness and Anarchy," p. 464.

Chapter 5

1. E. M. Jellinek, "Classics of the Alcohol Literature: Old Russian Church Views on Inebriety," *Quarterly Journal of Studies on Alcohol* 3, no. 4 (Mar. 1943): 663–67, noted: "The gravity of the problem in the Russian Middle Ages is indicated by the fact that inebriety was one of the few vices to which entire sermons were dedicated, while other vices were usually dealt with collectively" (p. 663). Early preachers against the abuse of drink were St. Theodosius Pecherskii (d. 1074), Abbot Daniel of Chernigov (early twelfth century), and St. Tikhon of Voronezh (eighteenth century), who was forced out of his bishopric and into retirement by the liquor merchants and by the government they pressured because of his unrelenting opposition to drink. See Olga Novikoff, "The Temperance Movement in Russia," *Nineteenth Century,* Sept. 1882, p. 443. For Tikhon's inveighing against Carnival and drink, see Gregory L. Freeze, "Institutionalizing Piety: The Church and Popular Religion, 1750–1850," in *Imperial Russia: New Histories for the Empire,* ed. Jane Burbank and David L. Ransel (Bloomington: Indiana University Press, 1998), pp. 224–26.

2. Quoted by Jellinek, "Classics of the Alcohol Literature," p. 663.

3. From the miracle tale of the Mother of God's appearance to St. Basil. See Eve Levin, "Miracles of Drunkenness: The Culture of Alcohol in Muscovite Hagiography and Miracle Tales," paper presented at the American Association for the Advancement of Slavic Studies Annual Conference, Seattle, WA, 1997.

4. "By defining alcohol abuse as a disease rather than as sin or a vice, especially for lay people, the ecclesiastical authors of miracle tales depicted them as deserving of healing. It became a virtue for family members, friends, and even strangers to bring them to pilgrimage sites for treatment, even by force if necessary" (ibid., p. 6). "Moscovite ecclesiastical authors were concerned about the disruptive social consequences [of drunkenness]" (ibid., p. 9).

5. Metropolitan Vladimir, "Arkhipastyrskii prizyv dukhovenstva i obshchestva k bor′be s p′ianstvom," *V bor′be za trezvost′*, no. 1 (1911): 32. Vladimir favored the excommunication of Leo Tolstoi and a lay temperance activist, Ivan Churikov.

6. Quoted by Segal, *Russian Drinking*, p. 329. A censorious British consul was puzzled by the tolerant Russian attitude toward the unfortunate drunk: "What is wanted is a change in public opinion. The sight of a drunken man causes no feeling of disgust." Stanley to Granville, Aug. 1, 1881, Odessa, as quoted by Dixon, "The Church's Social Role," p. 191 n. 40.

7. Bulgakovskii, *P′ianstvo*, p. 18.

8. On the early struggles of the church against the drunkenness of the people, see R. E. F. Smith and D. Christian, *Bread and Salt: A Social and Economic History of Food and Drink in Russia* (Cambridge, 1984), pp. 93, 137–42, 167–72.

9. In many ways, the clergy was a caste with frequent intermarriage among clerical families, as argued by Gregory L. Freeze, *The Parish Clergy in Nineteenth-Century Russia: Crisis, Reform, Counter-reform* (Princeton: Princeton University Press, 1983), pp. 173–78, 278–79. Therefore, if there is a hereditary factor in alcoholism, then the gene pool (as well as the occupational hazard of being offered drink at every rite and ritual) must have strongly reinforced the clergy's chances for alcoholism. D. G. Bulgakovskii, "Rol′ pravoslavnago dukhovenstva v bor′be s narodnym p′ianstvom," *ZhROONZ*, no. 6 (June 1900): 550, said that in Novgorod eparchy for the year 1880, fifteen priests were called before a clerical court for being obviously drunk. He noted that these were only the fifteen who were discovered. Segal, *Russian Drinking*, p. 147, stated that by the end of the nineteenth century, the clergy was making an effort to remain sober partly through improved morals and partly because of "punishments imposed upon drunkards by the Church administration."

10. Levin, "Miracles of Drunkenness," p. 4. In the nineteenth century some monasteries contained clinics for clerical alcoholics. See *Trezvye vskhody*, Apr.– May 1909, p. 65. Father Bulgakovskii admitted, "In some monasteries they drank literally day and night for want of anything to do." "Rol′," p. 547.

11. The inadequacies of seminary education were strongly emphasized in his memoirs (originally published in 1858): I. S. Belliustin, *Description of the Clergy in Rural Russia: The Memoirs of a Nineteenth-Century Parish Priest*, translated with an interpretative essay by Gregory L. Freeze (Ithaca: Cornell University Press, 1985), pp. 87–109.

12. At the 1912 All-Russian Congress of Church Temperance Workers, Father Krasnov from Riazan explained, "There is the influence of the social background out of which the clergy comes, the role of traditions inherited from fathers, grandfathers, and great-grandfathers; poverty, and the absence of broad spiritual

and cultural interests in the social spheres of the provincial clergy" (quoted by Segal, *Russian Drinking,* p. 147).

13. Belliustin, *Description,* p. 128. See Marina M. Gromyko, *Traditsionnye normy povedeniia i formy obshcheniia russkikh krest'ian XIX v.* (Moscow, 1986), pp. 34, 52, 56. Gromyko tends to understate the role of alcohol in these village customs. All the pre-Soviet works that I have consulted stress the association of *pomoch'* with drink. See, for example, Dr. N. V. Farmakovskii, "Materialy k bor'be s alkogolizmon v derevne," *Trudy komissii po voprosam ob alkogolizme i merakh borby s nim: Russkoe Obshchestvo Okhraneniia Narodnago Zdraviia,* nos. 10, 2 (1909), p. 1282.

14. Belliustin, *Description,* pp. 116, 126–27.

15. D. G. Bulgakovskii, "Die Rolle, welche der russischen Geistlichkeit im Kampfe mit der Trunksucht des Volkes zu Teil fällt." German summary by A. von Rothe, in *Alkoholismus* 3 (1902): 291–94.

16. Ivan Turgenev, "Two Landowners," in *Sketches from a Hunter's Album* (New York, 1990), p. 187.

17. Responses to a questionnaire on drinking distributed among rural clergy in 1908 reported that they drank with their parishioners "on holidays and during entire processions with the holy ikons." See the report of the survey given by P. Mirtov, in *Trudy pervago vserossiiskogo s"ezda po bor'be s p'ianstvom: S.-Peterburg 28 dekabria 1909 g.–6 ianvaria 1910 g.,* vol. 3, p. 1144. "Not only had churchmen in the past failed to warn their flock of the dangers of alcohol, but they had themselves succumbed to its temptations" (Dixon, "The Church's Social Role," p. 179).

18. See page 5 of the photo gallery in this volume.

19. The incident was reported in *Nedelia* 27, no. 19 (May 8, 1894): 596.

20. Bishop Mitrofan later became a representative in the Duma in 1907. See J. F. Hutchinson, "Science, Politics, and the Alcohol Problem in Post-1905 Russia," *Slavonic and East European Review,* 58, no. 2 (Apr., 1980):236.

21. S. A. Rachinskii, *Pis'ma k dukhovnomu iunoshestvu o trezvosti* (Kazan, 1898). Writing from Ufa in 1910, a priest exulted that there was at last in his area a clerical temperance society and credited the Ufa Consistory for allowing it. *Deiatel',* no. 4 (Apr. 1910): 66–67.

22. Gordon, *Russian Prohibition,* pp. 15–16.

23. P. Mirtov, "K voprosu o kurse ucheniia o trezvosti dlia dukhovnykh seminarii," *S"ezd* 2 (1910): 607.

24. James H. Krukones, "Satan's Blood, Tsar's Ink: Rural Alcoholism in an Official 'Publication for the People,' 1881–1917," *Russian History/Histoire russe* 18, no. 4 (1991): 439: "government objected to alcoholism for a variety of reasons, including the loss of economic productivity, the disruption of social order, and the undermining of public morality." Stephen P. Frank, "Confronting the Domestic Other: Rural Popular Culture and Its Enemies in Fin-de-Siècle Russia," in *Cultures in Flux: Lower-Class Values, Practices, and Resistance in Late Imperial Russia,* ed. Stephen P. Frank and Mark D. Steinberg (Princeton, 1994), pp. 3–4, argues that outsiders attempted to "colonize" the countryside, changing peasant culture in order to create sober peasants in their own image.

25. N. Kedrov, "Kipuchaia trezvennaia rabota," *V bor'be za trezvost'* 6, nos. 3–4 (1916). The account reported that the society's files were filled with testimonials from their members and their wives saying how their lives had changed for the better because of all these activities.

26. Ibid. Although the society observed religious rites, such as taking a pledge each month before the ikon of St. Nicholas, it was supported by the city duma, the governor of Saratov, the state Guardianship, professionals, and workers.

27. "Obshchestvo trezvosti v s. Il'inskom v lugakh, danilovsk. uezda, Iaroslav-skoi gubernii," *Prikhodskaia zhizn'* 5 (Apr. 1903): 202–6.

28. *Pervyi godichnyi otchet Spas-Zaulkovskago obshchestva trezvosti za 1910 god* (Moscow, 1911), p. 21.

29. See *Trezvye vskhody,* June–July 1909, p. 77. One report, written in 1899, gave a conservative estimate of the number of temperance societies organized in parishes. It claimed that there were only about 150 societies out of 30,000 parishes. See Bulgakovskii, "Rol'," p. 560.

30. *Trezvaia zhizn'* 4 (Dec. 1901): 605. In May 1905, one writer to *Trezvaia zhizn'* stated, "Our temperance society was organized at the instigation of the local priest, so we had no outside help" (p. 94).

31. A Bolshevik writer stressed that peasants attempted to free themselves from alcoholism by opposing taverns and taking oaths of sobriety. But what was required for success was an economic and social transformation in the countryside. See D. N. Voronov, *Zhizn' derevni v dni trezvosti* (Petrograd, 1916), p. 62.

32. *Trezvaia zhizn'* 4 (Dec. 1901): 601.

33. Arkadii M. Korovin, "La tempérance en Russie," in *Septième congrès contre l'abus des boissons alcooliques* (Paris, 1899–1900), p. 295.

34. Father Paul, "Pervaia Rossiiskaia Sergievskaia shkola trezvosti," *Trudy kommissii po voprosu ob alkogolizme, merakh bor'by s nim,* no. 10 (1909): 146–49. In 1915, the school celebrated its tenth anniversary. In all, 1,162 children of alcoholics were taught agricultural sciences as well as antialcohol propaganda. See *Rodnaia zhizn',* no. 38 (Sept. 26, 1915): 15–16; and Johnson, *Liquor Problem,* p. 165, who says that the society had two parish schools, with one class for girls, and claimed that the Trinity monastery school "was one of the most famous institutions of its kind in Russia."

35. By 1909, the property was worth more than 35,000 rubles. The library had 3,600 books. See *Rodnaia zhizn',* p. 18. In five years, 287 pupils were taught, and the dining room gave out 30,000 free meals to children and the homeless.

36. Ibid., p. 19.

37. Korovin, "La tempérance en Russie," p. 281.

38. *Rodnaia zhizn',* no. 26 (July 4, 1915).

39. For the history of this society, see Hedda, "Good Shepherds." For Father Rozhdestvenskii's liberal views concerning the necessity to liberate the church from state tutelage, see James W. Cunningham, *A Vanquished Hope: The Movement for Church Renewal in Russia, 1905–1906* (Crestwood, NY: St. Vladimir's Seminary Press, 1981), pp. 230–32 and p. 244 for his plea that the "white" (married) clergy should be allowed to be made bishops, one of the points advocated later by the Renovationists.

40. Hedda, "Good Shepherds," p. 55.

41. *VT,* nos. 126–27 (June–July 1905): 79.

42. Father Rozhdestvenskii gives the figure of 9,415 members in his report in *ZhROONZ* 10 (1900): 607. See also *Ves' Sankt Peterburg na 1906 god,* col. 1049.

43. By 1915, in addition to the factory societies, it had established a branch in the settlements of Martyshkino, Kronstadt, Tsarkoe Selo, and Oranienbaum. See Johnson, *Liquor Problem,* p. 164.

44. "Pamiati Vserossiiskago s"ezda po bor'be s p'ianstvom," *VT*, no. 193 (Jan. 1911): 1. Of the remaining four gold medals, two went to Finnish societies, one to a Lithuanian society, and one to Dr. Shor for his pathological anatomical collection showing the harmful effects of alcohol on the human organism. See Hedda, "Good Shepherds," p. 48, for the number of publications.

45. Dixon, "The Church's Social Role," p. 182.

46. See his obituary in *VT*, nos. 126–27 (June–July 1905): 79. Articles about him by Ivan Grebenshchikov appeared in *V bor'be za trezvost'*, nos. 7–8 (July–Aug. 1914): 7–17; nos. 9–10 (Sept.–Oct. 1914): 7–13; nos. 11–12 (Nov.–Dec. 1915): 25–35. Dr. A. M. Korovin, chair of the first Moscow Temperance Society, who knew Rozhdestvenskii, also wrote a memorial, saying how beloved he was among the workers who sought his help, not only Orthodox but also Lutherans and Catholics. See A. M. Korovin, "Pamiati sviashch. Aleks. Vas. Rozhdestvenskago," *VT*, no. 129 (Sept, 1905): 32–33. See also Dixon, "The Church's Social Role," p. 183.

47. Hedda, "Good Shepherds," p. 2.

48. Members of the Alexander Nevskii Temperance Society usually made pledges for longer than a year. See ibid., p. 56. W. Arthur McKee, "Sobering Up the Soul of the People: The Politics of Popular Temperance in Late Imperial Russia," *Russian Review* 58 (Apr. 1999): 221, claims that peasants equated taking a pledge not to drink with "charms." "The vow administered by Orthodox priests was in part a product of a magical conception of religion" (p. 224). It is doubtful that they thought they were doing anything other than promising not to drink for a certain period.

49. Herlihy, "Joy of the Rus'," pp. 131–47.

50. *O vrednykh sledstviiakh p'ianstva i dukhovnoe ot nego vrachevstvo*, 3d ed. (St. Petersburg, 1904), p. 23. The pamphlet is in the Helsinki Orthodox Library, 239/8.

51. By 1912, women were also chosen to be assistants. Father Mirtov called them "good workers." P. A. Mirtov, in *Trudy vserossiiskago s"ezda prakticheskikh deiatelei po bor'be s alkogolizmom* (Petrograd, 1915), vol. 2, pp. 303–4.

52. A. M. Korovin, "Dvizhenie trezvosti v Rossii," *ZhROONZ*, no. 4 (Apr. 1900): 374. Repeating the Jesus prayer, "Lord Jesus Christ, Son of God, have mercy on me," was an old Greek Orthodox practice adopted by the Russian Orthodox, who often add the words, "a sinner," to the invocation. Timothy Ware, *The Orthodox Church* (New York, 1993), p. 65.

53. *Trezvye vskhody*, nos. 7–10 (1910): 329–30. This form of a "trial" was later adapted by the League of the Militant Godless to put religion in the Soviet Union on trial in the 1920s.

54. This and the following statistics come from V. A. Akimov, "Prikhodskaia bor'ba s alkogolizmom," in *Trudy vserossiiskago s"ezda prakticheskikh deiatelei po bor'be s alkogolizmom*, vol. 2, pp. 17–22.

55. Ibid., p. 21. Father Akimov called for all parishes to keep similar records concerning their temperance activities so that a composite picture would emerge. Further, he urged that temperance statistics be compared to the composition of society as a whole to see if the proportion of those taking pledges equally represented their cohorts in society in general.

56. One worker walked more than 100 kilometers just to find a parish society where he could take a pledge. See I. Preobrazhenskii, "K bor'be s p'ianstvom v narode," *Deiatel'*, no. 8 (Aug. 1912): 186.

57. Father Ioann was canonized in 1964 by the emigrant church and in 1988 by the Orthodox Church in Russia. See Nadieszda Kizenko, "The Making of a Modern Saint: Ioann of Kronstadt and the Russian People, 1855–1917" (Ph.D. diss., Columbia University, 1995), p. 350. Some of his followers, known as Ioannites, were also devoted to abstinence from alcohol. Ioannites were considered too emotional, too antiestablishment in their rejection of the authority of the Synod, and too devoted to the person of Ioann and were censured by the Holy Synod in 1908. See J. Eugene Clay, "Orthodox Missionaries and 'Orthodox Heretics,' " in *Of Religion and Identity*, ed. Michael Khodarkovsky and Robert Geraci (Ithaca, NY: Cornell University Press, 2001), pp. 38–69.

58. N. Lebedev, "O. Ioann Kronshtadtskii," *V bor'be za trezvost'*, no. 2 (Mar.–Apr. 1914): 18. For accounts of the life of this somewhat controversial figure, see most recently Nadieszda Kizenko, *A Prodigal Saint: Father John of Kronstadt and the Russian People* (University Park: Pennsylvania State University Press, 2000); and also, Alla Selawry, *Johannes von Kronstadt, Starez Russlands, mit Selbstzeugnissen und dokumentarischen Belegen* (Basil, 1981); Karl Christian Felmy, *Predigt im orthodoxen Russland: Untersuchungen zu Inhalt und Eigenart der russischen Predigt in zweiten Hälften des 19. Jahrhunderts* (Göttingen, 1972).

59. "K istorii i sovremennom polozhenii tserkovnykh obshchestv trezvosti," *V bor'be za trezvost'*, no. 2 (Mar.–Apr. 1914): 33. At first, 25 persons inscribed themselves in the society but not all of them remained sober. The next year, hundreds joined and soon about 1,500 were on the books despite the fact that the entire number of inhabitants of both sexes in Kronstadt, numbered fewer than 5,000. The figure of 1,818 church temperance societies probably refers to urban societies. Other sources claimed there were 3,000 temperance societies in all of Russia by 1914.

60. Although nearly all contemporaries writing on the subject of temperance noted that for the most part Old Believers were abstemious in drink, if not complete teetotalers, a priest writing in the conservative journal *Deiatel'* claimed that there were Old Believers rich and poor who drank. "Starobriadcheskaia trezvost'," *Deiatel'*, no. 6 (June 1910): 96–99.

61. "K istorii i sovremennom polozhenii tserkovnykh obshechestv trezvosti," *V bor'be za trezvost'*, no. 2 (Mar.–Apr. 1914): 52.

62. Ibid., p. 41.

63. Ibid., p. 44.

64. Ibid., p. 47. Father Ioann was not attempting to impose middle-class morality on the members of his society so much as to eliminate poverty, which reduced their human dignity. Religiously conservative, he nevertheless publicly denounced the 1903 pogroms and the violence against Jews in Kishinev. Kizenko, *Prodigal Saint*, p. 243.

65. "K istorii i sovremennom polozhenii tserkovnykh obshchestv trezvosti," pp. 49–50.

66. Ministering to the poor and alcoholic marked conservative churches in the United States, as in Russia, but it also characterized the work of Dorothy Day, a Catholic anarchist who favored communal living (as did Leo Tolstoi). See "The Patron Saint of Paradox," *New York Times Magazine*, Nov. 8, 1998, pp. 44–47.

67. McKee, "Sobering Up," p. 212. For sympathetic accounts of Churikov and his temperance activities by a member of the intelligentsia who supported sectarians, see A. S. Prugavin, *"Brattsy" i trezvenniki iz oblasti religioznykh iskanii* (Mos-

cow, 1912). See also A. S. Prugavin, *Monastyrskiia tiur'my v bor'be s sektanstvom* (St. Petersburg, 1904), pp. 111–23.

68. For Tolstoi, see chapter 7.

69. McKee, "Sobering Up," p. 217, says Churikov was accused of adopting the sectarian *khlyst* (literally "whip," suggesting the acts of self-mortification they practiced) tenets. Clay, "Orthodox Missionaries," suggests that his enemies accused Churikov of not believing in the resurrection of the body, but in 1910, an investigation by the diocesan missionary council concluded that "Churikov and his followers were neither heretics nor sectarians" (p. 61).

70. Clay, p. 61.

71. Ibid., p. 62.

72. Other churchmen, including the missionary Dmitri Bogoliubov, also at one time supported Churikov. Clay, p. 61.

73. See McKee, "Sobering Up," pp. 220–21, who believes that in some way temperance advocates were attempting to incorporate peasant popular belief into liturgies and sermons. His argument conflates magic with religion. He cites signing in a book or being given oil as magical practices. But the rites of the Orthodox Church are full of such symbols. Common sense and experience showed people that signing a book and receiving oil did not confer sobriety but were merely symbolic of the desired goal.

74. Hedda, "Good Shepherds," pp. 6–7. In 1908, the hierarchy defrocked a popular priest and professor, Mikhail Petrov, associated with the Religious-Philosophical Society. He refused to run as a member of the Union of the Russian People, proclaiming that he supported the liberal Constitutional Democratic Party. Petrov wrote about the relationship of Christianity to contemporary social questions. The church authorities also defrocked Father Nikolai Ognev in the First Duma and five other priests of the Left in the Second Duma—moves that help to explain why the centrist party of the Octobrists opposed the hierarchy by supporting Churikov. In addition to harassing and defrocking liberal priests, the Synod tightened up censorship on church publications and even shut down several presses.

75. Cunningham, *Vanquished Hope*.

76. See chapter 8.

77. Jennifer Hedda, "The Quest for a Christian Politics: The Religious and Political Ideas of the Renovationist Clergy, 1905–1906" (typescript).

78. As late as 1913, Bishop Peter of Smolensk forbade his clergy to engage in temperance work. "Sv. Sinod o bor'be s p'ianstvom," *Deiatel'*, no. 6 (June 1913).

79. M. D. Chelyshev, *Rechi M. A. Chel'ysheva proiznesennyia v Tret'ei Gosudarstvennoi Dume o neobkhodumosti bor'by s p'ianstvom i po drugim voprosam* (St. Petersburg, 1912), p. 220. For a contrary view of the church's supposed silence on social questions, see Gregory L. Freeze, "Handmaiden of the State? The Church in Imperial Russia Reconsidered," *Journal of Ecclesiastical History* 36, no. 1 (Jan. 1985): 82–102.

80. The Guardianship itself included many members of the clergy, but it was a state and not a church organ.

81. Vladimir, Metropolitan of St. Petersburg, declared, "The people themselves were searching and found with joy an asylum from their despondent drunken life in such societies." *Golos tserkvi*, no. 10 (Oct. 1913): 4–5.

82. P. I. Poliakov, "Pravoslavnoe dukhovenstvo v bor'be s narodnym p'ianstvom," *ZhROONZ* 9 (1900): 564. Some of the peasants of Kostroma Province refused to drink liquor and signed an agreement to abstain. As a result, the head of the excise commission blamed Bishop Platon of Kostroma for the "illegal" preaching of priests against drink. Many peasants took the pledge not to drink from March 25 to September 1, the months of heaviest agricultural labor. The liquor merchants claimed that preaching temperance was unchristian. See David Christian, "The Black and Gold Seals: Popular Protests against the Liquor Trade on the Eve of Emancipation," in *Peasant Politics, Economy, Culture in European Russia, 1800–1917*, ed. Esther Kingston-Mann and Timothy Mixter (Princeton: Princeton University Press, 1990), pp. 261–93. Christian makes the point that the temperance movement was actually a boycott against the high prices and poor quality of vodka. That was true of many of the peasant participants in the temperance societies, but it would appear that the priests hoped for genuine temperance. D. G. Bulgakovskii marks this period as the beginning of temperance societies in the Russian Empire: the first was founded in Lithuania in 1858 and then in several other provinces: Saratov, Riazan, Ekaterinoslav, and Kursk and finally in nearly all of Russia. See his "Rol'," pp. 553–56. Sergei Shipov, *O trezvosti v Rossii* (St. Petersburg, 1859), pp. 31–36, also describes how the peasants of Kovno Province took an oath of abstinence. Both Nicholas I and Alexander II banned temperance societies under pressure from landowners who produced vodka. See *Tserkovnyi vestnik* 33, no. 35 (Aug. 30, 1907): col. 1115.

83. "Slovo i primer pastyriavernoe sredstvo protiv p'ianstva," from *Golos poriadka*, reprinted in *Deiatel'*, no. 6 (June 1910): 114. The Eparchy Archives are filled with complaints from tax farmers against the church's temperance societies. See "K voprosu o bor'be dukhovenstva s p'ianstvom," *Deiatel'*, no. 6 (June 1910): 95.

84. See A. V. Rozhdestvenskii, "Chto sdelalo pravoslavnoe dukhovenstvo dlia bor'by s narodnym p'ianstvom?" *ZhROONZ* 10 (1900): 583–617. Also, Bulgakovskii speaks of an *ukaz* of the Holy Synod dated July 5–22, 1889, that urged the clergy to form parish societies. Much earlier, in 1820, Tsar Alexander I issued an order to the Holy Synod demanding that it suppress drunkenness among the rural clergy; see Bulgakovskii, "Rol'," pp. 549, 556. By 1915, many urban parishes had such societies in St. Petersburg, including the Voniratyvskoe Society, the Matthew Society, the Ulianovskoe Society, and the Serafimovskoe Society. See Johnson, *Liquor Problem*, pp. 164–65.

85. Jiri Tilk, "Russia," in *Temperance of All Nations* (New York, 1893), p. 332.

86. A. M. Korovin, "Dvizhenie trezvosti v Rossii," *ZhROONZ*, no. 4 (Apr. 1900): 375.

87. Tilk, "Russia," p. 332.

88. Cited in Rozhdestvenskii, "Chto sdelalo," p. 606.

89. I. Preobrazhenskii, "K bor'be s p'ianstvom v narode," *Deiatel'*, no. 8 (Aug. 1912): p. 186.

90. Tilk, "Russia," pp. 332–33.

91. *Golos tserkvi*, no. 10 (Oct. 1913): 9.

92. The First All-Russian Congress on the Struggle against Drunkenness proclaimed that it would call a second meeting, but it never received permission from the Ministry of the Interior to do so because so many of the speeches were overtly political.

93. *V bor'be za trezvost'*, no. 5 (Sept.–Oct. 1914): 4.

94. "Otkrytoe pis'mo vsem obshchestvam i brat'iam trezvosti i vsem druz'iam naroda, trudiashchimsia nad spaseniem pogibaiushchikh ot p'ianstva," *Deiatel'*, no. 4 (Apr. 1911): 69–70; and "K voprosu o bor'be s alkogolizmom," *Deiatel'*, no. 9 (1913): 277.

95. In addition to members of the Holy Synod, in attendance were some high-ranking prelates: Metropolitan Vladimir, chair, Bishop Mitrofan, vice-chair, Archbishop Arsenii; Bishop Anastasii; Philip, rector of the Moscow Seminary; and archimandrites Dmitri, Modest, Nikodim, Feodosii, Antonii, and others. See "S″ezd po bor'be s alkogolizmom," *VT*, no. 212 (Aug. 1912): 1–19.

96. Arsenii, archbishop of Novgorod, "Rech', pri otkrytii protivoalkogol'nago s″ezda v Moskve 6-go avgusta 1912 goda," *Golos tserkvi*, no. 11 (Nov. 1912): 55.

97. Ibid., p. 59.

98. On hooliganism and alcoholism, see Joan Neuberger, *Hooliganism: Crime, Culture, and Power in St. Petersburg, 1900–1914* (Berkeley: University of California Press, 1993).

99. Arsenii, "Rech'," pp. 60–61.

100. Konstantin Vetlin, "Bor'ba s p'ianstvom," in *Trudy vserossiiskago s″ezda prakticheskikh deiatelei po bor'be s alkogolizmom*, vol. 2 (1915), p. 79.

101. Metropolitan Vladimir, "Slovo na molebne pred otkrytiem v Moskve protivoalkogol'nago s″ezda 6-go avgusta 1912 g.," *Golos tserkvi*, no. 10 (Nov. 1912): 1–2.

102. "S″ezd po bor'be s alkogolizmom," *VT*, 18. Johnson, *Liquor Problem*, p. 177.

103. Johnson, *Liquor Problem*, p. 177. Many priests faulted the state Guardianship for its lack of success. See G. B. and Y., "Letopis' bor'by s p'ianstvom," *Prikhodskaia zhizn'* 5 (Apr. 1903): 199–202.

104. Ellii Verkhovstinskii, in *Trudy vserossiiskago s″ezda prakticheskikh deiatelei po bor'be s alkogolizmom*, vol. 2, pp. 71–72.

105. Vetlin, "Bor'ba s p'ianstvom," in *Trudy vserossiiskago s″ezda prakticheskikh deiatelei po bor'be s alkogolizmom*, vol. 2, p. 75.

106. *Trudy vserossiiskago s″ezda*, vol. 2 (1915), pp. 67 and 96.

107. "Sv. Sinod o bor'be s p'ianstvom," *Deiatel'*, no. 6 (June 1913): 189. The French socialist newspaper *L'humanité* ridiculed the efforts of the clergy, calling the congress an exercise in hypocrisy and impotency since the clergy were "the greatest models for drunkenness in Russia." Furthermore, it claimed, proof that their efforts were ineffectual was that revenue from vodka was rising at a faster rate than the increase in population. Article reprinted in *Les annales antialcooliques*, Oct. 1912, 351.

108. "Sv. Sinod o bor'be s p'ianstvom," *Deiatel'*, no. 6 (June 1913): 190. See also P. Bel'tiukov, "O nekotorykh prichinakh slabago rasprostraneniia v narode trezvosti," *VT*, no. 158 (Feb. 1908): 17–19.

109. *VT*, no. 203 (Nov. 1911): 25.

110. Mitrofan, metropolitan of St. Petersburg, "Slovo v den' vserossiiskago prazdnika trezvosti," *Golos tserkvi*, no. 11 (Nov. 1913): 11–12. The founder of the All Russian Working Union of Christian Temperance Workers was a layman, Boris Il'ich Gladkov, born in Kursk Province in 1847. He studied law at the Imperial Kharkov University. He also founded the Circles of Christian Sober Youth. Within three years, he opened twenty-seven branches of the union and many youth circles.

111. For this and the following description see "Prazdnik trezvosti v g. S. Peter-burge," *VT*, no. 232 (Apr. 1914): 26–27. The Easter temperance holiday was cele-brated in Moscow with church services, sermons, and the distribution of litera-ture, including to the offices of the Guardianship as a pointed reminder that their temperance leadership was ineffectual.

112. "Davno pora!" *VT*, no. 230 (Feb. 1914): 1–2.

113. Hedda, "Good Shepherds," p. 33.

114. Ibid., pp. 53–54.

115. *Golos tserkvi*, no. 10 (Oct. 1913): 3.

116. I am indebted to Jennifer Hails Hedda for her periodization of clerical social-religious work and for her insights about the official church's take over of social movements after the 1905 revolution.

117. I. Aivazov, *Golos tserkvi*, no. 3 (Mar. 1914): 182. Aivazov noted: "Under the protection of the prelate, the ranking dignitary of the Russian Orthodox Church has sheltered, increased, and widened Orthodox activities in the struggle for sobri-ety" (p. 190). For more about Aivazov, see "Aivazov," in *Modern Encyclopedia of Religions in Russia and the Soviet Union*, ed. Paul Steeves (New York: Academic Press, 1988), vol. 1, pp. 70–72.

118. A cleric wrote anonymously in a church newspaper that in some instances the church had been too timid to preach abstinence because it went against the state's fiscal interests. He urged the clergy to speak up boldly for sobriety. "Tser-kov v bor'be s alkogolizmom," *Tserkovnyi vestnik*, Aug. 30, 1907, pp. 1114–17.

119. See, for example, M. Galkin, "O bor'be s p'ianstvom," *Prikhodskii sviash-chennik* 9 (Mar. 4, 1912): 5–8, in which the author criticizes the government for failing to support the church's efforts and even for hindering the work of temper-ance. I am grateful to Jennifer Hails Hedda for supplying me with this citation.

120. Father Innokentii Seryshev, "Monashestvo i p'ianstvo," *Krasnyi zvon*, Sept. 1909, pp. 171–174. I am indebted to Jennifer Hails Hedda for this citation.

121. For the activities of Father Gapon, see Hedda, "Good Shepherds," chap. 7.

122. "Dukhovenstvo v bor'be s p'ianstvom," *VT*, no. 202 (Oct. 1911): 29–30. Father Mirtov received permission from the minister of communications to sign up forty students from the ministry's school to take courses on alcoholism at the Alexander Nevskii Temperance Society in St. Petersburg.

123. Johnson, *Liquor Problem*, pp. 167–68, says that the state did what it could to discourage private temperance efforts in Russia.

124. *Trudy pervago vserossiiskago s''ezda po bor'be s p'ianstvom: S. Peterburg 28 dekabria 1909 g.-6 ianvaria 1910 g.*, vol. 3, p. 1181.

125. Hedda, "Good Shepherds," p. 54.

126. Deacon M. Sretenskii, *Pervyi godichnyi otchet Spas-Zaulkovskago Ob-shchestva Trezvosti za 1910 god* (Moscow, 1911), p. 30. Father Vladimir Vostokov, "K voprosu o bor'be s p'ianstvom," *Deiatel'*, no. 11 (1910): 215.

127. A. M. Korovin, "P'ianstvo vo Vladimirskoi gubernii," *VT*, no. 204 (Dec. 1911): 16.

128. The Living Church arose out of the turmoil associated with the confisca-tion of church property during the famine of 1921. When some priests refused to surrender holy objects, a violent persecution of those priests ensued. Metropolitan Veniamin of Petrograd was executed; Patriarch Tikhon was placed under house arrest. "A group of radical clergy used the covert backing of the secret police to set up a new church administration. Calling themselves 'Renovationists' and 'the

Living Church,' these parish priests and a handful of bishops embarked on a campaign to combine Orthodoxy with Bolshevism." See Edward E. Roslof, "Russian Orthodoxy and the Tragic Fate of Patriarch Tikhon (Bellavin)," in *The Human Tradition in Modern Russia,* ed. William B. Husband (Wilmington, DE, 2000), p. 88. For Lenin's approval of the Renovationist Movement, see Edward E. Roslof, "The Renovationist Movement in the Russian Orthodox Church, 1922–1946" (Ph.D. diss., University of North Carolina, 1994). The essence of the reform movement was "to make Orthodox Church practice more relevant to the Russian masses" (p. 3). See also Daniel Peris, *Storming the Heavens: The Soviet League of the Militant Godless* (Ithaca, NY: Cornell University Press, 1998), p. 2, "in 1922 the regime promoted a schism in the Church and supported the 'Renovationist' movement openly loyal to the Bolsheviks. True, pressure for reforming the Orthodox Church administration had existed for over twenty years, but recently opened Party archives indicate the Renovationist church was thoroughly controlled by the Bolsheviks."

129. Richard Stites, *Revolutionary Dreams: Utopian Vision and Experimental Life in the Russian Revolution* (New York, 1989), p. 121.

130. Daniel Peris, "Commissars in Red Cassocks: Former Priests in the League of the Militant Godless," *Slavic Review* 54, no. 2 (1995): 344–48.

Chapter 6

1. *Trudy Kommissii po voprosy ob alkogolizme i merakh bor'by s nim,* no. 3 (St. Petersburg, 1899), pp. 163–64.

2. *S"ezd* 3, no. 1 (1910): 160. A temperance writer also noted that women frequently acted as bootleggers. See his "K voprosu o merakh bor'by s tainoi prodazhei vina," *V bor'be za trezvost',* 1914, p. 59.

3. *Tserkovnyi vestnik* 50 (1915): pp. 1, 616.

4. *S"ezd* 3 (1910): 1157.

5. Stephen P. Frank, "Narratives within Numbers: Women, Crime, and Judicial Statistics in Imperial Russia, 1834–1913," *Russian Review* 55 (Oct. 1996): 560, calculated that 16 percent of the women bootleggers were peasant farmers, 25 percent were already engaged in retail selling, 12 percent were tavern keepers, and 17 percent were housewives.

6. See Frank, *Crime,* p. 153, "reports from many localities reported that bootlegging was the exclusive preserve of women" (p. 123). See also "O shinkarstve v Orlovskoi gubernii," *Deiatel',* no. 1 (Jan. 1911): 15, in which it was said that women spent their earnings from bootlegging on fashionable clothes and other finery, of which even their fathers and husbands approved.

7. Frank, "Narratives within Numbers," p. 558 n. 41.

8. I. Mordvinov, *S"ezd* 1 (1910): 296.

9. A. Ol'ginskii, "Zhenshchina i vodka," *VT,* no. 101 (May 1903).

10. Sidsel Eriksen, "Alcohol as a Gender Symbol," *Scandinavian Journal of History* 24 (1999): 52.

11. *Trudy,* vyp. 10 (1909), p. 1216.

12. Herlihy, "Joy of the Rus'," pp. 131–47.

13. S. Sumbaev, "Interesy russkoi derevni," *Vremennik zhivopisnoi Rossii* 1, no. 25 (1901): 230–31.

14. A. Bulovskii, "Le monpole de l'eau-de-vie en Russie et son influence sur la vie du peuple," Cinquième congrès international contre l'abus des boissons alcooliques, Brussels, 1897, p. 62.

15. See, for example, S. Shol'ts, "P'iantsvo i prestuplenie," *Izvestiia Moskovskoi gubernskoi zemskoi upravy,* no. 3, Mar. 1914, 5. According to Segal, *Russian Drinking,* p. 170: "The most frequently reported male to female ratio was about 11:1; however, various reports have placed the ratio of Russian male to female alcoholics as high as 18:1 and as low as 6:1." Some temperance literature hinted that wealthy women often drank at home alone and hid their addiction. For aristocratic women of Moscow and St. Petersburg in the eighteenth century who held drinking contests, see Lindsey Hughes, *Russia in the Age of Peter the Great* (New Haven: Yale University Press, 1998), p. 194.

16. Phillips, "Everyday Life," p. 203.

17. N. Rozanov, "Narodnaia russkaia satira na p'ianstvo," *V bor'ba za trezvost',* nos. 5–6 (May–June 1913): 37. He cites the collection of songs made by Academician A. V. Sobolevskii.

18. Segal, *Russian Drinking,* p. 156.

19. Eriksen, "Alcohol as a Gender Symbol," p. 47.

20. Segal, *Russian Drinking,* p. 12.

21. Christian, "Traditional and Modern Drinking Cultures," pp. 61–84.

22. Cited in Phillips, "Everyday Life," p. 202. For descriptions of working women's drinking, see Phillips, "In Defense of Their Families: Working-Class Women, Alcohol, and Politics in Revolutionary Russia," *Journal of Women's History* 11, no. 1 (spring 1999): 101–3.

23. D. Nikol'skii, "Uchastie zhenshchin v bor'be s alkogolizmom," *Deiatel',* no. 11 (Nov. 1907).

24. Eriksen, "Alcohol as a Gender Symbol," p. 49.

25. Quoted by W. A. Swanberg in his unpublished biography "Pussyfoot Johnson."

26. See Laurie Bernstein, *Sonia's Daughters: Prostitutes and Their Regulation in Imperial Russia* (Berkeley: University of California Press, 1995). See also A. Kuprin, *Yama (The Pit),* trans. Bernard Guilbert Guerney (New York, 1932).

27. Maria I. Pokrovskaia, "Prostitutsiia i alkogolizm", *ZhROONZ* 5–6 (1905): 216–23. The report was originally delivered on December 5, 1901.

28. Ibid., p. 218.

29. Ibid.

30. See Richard Stites, *The Women's Liberation Movement in Russia: Feminism, Nihilism, and Bolshevism, 1860–1930* (Princeton: Princeton University Press, 1978), pp. 202–3, 206, 208, 214–15, 218, 225–26, 229, 282, 291, 297, 307.

31. See, for example, her speech before the Society for the Preservation of Public Health, "Bor'ba s prostitutsiei," in *ZhROONZ,* no. 4 (Apr. 1990): 399–406.

32. "Trezvaia zhizn'," *Rodnaia zhizn',* no. 7 (1915).

33. Richard Stites, *Russian Popular Culture: Entertainment and Society since 1900* (Cambridge: Cambridge University Press, 1992), p. 18.

34. *S"ezd* 2 (1910): 569. Dr. Korovin made a survey of drinking habits of children aged seven to thirteen years in Moscow. See his article, "O bor'be s p'ianstvom v Gosudarsvennoi Dume i v Gosudarsvennom Sovete," *VT,* no. 156 (Dec. 1907). The Third Duma also investigated alcoholism in children; see *Prilozheniia k stenograficheskim otchetam gosudarstvennoi dumy,* vol. 3, nos. 439–562,

p. 34, in which it was recorded that when one of the children was asked, "Are you not ashamed to drink?" The child responded, "Why should I be ashamed? Auntie, mamma, uncle, and little sister drink; why should I not drink?"

35. N. G. Pomyalovsky (Pomialovskii), *Seminary Sketches* (Ithaca, NY: Cornell University Press, 1973), p. xxvi.

36. Johnson, *Liquor Problem*, pp. 172–73. I am reminded of the fact that when I was a teenager working in a bank, part of my pay was a carton of cigarettes each month.

37. E. Chebysheva-Dmitrieva, *Rol' zhenshchiny v bor'be s alkogolizmom* (St. Petersburg, 1904), p. 2. As far as I know, Russians did not advocate sterilization of male alcoholics as did some Germans. One German physician, Dr. Ploetz, described as "a pioneer worker in the field of race hygiene, contended that in the families of drinkers, first slightly degenerated children are begotten, then, with an increase in parental alcoholism, more degenerated. . . . There is an increased mortality and final sterility." Gordon, *Anti-alcohol Movement*, pp. 99–100. Gordon also quotes a French physician on the subject of degeneracy: "In his passion for alcohol the peasant becomes the cause of a morbid heredity, of social downfall. From the union of these degenerates follows either sterility, or a vitiated offspring *ab ovo*. The children retain an indelible stamp, the *stigmata* of alcoholism, and when they reach maturity, they procreate in their turn, weaklings, idiots, epileptics, brains of an arrested development, furrowed with misery and corrupted with sickness to which they soon succumb" (pp. 60–61).

38. On the supposedly scientific basis for this belief, see the report by D. N. Borodin in *S''ezd* 2 (1910): 490–93. Russians at least tested women independently of men for the effects of alcohol on their children. None of the experiments described in Gordon, *Anti-alcohol Movement*, pp. 83–115, appears to make a distinction between whether it was the drinking of the mother or the father that affected the child, although a chemist from the University of Basel, Professor von Bunge, claimed that if a man was a drinker, his daughter would be incapable of nursing her children.

39. D. Nikol'skii, "Uchastie zhenshchin v borb'e s alkogolizmom," *Deiatel'*, no. 11 (Nov. 1907): 169.

40. "Alkogolizm," in *Entsiklopedicheskii slovar'*, states that inherited alcoholic traits threatened to produce "the fundamental decadence of the population."

41. Metropolitan Vladimir, "Arkhipastyrskii prizyv dukhovenstva i obshchestva k bor'be s p'ianstvom," *Golos tserkvi*, no. 6 (June 1913): 28. Cristoph Wilhelm Hufeland wrote *Makrobiotik* in 1796. See James S. Roberts, *Drink, Temperance, and the Working Class in Nineteenth-Century Germany* (Boston, 1984), p. 4. Vladimir also cited English insurance figures that showed that those who did not drink at all paid from 8 to 10 percent less on their premiums. Again, according to English data, on average, nondrinkers lived ten years longer than drinkers. He said that in England (presumably in contrast to Russia) such a survey could be made because there were many teetotalers.

42. Dr. A. Korovin, "P'ianstvo vo Vladimirskoi gubernii," *VT*, no. 204 (Dec. 1911): 11.

43. E. Chebysheva-Dmitrieva, *Rol' zhenshchiny v bor'be s alkogolizmom* (St. Petersburg, 1904), p. 1. See also Stites, *Women's Liberation Movement*, p. 197. For her biography, see Marina Ledkovsky, Charlotte Rosenthal, and Mary Zirin, eds., *Dictionary of Russian Women Writers* (Westport, CT, 1994), pp. 126–28. Apparently

she went on to become active in the Soviet Society for the Struggle against Alcoholism. See Phillips, "Everyday Life," p. 174.

44. A. Ol'ginskii, "Zhenshchina i vodka," *VT*, no. 101 (May 1903): 30.

45. N. Rozanov, "Radost' dlia russkikh zhenshchin," *V bor'be za trezvost'*, no. 5 (1914): 27–28.

46. D. Nikol'skii, "Uchastie zhenshchin v bor'be s alkogolizmom," *Deiatel'*, no. 11 (Nov. 1907): 168.

47. *New York Times*, Nov. 19, 1914, p. 1.

48. E. A. Kivonosova donated 120 rubles to the Kazan Temperance Society in 1894: *VT*, no. 2 (Feb. 1894): 7. M. M. Antonova is mentioned as a benefactor of the Sergievskii Society: *VT*, no. 6 (June 1895): 13. E. M. Dukhovskaia founded one of the two temperance societies of Kharkov, in the village of Novo Merchik in Valkovskii County: *VT*, no. 6 (June 1895): 25. In 1897, Countess S. V. Panina offered a large number of books to a temperance society affiliated with a face powder factory on the condition that the society maintain the collection. See Dr. Alexandre Korowin [Korovin], "La tempérance en Russie," p. 284. Countess Panina became the assistant minister of education under the Provisional Government. See Daniel T. Orlovsky, "The Provisional Government and Its Cultural Work," in *Bolshevik Culture: Experiment and Order in the Russian Revolution*, ed. Abbott Gleason, Peter Kenez, and Richard Stites (Bloomington: Indiana University Press, 1985), p. 46.

49. *Pervyi Zhenskii Kalendar' na 1903 god*, ed. P. N. Arian (St. Petersburg, 1903), pp. 484–525. In her new and exhaustive survey of women's secular charitable organizations, Adele Lindenmeyr does not bring up the subject of temperance societies since there was so little evidence for any such activity among women. See her *Poverty Is Not a Vice: Charity, Society, and the State in Imperial Russia* (Princeton: Princeton University Press, 1996).

50. The letter is published in *Vrachebnaia gazeta* 9 (1902): 334. Later, Chebysheva-Dmitrieva reported how, in 1901 and 1902, she wrote to "several thousand women physicians, teachers in lower or middle schools, wives and daughters of clerks, businessmen, and various liberal professions." She asked for help in creating the new society; she received, she says, not a single response. See her report, "Rol' zhenshchiny v bor'be s alkogolizmom," in *Trudy pervago vserossiiskago s'ezda po bor'be s p'ianstvom*, vol. 3, pp. 1193–200. For the founding of the Society for the Preservation of Women's Health, see "Khronika," *Zhurnal russkago obshchestva okhraneniia narodnago zdraviia*," no. 12 (Dec. 1898): 931. This society for women was more than a lecture club and library. Women were to do exercises, rent skating rinks, arenas, riding halls, and swimming pools, and go on excursions and walks and to dances. They hoped to issue their own journal, books, and brochures to educate women about proper food, care of the skin and hair, and what clothes to wear for their health. Members would adopt healthy lifestyles and influence others by their example. Membership dues for charter members were 10 rubles for the first year and 6 rubles thereafter, or a lifetime membership for 100 rubles. Only women could become active members, but men could be honorary members (if they paid 200 rubles). As a badge of membership, women could wear a special charm on their watch chain. The first president was Dr. M. M. Volkova.

51. Other members were Kortik, Orlova, Burgard, Kopets, Petichinskaia, Rognieva, Count P. P. Bel'tiukkov, Countess E. V. Saburova, Countess V. S. Golenisheva-Kutuzova, Academician Prince I. R. Tarkhanov, Academician N. P.

Ivanovskii (chair of the St. Petersburg Temperance Society), S. A. Smirnov (publisher of the journal *Trezvost'*), Dr. N. I. Grigor'ev, A. N. Borodin, Professor Maliev, women doctors Pokrovskaia, Shneman, and Reshetnikova, Dr. N. S. Uvarov (inspector of the Medical Administration), V. I. Skabichevskii, and many others over time; see *Deiatel'*, no. 1 (1905): 44.

52. "Otdel bor'by s alkogolizmom zhenshchin i detei pri obshchestve okhraneniia zdorov'ia zhenshchny v Sankt Peterburge," *VT*, no. 909 (Jan. 1904): 51–56.

53. Ibid., p. 52.

54. Ibid., p. 44.

55. "Otdel bor'by s alkogolizmom zhenshchin i detei pri obshchestve okhraneniia zdorov'ia zhenshchny v Sankt Peterburge," *VT*, no. 909 (Jan. 1904): 51–56.

56. D. Nikol'skii, "Uchastie zhenshchin v bor'be s alkogolizmom," *Deiatel'*, no. 11 (Nov. 1907).

57. R. Baudouin de Courtenay, "Nyneshnii fazis bor'by s alkogolizmom v Rossii," in *Trudy pervago zhenskago s"ezda pri russkom zhenskom obshchestve v S. Peterburge* (St. Petersburg, 1909), pp. 749–53.

58. Stites, *Women's Liberation Movement*, p. 197.

59. R. Baudouin de Courtenay, "Iz oblasti sovremennago etiko-sotsial'nago dvizheniia," *Soiuz zhenshchin*, nos. 5–6 (May–June 1908): 20–25. She criticized the weak development of temperance activity in Russia: "Readers of Polish temperance journals often ask me why our schools do not teach, as in Sweden and in England, about the harm of alcoholism. Why do we not have even ten teachers who advocate temperance?" (p. 22). She went on to say that teachers in St. Petersburg were indifferent to the idea of teaching courses on the harm of alcohol. Despite all the obstacles in St. Petersburg against inserting antialcohol courses into the curriculum, much could be done if the intelligentsia became aware of the need for such education. As many temperance advocates noted, women and members of the intelligentsia did not appear to be supportive of those advocating abstinence.

60. I have found no evidence that Russian doctors were acquainted with J. Eberle's paper published in 1833 in America, which stated: "The majority of children born to mothers who are heavy drinkers are weak and sickly and few of them reach adolescence." See Jean-Charles Sournia, *A History of Alcoholism* (Cambridge, MA, 1990), p. 33.

61. "1911 god," *VT*, no. 205 (Jan. 1912): 2.

62. *VT*, no. 206 (Feb. 1912): 28.

63. G. Fomin, in *VPONT*, no. 21 (1905).

64. M. D. Chelyshev, "Otkrytoe pis'mo k russkim zhenshchinam," *VT*, no. 232 (Apr.–May 1914): 1–5.

65. Ibid., p. 5.

66. Ibid.

67. "Otnoshenie zhenshchiny i alkogolizmy," *Deiatel'*, no. 2 (Jan. 1905): 58.

68. N. I. Grigor'ev, "Zhenshchina v bor'be s p'ianstvom," *VT*, no. 196 (Apr. 1911): 12–20; *VT*, no. 230 (Feb. 1914): 67.

69. Conversely, in 1914, Dr. A. Verzhbitskii appealed exclusively to women of the intelligentsia, writing an open letter to them that begged them to be models of sobriety and to work for a sober environment. He ended his plea: "Russian women of the intelligentsia, mother and housewife, help us!" See "Otkrytoe pis'mo k russkoi intelligentsii," *V bor'be za trezvost'*, no. 1 (Jan.–Feb. 1914): 6–7.

70. For American women temperance leaders, see Charles A. Isetts, "A Social Profile of the Women's Temperance Crusade: Hillsboro, Ohio," in *Alcohol, Reform, and Society: The Liquor Issue in Social Context,* ed. Jack S. Blocker, Jr. (Westport, CT, 1979), p. 108.

71. Stites, *Women's Liberation Movement,* p. 288; *Zhenskoe delo,* no. 15 (Aug. 1, 1914).

72. A. I. Tomlina, "Vospominaniia o kongresse 1903 goda vsemirnago khristianskago soiuza trezvosti zhenshchin," *Russkaia starina* (Mar. 1916), pp. 460–74. For the association of alcohol with Russian hospitality, see Herlihy, "Joy of the Rus'," pp. 131–47. Russian women of the aristocracy and of the intelligentsia probably felt they had few opportunities to affect the drinking habits of workers and peasants.

73. Phillips, "Everyday Life," p. 176.

74. Ibid., p. 178 n. 33.

75. Ibid., p. 185. For more aversion techniques, see Herlihy, "Joy of the Rus'," pp. 140–41.

76. Reprinted from *VT* in *Zhenskoe delo,* no. 11 (June 1, 1911): 56.

77. Ibid.

78. Published in *VT,* no. 164 (Aug. 1908): 10–12.

79. "Zhaloba krest'ianok," *Nizhegorodskii listok,* no. 152 (June 6, 1899): 2.

80. V. A. Akimov, "Prikhodskaia bor'ba s alkogolizmom," in *Trudy vserossiiskago s"ezda prakticheskikh deiatelei po bor'be s alkogolizmom,* vol. 2, pp. 17–22.

81. See Laurie Manchester's paper, "Gender and Pastoral Care: Shifting Conceptions of Parish Service and the Role of Clerical Women in Imperial Russia," presented at the Annual Meeting of the New England Slavic Association, Wellesley College, Wellesley, MA, Apr. 18, 1997.

82. P. Bel'tiukov, "Pechal'noe iavlenie v dele bor'by s p'ianstvom," *VT,* no. 152 (Aug. 1907): 25–26.

83. A. M. Korovin, "Dvizhenie trezvosti v Rossii," *ZhROONZ,* no. 4 (Apr. 1900): 375–76.

84. Father Paul, "Pervaia rossiiskaia Sergievskaia shkola trezvosti," in *Trudy kommissii po voprosu ob alkogolizm, merakh bor'by s nim,* no. 10 (St. Petersburg, 1909), 148. Apart from Smith's name, we know little about her.

85. See N. Mirovich, *Iz istorii zhenskago dvizheniia v Rossii* (Moscow, 1898), p. 4.

86. In the United States, the Women's Christian Temperance Union split in two over the issue of suffrage. Unlike in Russia, women fought first for temperance and then some of them for suffrage.

87. E. A. Chebysheva-Dmitrieva, "Chto dal i vserossiiskii s"ezd po bor'be s p'ianstvom dlia pedagogov i shkol'nykh vrachei?" *ZhROONZ,* no. 8 (Aug. 1911): 39.

88. Ibid., p. 40.

89. T. Ch., "Opiat' o zelenom zmee," *Zhenskoe delo,* no. 11 (June 1, 1915): 2.

90. The resolutions are reprinted in their entirety in *Soiuz zhenshchin,* no. 12 (1909): 19; in *Zhenskaia mysl'* (Kiev), January 15, 1910; and in V. A. Chernevskii, *K voprosu o p'ianstve,* pp. 60–61.

91. Quoted in Hutchinson, "Science, Politics, and the Alcohol Problem," p. 249.

92. D. Nikol'skii, "Uchastie zhenshchin v bor'be s alkogolizmom," *Deiatel'*, no. 11 (Nov. 1907): 170.

93. *Prilozheniia k stenograficheskim otchetam gosudarstvennoi dumy:* vol. 3, nos. 439–502, p. 45.

94. Ibid.

95. In the United States, women obtained suffrage in 1920, one year after prohibition.

96. Protestant countries were the first to produce temperance societies: the United States in 1808, Norway in 1836, and Sweden in 1857. The first international temperance organization, the Order of Good Templars, was established in 1851 in Utica, New York, and then spread to Canada, Great Britain, and Scandinavia. Hutchinson, "Medicine, Morality, and Social Policy," p. 203, noted, "From England and Germany, the temperance movement spread to Finland and Russia." According to Jack S. Blocker, Jr., the Anti-saloon League in the United States based "its support among conservative middle-class Protestants." See his "The Modernity of Prohibitionists: An Analysis of Leadership Structure and Background," in *Alcohol, Reform, and Society: The Liquor Issue in Social Context* (Westport, CT, 1979), p. 166. There were Catholic temperance movements, but they were in the minority. See Jack S. Blocker, Jr., *American Temperance Movements: Cycles of Reform* (Boston, 1989), pp. xii–xiii. "Evangelical Protestant lay people and clergy have usually provided the bulk of temperance leadership and grass-roots support. At times, however, nonevangelical Protestants have played key roles, and the existence of the Catholic Total Abstinence Union and other Roman Catholic temperance associations indicates the persistent presence of non-Protestant temperance folk" (p. xiii–xiv). Denmark and Sweden appear to be exceptions. Although they were Protestant countries, women were not particularly active in promoting temperance. See Eriksen, "Alcohol as a Gender Symbol," p. 55.

97. Grigor'ev, "Zhenshchina."

98. "Bor'ba zhenshchin s p'ianstvom," *Zhenskoe delo*, no. 11 (June 1, 1911): 56.

99. Speaking of the temperance movement in Scandinavia, Gordon, *Anti-alcohol Movement*, pp. 11–12, noted, "But the temperance movement there was Anglo-American in origin, and bore the familiar Anglo-Saxon stamp." Dixon, "The Church's Social Role," p. 179: "It [temperance movement] spread to Finland and Russia from Britain and Germany." See L. V. Evdokimov, "Bor'ba s p'iantsvom," *Russkii invalid*, no. 17 (1910): "Russia is one hundred years behind America, where the first temperance society was founded in 1808, and is some decades behind Europe. . . . In Finland, the antialcohol movement began in the 30s of the last century and was renewed in 1860; in the Baltic area, such movements arose in 1836 and flourished only from the year 1891."

100. Steven C. Hause and Anne R. Kenney, "The Limits of Suffragist Behavior: Legalism and Militancy in France, 1876–1922," *American Historical Review* 86, no. 4 (Oct. 1981): 794–95.

101. L. V. Evdokimov, "Bor'ba s p'ianstvom," *Russkii invalid*, no. 21 (Jan. 1910).

102. Manchester, "Gender and Pastoral Care," p. 11.

103. V. M. Skvortsov, *Bogoslavskoe obshchestvo trezvosti i bor'ba so shtundoiu* (Kiev, 1895), p. 3.

104. "Sv. Sinod o bor'be s p'ianstvom," *Deiatel'*, 18, no. 6 (June 1913).

105. On Kalmykova's remarkable career, see George Woodcock and Ivan Avak-umovic, *The Doukhobors* (Toronto, 1968), pp. 68–75. According to V. M. Skvort-sov, in a discussion held on October 23, 1900, and reported in *Kommissii po vo-prosy ob alkogolizm,* ed. M. N. Nizhegorodtsev (St. Petersburg, 1909), p. 750, the Dukhobors "gladly consumed spirits up to 1886, but as soon as Luker'ia Kalmy-kova became their chief, she demanded that all Dukhobors end their use of alco-holic drinks." His date, however, does not seem accurate, since she died in De-cember 1886. A. N. Shabanova, a feminist leader, wrote an article on Kalmykova, "Zhenshchina v russkom sektantsve," *Zhenskoe delo,* Jan. 24, 1910, pp. 3–4, without mentioning her ban on alcohol.

106. I. Popov, "Bor'ba s p'ianstvom," *Zhenskoe delo,* Sept. 2, 1914, 1.

107. Levin, "Miracles of Drunkenness," pp. 5–6.

108. Eriksen, "Alcohol as a Gender Symbol," p. 60.

109. Leo Tolstoi, "What's Then to Be Done?" in *The Complete Works of Count Tolstoy,* ed. Leo Wiener, vol. 19 (Boston, 1904–1905), p. 64.

110. Stevens, *Through Russia on a Mustang,* p. 320. "Among the cheap chromos that adorn the walls of village tea-houses and traktirs one of the most familiar scenes is a drunken moujik on the ground and his wife beating him in no gin-gerly manner" (p. 321).

111. L. V. Evdokimov, "Vino v okopakh?" *Russkii invalid,* no. 289 (Dec. 13, 1914).

Chapter 7

1. *Tolstoy's Letters,* vol. 2, *1880–1910,* ed. and trans. R. F. Christian (University of London, 1978), no. 321, n. 5.

2. Reardon, *Temperance Movement,* p. 4.

3. For an account of Tolstoi's spiritual odyssey written in 1879, see his *Confession.*

4. Ibid., p. 432. There has been much discussion concerning the roots of Tol-stoi's ascetic ethic. Pål Kolstø has commented: "There is convincing evidence to suggest that the strong ascetic element in Tolstoi's ethics may best be understood in the context of Eastern Christian monasticism and not primarily as a distant echo of Buddhism or Stoicism. Tolstoi's ideal of indifference to scorn, pain and desire seems to have been molded on the Orthodox idea of passionlessness, *apath-eia* (Church Slavonic: *bezstrastie*). Both the Greek fathers and the Russian novelist insisted that true love can spring forth from our heart only insofar as we have managed to quench our lusts and passions." See Pål Kolstø, "Leo Tolstoy, a Church Critic Influenced by Orthodox Thought," in *Church, Nation, and State in Russia and Ukraine,* ed. Geoffrey A. Hosking, (New York: St. Martin's Press, 1991), pp. 159–60.

5. *Izvestiia Tolstovskogo Muzeia* (St. Petersburg), nos. 3–5 (1911), 11. He was the 221st to sign. As a young man, he had been influenced by the austere teaching of the Hussites.

6. Vladimir Bonch-Bruevich, "Itogi 'Soglasiia protiv p'ianstva,' " *Izvestiia Tol-stovskogo Muzeia,* nos. 3–5 (1911): 22–24. The writers were P. I. Viriukov, M. A. Shmidt, I. I. Gorbunov-Posadov, K. M. Fofanov, I. I. Iasinskii, A. S. Prugavin, N. Kasatkin, S. T. Semenov, P. A. Bulanzh(e)?, F. A. Zheltov, N. N. Miklukho-Maklai, G. Masaryk, P. I. Makushina, and N. N. Ge. Bonch-Bruevich became a Social

Democrat in the 1890s and a specialist in the Russian sectarian movement. He was close to the Skoptsy and managed to collect their papers. After the 1917 revolution, he was a trusted associate of Lenin and an administrator of the Council of the People's Commissars until 1920. His interest in preserving Tolstoi's papers and making contacts with Tolstoian exiles shows that he regarded Tolstoi as a sectarian and political dissident. See Laura Engelstein, *Castration and the Heavenly Kingdom: A Russian Folktale* (Ithaca: Cornell University Press, 1999), passim. In November and December 1917, he was put in charge of a committee to quell riots fueled by alcohol. See Neil Weissman, "Prohibition and Alcohol Control in the USSR: The 1920s Campaign against Illegal Spirits," *Soviet Studies* 38 (July 1986): 350.

7. *Tolstoi's Letters*, vol. 2, p. 436. It seems that Tolstoi did not always forbid guests to drink, as his wife observed on August 28, 1898, on the occasion of Lev's seventieth birthday: "P. V. Preobrazhenskii started to drink to Lev Nikolaevich's health in white wine, then made a clumsy speech which everyone deliberately ignored. One can hardly *drink* to L-N's health, since he preaches total abstinence." See *The Diaries of Sophia Tolstoy*, ed. O. A. Golinenko et al., trans. Cathy Porter (New York, 1985), p. 336.

8. Tilk, "Russia," p. 333. Perhaps the membership numbers include the village Tolstoi invited to sign pledges in 1897.

9. *Diaries of Sophia Tolstoy*, p. 220. The translation of *vino* as "wine" here should probably be "liquor" (i.e., vodka).

10. Nathan H. Dole, *Life of Count Lyof N. Tolstoi* (New York, 1911), pp. 322–23.

11. Tolstoi, *Confession*, p. 22.

12. "Dlia chego liudi odurmanivaiutsia?" was published in English in the *Contemporary Review* in 1891, and in the same year it appeared as the introduction to Dr. P. S. Alekseev's book *O p'ianstve* (On Drunkenness) (Moscow). As early as 1886, Alekseev asked Tolstoi to write an antialcohol play, which he did, *Vlast' t'my* (The Power of Darkness). Tolstoi wrote to I. I. Repin: "I've been editing some books on drunkenness. There are two by Dr. Alekseev (which will be coming out any day), another is with the censor, and a third is being reprinted, and I keep thinking about a booklet on the same subject myself." See *Tolstoy's Letters*, vol. 2, p. 436. Despite this close collaboration of two antialcohol leaders, they became estranged by 1897. Dr. Alekseev believed the cause was that he was an employee of the state and the purist Tolstoi felt the state was evil in purveying alcohol so he would have no further relations with him.

13. L. N. Tolstoi, "Dlia chego liudi odurmanivaiutsia?" *Polnoe sobranie sochinenii*, ed. V. G. Chertkov (Moscow, 1933), vol. 27, p. 282.

14. *Tolstoy: Plays*, vol. 1, *1856–1886*, trans. Marvin Kantor with Tanya Tulchinsky (Evanston, IL: Northwestern University Press, 1994), pp. 167–85.

15. Ibid., p. 175.

16. Ibid., p. 185.

17. The purpose of this publishing endeavor was to bring good literature as cheaply as possible to a broad audience. Even after 1897 when Tolstoi no longer wrote for Posrednik, the publishing house produced moralistic literature, including temperance propaganda. See Jeffrey Brooks, *When Russia Learned to Read: Literacy and Popular Literature* (Princeton: Princeton University Press, 1985), pp. 337–40; McReynolds, *News under Russia's Old Regime*, pp. 172–73.

18. *I. E. Repin i L. N. Tolstoi*, vol. 1: *Perepiska s L. N. Tolstym i ego sem'ei* (Moscow, 1949), p. 14, and n. 3 on p. 106.

19. *Tolstoy's Letters,* vol. 2, no. 326.

20. In a letter dated October 9, 1909, Tolstoi wrote: "Yesterday M. D. Che-lyshev came. A combination of intelligence, vanity, and play-acting and a peasant's common sense, independence and subordination. I can't describe him, but he is very interesting." *Tolstoy's Letters,* vol. 2, p. 729. Tolstoi's wife also mentioned Che-lyshev in her diary: "Mikl. Dm. Chelyshchev [*sic*], a Duma member, arrived from Samara. A large, loud, clever man, he has devoted his life's work to the abolition of vodka." See *Diaries of Sophia Tolstoy,* p. 648.

21. A photocopy of Tolstoi's letter to Chelyshev on making the label was shown at the 1911 exhibit on Tolstoi in Moscow after his death. See *Tolstovskii ezhegodnik, 1911, Izvestiia Tolstovskogo Muzeia,* nos. 3–5 (1911): 26, for a photograph of the document placed in the Tolstoi Museum in St. Petersburg.

22. Johnson, *Liquor Problem,* p. 187. See also *New York Times,* Nov. 19, 1914.

23. For an explanation of Tat'iana Day and its association with drunken students, see *Entsiklopediia zimnikh prazdnikov* (St. Petersburg, 1995), pp. 287–91, where V. A. Giliarovskii is quoted as saying that in fact *sp'iana* (in a drunken state) and Tat'iana not only rhymed but the word described the holiday. A. P. Chekhov, the writer-doctor, was quoted as saying that on that day students drank everything in Moscow except the river, and not that only because it was frozen.

24. Had Tolstoi lived, he would have been pleased to know that a student temperance worker made a rousing speech to fellow students against alcohol on Tat'iana Day in 1914. He told students that they could still be joyous without alcohol. "The mind loses its sharpness and the force of thoughts weakens," he proclaimed. He warned students that alcohol would redden and wrinkle their faces, fade their eyes, stoop their bodies, and turn their hair gray. A. Riabov, "K studentam-tovarishcham," *VT,* no. 231 (Mar. 1914): 13–16.

25. An article by S. Kavelin reprinted in *Deiatel',* no. 14 (1911): 4.

26. Ibid., p. 45.

27. *Why People Become Intoxicated,* in *The Complete Works of Count Tolstoy,* ed. Leo Wiener, vol. 19 (1905), p. 360, n. 1.

28. See Joseph R. Gusfield, *Symbolic Crusade: Status Politics and the American Temperance Movement* (Urbana, IL, 1963), who argued that the American temperance movement was largely the attempt of a narrowly puritanical middle class to impose its values on the lower classes. This model, I argue, does not sufficiently explain the formation of temperance societies in Russia by workers themselves or by professional classes who attempted to reform the educated class.

29. Alekseev, *O p'ianstve,* p. 25.

30. See his introduction to Alekseev, *O p'ianstve,* pp. 6–27, "Dlia chego liudi odurmanivaiutsia?" Originally from Moscow, Alekseev served as a doctor for the government in Siberia, returned to Riga, and lived there until his death in August 1913.

31. *ZhROONZ,* nos. 10–11 (1912): 70. The congress took place from December 1909 to January 1910. D. N. Borodin read a letter to the congress written to him from Tolstoi congratulating the physicians who organized the congress and setting forth his religious views: "I am very happy to contribute as much as possible to your beautiful purpose. The more I see the evil proceeding from drunkenness (and I see this evil in frightful measure), and the more often I have the chance to speak of this evil to those suffering from it, the more I am convinced that the

rescue from it primarily, if not exclusively, is in the realization of the destruction it wreaks, not on the body, but on the soul."

32. *ZhROONZ*, nos. 10–11 (1912): 108

33. In his lecture on Tolstoi's brochures presented at the 1909–10 congress, Grigor'ev pointed out that Tolstoi was not like most temperance workers, who spoke of the physical harm to the drinker and his offspring. Tolstoi defined drunkenness as the "sin of intoxication, which consists in producing an artificial excitation of one's bodily and mental forces." "The Christian Teaching," in *Miscellaneous Letters and Essays by Count Lev N. Tolstoy,* trans. and ed. Leo Wiener (London, 1904), vol. 20, p. 381.

34. *ZhROONZ*, nos. 10–11 (1912): 112.

35. D. G. Bulgakovskii, *Gore goremychnoe* p. 17.

36. Johnson, *Liquor Problem,* p. 189.

37. See Weissman, "Prohibition and Alcohol Control," p. 350.

38. Tolstoi, *Polnoe sobranie sochinenii,* vol. 27, p. 612.

39. Johnson, *Liquor Problem,* pp. 81–82.

40. *Ves' Sankt-Peterburg* for the year 1896 listed 200 members, a library of 230 volumes, and events such as literary evenings. The same city directory continued to list the organization each year; the last one I consulted, for 1909, revealed a steady, but not growing, membership.

41. Tilk, "Russia," p. 334, says that these societies were in Tobolsk Province and Enisei Province near the Chinese border. According to Johnson, *Liquor Problem,* p. 77, "It was a woman who founded the first really successful temperance society in Finland thirty years ago."

42. In the Baltic holdings of the Russian Empire, most of the temperance literature was published in German. Johnson, *Liquor Problem,* pp. 109–10.

43. Ibid., p. 83. Membership in temperance societies in Finland went from 80 in 1877 to 9,801 in 1886.

44. Ibid., p. 91.

45. For the politics of temperance activities in Finland, see Irma Sulkunen, *History of the Finnish Temperance Movement: Temperance as a Civic Religion* (Lewiston, NY, 1990).

46. Johnson, *Liquor Problem,* p. 100.

47. Ibid., p. 101. Even without imperial sanction, a variety of Protestant temperance societies sprang up in the Latvian lands influenced by the American example.

48. Ibid., pp. 102–3.

49. Among the larger cities, temperance societies were formed in Odessa in 1891, Kazan in 1892, and Moscow in 1895. They were all formed for workers. A. M. Korovin, "Dvizhenie trezvosti v Rossii," *ZhROONZ*, no. 4 (Apr. 1900): 375.

50. Ibid., p. 333. Some of the early prominent members were Father Mikhailovskii, Father Ioann of Kronstadt, Senator Barikov, Professor I. Wagner, Count Tol', Prince L. Obolenskii, Professor Jacoby, and Dr. Smolenskii. The society was well supported by its wealthier members.

51. *Deiatel',* nos. 8–9 (Aug.–Sept. 1897): 480.

52. Johnson, *Liquor Problem,* pp. 164–65.

53. A. M. Korovin, "Dvizhenie trezvosti v Rossii," *ZhROONZ*, no. 4 (Apr. 1900): 375.

54. Ibid., p. 377.

55. Dr. S. N. Danillo made a special plea in the journal *Novoe vremia* for donations for a new clinic to be sent to him at the Military Medical Academy. "Chto delat' dlia bor'by s p'ianstvom," *Deiatel'*, no. 12 (Jan. 1910): 165. It does not appear that there were at that date clinics for women and children.

56. "Narodnyi dom E. L. Nobelia," *VPONT* 3, no. 19 (July 21, 1905): 406–8.

57. "1911 god," *VT*, no. 205 (Jan. 1912): 1–2.

58. *VT*, no. 203 (Nov. 1911).

59. A. M. Korovin, "Dvizhenie trezvosti v Rossii," *ZhROONZ*, no. 4 (Apr. 1900): 378.

60. Tolstoi had participated in taking the census in the industrial area near where he lived. Seeing firsthand the dreadful poverty in the industrial section near his home, he recorded his experiences and analyzed the causes of poverty in his long essay *What Then Should Be Done?*, written in 1884–85.

61. "Desiatiletie (1898–1908 g.) Kozhevnicheskago otdeleniia l-go Moskovskago Obshchestva Trezvosti," *VT*, no. 165 (Sept. 1908): 22–25. I. F. Bordman, an administrator of the Tsindel factory, was one of the chief mentors and financial supporters of the First Moscow Temperance Society (he gave more than 100 rubles of his own money). The owners of the factory gave more than a thousand rubles for tearooms and libraries. The major donors were listed—all of them laymen. Even the Guardianship of Public Sobriety contributed a sum of 5,000 rubles over the years.

62. "Otkrytie vystavki po alkogolizmu v g. Moskve," *VT*, no. 168 (Dec. 1908): 4–5.

63. *A Radical Worker in Tsarist Russia: The Autobiography of Semën Ivanovich Kanatchikov*, p. 93.

64. Schneiderman, *Sergei Zubatov*, pp. 81–82.

65. R. K. Valeev, I. M. Ionenko, and I. P Tagirov, "Kazan' v 1917 gody," in *Stranitsy istorii goroda Kazani* (Kazan, 1981).

66. A. M. Korovin, "Dvizhenie trezvosti v Rossii," *ZhROONZ*, no. 4 (Apr. 1900): 376.

67. "Otkrytie bol'nitsy dlia alkogolikov," *Deiatel'*, no. 4 (Apr. 1896): 201.

68. Ibid., p. 206.

69. "Lechebnitsa dlia alkogolikov," *Deiatel'*, no. 3 (Mar. 1896): 162.

70. Ibid., p. 164.

71. L. O. Darkshevich, "Doklad glavnago vracha bol'nitsy komitetu obshchestva trezvosti 1 iunia," *Deiatel'*, no. 7 (July 1896): 400; A. Chekhov, "Alkogolizm i vozmozhna s nim bor'ba," *Novoe vremia*, no. 7441, reprinted in *Deiatel'*, no. 12 (Dec. 1896): 649–55.

72. Darkshevich, "Doklad glavnago vracha bol'nitsy komitetu obshchestva trezvosti: 1 iunia," p. 403.

73. A. Solov'ev, "Chto delat' dlia bor'by s p'ianstvom," *Deiatel'*, no. 12 (Jan. 1910): 165.

74. "Protokol ocherednago zasedaniia komitet Kazanskago obshchestva trezvosti 7 ianvaria," *Deiatel'*, no. 2 (Feb. 1902): 95.

75. "Popechitel'stvo o narodnoi trezvosti," *Deiatel'*, no. 3 (Mar. 1910): 51.

76. See chapter 5 for Galkin's transformation into the atheist Gorev after 1917.

77. Father Mikhail Galkin, "K bor'be s p'ianstvom," *Deiatel'*, no. 4 (Apr. 1910): 60–61.

78. Ibid., p. 53.

79. The Kazan Temperance Society's strong religious ties are revealed by the fact that it formed a committee to help find the Mother of God ikon, which had been stolen from the Kazan monastery; they offered 300 rubles as a reward to anyone who found and returned it. *VT*, no. 124 (1905).

80. *Nedelia* 27, no. 198 (May 1894): 595–96.

81. *Otchet po deiatel'nosti soveta Odesskogo obshchestva dlia bor'by s p'ianstvom za 1894* (Odessa, 1895), pp. 11–12.

82. For commentary on the failure of the official sobriety days in Odessa, see "Dni 'trezvosti' v Odessa," *Odesskaia pochta*, no. 1914 (Apr. 11, 1914): 3; "Bor'ba s p'ianstvom v Odessa," *Odesskaia pochta*, no. 1928 (Apr. 25, 1914): 3; and "Dni nashi zhizni," *Odesskaia pochta*, no. 1932 (Apr. 29, 1914). For the success of the dry days in St. Petersburg, see "Prazdnik trezvosti v. g. S. Peterburge," *VT*, no. 232 (Apr. 1914).

83. For a breakdown by area and by name of where the money was distributed, see "Denezhnaia pomoshch ot popechitel'stve o narodnoi trezvosti, raznym uchrezhdeniiam po bor'be s p'ianstvom," *VT*, nos. 150–51 (June–July 1907): 37–39.

84. "Trezvost' i zheleznyia dorogi," *VT*, no. 250 (Oct. 1915): 11.

85. A. Riabov, "K studentam-tovarishcham," *VT*, no. 231 (Mar. 1914), pp. 13–16.

86. A. M. Korovin, "Dvizhenie trezvosti v Rossii," *ZhROONZ*, no. 4 (Apr. 1900): 379–80.

87. For Russian professions, see Balzer, *Russia's Missing Middle Class.*

88. See Joseph Bradley, "Voluntary Associations, Civic Culture, and *Obshchestvennost'* in Moscow," in *Between Tsar and People: Educated Society and the Quest for Public Identity in Late Imperial Russia.* ed. Edith W. Clowes, Samuel D. Kassow, and James L. West (Princeton: Princeton University Press, 1991).

89. Tolstoi condemned poverty in Moscow as a consequence of industrialization. See his *Tak chto zhe nam delat'* (What Then Must We Do?), finished in 1886, first published 1902. See the English translation in *The Complete Works of Count Tolstoy*, vol. 19 (1905), pp. 337–63.

Chapter 8

1. A. M. Korovin, "Vysochaishii manifest 17 oktabria i bor'ba s p'ianstvom," *VT*, no. 130 (Oct. 1905): 3, 4.

2. Ibid. A writer for *Pravda* felt that workers drank because they could not form labor unions. S. S. Danilov [D. Ianov], "Bor'ba s p'ianstvom," *Pravda*, no. 25 (May [June 7] 1912): 1–2.

3. George E. Snow, "Socialism, Alcoholism, and the Russian Working Classes before 1917," in *Drinking: Behavior and Belief in Modern History*, ed. Susanna Barrows and Robin Room (Berkeley: University of California Press, 1991), p. 251.

4. A. P., "Alkogolizm i rabochii klass," *Pravda*, no. 11 (May 5 [18], 1912): 4–5 (160–61). Earlier, the Belgian socialist leader for temperance Professor Vandervelde had much the same message: "We socialists have reason to speak this way. An alcoholized people are incapable of socialist organization. It is good for sterile rioting, for attempting *coups de force,* which an implacable repression directly crushes. It cannot organize, cannot march to the conquest of a better state." See Gordon, *Anti-alcohol Movement*, p. 175.

5. Hutchinson, "Science, Politics, and the Alcohol Problem," p. 247.

6. *Trudy pervago vserossiiskago s"ezda po bor'be s p'ianstvom.* In 1911, an article in *Vestnik trezvosti* complained that as soon as the congress was over, the special commission ceased its activities. See no. 193 (Jan. 1911): 1.

7. *Trudy pervago vserossiiskago s"ezda po bor'be s p'ianstvom.*

8. Hutchinson, "Science, Politics, and the Alcohol Problem," p. 248.

9. See ibid., pp. 249–50, for resolutions giving more rights to ethnic minorities, local self-government, and to workers' organizations.

10. The clergy attempted to show that scientists such as the physicians Nizhe-gorodtsev and Dril' and even the heretic Lev Tolstoi agreed that "drunkenness comes from the absence of religious consciousness and only the awakening of religious consciousness will save people from drunkenness." "Slovo i primer pastyria-vernoe sredstvo protiv p'ianstva," reprinted from *Golos poriadka* in *Deiatel'*, no. 6 (June 1910): 114.

11. *Sotsial-demokrat*, no. 9 (1909). The results of these questionnaires were given in papers at the congress by V. I. Magindov, "On Alcoholism among Petersburg Workers," and by O. A. Kaspar'iants, "Alcoholism and Baku Workers."

12. N. I. Letunovskii, *Leninskaia taktika ispol'zovaniia legal'nykh vserossiiskhikh s"ezdov v bor'be za massy v 1908–1911 godakh* (Moscow, 1971), pp. 35–44.

13. An American temperance activist wrote of how the government thwarted the workers at the congress: "the police suppressed the whole movement and all attempts of these wageworkers to organize temperance propaganda have been mercilessly crushed." See Gordon, *Anti-alcohol Movement*, p. 162.

14. I. D. Strashun, *Russkaia obshchestvennaia meditsina v period mezhdu dvumia revoliutsiiami, 1907–1917* (Moscow, 1964), p. 143.

15. Ibid. But at the closing session on the next day, they read a toned-down version of the resolution.

16. Ibid., p. 145.

17. Hutchinson, "Science, Politics, and the Alcohol Problem," pp. 232–33.

18. "O bor'be s p'ianstvom v Gosudarsvennoi Dume i v Gosudarstvennom Soviete," *VT*, no. 156 (Dec. 1907): 4.

19. *Deiatel'*, no. 10 (1904): 368. See also Johnson, *Liquor Problem*, p. 186.

20. The article in *Deiatel*, no. 10 (1904): 368–69, reprinted from the *Izvestiia* of the Moscow City duma, reasoned that the average consumption of vodka per inhabitant per year yielded the treasury 6 rubles per year. But only half of that amount was profit from the monopoly, so the amount needed to replace vodka profits from Samara would be 3 rubles for each of its 100,000 inhabitants. That sum could easily be gained from the money saved from not buying vodka and from the increase of working days not lost to drunkenness. He would raise real estate taxes by 4 percent in order to give or "pay the state for not selling vodka in the city."

21. Johnson, *Liquor Problem*, p. 187. Dr. Grigor'ev saluted Chelyshev, saying, "many tens and hundreds of thousands of people are indebted to you for your energy in this struggle against drunkenness and your name as apostle of sobriety will be retained forever in the history of Russia." "Bor'ba za trezvost'," *VT*, no. 204 (Dec. 1911): 2.

22. Hutchinson, "Science, Politics, and the Alcohol Problem" p. 235.

23. *ZhROONZ*, nos. 10–11 (1912): 112.

24. "Bor'ba za trezvost' v Gosudarstvennoi Dume," *VT*, no. 204 (Dec. 1911):

1. Previously, "the local authorities had authority to close up private shops, but they had no such control over the government monopoly establishments. There was nothing to be gained [for peasants], therefore, in forbidding the private shops, which paid them a revenue, when the government stores continued, which paid them no revenue."

25. The bottles were to be larger and not easily opened, unlike the easy peel-off lids on plastic containers of about six ounces of vodka available in Russia in the late 1990s.

26. Walter Laqueur, *Black Hundred: The Rise of the Extreme Right in Russia* (New York, 1993), pp. 17–23.

27. Hutchinson, "Science, Politics, and the Alcohol Problem," p. 237.

28. "1911 god," *VT*, no. 205 (Jan. 1912): 1.

29. A. Sobolevskii, "Pokhod protiv p'ianstva," *Deiatel'*, no. 12 (Dec. 1911): 312.

30. Ibid., p. 113. There are numerous examples of places in which the local villages actually did force the closing of shops. See *Deiatel'*, nos. 9–10 (1902): 437. Since 1891, village assemblies were allowed the right to ban liquor stores in their districts, and 24,299 bans were enacted in that year and from 1892 to 1894 as many as 39,881 bans were issued. See A. M. Korovin, "Dvizhenie trezvosti v Rossii," *ZhROONZ*, no. 4 (Apr. 1900): 373.

31. I. Diomidov, "Vinnaia monopoliia i golod," *VT*, nos. 210–11 (June–July 1912): 42.

32. G. Kucherovskii, "K voprosu po bor'be s p'ianstvom," reprinted from *Kolokol* in *Deiatel'*, no. 11 (1911): 265.

33. Ibid., pp. 266–67.

34. Johnson, *Liquor Problem*, p. 169.

35. R. Hercod, *La prohibition* (Westerville, OH, 1919), p. 4.

36. Johnson, *Liquor Problem*, p. 182. Hercod, *La prohibition*, p. 4, stated that gross receipts from vodka sales amounted to 547 million rubles in 1904 and grew to 936 million in 1914.

37. Johnson, *Liquor Problem*, p. 183. See Neuberger, *Hooliganism*, p. 125: "Alcohol abuse, not surprisingly, was cited more often than any other factor, on the left and the right, as a sign of social decay and a cause of hooliganism."

38. Johnson, *Liquor Problem*, pp. 185–86.

39. V. N. Kokovtsev, *Out of my Past: The Memoirs of Count Kokovtsev,* ed. H. H. Fisher, trans. L. Matveev (Stanford, 1935), p. 444.

40. Robert D. Warth, *Nicholas II: Life and Reign of Russia's Last Monarch* (Westport, CT, 1997), p. 169.

41. For a description and analysis of the political significance of the tercentenary celebration, see Wortman, *Scenarios of Power*, pp. 439–80; with reference to the temperance societies marching, see p. 460. For 1913 closing of vodka shops, see Christian, "Prohibition in Russia," p. 90.

42. Johnson, *Liquor Problem*, p. 191. See also Hercod, *La prohibition*, p. 4.

43. Johnson, *Liquor Problem*, p. 192.

44. Ibid., pp. 180–86. The newspapers of St. Petersburg published the names of twenty-four members of the state Council who profited from the sale of vodka.

45. Hercod, *La prohibition*, p. 4, reported that Bark yielded to demands made by communal assemblies to suppress the sale of vodka.

46. Ibid., p. 5.

47. Johnson, *Liquor Problem*, pp. 174–75. The governor of Kuban Territory blamed cultural rituals for the abuse of alcohol as well as the false belief that vodka gives strength and helps in healing. He said science showed that, apart from initial stimulation, people become weaker.

48. Gordon, *Russian Prohibition*, p. 13.

49. Ibid., p. 14.

50. Hercod, *La Prohibition*, pp. 9–22.

51. E. A. Chebysheva-Dmitrievna, "M. D. Chelyshev i russkaia zhenshchina v bor'be s alkogolizmom," *Rodnaia zhizn'*, nos. 45–46 (November 16–21, 1915): 13.

52. Ibid., p. 14. A. N. Antisferov et al., *Russian Agriculture during the War* (New Haven, CT: Yale University Press, 1930), p. 120, also make use of the Poltava statistics.

53. Hercod, *La Prohibition*, pp. 5–6, was among the few to say that the reports in the press of the use of substitutes and illegal distillation were exaggerated. *Braga* is a type of homemade beer, kumiss is fermented mare's milk, and *kinderbalsaam* is a kind of liniment.

54. *Rodnaia zhizn'*, no. 38 (Sept. 26, 1915): 10–11. See also Hercod, *La Prohibition*, p. 5.

55. Christian, "Prohibition in Russia," p. 95.

56. *Rodnaia zhizn'*, no. 43 (Oct. 31, 1915): 12.

57. Ibid.

58. N. Rozanov, "Narodnyi—ili prikhodskii dom?" *V bor'be za trezvost'*, nos. 3–4 (Mar.–Apr. 1916): 3–16.

59. Orlando Figes, *A People's Tragedy: The Russian Revolution, 1891–1924* (New York, 1996), p. 307. See also Robert B. McKean, *St. Petersburg between the Revolutions: Workers and Revolutionaries, June 1907–February 1917* (New Haven CT: Yale University Press, 1990), p. 468: "In the highly charged atmosphere of the capital, the sudden bread crisis acted as the trigger for the outpouring of workers and bourgeois inhabitants' political alienation from the regime."

60. McKean, *St. Petersburg*, p. 468.

61. Robert E. Jones, "Ukrainian Grain and the Russian Market in the Late Eighteenth and Early Nineteenth Centuries," in *Ukrainian Economic History: Interpretive Essays*, ed. I. S. Koropeckyj (Cambridge: Harvard University Press, 1991), pp. 212–21.

62. James Bater, *St. Petersburg: Industrialization and Change* (London, 1976), p. 144.

63. Paul P. Gronsky, *The War and the Russian Government: The Central Government* (New Haven, CT: Yale University Press, 1929), p. 282.

64. S. O. Zagorsky, *State Control of Industry during the War* (New Haven, CT: Yale University Press, 1928), p. 163. See also George P. Pavlovsky, *Agricultural Russia on the Eve of the Revolution* (New York, 1968), p. 45: "This other great centre of population [Petrograd] and industry, situated in the extreme North-West corner of the empire, amid districts by nature ill-adapted to the development of farming, depended on supplies transported to it over very long distances, mostly by rail."

65. Gronsky, *War*, p. 269.

66. Zagorsky, *State Control*, p. 164.

67. Ibid., pp. 163–64. Lars T. Lih, *Bread and Authority in Russia, 1914–1921* (Berkeley: University of California Press, 1990), p. 14, notes that as early as 1915,

authorities feared that peasants would not deliver grain to market because of their self-sufficiency, a result of the vodka prohibition.

68. K. I. Zaitsev, N. V. Dolinsky, and S. S. Demonthenov, *Food Supply in Russia during the World War* (New Haven, CT: Yale University Press, 1930), pp. 342–48.

69. Ibid., p. 342.

70. Gronsky, *War*, p. 294.

71. Christian, "Prohibition in Russia," p. 95.

72. Italics are mine to indicate that there had already been a problem with *samogon* before the Bolsheviks came to power. Lih, *Bread and Authority*, p. 121. Neuberger, *Hooliganism*, p. 125, reports that a survey made by the Holy Synod in 1913 complained of illegal liquor being produced in the countryside.

73. Ibid., pp. 107–8.

74. N. Kedrov, "Kipuchaia trezvennaia rabota," *V bor'be za trezvost'* 11, nos. 3–4 (Mar.–Apr. 1916).

75. Leopold H. Haimson, "Russian Workers' Political and Social Identities: The Role of Social Representations in the Interaction between Members of the Labor Movement and the Social Democratic Intelligentsia," in *Workers and Intelligentsia in Late Imperial Russia: Realities, Representations, Reflections*, ed. Reginald E. Zelnik (Berkeley: University of California Press, 1999), pp. 145–71. Hamison concedes that the "February revolution actually did begin in the conditions of a hunger rebellion" (p. 150).

76. Zagorsky, *State Control*, p. 163; and Antsiferov et al., *Russian Agriculture*, p. 192.

Chapter 9

The epigraph to this chapter is from Johnson, *Liquor Problem*. Johnson continues: "The monopoly was overthrown by the exigencies of war, but its days long since, like the days of serfdom seventy-five years ago, had been numbered" (p. 171).

1. It is also possible that the tsar was influenced by members of the imperial family, several of whom were not only honorary patrons of various societies, but also actively engaged in promoting the cause and donating large sums of money to it, including Prince Ol'denburg, Grand Duke Sergei and his wife Elizaveta, Grand Duke Konstantin Konstantinovich, and Grand Duke Nikolai Nikolavich. We know that as early as 1896, the tsar himself donated a People's House to the Guardianship in St. Petersburg, see Luigi Villari, *Russia under the Great Shadow* (London, 1905), pp. 30–31.

2. Even Baron Meyendorf, an Octobrist member of the Third Duma, thus a moderate, called for civil liberties, reduced police powers, a better educational system, and a reformed judicial administration. Other temperance leaders demanded universal suffrage, the nationalization of insurance companies, and, of course, the outright abolition of the State Vodka Monopoly. See Hutchinson, "Science, Politics, and the Alcohol Problem," pp. 240–43.

3. A. M. Korovin, *ZhROONZ*, no. 9 (1899): 844.

4. According to Abbott Gleason, "*obshchestvennost'* has some sense of the English word 'public.'" See "The Terms of Russian Social History," in *Between Tsar and People: Educated Society and the Quest for Public Identity in Late Imperial Rus-*

sia, ed. Edith W. Clowes, Samuel D. Kassow, and James L. West (Princeton: Princeton University Press, 1991), pp. 21–22. See also Joseph Bradley, "Voluntary Associations," p. 131: "the term *obshchestvennost'* signified the public sphere, a sense of public duty and civic spirit, increasingly in an urban context, and the groups possessing those values."

5. E. N. Chernov, *Sistematicheskii katalog otchestvennykh periodicheskikh i pro-dolzhaiushchikhsia izdanii po meditsine* (Leningrad, 1965), with a section on alcoholism.

6. Lilian Lewis Shiman, *Crusade against Drink in Victorian England* (New York: St. Martin's Press, 1988), p. 245.

7. A. Korovin, "Neotlozhnoe delo," *VT,* no. 159 (Mar. 1908): 2.

8. "Miting trezvosti," *VT,* no. 231 (Mar. 1914): 17.

9. Frank, *Crime,* p. 296.

10. Johnson, *Liquor Problem,* pp. 167–68.

11. "Mirskaia bor'ba s p'ianstvom," *Deiatel',* no. 6 (June 1911): 130–31.

12. Ibid., p. 131.

13. Johnson, *Liquor Problem,* p. 171.

14. Ibid. Johnson quotes Dr. Kelnyck, author of *Drink Problem,* as his authority for the allegation that some doctors were sent to Siberia.

15. A. B. Balov, "Vinnaia monopoliia i narodnaia trezvost'," *Otdel obshechest-vennoi gigieny Vrachebnoi gazety,* no. 24 (1906): 65.

16. Mark Steinberg, "The Injured and Insurgent Self: The Moral Imagination of Russia's Lower-Class Writers, in *Workers and Intelligentsia in Late Imperial Russia: Realities, Representations, Reflections,* ed. Reginald E. Zelnik (Berkeley: University of California Press, 1999), pp. 320–21.

17. Ibid., p. 321.

18. A. I. Khrushchev, "Trezvennaia petitsiia Gosudarstvennoi Dume," *VT,* no. 157 (Jan. 1908): 14.

19. William Wagner uses the same image: "Reform of women's rights became the Trojan Mare through which Russian civil law, and then Russian society, would be transformed in accordance with the values, ideals, and professional aspirations of the progressive jurists." See "The Trojan Mare: Women's Rights and Civil Rights in Late Imperial Russia," in *Civil Rights in Imperial Russia,* ed. Olga Crisp and Linda Edmondson (Oxford, 1989), p. 78.

20. Gleb Botkin, *The Real Romanovs as Revealed by the Late Czar's Physician and His Son* (New York, 1931), pp. 91–92.

Epilogue

1. Rheta Childe Dorr, *Inside the Russian Revolution* (New York, 1917), p. 150.

2. Of Alexander III it was reported, "His one vice was an immoderate love of brandy, which he consumed in large quantities with his companion, the court commandant P. A. Cherevin, hiding his bottle in a jackboot to avoid the empress's suspicious eye" (Wortman, *Scenarios,* vol. 2, p. 27).

3. Mark D. Steinberg and Vladimir M. Khrustalëv, *The Fall of the Romanovs* (New Haven, CT: Yale University Press, 1995), p. 149.

4. Ibid., p. 177.

5. Ibid., p. 281.

6. John E. Hodgson, *With Denikin's Armies* (London, 1932), p. 79.

7. White, *Russia Goes Dry*, p. 17.

8. Helena Stone, "The Soviet Government and Moonshine, 1917–1929," *Cahiers du monde russe et soviétique* 27 (July–Dec. 1986): 359–92. See also Weissman, "Prohibition and Alcohol Control," pp. 349–68.

9. Daniel Tarschys, "The Success of a Failure: Gorbachev's Alcohol Policy, 1985–88," *Europe-Asia Studies* 45, no. 1 (1993): 18.

10. As quoted by White, *Russia Goes Dry*, p. 19. For the continuity of workers' drinking habits after the 1917 revolution, see Kate Transchel, "Liquid Assets: Vodka and Drinking in Early Soviet Factories," in *The Human Tradition in Modern Russia*, ed. William B. Husband (Wilmington, DE, 2000), pp. 129–41.

11. Husband, *"Godless Communists,"* p. 89.

12. Ibid., p. 195 n. 90.

13. Stites, *Revolutionary Dreams*, p. 118.

14. Susan Gross Solomon, "Social Hygiene and Soviet Public Health, 1921–1930," in *Health and Society in Revolutionary Russia*, ed. Susan Gross Solomon and John F. Hutchinson (Bloomington: Indiana University Press, 1990), p. 175.

15. Ibid., p. 188.

16. White, *Russia Goes Dry*, p. 23. Marshal Budenny and the poet Vladimir Maiakovskii were among the members. Maiakovskii drew the cartoon, "Nicholas the Last," shown on the cover of this book.

17. Ibid., p. 27.

18. V. Treml, *Alcohol in the USSR* (Durham, NC: Duke University Press, 1982), p. 69.

19. Caesar Korolenko, Vladimir Minevich, and Bernard Segal, "The Politicization of Alcohol in the USSR and Its Impact on the Study and Treatment of Alcoholism," *International Journal of the Addictions* 29, no. 10 (1994): 1270.

20. For this and much of the following, see White, *Russia Goes Dry*.

21. Aleksandre Nemtsov, "To Live or Drink?" *Current Digest of the Post Soviet Press* 46, no. 13 (Aug. 17, 1994): 8.

22. The lasting effect was a reduction of 40 percent of Russia's capacity for producing vodka. See Dmitry Pushkar, "The Anti-Alcohol Decree Is Still Felt," *Moscow News*, no. 19 (May 19–25, 1995): 14.

23. O. A. Balunov and Bernard Segal, "Development and Organization of Services for Alcoholics in Leningrad, USSR," *International Journal of the Addictions* 20, no. 1 (1987): 101.

24. Tarschys, "Success of a Failure," p. 11.

25. Robert B. Davis, "Drug and Alcohol Use in the Former Soviet Union: Selected Factors and Future Considerations," *International Journal of the Addictions* 29, no. 3 (1994): 309.

26. Korolenko, Minevich, and Segal, "The Politicization of Alcohol in the USSR," p. 1271.

27. Stephen Handelman, "Not Licking Liquor," *Spectator*, Nov. 12, 1988, pp. 16–18.

28. Korolenko, Minevich, and Segal, "The Politicization of Alcohol in the USSR," pp. 1273–74.

29. P. M. Fleming, A. Meyroyan, and I. Klimova, "Alcohol Treatment Services in Russia: A Worsening Crisis," *Alcohol and Alcoholism* 29, no 4 (1994): 357.

30. Ibid.

31. By 1988 the ministries, complaining that moonshiners took one-third of all revenues coming from the sale of alcohol, forced Gorbachev to reverse some of his restrictions.

32. Thomas Kirn, "Branch of Medicine Called 'Narcology' Spearheads Aggressive Soviet Campaign against Alcoholism," *Journal of American Medical Association* 258, no. 7 (Aug. 21, 1987): 886.

33. Ibid.

34. Tarschys, "Success of a Failure," pp. 22–23.

35. Laurie Garrett, "Russia Losing a War on Alcoholism," *Newsday,* Dec. 7, 1997. See also *Current Digest of the Post-Soviet Press,* 65, no. 36 (1993): 27.

36. Tarschys, "Success of a Failure," p. 23. See also "Russia's Anti-Drink Campaign: Veni, Vidi, Vodka," *Economist,* Dec. 23, 1989, pp. 50–54.

37. *Current Digest of the Post-Soviet Press* 65, no. 24 (1993): 24–25.

38. Daniel Williams, "Vodka Tonic: Russia Gets a Boost, Headache May Follow," *Washington Post,* Oct. 20, 1997, p. A20.

39. Judy Stark, "Russians Can Toast 1992 with St. Petersburg Vodka," *St. Petersburg Times,* Dec. 17, 1991, Business section, p. 1E.

40. Martha Meisels, "Askalon Ships 11,000 Bottles of Vodka to Help Slake Thirst of Russian Market," *Jerusalem Post,* Feb. 4, 1992, Economics section.

41. Inga Saffron, "Russians Drowning in Sea of Vodka—Foreign Vodka," *The Gazette* (Montreal), Nov. 28, 1996, p. B5.

42. Bruce Barnard, "EU Calls for Russia to Halt Planned Vodka Import Curbs," *Journal of Commerce,* Dec. 13, 1996, p. 4A.

43. The Hieie Brewery in Itoman city on Okinawa produces awamori, a fine powerful distilled rice wine. On bottles of its "Summit" brand are the faces of Boris Yeltsin and Vladimir Putin, a big selling point. See David Williams, "Powerful Japanese Liquor Gives Up Boris Yeltsin," Agence France Presse, International News, Apr. 2, 2000.

44. Anita Snow, "Vodka Ad Stirs Ire of Cubans," *Providence Journal-Bulletin,* Aug. 10, 2000, p. A2.

45. "Russia's Un-Orthodox Business," *Christian Century,* Jan. 18, 1997, pp. 6–7.

46. Danna Kromhourt, "Reversibility of Rise in Russian Mortality Rates," *Lancet,* Aug. 9, 1997, pp. 379–80. See also "Russian Men Face Hard, Short Lives," *St. Petersburg Times,* Nov. 28, 1997, quoted in Stockholm Centre on Health of Societies in Transition, *Newsletter,* no. 4, Mar. 1, 1998, pp. 3–4: "Russian men can expect to die 14 years before Russian women—the largest such gender gap in the world. At current mortality rates, a 16-year old boy has a 54 percent chance of making it to 60. Alcohol is a leading bane of Russian public health. Russian men drink a lot. They die from alcohol poisoning, either from overdoses or from contaminated bootleg drink. Each life lost prematurely amounts to $10,000 per year in the country." According to Evgeny Primakov, when he was prime minister of Russia, more Russians died annually from alcohol poisoning, about thirty to forty thousand persons, than during the entire ten years of the Afghanistan War. See Geoffrey York, "Russia's Vodka Culture," *Globe and Mail* (Canada), Dec. 31, 1998, p. 4.

47. Barry Renfrew, "At Russia's Beaches, Drinking, Drowning Go Hand in Hand," *Providence Journal,* June 30, 1999, p. A2.

48. "Divorce and Drinking: An Analysis of Russian Data," *Journal of Marriage and the Family* (Nov. 1994): 805–12.

49. "Vodka Production Declines," *Kommersant,* Oct. 2, 2000, p. 2.

50. Maksim Zhukov, "Zyuganov Is Not Afraid of Promises," *Russian Press Digest,* Feb. 10, 2000.

51. Edmund L. Andrews, "Volleying over Vodka: Russia and Georgia Duel on Trade," *International Herald Tribune,* Sept. 27, 1997, Finance Section, p. 13.

52. Aleksei Tarason, "If Russia Does Die, It Will Be from Fake Vodka," *Current Digest of the Post-Soviet Press,* July 9, 1997, pp. 5–6. Of the 2,000 survivors of the Chernobyl cleanup living in 1994, only 500 to 600 will still be alive in the year 2000 because of suicide and alcohol poisoning (*Current Digest of the Post Soviet Press,* Sept. 28, 1994, pp. 15–17), and the suicide rate in Russia is more than three times that of the United States (Toni Nelson, "Russia's Population Sink," *World Watch* 9, no. 1 [Jan.–Feb., 1996]: 22–23).

53. Michael Wines, "She's in the Kitchen, and She's Not Making Blinis," *New York Times,* International, July 25, 2000, p. A4.

54. Michael Specter, "Russia Takes Aim at Vodka Bacchanalia," *International Herald Tribune,* Jan. 22, 1997, p. 2.

55. Vladimir Bukovsky, "Who Resists Gorbachev?," *Quadrant* 33, no. 5 (May 1989): 8–16.

56. "Talking Vodka Bottle Hits Russia," abcNews.com, Mar. 26, 2001.

57. Nemtsov, "To Live or Drink?," p. 8. American adults annually consume about eight liters, or less than half the Russian consumption. Russian alcohol consumption figures vary with estimates ranging from thirteen liters to twenty-five liters per person per year. See RFE/RL *Newsline,* Dec. 16, 1999, p. 5.

58. "Three Dead in Russian Vodka Gang War," Agence France Presse, Jul. 12, 2000.

59. "The State Is Attacking Its Own Vodka Plant," Agence France Presse, citing *Segodnia,* Aug. 7, 2000. See also Fred Weir, "In Russia, Hostile Takeover Takes on a New Meaning," *Christian Science Monitor,* Aug. 8, 2000, sec. 2, p. 7.

60. Patrick E. Tyler, "With Bunkers Manned, Vodka War Is in Stalemate," *New York Times,* Aug. 8, 2000, p. A4. The head of the State Tax Service, Alexander Pochinok, claimed in 1997 that 70 percent of Russia's vodka market consisted of moonshine alcohol. See Lena Berezanskaya, "Government Ups Spirit Duties," *St. Petersburg Times,* June 2–8, 1997, Business section, p. 1.

61. William K. Rashbaum, "A Smuggling Operation with a Russian Twist," *New York Times,* Aug. 19, 2000, pp. A1, A15.

62. Radio Free Europe/Radio Liberty Newsline, Feb. 4, 2000. In 1997, fake vodka seized by Moscow police was converted into brake fluid and windshield cleaner. See *Russia Today,* July 1997, p. 1 (http://www.russiatoday.com).

63. *San Diego Union-Tribune,* Aug. 26, 2000, p. A22. Since it is so difficult for Russia to collect taxes, it keeps raising them. As a result, only 2 percent of its present budget comes from alcohol taxes, compared to 20 percent under the Soviet system and 33 percent under the tsarist regime. See "Gen. Kulikov Has Worked Out a New Collection Plan," *Current Digest of the Post Soviet Press,* 49, no. 7 (Mar. 19, 1997).

64. Stockholm Centre on Health of Societies in Transition, *Newsletter,* no. 12 (Apr. 20, 2000), p. 5.

65. Neela Banerjee, "Vodka Sheds Proletarian Chains: Russian Distillers Courting a Higher Class of Drinker," *New York Times,* June 5, 1999, Business section, p. 1.

66. "Drink to Me Only: Russia's Battle with the Bottle," Agence France Presse, Mar. 3, 2001.

67. York, "Russia's Vodka Culture," p. 6.

68. Davis, "Drug and Alcohol Use in the Former Soviet Union: Selected Factors and Future Considerations": "Gorbachev's attack on drinking was the first in a series of unpopular government policies that would eventually lead to his downfall" (p. 303).

69. "Russia Denies Vodka Price Increase," AP Online, Moscow, Feb. 15, 2000.

BIBLIOGRAPHY

•

•

• Selected Periodicals

Alcohol and Alcoholism
Alkogolizm
Alkoholfrage
Alkoholismus
Arkhiv psikhiatrii
Birzhevye vedomosti
Bor'ba s netrezvost'iu v Kishi-
    nevskoi eparkhiu
Bor'ba s p'ianstvom
British Medical Journal
Charitsynskii trezvenik
Chernigovskie eparkhial'nye ve-
    domosti
Current Digest of the Post Soviet
    Press
Deiatel'
Deiatel' trezvosti
Delo trezvosti v Moskovskoi
    Eparkhii
Drug trezvosti
Drug zhenshchina
Druz'iia trezvosti
Etnograficheskoe obozrenie
Etnografiia
Golos Moskvy
Golos tserkvi
International Journal of the Ad-
    dictions
Istoricheskii vestnik
Iuridicheskii vestnik
Iuzhno-Russkaia meditsinkaia
    gazeta
Izvestiia Moskovskoi Gubernskoi
    zemskoi upravy

Journal of Religious History
Journal of the American Medical
    Association
K svetu
Kalendar' druzhei trezvosti
Khersonskie eparkhial'nye vedo-
    mosti
Kievskie eparkhial'nye vedomosti
Kooperativnaia zhizn'
Kurskie eparkhial'nye vedomosti
La presse medicale
Les annales antialcooliques
Listok trezvosti. Supplement to
    Prikhodskaia zhizn'
Listok trezvosti dlia shkol'nikov.
    Supplement to Trezvaia
    zhizn'
Muzei truda
Narodnaia trezvost'. Supplement
    to Trezvye vskhody
Nedelia
Odesskaia pochta
Otrezvlenie
Pervyi antiaklogol'nyi kalendar'
Pravda
Prazdnik trezvosti
Prikhodskaia zhizn'
Prikhodskii sviashchennik
Promyshlennost' i zdorov'e
Ranee utro
Rodnaia zhizn'
Russkii arkhiv
Russkii invalid
Russkii vedomosti

Russkoe bogatstvo
Sel'skii vestnik
Sila trezvosti
Soiuz zhenshchin
Sotsialogicheskie issledovaniia
Sovetskoe zdravookhranenie
Trezvaia zhizn'
Trezvoe slovo
Trezvost'
Trezvost' i berezhlivost'
Trezvye vskhody
Trudovaia pomoshch'
Tsaritsynskii trezvennik
Tserkovnyi vestnik
Utro Rossii
V bor'be za trezvost'
Vestnik popechitel'stv o narodnoi
    trezvosti (VPONT)

Vestnik trezvosti (VT)
Voennyi sbornik
Voprosy nervno-psikhicheskoi
    meditsiny
Vrach'
Vrachebnaia gazeta
Vremennik zhivopisnoi Rossii
Vserossiiskii vestnik trezvosti
Za trezvost'
Zaria trezvosti
Zelenoi zmei
Zemskoe delo
Zhenskaia mysl'
Zhenskoe delo
Zhurnal Russkogo obshchestva
    okhraneniia narodnago zdra-
    viia (ZhROONZ)

Primary Sources

Abtekan, O. O p'ianstve. Moscow, 1910.
Adams, Charles Francis, ed. The Memoirs of John Adams. Vol. 2. Philadelphia, 1874.
Afanas'ev-Chuzhbinskii, A. Poezdka v iuzhnuiu Rossiiu. 2 vols. St. Petersburg, 1863.
Aksakov, A. Soderzhanie piteinykh kak prosteishaia mera protiv p'ianstva i narusheniia pravil ustava o piteinom sbore. St. Petersburg, 1874.
Alekseev, Piotr S. O p'ianstve s predisloviem Gr. L. N. Tolstago. Moscow, 1891.
———. Alkogolizm. Riga, 1898.
———. Chem pomoch velikomu goriu? Kak ostanovit' p'ianstvo? Moscow, 1906.
"Alkogolizm." Entsiklopedicheskii slovar'. Vol. 1, pp. 453–55. St. Petersburg: Brokhaus and Efron, 1890.
Alkogolizm i bor'ba s nim: Komissiia po voprosu ob alkogolizme. St. Petersburg, 1909.
Atkinson, Thomas Witlam. Travels in the Regions of the Upper and Lower Amoor (and the Russian Acquisitions on the Confines of India and China). New York, 1860.
Babushkin, A. Boites' khmel'nogo! Moscow, 1902.
Baird, Robert. Istoriia obshchestv vozderzhaniia v. Severno-Amerikanskikh S. Sh. St. Petersburg, 1843.
Bankov, D. N. Bibliograficheskii ukazatel' po obshchestvennoi meditsinskoi literature za 1890–1905 gg. Moscow, 1907.
Bekhterev, V. M. Alkogolizm i bor'ba s nim. Leningrad, 1927.
———. "Russia without Vodka." In The Soul of Russia, ed. Winifred Stephens. London, 1916.
Belliustin, I. S. Description of the Clergy in Rural Russia: The Memoirs of a Nineteenth-Century Parish Priest. Trans. with an interpretative essay by Gregory L. Freeze. Ithaca: Cornell University Press, 1985.

Berezin, P. V. *Na sluzhbe zlomu delu: Khronika iz zhizni na vinokurennykh zavo-dakh.* Moscow, 1900.

Bericht des III. internationales Congresses gegen den Missbrauch geistiger Getränken ... Christiania von 3.5. September 1890. Christiania, 1891.

Bericht über den V. internationalen Kongress zur Bekampfung des Missbrauchs geistiger Getränken. Basel 20–22 August 1896. Basel, 1897.

Bericht über den XI. internationalen Kongress gengen den Alkoholismus abgehalten in Stockholm von 28 Juli–3 August, 1907. Stockholm, 1908.

Beseda o p'ianstve. Afonskago Russkago Panteleimonova monastyria. 9th ed. Moscow, 1913.

Blashke, R. E. *Ukazatel' knig i zhurnal'nykh statei po voprosam zhenskago sel'skokhoziaistvennago obrazovaniia.* St. Petersburg, 1905.

Bludorov, N. P. *Polnyi sistematicheskii ukazatel' knig, broshuir, zhurnalov, listkov, a takzhe svetovykh kartin i drugikh nagliadnylh posobii po alkogolizmu.* St. Petersburg, 1912.

———. *Sistematicheskii ukazatel' knig i nagliadnykh posobii po alkogolizmu.* 2d ed. St. Petersburg, 1914.

Bochkarev, V. N. *Moskovskoe gosudarstvo.* Vols. 15–17. St. Petersburg, 1914.

Borodin, D. N. *Kalendar' dlia trezvennikov.* St. Petersburg, 1893.

———. *Lechebnitsy dlia alkogolikov.* St. Petersburg, 1893.

———. *Vinnaia monopoliia.* St. Petersburg, 1899.

———. *Kabak i ego proshloe.* St. Petersburg, 1906.

———. *Itogi vinnoi monopolii i zadachi budushchago.* St. Petersburg, 1908.

———. *Doklad na pervom Vserossiiskom s''ezde po bor'be s p'ianstvom.* St. Petersburg, 1910.

———. *P'ianstvo sredi detei.* St. Petersburg, 1910.

———. *V zashechitu trezvosti.* St. Petersburg, 1915.

Brandt, Boris Filippovich. *Bor'ba s p'ianstvom za granitsei i v Rossii.* Kiev, 1897.

Bulgakovskii, D. G. *P'ianstvo. Izrecheniia o p'ianstve, zaimstvovannyia iz Sviash-chennago Pisaniia, i mneniia o nem drevniago i novago vremeni.* St. Petersburg, 1898.

———. *Novaia russkaia khrestomatiia.* St. Petersburg, 1900.

———. "Rol' pravoslavnago dukhovenstva v bor'be s narodnym p'ianstvom." *ZHROONZ* No. 6 (June 1900): 545–64.

———. *Alfabetnyi ukazatel' knig i statei protiv p'ianstva v noveishei russkoi litera-ture i pamiatnikakh drevne-russkoi pis'mennosti.* 2d ed. Moscow, 1902.

———. *Ocherk deiatelnosti popechitel'stva o narodnoi trezvosti za vse vremia ikh sushchestvovaniia [1895–1909] v dvukh chastiakh.* St. Petersburg, 1910.

———. *Gore goremychnoe.* 3d ed. Moscow, 1911.

Bunge, G. *O vrede p'ianstva.* St. Petersburg, 1897.

Bunge, Gustave von. *The Alcohol Question.* Westerville, OH, 1907.

Buslaev, F. *Istoricheskie ocherki russkoi narodnoi slovesnosti i iskusstva.* Vol. 1. St. Petersburg, 1861.

Bykov, N. P. *Sbornik statei, zakona i pravitel'stvennykh rasporiazhenii.* Kaluga, 1876.

Byt' pomeshchichikh krestan na Podole, Volyne i Ukraine. Kiev, 1859.

Calkins, Raymond. *Substitutes for the Saloon.* 2d ed. Boston, 1919.

Charushin A. A. "*Trezvaia Rus'*": *Izvestiia Arkhangel'skago obsch. izucheniia rus-skago severa.* Archangel, 1914.

Chebysheva-Dmitrievna, E. *Rol' zhenshchiny v bor'be s alkogolizmom.* St. Petersburg, 1904.

Chekhov, Anton. *The Oxford Chekhov.* Vol. 8, *Stories,* 1895–1897. Trans. and ed. Ronald Hingley. London: Oxford University Press, 1965.

Chelyshev, M. D. *Rechi M. A. Chel'ysheva prouznesennyia v tret'ei Gosudarstvennoi Dume o neobkhodumosty bor'be s p'ianstvom i po drugom voprosam.* St. Petersburg, 1912.

Chernevskii, V. A. *K voprosu o p'ianstve vo vladimirskoi gubernii.* Vladimir, 1911.

Cinquième congrès international contre l'abus des boissons alcooliques. Brussels, 1897.

Compte-rendu du Quatrième congrès internationale . . . La Haye . . . du 15–18 août 1893. The Hague, 1893.

Considérant, Nestor. *La Russie en 1856: Souvenirs de voyage.* 2 vols. Brusells, 1857.

Crafts, Wilbur F., et al. *Intoxicating Drinks and Drugs in All Lands and Times.* 10th ed. Washington, DC, 1909.

Cross, Samuel Hazard, and Olgered P. Sherbowitz-Wetzor, eds. *The Russian Primary Chronicle.* Cambridge: Harvard University Press, 1953.

Custine, Astolphe de. *La Russie en 1839.* 4 vols. Paris, 1845.

Dembo, Grigorii I. *Alkogolizm i bor'ba s nim.* Kiev, 1900.

———. *L'esquisse sur l'actualité de la Commission pour l'étude de l'alcoolisme (1898–1900).* St. Petersburg, 1900.

———. *Ocherki deiatel'nosti komissii po voprosu ob alkogolizme za 15 let, 1898–1913.* St. Petersburg, 1913.

Derevnia i zapreshchenie prodazhi pitei v. Moskovskom uezde. Moscow, 1915.

Deriuzhinskii, V. F. *Politseiskoe pravo.* St. Petersburg, 1908.

Desiatyi s''ezd russkikh vrachei v pamiat' N. I. Pirogova. Moscow, 1907.

Dixième congrès contre l'abus des boissons alcooliques. Budapest, 1905.

Dmitriev, V. K. *Kriticheskiia izsledovanie o potreblenii alkogolia v Rossii.* Moscow, 1911.

Dnevnik chetvertogo s''ezda russkikh vrachei. Moscow, 1891.

Dnevnik sed'mogo s''ezda russkikh vrachei. Kiev, 1899.

Dnevnik shestogo s''ezda russkikh vrachei. Kiev, 1896.

Dobrovol'skii, N. S. *Znachenie kreditnykh tovarishchestv v dele otrezvleniia naroda i uchastie v nem dukhovenstva.* St. Petersburg, 1910.

———. *K voprosu o narodnom p'ianstve.* Moscow, 1914.

Dogel', I. M. *Spirtnye napitki, zdorov'e i nravestvennost'.* Kazan, 1912.

Dogel', I. M., and A. T. Solov'ev. *Spirtnye napitki, kak neschastie cheloveka.* Kazan, 1904.

Dole, Nathan H. *Life of Count Lyof N. Tolstoi.* New York, 1911.

Dorchester, D. *The Liquor Problem in All Ages.* New York, 1884.

Dorr, Rheta Childe. *Inside the Russian Revolution.* New York, 1917.

Dostoyevsky, Fyodor. *Crime and Punishment.* 2d ed. Ed. George Gibian. New York: Norton, 1975.

———. *The Village of Stepanchikovo and Its Inhabitants.* Ithaca, N.Y.: Cornell University Press, 1983.

Douzième Congrès contre l'abus des boissons alcooliques. London, 1909.

Dril', D. A. *Maloletnie prestupniki: Etiud po voprosu o chelovecheskoi prestupnosti, eia faktorakh i sredstvakh bor'by s nei.* 2 vols. Moscow, 1884–88.

———. *Brodiazhestvo i nishchenstvo i mery bor'by s nimi.* St. Petersburg, 1898.

Dril', D. A. "Nekotorye iz prichin massovogo alkogolizma i vopros o sredstvakh bor'by s nim." In *Trudy postoiannoi kommissii po voprosu ob alkogolizme*. St. Petersburg, 1898.

———. *Prestupnost' i prestupniki (ugolovno-psikhologicheskie etiudy)* St. Petersburg, 1899.

———. *Odin iz voprosov sotsial'nago. zakonodatel'stva*. St. Petersburg, 1908.

———. *Ugolovnoe Pravo: Lektsii, chitannye prof. A. A. Drilem na ekonomicheskom otdelenii v 1909–1910 akad. gody*. St. Petersburg, 1909.

———. *Uchenie o prestupnosti i merakh bor'by s nimi*. St. Petersburg, 1912.

Dumas, Alexander (père). *Voyage en Russie*. Paris, 1960.

Durova, Nadezhda. *The Cavalry Maiden: Journals of a Russian Officer in the Napoleonic Wars*. Trans. Mary Fleming Zirin. Bloomington: Indiana University Press, 1989.

Dzhunkovskii, General-Maior. *Kratkii obzor deiatel'nosti Moskovskago stolichnago popechitel'stva o narodnoi trezvosti za 10 let*. Moscow, 1911.

Eddy, Richard. *Alcohol in History: An Account of Intemperance in All Ages, Together with a History of the Various Methods Employed for Its Removal*. New York, 1887.

Efimenko, A. A. *Issledovaniia narodnoi zhizni*. Moscow, 1884.

Ekk, Nikolia. *Opyt obrabotki statischeskikh dannykh o smertnosti v Rossii*. St. Petersburg, 1888.

Engel'gardt, A. N. *Pisma iz derevni*. Moscow, 1937.

Ezerskii, Fedor V. *Institut trezvennikov*. St. Petersburg and Moscow, 1913.

Favr, V. V. *Sposoby obshchestvennoi-gosudarstvennoi borb'y s p'ianstvom*. Khar'kov, 1908.

Ferguson, William P. F. *The Canteen in the U.S. Army: A Study of Uncle Sam as a Grog-Shop Keeper*. Chicago, 1900.

Filaret (Amfiteatrov). *Besedy*. 2 vols. Kiev, 1849.

Filaret (Drozdov). *Slova i rechi*. 3 vols. Moscow, 1847–61.

Filaret (Gumilevskii). *Slova i besedy*. 2 vols. Moscow, 1850.

Fisher, Dr. *Kak deistvuiut spirtnye napitki na cheloveka*. Moscow, 1901.

Forel', Auguste. *Protiv p'ianstva*. Moscow, n.d.

Fraser, John Foster. *Russia of To-day*. London, 1915.

Fridman, M. M. *Vinnaia monopoliia*. 2 vols. St. Petersburg, 1914–16.

———. *Kazennaia vinnaia monopoliia*. 2 vols. St. Petersburg, 1912–14.

Friedmann, M. I. "The Drink Question in Russia." In *Russia: Its Trade and Commerce*, ed. Arthur Raffalovich. London, 1918.

Gaginskii, (Father) Vasilii. *P'ianstvo, ego vrednyia posledstviia i sredstva k ogranicheniiu ego*. Perm, 1896.

Gautier, Théophile. *Voyage en Russie*. Paris, 1901.

Gersevanov, N. [A. G.]. *O p'ianstve v Rossii i sredstvakh istrebleniia ego*. Odessa, 1845.

Gerver, A. V. "Ob osnovnykh zadachakh Eksperimental'no-Klinicheskago Instituta po izucheniiu alkogolizma." *Obozrenie psikhiatrii*, nos. 8–12 (Aug.–Dec., 1913).

Godnev, I. V. *Rech', proiznesennaia v obshchem sobranii G.-noi D.-y 14 iiunia 1916*. St. Petersburg, 1917.

Golitsyn, N. N. *Bibliograficheskii slovar' russkikh pisatel'nits*. St. Petersburg, 1889. Reprint, Leipzig, 1974.

Gorbunov-Posadov, Ivan Ivanovich. *K uchiteliam nachal'noi srednei i vysshei shkoly v bor'be s narodnym p'ianstvom.* Moscow, 1912.

Gordon, Ernest B. *The Anti-alcohol Movement in Europe.* New York, 1913.

———. *Russian Prohibition.* Westerville, OH, 1916.

Gordon, G. I. *Alkogolizm sredi uchashchikhsia: Vtoroi Vserossiiskii s"ezd po pedagogicheskoi psikhologii.* St. Petersburg, 1910.

Gorev, M. *Kak trezvenniki ezdili na Valaam.* 2d ed. St. Petersburg, 1909.

Gosudarstvennaia Duma. *Stenograficheskie otchety.* St Petersburg, 1906–1916.

Great Britain. Foreign Office. Confidential print, ed. D. C. V. Lieven. Pt. I, series A, Russia, 1959–1914, vol. 2. Stanley to Granville, 1 Aug. 1881, Odessa. vol. 4, 1983.

———. Letter from Sir Edwin O'Connor to the Marquis of Salisbury, Jan. 14, 1897. Miscellaneous Series, no. 416. *Report on the Drink Question in Russia.*

Griaznov, Pavel. *Opyt sravnitel'nogo izucheniia gigienicheskikh uslovii krest'ianskogo byta i mediko-topografiia cherepovetskogo uezda.* St. Petersburg, 1880.

Grigor'ev, N. I. *Russkie obshchestva trezvosti, ikh organizatsiia i deiatel'nost' v 1892–93 g.* St. Petersburg, 1894.

———. *Alkolgolizm i prestupleniia v g. S. Peterburge po materialam S. Petroburgkikh gorodskikh bolnits i Arkhiva.* St. Petersburg, 1900.

———. *Biblioteka izdanii po voprosu o bor'be s p'ianstvom.* St. Petersburg, 1900.

———. *Alkogolizm kak obshchestvennoe zlo: Materialy dlia g. S.-Peterburga.* St. Petersburg, 1908.

Grigorii (Postnikov). *Besedy s dukhovenstvom Kazanskoi eparkhii.* St. Petersburg, 1855.

Gusev, A. M., and A. A. Rodnykh. "Biografii zhenshchin." In *Sistematicheskii i khronologicheskii katalog biblioteki, bibliofila i bibliografa Ia. F. Berezina-Shiriaeva,* vol. 1. St. Petersburg, 1900.

Hamilton, Harriet Georgina. *My Russian and Turkish Journals.* London, 1917.

Haxthausen, August von. *Studies on the Interior of Russia.* Ed. with an introduction by S. Frederick Starr. Trans. Eleanore L. M. Schmidt. Chicago: University of Chicago Press, 1972.

Hayler, Guy. *The World's Fight against Alcoholism.* Glasgow, 1911.

———. *Prohibition Advance in All Lands: A Study of the World-wide Character of the Drink Question.* 2d rev. ed. Westerville, OH, 1914.

Hercod, Robert. *La prohibition de l'alcool en Russie.* Westerville, OH, 1919.

———. *The Prohibition of Alcohol in Russia.* Westerville, OH, n.d.

Hodgson, John E. *With Denikin's Armies.* London, 1932.

Huitième congrès contre l'abus des boissons alcooliques. Vienna, 1901.

I. E. Repin i L. N. Tolstoi, I, *Perepiska s L. N. Tolstym i ego sem'ei.* Moscow, 1949.

Iakolev, V. Ia. "Biudzhet russkogo rabochego," *Obshchestvennyi vrach,* 9 (1911): 96–106.

Iakushkin, E. I. "Grazhdanskoe i ugolovnoe pravo rabochikh." In *Obychnoe pravo: Materialy dlia bibliografii obychnago prava.* 2d ed., no. 1, pp. 4–32. Moscow, 1910.

Ianzhul, I. "Istoriia p'ianstvo i bor'ba s nim." *Trudovaia pomoshch,* June 1908, pp. 1–43.

Ilinskii, P. *Pit'e i krepkie napitki.* St. Petersburg, 1907.

Innokentii (Smirnov). *Sochineniia.* 3 vols. St. Petersburg, 1847.

Ivanov, N. *Sbornik uzakonenii o popechitel'stvakh o narodnoi trezvosti.* Moscow, 1910.

Izvestiia Vserossiiskogo s"ezda prakticheskikh deiatelei po bor'be s p'ianstvom. Petrograd, 1912–16.

Jellinek, E. M. "Classics of the Alcohol Literature: Old Russian Church Views on Inebriety." *Quarterly Journal of Studies on Alcohol* 3, no. 4 (Mar. 1943): 663–67.

Johnson, William E. *The Liquor Problem in Russia.* Westerville, OH, 1915.

K voprosu o p'ianstve i ego lechenii v spetsial'nykh zavedniiakh dlia p'ianits. Moscow, 1887.

Kalendar' druzei trezvosti. Iaroslav', 1903–5, 1907, 1910.

Kanatchikov, S. *A Radical Worker in Tsarist Russia: The Autobiography of Semën Ivanovich Kanatchikov.* Ed. and trans. Reginald E. Zelnik. Stanford, CA: Stanford University Press, 1986.

Kanel', V. I. *Alkogolizm i shkola.* Moscow, 1910.

———. "Fabrika i alkogolizm." *Obshchestvennyi vrach* 2 (1912): 242–55; 3 (1913): 390–401.

———. *Alkogolism i bor'ba s nim.* St. Petersburg, 1914.

Kapustin, M. Ia. *Osnovnye voprosy zemskoi meditsiny.* St. Petersburg, 1889.

Kefershtein, F. *Rabochee dvizhenie i alkogolizm.* Moscow, 1906.

Kelynack, Theophilus N. *The Drink Problem of To-day.* New York, 1916.

Knox, Sir Alfred. *With the Russian Army, 1914–1917.* New York, 1921.

Kokovtsov, V. N. *Iz moego proshlogo.* 2 vols. Paris, 1933.

———. *Out of My Past: The Memoirs of Count Kokovtsev.* Ed. H. H. Fisher, trans. L. Matveev. Stanford, CA: Stanford University Press, 1935.

Kolpakov, M. I. *K voprosu ob alkogolizme v S. Peterburge i o merakh obshchestvennoi bor'by s nim v sviazi s ustroistvom spetsial'nyk lechebnikh dlia alkogolikov.* St. Petersburg, 1896.

Komarov, P. N. *Trezvennoe delo v Tomskoi eparkhii.* Tomsk, 1912.

Kondyrev, Viktor. *Sapogi—Litso Ofitsera.* London, 1985.

Kongress gegen den Alkoholismus abgehalten in Wien, 9–14 April 1903. Leipzig and Vienna, 1903.

Kongress VIII: Bericht über der VIII. internationalen Kongress zur Bekämpfung des Missbrachs geistiger Getränken. Vienna, 1901.

Koni, A. F. *Sobranie sochinenii.* 8 vols. Moscow, 1966–69.

Koren, John. *Economic Aspects of the Liquor Problem.* Boston, 1899.

———. *Alcohol and Society.* New York, 1916.

Korovin, Arkadii M. *Obshchestvennaia bor'ba s p'ianstvom, v sviazi s ustroistvom lechebnits dlia alkogolikov v Anglii, Shveistsarii i Germanii.* Moscow, 1895.

———. *Posledstviia alkogolizma i bor'ba s nim.* Moscow, 1896.

———. *Dvizhenie trezvosti v Rossii.* St. Petersburg, 1900.

———. *Opyt analiza glavnykh faktorov lichnogo alkogolizma.* Moscow, 1907.

———. *Dipsomaniia kak ritm i istoshchenie.* Moscow, 1910.

———. *Bor'ba s alkogolizmom kak neobkhodimoe uslovie pri uluchshenii rabochago byta.* St. Petersburg, 1911.

———. *Obzor meropriatii protiv alkogolizma.* Moscow, 1911.

Kostomarov, N. *Ocherk domashnei zhizni nravov velikorusskago naroda v XVI i XVII stoletiiakh i starinnye zemskie sobory.* 3d ed. St. Petersburg, 1887.

Kovalevskii, P. J. *P'ianstvo: Ego prichiny i lechenie.* Kharkov, 1888.

Kovalevskii, P. J. *Ivrognerie: Ses causes et son traitement.* Trans. Woldemar de Holstein. Kharkov, 1889.

Krassnoff, General P. N. *From Double Eagle to Red Flag.* 2 vols. New York, 1927.

Kratkii obzor deiatel'nosti Moskovskago stolichnago popechitel'stva o narodnoi trezvosti za 10 let. Moscow, 1911.

Kratkii ocherk deiatel'nosti S. Peterburgskago gorodskogo popechitel'stva o narodnoi trezvosti, 1898–1908. St. Petersburg, 1908.

Kratkii ocherk deiatel'nosti S. Peterburgskago gorodskogo popechitel'stva o narodnoi trezvosti, 1898–1912. St. Petersburg, 1913.

Kratkii spisok knig po alkogol'nomu voprosu dlia shkol'noi bibloteki i samoobrazovaniia. St. Petersburg, 1914.

Krol', T. *K voprosu o vliianii alkogolia na zabolevaemost', smertnost' i prestupnost'.* St. Petersburg, 1907.

Kuprin, A. *The Duel.* New York, 1916.

———. *Yama (The Pit).* Trans. Bernard Guilbert Guerney. New York, 1932.

———. "Night Duty." In *The Garnet Bracelet and Other Stories.* Moscow, 1938.

Kuropatkin, General A. N. *The Russian Army, and the Japanese War, Being Historical and Critical Comments on the Military Policy and Power of Russia and on the Campaign in the Far East.* 2 vols. London, 1909.

Lavrov, D. *Protiv p'ianstva.* Moscow, 1893.

———. *K studenchestvu.* Moscow, 1910.

———. *Vliianie alkogol'nykh napitkov na cheloveka: Dve lektsii.* Moscow, 1913.

Le Play, P. G. F. *Les ouvriers européens.* 2d ed. 6 vols. Paris, 1877–79.

Legrain, M. *Sotsial'noe vyrozhdenie i alkogolizm.* Tver, 1896.

Leskov, N. S. *Gens de Russie.* Paris, 1906.

———. *Sobranie sochinenii.* 11 vols. Moscow, 1956.

———. *Satirical Stories.* New York, 1965.

Liubimov, N. A. *Dnevnik uchastnika Pervogo Vserossiiskago s"ezda po bor'be s narodnym p'ianstvom.* Moscow, 1911.

Livanskii, I. V. *Orlovskie otgoloski Vserossiiskogo protivo-alkogol'nago s"ezda.* Moscow, 1915.

Lositskii, A. I., and I. Chernyshev. *Alkogolism peterburgskikh rabochikh.* St. Petersburg, 1913.

Materialy po istorii sovremennogo protivo alkogol'nogo dvizheniia v Rossii. St. Petersburg, 1913.

McCormick, Frederick. *The Tragedy of Russia in Pacific Asia.* 2 vols. London, 1909.

Minor, Lazar S. *K voprosu o p'ianstve i ego lechenii spetsial'nykh zavedeniiakh dlia p'ianits.* Moscow, 1887.

Mirovich, N. *Iz istorii zhenskago dvizheniia v Rossii.* Moscow, 1898.

Neuvième congrès contre l'abus des boissons alcooliques. Bremen, 1903.

Nikol'skii, D. P. *K voprosu o p'ianstve i ego lechenii spetsiäl'nykh zavederiiakh dlia p'ianits.* Moscow, 1898.

Novikoff, Olga. "The Temperance Movement in Russia." *Nineteenth Century* 67 (Sept. 1882): 439–59.

O narodnoi trezvosti. Moscow, 1900.

O p'ianstve i drugikh khudykh privychkakh. Kiev, 1893.

O vrednykh sledstviiakh p'ianstva i dukhovnoe ot nego vrachevstvo. 3d ed. St. Petersburg, 1904.

Onzième congrès contre l'abus des boissons alcooliques. Stockholm, 1907.

Otchet Kazanskago obshchestva Trezvosti. Kazan, 1895, 1905, 1906–1910.

Otchet Moskovskago stolichnago popechitel'stva . . . za 1901. Moscow, 1900.

Otchet Moskovskago stolichnago popechitel'stva . . . za 1902. Moscow, 1903.

Otchet Moskovskago stolichnago popechitel'stva o narodnoi trezvosti za 1903 g. Moscow, 1904.

Otchet Moskovskago stolichnago popechitel'stva . . . za 1904. Moscow, 1905.

Otchet Moskovskago stolichnago popechitel'stva za 1907 g. Moscow, 1908.

Otchet Moskovskago stolichnago popechitel'stva za 1915 g. Moscow, 1916.

Otchet o deiatel'nosti Moskovskago stolichnago popechitel'stva o narodnoi trezvosti za 1901 g. Moscow, 1902.

Otchet po deiatel'nosti soveta Odesskogo obshchestva dlia bor'by s p'ianstvom za 1894. Odessa, 1895.

Otchet po S. Peterburgskomu gorodskomu popechitel'stvu o narodnoi trezvosti. Peterburgskoe gor. popechitel'stvo o narodnoi trezvosti. St. Petersburg, 1899, 1904.

Otchet S. Peterburgskago obshchestvo trezvosti. St. Petersburg, 1892, 1894–97.

Otchet S. Peterburgskago obsheshtva trezvosti. St. Peterburg, 1898.

Otrezvlenie rabochikh; statisticheskoe obsledovanie: Obshchestvo fabrikantov moskovskago raiona. Moscow, 1915.

Ozerov, I. kh. *Atlas Diagramm po economicheskin voprosam: Alkogolizm i bor'ba s nim.* Moscow, 1909.

Pervyi godichnyi otchet Spas-Zaulkovskgakgo obshchestva trezvosti za 1910 god. Moscow, 1911.

Pervyi Zhenskii Kalendar' na 1903 god. Ed. P. N. Arian. St. Petersburg, 1903.

Petrov, G., ed. *Doloi p'ianstvo: Sbornik statei.* St. Petersburg, 1903.

Politovsky, Eugene S. *From Libau to Tsushima: A Narrative of the Voyage of Admiral Rojdestvensky's Fleet to Eastern Seas, Including a Detailed Account of the Dogger Bank Incident.* New York, 1908.

Pomyalovsky, N. G. *Seminary Sketches.* Trans. Alfred Kuhn. Ithaca: Cornell University Press, 1973.

Prilozheniia k stenograficheskim otchetam gosudarstvennoi dumy: Tretii sozyv, sessiia tret'ia 1909–1910 gg. Vol. 3, nos. 439–562. St. Petersburg, 1911.

Promyshlennost' i zdorov'e, ed. A. V. Pogozhev. St. Petersburg, 1902.

Prugavin, A. S. *Monastyrskiia tiur'my v bor'be s sektanstvom.* St. Petersburg, 1904.

———. *"Brattsy" i trezvenniki iz oblasti religioznykh iskanii.* Moscow, 1912.

Pryzhov, Ivan G. *Ocherki, stat'i, pis'ma.* Ed. M. S. Al'tman. Moscow, 1934.

———. *Istoriia kabakov v Rossii v sviazi s istoriei russkago naroda.* Moscow, 1991.

Rachinskii, S. A. *Pis'ma k dukhovnomu iunoshestvu o trezvosti.* Kazan, 1898.

Reardon, James M. *The Temperance Movement in Russia,* Minneapolis, 1905.

Rozhdestvenskii, A. *Azbuka trezvosti.* St. Petersburg, 1902.

Russkie obshchestva trezvosti, ikh organizatsiia deiatel'nost v 1892–93 g. St. Petersburg, 1894.

Russkoe Obshchestvo Okhrananeniia Narodago Zdraviia. Trudy komissii po voprosu ob alkogolizme. St. Petersburg, 1899.

Septième congrès contre l'abus des boissons alcooliques. Paris, 1899–1900.

Sherwell, Arthur, *The Russian Vodka Monopoly.* London, 1915.

Shipov, Sergei. *O trezvosti v Rossii.* St. Petersburg, 1859.

Sikorskii, I. A. *Alkogolizm v Rossii v XIX stoletii i bor'ba s nim.* Kiev, 1899.

Sixième international congrès contre l'abus des boissons alcooliques. Brussels, 1897.

Skarzhinski, L. B. *L'alcool et son histoire en Russie.* Paris, 1902.

Skvortsov, V. M. *Bogoslavskoe obshchestvo trezvosti i bor'ba so shtundoiu.* Kiev, 1895.

Sretenskii, Deacon M. *Pervyi godichnyi otchet Spas-Zaulkovskago Obshchestva Trez-vosti za 1910 god.* Moscow, 1911.

Steveni, William. *The Russian Army from Within.* New York, 1914.

Stevens, Thomas. *Through Russia on a Mustang.* New York, 1891.

Tian-Shanskaia, Olga Semyonova. *Village Life in Late Tsarist Russia.* Ed. David L. Ransel. Bloomington: Indiana University Press, 1993.

Tilk, Jiri. "Russia." In *Temperance of All Nations.* New York, 1893.

Tolstoy, Leo. *The Complete Works of Count Tolstoy.* Ed. Leo Wiener. 24 vols. Boston, 1904–1905.

———. *Polnoe sobranie sochenenii.* Ed. V. G. Chertov. 90 vols. Moscow, 1928–.

———. *A Confession and Other Religious Writings.* New York, 1987.

———. *Tolstoy: Plays.* Vol. 1, 1856–1886. Trans Marvin Kantor with Tanya Tulchinsky. Evanston, IL: Northwestern University Press, 1994.

Tolstovskii ezhegodnik, 1911. Izvestiia Tolstovskogo Muzeia, nos. 3–5 (1911).

Tolstoy, Lev. N. [Tolstoi, Leo N.]. *Tolstoy's Letters.* Vol. 2, 1880–1910. Ed. and trans. R. F. Christian. London: University of London, 1978.

Tolstoy, Sophia. *The Diaries of Sophia Tolstoy.* Ed. O. A. Golinenko et al. Trans. Cathy Porter. New York, 1985.

Tolstoy, Tatiana. *The Tolstoy Home: Diaries of Tatiana Sukhotin-Tolstoy.* New York: Columbia University Press, 1951.

Treizième congrès contre l'abus des boissons alcooliques. The Hague, 1911.

Trudy kommissii po voprosu ob alkogolizme i merakh bor'by s nim. Russkoe obshchestvo Okhraneniia Narodnago Zdraviia. St. Petersburg, 1899–1909.

Trudy pervago vserossiiskago s''ezda po bor'be s p'ianstvom: S.-Peterburg 28 dekabria 1909 g.–6 ianvaria 1910 g. (*S''ezd*) 3 vols. St. Petersburg, 1910.

Trudy pervago zhenskago s''ezda pri Russkom zhenskom obshchestve v S. Peterburg. St. Petersburg, 1909.

Trudy postoiannoi komissii po voprosu ob alkogolizme. Vols. 1–14. St. Petersburg, 1913.

Trudy vserossiiskago s''ezda prakticheskikh deiatelei po bor'be s alkogolizmom, sostoiavshegosia s 6 do 12 avgusta 1912 g. v Moskve. 3 vols. Petrograd, 1914–16.

Trudy vtorogo s''ezda otechestvennykh psikhiatrov. Kiev, 1907.

Trudy vtorogo s''ezda russkikh vrachei v Moskve. 2 vols. Moscow, 1887.

Turgenev, Ivan. *Sketches from a Hunter's Album.* New York, 1990.

Verhandlungen der II. Internationalen Versammlung gegen den Missbrauch geistiger Getränken in Zürich von 8. bis 11. September 1887. Zürich, 1888.

Ves' Sankt Peterburg na 1906 god: Adresnaia i spravochnaia kniga S. Peterburga. St. Petersburg, 1907.

Viazemskii, M. K. *Bibliografiia po voprosu ob alkogolizme.* Moscow, 1909.

Villari, Luigi. *Russia under the Great Shadow.* London, 1905.

Voronov, D. N. *Zhizn' derevni v dni trezvosti.* Petrograd, 1916.

White, P. S., and H. R. Pleasants. *The War of Four Thousand Years.* Philadelphia, 1846.

Witte, Sergei. *The Memoirs of Count Witte.* Trans and ed. Sidney Harcave. Armonk, NY, 1990.

Secondary Sources

Agursky, Mikhail. "Caught in a Cross Fire: The Russian Church between Holy Synod and Radical Right (1905–1908)." In *Orientalia Christiana Periodica,* fasc. 1, vol. 50, pp. 126–96. Rome, 1984.

Aleksandrov, V. A. *Sel'skaia obshchina v Rossii.* Moscow, 1966.

———. *Obychnoe pravo krepostnoi derevni Rossii XVIII–nachalo XIX v.* Moscow, 1984.

Alkogolizm kak nauchnaia i bytovaia problema. Moscow, 1928.

Andreev, Leonid N. *Povesti i rasskazy.* Moscow, 1957.

Anokhina, L. A., and M. N. Shmeleva. *Kul'tura i byt kolkhoznikov Kalininskoi oblasti.* Moscow, 1964.

Anschedl, Eugene. *The American Image of Russia, 1775–1917.* New York, 1974.

Antisferov, A. N., et al. *Russian Agriculture during the War.* New Haven, CT: Yale University Press, 1930.

Apostolov, I. I. "Alkogolizm i garmoniia patologii." *Sotsiologischeskie issledovaniia,"* no. 6 (1987).

Avakumoviv, Ivan. *The Doukhobors.* Toronto, 1968.

Balzer, Harley D., ed. *Russia's Missing Middle Class: The Professions in Russian History.* Armonk, NY, 1996.

Barchugov, P. V. *Revoliutsionnaia rabota bol'shevikov v legal'nykh rabochikh organizatsiiakh (1907–1911).* Rostov, 1963.

Barrows, Susanna, Joseph Gusfeld, and Robin Room, eds. *Drinking: Behavior and Belief in Modern History.* Berkeley: University of California Press, 1991.

Bater, James. *St. Petersburg: Industrialization and Change.* London, 1976.

Benjamin, Walter. *Moscow Diary.* Cambridge: Harvard University Press, 1986.

Berliand, A. S., ed. *Alkogolizm v khudozhestvennoi literatura: Khrestomatiia.* Moscow, 1930.

Bernshtam, Tat'iana Aleksandrovna. *Russkaia narodnaia kul'tura pomor'ia v XIX— nachale XX v.* Leningrad, 1983.

Bernstein, Laurie. *Sonia's Daughters: Prostitutes and Their Regulation in Imperial Russia.* Berkeley: University of California Press, 1995.

Blocker, Jack S., Jr. "The Modernity of Prohibitionists: An Analysis of Leadership Structure and Background." In *Alcohol, Reform, and Society: The Liquor Issue in Social Context.* Westport, CT, 1979.

———. *American Temperance Movements: Cycles of Reform.* Boston, 1989.

Bograd, V. E. *Zhurnal "Otchestvennye Zapiski," 1839–1848.* Moscow, 1985.

Bolonev, F. F. *Narodnyi kalendar: Semeiskikh Zabaikal'ia.* Novosibirsk, 1978.

Bonnell, Victoria E. *The Russian Worker: Life and Labor under the Tsarist Regime.* Berkeley: University of California Press, 1983.

Borodin, Ruth. *Women and Temperance: The Quest for Power and Liberty, 1873–1900.* Philadelphia: Temple University Press, 1981.

Bradley, Joseph. *Muzhik and Muscovite: Urbanization in Late Imperial Russia.* Berkeley: University of California Press, 1985.

———. "Voluntary Associations, Civic Culture, and *Obshchestvennost'* in Moscow." In *Between Tsar and People: Educated Society and the Quest for Public Identity in Late Imperial Russia,* ed. Edith W. Clowes, Samuel D. Kassow, and James L. West. Princeton: Princeton University Press, 1991.

Brooks, Jeffrey. *When Russia Learned to Read: Literacy and Popular Literature.* Princeton: Princeton University Press, 1985.

Brower, Daniel R. *The Russian City between Tradition and Modernity: 1850–1900.* Berkeley: University of California Press, 1990.

Brown, Julie V. "The Professionalization of Russian Psychiatry, 1857–1911." Ph.D. diss., University of Pennsylvania, 1981.

———. "Revolution and Psychosis: The Mixing of Science and Politics in Russian Psychiatric Medicine, 1905–13." *Russian Review* 46 (1987): 283–302.

———. "Social Influences on Psychiatric Theory and Practice in Late Imperial Russia." In *Health and Society in Revolutionary Russia.* Ed. Susan Gross Solomon and John F. Hutchinson. Bloomington: Indiana University Press, 1990.

Burds, Jeffrey. *Peasant Dreams and Market Politics: Labor Migration and the Russian Village, 1861–1905.* Pittsburgh: University of Pittsburgh Press, 1998.

Bushnell, John. "The Tsarist Officer Corps, 1881–1914: Customs, Duties, Inefficiency." *American Historical Review* 86, no. 4 (Oct. 1981): 753–80.

———. *Mutiny amid Repression: Russian Soldiers in the Revolution of 1905–1906.* Bloomington: Indiana University Press, 1987.

Busygin, E. P. *Sel'skaia zhenshchina v semeinoi i obshchestvennoi zhizni.* Kazan, 1986.

Busygin, E. P., I. V. Zorin, and E. V Mikhailichenko. *Obshchestvennyi i semeinyi byt russkogo sel'skogo naseleniia Srednego Povolzh'ia.* Kazan, 1988.

Cherrington, Ernest Hurst, et al., eds. *Standard Encyclopedia of the Alcohol Problem.* Westerville, OH, 1929.

Chicherov, V. I. *Zimnii period russkogo zemledel'cheskogo kalendaria XVI–XIX vekov.* Moscow, 1957.

Christian, David. "Traditional and Modern Drinking Cultures in Russia on the Eve of Emancipation." *Australian Slavonic and East European Studies* 1, no. 1, (1987): 61–84.

———. *"Living Water": Vodka and Russian Society on the Eve of Emancipation.* Oxford: Oxford University Press, 1990.

———. "The Black and Gold Seals: Vodka and the Abolition of Serfdom in Russia." In *Peasant Politics, Economy, Culture in European Russia, 1800–1917,* ed. Esther Kingston-Mann and Timothy Mixter. Princeton: Princeton University Press, 1990.

———. "Prohibition in Russia, 1914–1925." *Australian Slavonic and East European Studies* 9, no. 2 (1995): 89–118.

Clay, J. Eugene. "Orthodox Missionaries and 'Orthodox Heretics.' " In *Of Religion and Identity,* ed. Michael Khodarkovsky and Robert Geraci. Ithaca, NY: Cornell University Press. 2001. 38–69.

Crisp, Olga, and Linda Edmondson, eds. *Civil Rights in Imperial Russia.* Oxford, 1989.

Cunningham, James W. *A Vanquished Hope: The Movement for Church Renewal in Russia, 1905–1906.* Crestwood, NY, 1981.

Dixon, Simon. "The Church's Social Role in St. Petersburg, 1880–1914." In *Church, Nation, and State in Russia and Ukraine,* ed. Geoffrey Hosking. New York, 1991.

Douglas, Mary, ed. *Constructive Drinking: Perspectives on Drink from Anthropology.* Cambridge: Cambridge University Press, 1987.

Dubinin, M. "New Martyr Archpriest Michael Edlinsky." *Orthodox Life* 39, no. 2 (1989): 16–26.

Dunn, Stephen P., and Ethel Dunn. *The Peasants of Central Russia.* New York, 1967.

Edmondson, Linda Harriet. *Feminism in Russia, 1900–17*. Stanford, CA: Stanford University Press, 1984.

Edmondson, Linda, ed. *Women and Society in Russia and the Soviet Union*. Cambridge: Cambridge University Press, 1992.

Engelstein, Laura. *The Keys to Happiness: Sex and the Search for Modernity in Fin-de-Siècle Russia*. Ithaca: Cornell University Press, 1992.

———. *Castration and the Heavenly Kingdom: A Russian Folktale*. Ithaca: Cornell University Press, 1999.

Entsiklopediia zimnikh prazdnikov. St. Petersburg, 1995.

Eriksen, Sidsel. "Alcohol as a Gender Symbol." *Scandinavian Journal of History* 24 (1999): 45–73.

Erofeev, Benedict. *Moscow Circles*. Trans. J. R. Dorrell. New York, 1981.

Fahey, David M., ed. *The Collected Writings of Jessie Forsyth, 1847–1937: The Good Templars and Temperance Reform on Three Continents*. Lewiston and Queenston, 1988.

Fasmer, M. *Etimologicheskii slovar' russkago iazyka*. Moscow, 1967.

Fedorov, Vladimir A. "Krest'ianskoe trezvennoe dvizhenie 1858–1859 gg." *Revoliutsionnaia situatsiia v Rossii v 1859–1861 gg*. 1 (1960): 133–48.

———. *Krest'ianskoe dvizehenie v tsentral'noi Rossii, 1800–1860*. Moscow, 1980.

Felmy, Karl Christian. *Predigt im orthodoxen Russland: Untersuchungen zu Inhalt und Eigenart der russischen Predigt in zweiten Hälften des 19. Jahrhunderts*. Göttingen, 1972.

Figes, Orlando. *A People's Tragedy: The Russian Revolution, 1891–1924*. New York, 1996.

Fleming, P. M., A. Meyroyani, and I. Klimova. "Alcohol Treatment in Russia: A Worsening Crisis." *Alcohol and Alcoholism* 29, no. 4 (1994): 357–62.

Florovsky, G. "The Social Problem in the Eastern Orthodox Church." In *Christianity and Culture: Collected Works*, vol. 2. Belmont, MA, 1974.

Frank, Stephen P. *Crime, Cultural Conflict, and Justice in Rural Russia, 1856–1914*. Berkeley: University of California Press, 1999.

Frank, Stephen P. "Cultural Conflict and Criminality in Rural Russia, 1861–1900." Ph.D. diss., Brown University, 1987.

———. "Simple Folk, Savage Customs? Youth, Sociability, and the Dynamics of Culture in Rural Russia, 1861–1914." *Journal of Social History*, 25, no. 4 (1992): 711–36.

———. "Narratives within Numbers: Women, Crime, and Judicial Statistics in Imperial Russia, 1834–1913." *Russian Review* 55, no. 4 (Oct. 1996): 541–66.

Frank, Stephen P., and Mark D. Steinberg, eds. *Cultures in Flux: Lower-Class Values, Practices, and Resistance in Late Imperial Russia*. Princeton: Princeton University Press, 1994.

Frank, Waldo. *Dawn in Russia: The Record of a Journey*. New York, 1932.

Frankel, B. Gail, and Paul C. Whitehead. *Drinking and Damage: Theoretical Advances and Implications for Prevention*. New Brunswick, NJ, 1981.

Freeze, Gregory L. *The Parish Clergy in Nineteenth-Century Russia: Crisis, Reform, Counter-reform*. Princeton: Princeton University Press, 1983.

———. "Handmaiden of the State? The Church in Imperial Russia Reconsidered." *Journal of Ecclesiastical History* 36, no. 1 (Jan. 1985): 82–102.

———. "Institutionalizing Piety: The Church and Popular Religion, 1750–1850." In *Imperial Russia: New Histories for the Empire*, ed. Jane Burbank and David L. Ransel. Bloomington: Indiana University Press, 1998.

Frieden, Nancy Mandelker. *Russian Physicians in an Era of Reform and Revolution, 1856–1905.* Princeton: Princeton University Press, 1981.

Fuller, William C., Jr. *Civil-Military Conflict in Imperial Russia, 1881–1914.* Princeton: Princeton University Press, 1985.

Gabriel, Richard. *The New Red Legion: An Attitudinal Portrait of the Soviet Soldier.* Westport, CT, 1980.

Gamalia N. F. "Pervyi vserossiiskii s"ezd po bor'be s p'ianstvom." In *Sobranie sochineniia.* Vol. 3. Moscow, 1958.

Gargarin, Ivan Sergeevich. *The Russian Clergy.* 1872. Trans. from the French by C. Du Gard Makepeace. Reprinted with an introduction and bibliography by Gregory Freeze. Newtonville, MA, 1976.

Gleason, Abbott, Peter Kenez, and Richard Stites, eds. *Bolshevik Culture: Experiment and Order in the Russian Revolution.* Bloomington: Indiana University Press, 1985.

Golosenko, I. D. "Russkoe p'ianstvo: mify i real'nost'." *Sotsiologicheskie issledovaniia* 13, no. 3 (1986): 203–9.

Gorshkov, M. K., and F. E. Sheregi. "O bor'be s p'ianstvom i alkogolizmom." *Sotsiologicheskie issledovaniia,* no. 1 (1986): 42–49.

Granovskii, L. B. *Obshchestvennoe zdravookhrannenie i kapitalizm.* Moscow, 1907.

Greenwell, Harry J. *Mirrors of Moscow.* London, 1929.

Gromyko, Marina M. *Trudovye traditsii russkikh krest'ian Sibiri (XVII-pervaia polovina XIX v).* Novosibirsk, 1975.

———. *Traditsionnye normy povedeniia i formy obshcheniia russkikh krest'ian XIX v.* Moscow, 1986.

Gronsky, Paul P. *The War and the Russian Government: The Central Government.* New Haven, CT: Yale University Press, 1929.

Guberman, I. *Bekhterev: Stranitsy zhizni.* Moscow, 1977.

Gurko, Vladimir Iosif. *Features and Figures of the Past: Government Opinion in the Reign of Nicholas II,* ed. J. E. Wallace Sterling et al. Stanford, CA: Stanford University Press, 1939.

Gusfield, Joseph R. *Symbolic Crusade: Status Politics and the American Temperance Movement.* Urbana, IL, 1963.

Guthrie, K. B. *Through Russia from St. Petersburg to Astrakhan and the Crimea.* Vols. 1 and 2. London, 1874. Reprint, NY, 1970.

Haimson, Leopold H. "Russian Workers' Political and Social Identities: The Role of Social Representations in the Interaction between Members of the Labor Movement and the Social Democratic Intelligentsia." In *Workers and Intelligentsia in Late Imperial Russia: Realities, Representations, Reflections,* ed. Reginald E. Zelnik. Berkeley: University of California Press, 1999.

Hause, Steven C., and Anne R. Kenney. "The Limits of Suffragist Behavior: Legalism and Militancy in France, 1876–1922." *American Historical Review* 86, no. 4 (Oct. 1981): 781–806.

———. *Women's Suffrage and Social Politics in the French Third Republic.* Princeton: Princeton University Press, 1987.

Hedda, Jennifer Elaine. "Good Shepherds: The St. Petersburg Pastorate in the Emergence of Social Activism in the Russian Orthodox Church, 1855–1917." Ph.D. diss., Harvard University, 1998.

Herlihy, Patricia. " 'Joy of the Rus': Rites and Rituals of Russian Drinking." *Russian Review* 50 (Apr. 1991): 131–47.

Hughes, Lindsey. *Russia in the Age of Peter the Great*. New Haven: Yale University Press, 1998.

Hryniuk, S. M. "The Peasant and Alcohol in East Galicia in the Late Nineteenth Century; a Note." *Journal of Ukrainian Studies* 20, no. 1 (1986): 75–85.

Husband, William B. *"Godless Communists": Atheism and Society in Soviet Russia, 1917–1932*. DeKalb: Northern Illinois University Press, 2000.

Hutchinson, John F. "Medicine, Morality, and Social Policy in Imperial Russia: The Early Years of the Alcohol Commission." *Histoire sociale/Social History* 7 (Nov. 1974): 202–26.

———. "Science, Politics, and the Alcohol Problem in Post-1905 Russia." *Slavonic and East European Review* 58, no. 2 (Apr. 1980): 232–54.

———. *Politics and Public Health in Revolutionary Russia, 1890–1918*. Baltimore: Johns Hopkins University Press, 1990.

Idel'chik, Kh. I., M. I. Aruin, and A. I. Nesterenko. "1 Vserossiiskii s"ezd po bor'be s p'ianstvom." *Sovetskoe zdravookranenie*, no. 2 (1972): 61–65.

Ignashev, D. Nemec, and S. Krive, eds. *Women and Writing in Russia and the USSR: A Preliminary Bibliography of English-Language Sources*. Northfield, MN: Carleton University, 1987.

Isetts, Charles A. "A Social Profile of the Women's Temperance Crusade: Hillsboro, Ohio." In *Alcohol, Reform, and Society: The Liquor Issue in Social Context*, ed. Jack S. Blocker, Jr. Westport, CT, 1979.

Istoriia dorevoliutsionnoi Rossii v dnevnikhakh i vospominaniiakh. Annotirovannyi ukazatel' knig i publikatsii v zhurnalakh. Nauchnoe rukovodstvo, redaktsiia i vvedenie prof. P. A. Zaionchkovskogo. 4 vols. in 11. Moscow, 1976–86.

Ivanits, Linda J. *Russian Folk Belief*. Armonk, NY, 1989.

Ivanov, Iu. G. *Kniga o vodke*. Smolensk, 1995.

Iz istorii sem'i i byta sibirskogo krest'ianina XVII-nachala XX v. Novosibirsk, 1975.

Jones, Ellen. *Red Army and Society: A Sociology of the Soviet Military*. Boston, 1985.

Jones, Robert E. "Ukrainian Grain and the Russian Market in the Late Eighteenth and Early Nineteenth Centuries." In *Ukrainian Economic History: Interpretive Essays*, ed. I. S. Koropeckyj. Cambridge: Harvard University Press, 1991.

Kader, Boris. *Life, I Salute You*. Cambridge, 1945.

Kahan, Arcadius, *The Plow, the Hammer, and the Knout: An Economic History of Eighteenth Century Russia*. With the editorial assistance of Richard Hellie. Chicago: University of Chicago Press, 1985.

Kalendarnye obychai i obriady v stranakh zarubezhoi Evropy XIX-nachalo XX v. Moscow, 1983.

Kalinovskaiia, V. N. "K izucheniiu drevneishikh russkikh pouchenii i slov protiv p'ianstva." In *Drevnerusskaia literatura: Istochnikovedenie*. Leningrad, 1984.

Keep, John L. H. *Soldiers of the Tsar: Army and Society in Russia, 1462–1874*. Oxford: Clarendon Press, 1985.

Kizenko, Nadieszda. "The Making of a Modern Saint: Ioann of Kronstadt and the Russian People, 1855–1917." Ph.D. diss., Columbia University, 1995.

———. *A Prodigal Saint: Father John of Kronstadt and the Russian People*. University Park: Pennsylvania State University Press, 2000.

Klein, B. "Sila na dobro." *Neman*, no. 3 (Nov. 1987): 166–170.

Kniazeva, G. V. *Bor'ba bol'shevikov za sochetanie nelegal'noi partinoi raboty v gody reaktsii, 1907–1911*. Moscow, 1967.

Koenker, Diane. *Moscow Workers and the 1917 Revolution*. Princeton: Princeton University Press, 1981.

Kolstø, Pål. "Leo Tolstoy, a Church Critic Influenced by Orthodox Thought." In *Church, Nation, and State in Russia and Ukraine*, ed. Geoffrey A. Hosking. New York: St. Martin's Press, 1991.

Korzhulkhina, T. P. "Bor'ba s alkogolizom v 20-kh-nachal 30-kh godov." *Voprosy istorii*, no. 9 (1985).

Kourennoff, Paul M., and George St. George. *Russian Folk Medicine*. New York, 1971.

Krukones, James H. *To the People: The Russian Government and the Newspaper Sel'skii vestnick ("Village Herald"), 1881–1917*. New York, 1987.

———. "Satan's Blood, Tsar's Ink: Rural Alcoholism in an Official 'Publication for the People,' 1881–1917." *Russian History/Histoire russe* 18, no. 4 (1991): 435–56.

Kubanskie stranitsy: Etnicheskie i kul'turno-bytovye protsessy na Kubani. Moscow, 1967.

Kuz'min, S. A., et al. *Ukazateli soderzhaniia russkikh dorevoliutsionnykh gazet: Bibliograficheskii ukazatel'*. Leningrad, 1986.

Lambert, W. R. *Drink and Sobriety in Victorian Wales, c. 1820–c. 1895*. Cardiff: University of Wales Press, 1983.

Laqueur, Walter. *Black Hundred: The Rise of the Extreme Right in Russia*. New York, 1993.

Larin, Iu. *Novye zakony protiv alkogolizma*. Moscow, 1929.

LeDonne, John P. "Indirect Taxes in Catherine's Russia. II. The Liquor Monopoly." *Jahrbücher für Geschichte Osteuropas* 24, no. 2 (1976): 174–207.

Lebedeva, A. A. "K istorii formirovaniia russkogo naseleniia Zabaikal'ia, ego khoziaistvennogo i semeinogo byta (XIX-nachala XX v)." In *Etnografiia russkogo naseleniia Sibiri i Srednei Azii*. Moscow, 1969.

Ledermann, Sully. *Alcool, alcoolisme, alcoolisation*. 2 vols. Paris, 1956 and 1964.

Ledkovsky, Marina, Charlotte Rosenthal, and Mary Zirin, eds. *Dictionary of Russian Women Writers*. Westport, CT, 1994.

Letunovskii, N. I. *Leninskaia taktika ispol'zovaniia legal'nykh vserossiiskhikh s"ezdov v bor'be za massy v 1908–1911 godakh*. Moscow, 1971.

Levin, Eve. "Miracles of Drunkenness: The Culture of Alcohol in Muscovite Hagiography and Miracle Tales." Paper presented at the American Association for the Advancement of Slavic Studies Annual Conference, Seattle, WA, 1997.

Lih, Lars T. *Bread and Authority in Russia, 1914–1921*. Berkeley: University of California Press, 1990.

Lincoln, W. Bruce. *The Great Reforms: Autocracy, Bureaucracy, and the Politics of Change in Imperial Russia*. DeKalb: Northern Illinois University Press, 1990.

Lindenmeyr, Adele. *Poverty Is Not a Vice: Charity, Society, and the State in Imperial Russia*. Princeton: Princeton University Press, 1996.

Lotova, E. I. *Russkaia intelligentsiia i voprosy obshchestvennoi gigieny*. Moscow, 1962.

Luker, Nicholas. *Alexander Kuprin*. Boston, 1978.

Manchester, Laurie. "Gender and Pastoral Care: Shifting Conceptions of Parish Service and the Role of Clerical Women in Imperial Russia." Paper presented at the Annual Meeting of the New England Slavic Association, Wellesley College, Wellesley, MA, Apr. 18, 1997.

McKean, Robert B. *St. Petersburg between the Revolutions: Workers and Revolutionaries, June 1907–February 1917.* New Haven, CT: Yale University Press, 1990.

McKee, W. Arthur. "Taming the Green Serpent: Alcoholism, Autocracy, and Russian Society, 1881–1914." Ph.D. diss., University of California, Berkeley, 1997.

———. "Sobering Up the Soul of the People: The Politics of Popular Temperance in Late Imperial Russia." *Russian Review* 58 (Apr. 1999): 212–43.

McReynolds, Louise. *The News under Russia's Old Regime: The Development of a Mass-Circulation Press.* Princeton: Princeton University Press, 1991.

Menning, Bruce W. *Bayonets before Bullets: The Imperial Russian Army, 1861–1914.* Bloomington: Indiana University Press, 1992.

Miller, Martin A. *Freud and the Bolsheviks: Psychoanalysis in Imperial Russia and the Soviet Union.* New Haven, CT: Yale University Press, 1998.

Modern Encyclopedia of Religions in Russia and the Soviet Union, Ed. Paul Steeves. New York: Academic Press, 1988–.

Nemtsov, Aleksandre. "To Live or Drink?" *Current Digest of the Post Soviet Press* 46, no. 13 (Aug. 17, 1994).

Neuberger, Joan. *Hooliganism: Crime, Culture, and Power in St. Petersburg, 1900–1914.* Berkeley: University of California Press, 1993.

Orlovsky, Daniel T. "The Provisional Government and Its Cultural Work." In *Bolshevik Culture: Experiment and Order in the Russian Revolution,* ed. Abbott Gleason, Peter Kenez, and Richard Stites. Bloomington: Indiana University Press, 1985.

Osipov, V. P. *Bekhterev.* Moscow, 1947.

Pavlovsky, George P. *Agricultural Russia on the Eve of the Revolution.* New York, 1968.

Pechenuk, Volodimir, "Temperance and Revenue Raising: The Goals of the Russian State Liquor Monopoly, 1894–1914." *New England Slavonic Journal* 1 (1980): 35–48.

Peris, Daniel. "Commissars in Red Cassocks: Former Priests in the League of the Militant Godless." *Slavic Review* 54, no. 2 (1995): 344–48.

———. *Storming the Heavens: The Soviet League of the Militant Godless.* Ithaca, NY: Cornell University Press, 1998.

Phillips, Laura Lynne. "Everyday Life in Revolutionary Russia: Working Class Drinking and Taverns in St. Petersburg, 1900–1929." Ph.D. diss., University of Illinois at Urbana-Champaign, 1993.

———. "In Defense of Their Families: Working-Class Women, Alcohol, and Politics in Revolutionary Russia." *Journal of Women's History* 11, no. 1 (spring 1999): 97–120.

———. *Bolsheviks and the Bottle: Drink and Worker Culture in St. Petersburg, 1900–1929.* DeKalb: Northern Illinois University Press, 2000.

Pokhlebkin, V. V. *Istoriia vodki.* Moscow, 1991.

Prestwich, Patricia E. *Drink and the Politics of Social Reform: Antialcoholism in France since 1870.* Palo Alto, 1988.

Ravitch, Michael L. *The Romance of Russian Medicine.* New York, 1937.

Rich, David Allan. *The Tsar's Colonels: Professionalism, Strategy, and Subversion in Late Imperial Russia.* Cambridge: Harvard University Press, 1998.

Roberts, James S. *Drink, Temperance, and the Working Class in Nineteenth-Century Germany.* Boston, 1984.

Rohrabaugh, W. J. *The Alcoholic Republic: An American Tradition.* New York: Oxford University Press, 1979.

Roslof, Edward E. "The Renovationist Movement in the Russian Orthodox Church, 1922–1946." Ph.D. diss., University of North Carolina, 1994.

———. "Russian Orthodoxy and the Tragic Fate of Patriarch Tikhon (Bellavin)." In *The Human Tradition in Modern Russia.* Ed. William B. Husband. Wilmington, DE, 2000.

Schneiderman, Jeremiah. *Sergei Zubatov and Revolutionary Marxism: The Struggle for the Working Class in Tsarist Russia.* Ithaca, 1976.

Schulkin, Marc Lee. "The Politics of Temperance: Nicholas II's Campaign against Alcohol Abuse." Ph.D. diss., Harvard University, 1985.

Segal, Boris. *Russian Drinking: Use and Abuse of Alcohol in Pre-revolutionary Russia.* New Brunswick, NJ, 1987.

Selawry, Alla. *Johannes von Kronstadt, Starez Russlands, mit Selbstzeugnissen und dokumentarischen Belegen.* Basel, 1981.

Shiman, Lilian Lewis. *Crusade against Drink in Victorian England.* New York, 1988.

Shlapentokh, Dmitry. "Drunkenness and Anarchy in Russia: A Case of Political Culture," *Russian History/Histoire russe,* 18, no. 4 (1991): 457–500.

Smirnova, K. V., G. V. Chiniaeva, V. O. Smirnov, and M. I. Gogolashchvili. *Vodochnyi kopol' Petr Arsen'evich Smirnov i ego potomki.* Moscow, 1999.

Smith R. E. F., and D. Christian. *Bread and Salt: A Social and Economic History of Food and Drink in Russia.* Cambridge, 1984.

Snow, George E. "Socialism, Alcoholism, and the Russian Working Classes before 1917." In *Drinking: Behavior and Belief in Modern History,* ed. Susanna Barrows and Robin Room. Berkeley: University of California Press, 1991.

Snow, George E. "Alcoholism in the Russian Military: The Public Sphere and the Temperance Discourse, 1883–1917," *Jahrbücher für Geschichte Osteuropas* 45, no. 3 (1997): 417–31.

Solomon, Susan Gross. "Social Hygiene and Soviet Public Health, 1921–1930." In *Health and Society in Revolutionary Russia,* ed. Susan Gross Solomon and John F. Hutchinson. Bloomington: Indiana University Press, 1990.

Sournia, Jean-Charles. *A History of Alcoholism.* Cambridge, MA, 1990.

Stavrou, Theofanis G., ed. *Art and Culture in Nineteenth-Century Russia.* Bloomington: Indiana University Press, 1983.

Steinberg, Mark D., and Vladimir M. Khrustalëv. *The Fall of the Romanovs.* New Haven, CT: Yale University Press, 1995.

Stites, Richard. *The Women's Liberation Movement in Russia: Feminism, Nihilism, and Bolshevism, 1860–1930.* Princeton: Princeton University Press, 1978.

———. *Revolutionary Dreams: Utopian Vision and Experimental Life in the Russian Revolution.* New York, 1989.

———. *Russian Popular Culture: Entertainment and Society since 1900.* Cambridge: Cambridge University Press, 1992.

Stone, Helena. "The Soviet Government and Moonshine, 1917–1929," *Cahiers du monde russe et soviétique* 27 (July–Dec. 1986): 359–79.

Stranitsy istorii goroda Kazani. Kazan, 1981.

Strashun, I. D. *Russkaia obshchestvennaia meditsina v period mezhdu dvumia revoliutsiami: 1907–1917.* Moscow, 1964.

Sulkunen, Irma. *History of the Finnish Temperance Movement: Temperance as a Civic Religion.* Lewiston, NY. 1990.

Surh, Gerald D. "A Matter of Life or Death: Politics, Profession, and Public Health in St. Petersburg before 1914," *Russian History/Histoire russe* 20, nos. 1–4 (1993): 125–46.

Swift, E. Anthony. "Fighting the Germs of Disorder: The Censorship of Russian Popular Theater, 1888–1917." *Russian History/Histoire russe* 18, no. 1 (spring 1991): 1–49.

———. "Workers' Theater and 'Proletarian Culture' in Prerevolutionary Russia, 1905–17." In *Workers and Intelligentsia in Late Imperial Russia: Realities, Representations, Reflections,* ed. Reginald E. Zelnik. Berkeley: University of California Press, 1999.

Tarschys, Daniel. "The Success of a Failure: Gorbachev's Alcohol Policy, 1985–88." *Europe-Asia Studies* 45, no. 1 (1993): 7–25.

Terras, Victor, ed. *Handbook of Russian Literature.* New Haven, CT: Yale University Press, 1985.

Thurston, Gary, "The Impact of Russian Popular Theatre, 1886–1915." *Journal of Modern History* 55, no. 2 (1983): 237–67.

———. *The Popular Theatre Movement in Russia, 1862–1919.* Evanston, IL: Northwestern University Press, 1998.

Transchel, Kate. "Liquid Assets: Vodka and Drinking in Early Soviet Factories." In *The Human Tradition in Modern Russia,* ed. William B. Husband. Wilmington, DE, 2000.

Treml, V. *Alcohol in the USSR.* Durham, NC: Duke University Press, 1982.

Von Laue, Theodore H. *Sergei Witte and the Industrialization of Russia.* New York, 1974.

Warth, Robert D. *Nicholas II: Life and Reign of Russia's Last Monarch.* Westport, CT, 1997.

Weissman, Neil. "Prohibition and Alcohol Control in the USSR: The 1920s Campaign against Illegal Spirits." *Soviet Studies* 38 (July 1986): 349–68.

White, Stephen. *Russia Goes Dry: Alcohol, State, and Society.* Cambridge: Cambridge University Press, 1996.

Wirtschafter, Elise Kimerling. *From Serf to Russian Soldier.* Princeton: Princeton University Press, 1988.

Wise, Andrew Kier. "The Russian Government and Temperance, 1894–1914." M.A. thesis, University of Virginia, 1990.

Woodcock, George, and Ivan Avakumovic. *The Doukhobors.* Toronto, 1968.

Wortman, Richard S. *Scenarios of Power: Myth and Ceremony in Russian Monarchy.* Vol. 2, *From Alexander II to the Abdication of Nicholas II.* Princeton: Princeton University Press, 2000.

Zabludovskii, P. E. *Istoriia otechestvennoi meditsiny.* Moscow, 1960.

Zagorsky, S. O. *State Control of Industry during the War.* New Haven, CT: Yale University Press, 1928.

Zaionchkovskii, P. A. *Samoderzhavie i russkaia armiia na rubezhe XIX–XX stoletii, 1881–1903.* Moscow, 1973.

———. *The Russian Autocracy under Alexander III.* Ed. and trans. David R. Jones. Gulf Breeze, FL, 1976.

Zaitsev, K. I., N. V. Dolinsky, and S. S. Demonthenov. *Food Supply in Russia during the World War.* New Haven, CT: Yale University Press, 1930.

INDEX